ADVENTURES
of an
URBAN EXPLORER
THE 100 COUNTRY CHALLENGE

ADVENTURES of an URBAN EXPLORER

THE 100 COUNTRY CHALLENGE

All the best

JIM PARKES MBE JP

BREWIN BOOKS

First published by
Brewin Books Ltd, 56 Alcester Road,
Studley, Warwickshire B80 7LG in 2006
www.brewinbooks.com

ISBN 1 85858 288 1

A Cataloguing in Publication Record
for this title is available from the British Library

Typeset in Bembo
Printed in Great Britain by
Cromwell Press Ltd.

Dedicated to Lily Rose, My granddaughter
In the hope of inspiring a thirst for round the world adventures.

Acknowledgements
Many thanks to my daughter Leigh and her husband Richard
for reviewing and presenting my thoughts in a readable form.

Contents

Introduction   xi

1   Discovering a Whole World Perspective on Life   1
  Bullied by a cockerel and Hitler's Bombs
  My best friend a brick wall
  Good fortune as my first job lasts five minutes

2   The Journey begins in Weston-Super-Mare   10
  Colliding with a police van in Paris
  Arrested by the Russians in East Germany
  Driving an ambulance across Russia

3   Travelling by Royal Appointment   26
  King Asantehene wants the Crown Jewels back
  Celebrity Pied Pipers promote the Duke of Edinburgh's Award
  Hypothermia drama in Canada and vampire bats attack in the Caribbean

4   Punishments that fit the crime - A World Wide Perspective   38
  The loss of a limb or Community Service?
  The unequal treatment of women - "Honour Killings"
  Justification of the death penalty?

5   Spiritual Enlightenment in India   60
  Stalked by a Tiger
  Removed from a train at gunpoint
  Working with Mother Teresa - Reception at her home

6   Climbing the Great Wall of China   74
  The pre-Tiananmen Square Massacre Meeting
  The surrender of Hong Kong
  The Chinese Refugee Dilemma

7   Serving the Community in Nairobi   86
      Arrested in Uganda and Kenya
      Near death experience on Mount Kenya
      On Safari in Amboseli
8   To fly or not to fly - Terrorists rule OK?   95
      Chinese oppression of Buddhist Tibetans
      State of emergency in Nepal
      Kashmiri terrorist attack on the Indian Parliament
9   Dodging rockets in the "Cradle of Civilisation"   102
      Life in Israel, Syria, Lebanon and Jordan
      Surviving the "Jerusalem Syndrome"
      Encounter with Hizbullah terrorists
10 The event that killed Apartheid   112
      Meeting Nelson Mandela and Desmond Tutu
      Cape Town Cathedral riot
      The Garden of Eden for UK Wrinklies
      Transformation of Soweto
      Deported from Mozambique in the back of a lorry
11 Evaluation of Government Propaganda   129
      Manipulation of the Press
      The Suppression of the Facts - The role of the Media
      The justification of travel
      Operation "Drive Out Trash" in Zimbabwe
12 A South American Adventure   151
      A car bomb in Argentina
      Volcanic eruption in Mexico
      Arrests in Ecuador and Columbia and a mugging in Peru
      A week in a love hotel
13 Interact with a visitor from Outer Space -   166
    Religion, a positive or destructive force within society?
      "No one religion can claim to be better than another as all are
      based on doing good for others". Dalai Lama.
      "Just enough religion to hate one another but not enough
      to love one another". Jonathan Swift.
14 Surviving in South East Asia   178
      Racial conflicts in Malaysia, Sri Lanka and Borneo
      Brutality of the Khmer Rouge in Cambodia
      Vietnam War Crimes Museum
      Attacked by an Orang-utan

15 Three American Adventures   191
    Triangles based on music, gambling, entertainment and obesity
    Tributes to the Civil Rights Movement
    Sporting welcome in Barbados
    Life in Cuba under Castro
16 Around the World in 40 days   206
    Tamil Terrorist attack in Colombo
    The Vicar eaten by cannibals in Fiji
    Ringing the Peace Bell in Hiroshima
    Adrift in the China Sea
17 Sport - The Opium of the Masses?   219
    A constructive or destructive force within society?
    Can sport be defined as a religion?
    The political exploitation of sport?
    World Cup Black Magic
18 Residing in the home of Osama Bin Laden   234
    Afghanistan, Turkey, Iran and Pakistan -
    Four of the most volatile countries on Earth
    Has the liberation of Afghanistan been justified?
    What next - a bullet or a smile?
19 Journey's End in West Africa   252
    100 Countries visited - Ghana reunion
    Reality of modern day slavery, voodoo and corruption
    Royal funds for trees and monkeys myth destroyed
    Nigerian missionaries lead Anglican revival in the UK
    A Near Death Experience with King Mboutcheko in Cameroon

Introduction

On my retirement I finally had the time to reflect on a lifetime of travel, much of which involved accompanying young people. During the past 45 years, 100 countries have already been visited and are featured in this book.

Two methods of reflection and communication are currently being undertaken, interactive public speaking and interactive essay writing. Both mediums are aimed at engaging listeners and readers in a series of situations and moral dilemmas. Two words summarise my approach to life - optimism and opportunism. Although I am a great optimist and can see something good in almost every situation it does not stop me looking both ways when crossing a one way street. An adventurous approach linked to a risk appraisal of any situation has enabled me to survive many dangerous situations including race riots, car bombs, terrorist attacks, muggings, cyclones, and arrests.

My interpretation of being an opportunist revolves around reacting to an opportunity that wasn't pre-planned, that would position me at an event or in contact with people to whom I would normally be denied access. Examples include being invited to Mother Teresa's home and attending the remembrance service at Cape Town Cathedral led by Nelson Mandela and Desmond Tutu that was the last major event prior to the scrapping of Apartheid. History was made that day.

The essays in this book reflect my definition of myself as an Urban Explorer. This is not a book about climbing mountains, walking to the North or South Pole, riding rapids or trekking across deserts or through jungles. It is about towns and cities, people and events. Although countries such as Iran, Lebanon or Afghanistan may not feature in the travel plans of the average tourist, many of the

100 countries I have visited do. Sitting outside a street café armed only with a local newspaper, watching the world go by may seem boring. The bonus comes with the casual conversation struck up with a passer-by or participating in events featured in the paper that otherwise might have been missed.

The following essays fall into two groups, the larger group concentrating on people and events in countries linked by touching borders, politics, terrorism or armed conflict. The smaller group focuses on topics encountered across the whole world and includes an evaluation of religion, sport, crime, punishment, press coverage and government control of the media. This group provides the highest level of interaction as you are challenged to review the impact of religion on world politics or whether a punishment for a crime should involve community service or amputation.

With the aid of facts or opinions I aim to challenge you intellectually. It does not matter if you agree or disagree. Feel free to rant at my evaluation or throw the book against the wall in anger. I will have achieved my aim of interacting with you. A greater achievement would be if you adopted a more enquiring role when travelling abroad. Seek out the local characters that can lift the superficial veil that may mask what life is really like in that country.

J.S. Parkes MBE JP.

1

Discovering a Whole World Perspective on Life

Bullied by a cockerel and Hitler's Bombs
My best friend a brick wall
Good fortune as my first job lasts five minutes

My journey of discovery started in 1961 during a collision with a van full of armed police officers in Paris. Here I am, 100 countries later in 2005, after surviving a near death experience when a tyre blew out at 60mph on a road in Cameroon in the company of the King of Batoussam.

That first incident with the French police on my first international trip was to be a characteristic of many events and incidents to follow! Two things soon became apparent to readers of press reports and to friends and relatives following my adventures. The first is that it was almost inevitable that something dramatic would happen to me whilst abroad and secondly, that I would escape unscathed.

It became a joke that friends would check my next itinerary to ensure they were not going to the same country at the same time as me. Something always seemed to happen before, during or after my visit. In later years "Lucky Jim" was used regularly by headline writers. A more recent favourite headline of mine read, "Brummie OAP is the new Phileas Fogg". An evaluation of the accuracy of the term "Lucky Jim" is undertaken in the final essay where a more profound description is considered.

In reading this book I'm sure you will agree that I have led a charmed life when abroad. Some of the public order incidents I've survived are listed below:

An airline office bomb in Athens.
A Hindu and Malaysian wedding riot in Kuala Lumpur.
Pre-Tiananmen Square massacre meetings with students in Beijing.
The state of emergency in Nepal following Maoist terrorist attacks.
A Tamil terrorist attack on my hotel in Sri Lanka.

Kashmiri Separatists attacking the Delhi Parliament.
Street riots in Capetown at the funeral of Chris Hani.
A Brazil car bomb killing a top reporter investigating police corruption.
A pitched battle between Tabasca Indians and riot police in Mexico City.
The Japanese embassy siege in Lima.
Israeli rocket attacks in Beirut on the Hizbullah.
A car bomb in Nicosia.
Riots at a football match in Larnaka.
A bus bomb killing 19 in Tel Aviv.
An attempted mugging in Peru and New Orleans.
A tear-gas attack at a Test Match in Pakistan.
An oil refinery explosion in Bangkok.
A car bomb attack in Istanbul.
Adverse weather conditions include:
A typhoon in Japan.
Flash floods in Brazil.
A cyclone in Fiji.
A dust storm and volcanic eruption in Mexico.
Floods in Prague and neighbouring countries.
A North Atlantic storm whilst cruising.

War zones and places of past atrocities I've experienced include:

Pol Pot's Killing Fields and a map of skulls in Cambodia.
The Japanese "Death Railway" in Thailand.
A memorial marking the A bomb destruction of Hiroshima.
The American War Crimes Museum in Vietnam.
The Berlin Wall and "Check point Charlie".
The US embassy where US hostages were held in Tehran.
The Chinese occupancy of Tibet.
An encounter with Bosnian gangsters.
Travelled through Russian occupied Poland and East Germany during the Cold War.
Visited the Shinto Shrine to Japanese airman and sailors who were involved in Kamikaze attacks.
Zimbabwe - "Drive out trash".

In my role as a youth leader, projects that have supported young people on International exchanges that have helped improve the environment and the quality of life for those less fortunate. These include:

The construction of a well in and Indian village and a road link to another isolated village.
Working in an Indian village sponsored by Mother Teresa.
Planting saplings in Portugal in 1962 at an International Work Camp. It is now a fully-fledged forest.
Planted a commemorative tree in Israel and trees in West Berlin on a man made mountain of rubble from the bombing of Berlin in World War II.
A conservation project in Trinidad.
Work in a shantytown in Nairobi.
Preservation of tigers in the Corbett National park in India.
Assisting in a workshop for the disabled in Hong Kong.
Working in an asylum in Germany.

In addition to that first Paris confrontation with the police there have been other dramatic confrontations including my arrest by Russian troops in East Germany on two separate occasions. Among the holding cells I've frequented include those in Uganda (Yellow fever), Ecuador (Three Presidents), Columbia (Military coup) Mozambique (Visa) and Kenya (tea money). No charges were ever made.

There were road accidents in Mexico, India, Peru, Cameroon and Russia. Again no charges. Money changed hands with corrupt police in Poland, Benin and Nigeria to avoid difficult situations.

I was grabbed by an orang-utan in Borneo and had a snake thrust in my face whilst in a taxi in Bombay. Surprisingly the only injuries in 45 years of travel have been a gashed wrist and ankle as a boat capsized off Thailand. There were close calls when dune buggy racing in the Dubai desert and when a turbo jet ferry drifted out of control in the China Sea off the Island of Macao. Being water bombed in Venezuela was not a pleasant experience.

Places of major historical and cultural interest include climbing the pyramids in Egypt, Peru and Mexico, walking the Great Wall of China, exploring the Taj Mahal and walking in Jesus' footsteps in Jerusalem.

The wonders of nature I have experienced include the Aurora Borealis, the Grand Canyon, the Amazon Basin, Niagara Falls, Victoria Falls, Iguacu Falls and the Giants Causeway.

There have been four out-of-body experiences including watching my life flash before my eyes whilst wrestling with the wheel of an out of control ambulance when driving in a storm in Russia.

I have met many people who have had a major influence on world affairs or have expanded the boundaries of achievement. There was a reception with Mother Teresa at her home in Calcutta, a meeting with Nelson Mandela in South

Africa, listening to Bishop Desmond Tutu in the Cape Town Cathedral and receiving a copy of the Little Red Book from Chairman Mao. I have also interviewed and worked with the Sultan of Brunei, Lord Hunt, Sir Stanley Matthews, Brian Clough, Robert Swan, David Bellamy, Dame Mary Peters and Chris Bonington. I have conversed with her majesty The Queen when receiving my MBE at Buckingham Palace. There has been considerable time spent with two Kings and three Princes and frustratingly I have been the thickness of a wall away from an interview with Castro while in Cuba.

Reflecting back on my childhood and teenage years I can find nothing that would suggest I would become an avid traveller. My family background was working class, in the time when that meant being at the bottom of the pile. I lived in a rented house in Birmingham whose only external door opened onto the pavement. I had to walk past the communal wash house to get to the outside toilets at the end of the block. Walking through the cold, snow, rain and fog in my underclothes left me with a lasting gratitude for indoor toilets!

Another luxury for me now is hot water. After all this time I still savour the sensation of splashing instant hot water on my face each morning. Working class houses didn't have electricity in the 1930s. Gas mantles provided light and water for washing had to be boiled in a kettle with baths taken in a tin bath in front of the fire.

In the 1930s and 40s your place in the social pecking order was related to your parents occupations. My father drove a scrap metal lorry and my mother was a charwoman. This was the new name to describe and replace the title of servant that had become unfashionable. My mother worked for a number of the nouveau riche families that had made their money during the Black Country Industrial Revolution. They were building large houses on the Newton Road only 100 yards away from our block of old cottages. As an only child from such a working class background there was never the chance of having friends of my own age from any of those families.

My mother's employers treated her graciously and she in turn knew what was expected of her. She had been well trained by her mother who, around 1900, was in service to Lady Scott of Barr Hall. Servants, maids, butlers, gardeners etc. were expected to raise their hats or curtsey as Lady Scott drove through the estate in her horse drawn carriage. My mother maintained the tradition and I was expected to tip my cap if we met any of her employers while out shopping. When I was born one of my mother's employers gave her a silver spoon in a case so that it could be said in later life that I was above average because I had been born with a silver spoon in my mouth.

The lack of children my own age to play with probably contributed to my shyness and even now I have feelings of unease when I am at events involving complete strangers. A strict upbringing also contributed to an early lack of confidence. My mother ruled with an iron tongue. If that didn't work it would be, "Wait till your father gets home". That meant one thing - the strap. The strap in question was worn as a belt and also used to sharpen cut-throat razors. The seriousness of the offence depended on how many blows of the strap were administered.

Another factor that probably led to my difficulty in showing affection was that affection was never shown between my parents. I never saw them kiss or hug at home or even hold hands in public.

It is sad to record that my best friend for much of my childhood was a brick wall. Just behind our cottage was Red House Park. On the outset of the German bombing attacks on Birmingham a garage to accommodate fire engines was built in the park. There was also a searchlight unit positioned nearby. Opposite our front door, across the road, was a communal air raid shelter. When the sirens went off everyone would rush to the shelter. I would be with my mother; my father, because of his deafness, was on duty as an Air Raid Warden rather than as a soldier called up to fight the Germans. We would cower in the shelter listening to the planes overhead, the sounds of anti aircraft guns and of the bombs exploding. One of the big targets was the Kynoch Ammunition factory in Perry Barr just three miles away. Sometimes stray bombs would fall on local houses.

When the war finally ended it was then that the brick wall, which was the side of the fire engine garage, became my best friend. The wall's face was about 20ft high and 22 yards long. There were no windows or doors. There was a smooth concrete area in front of the wall. Depending on the time of year I would either chalk a goal, wickets or a tennis net on the wall. In the Winter I would kick a football to score goals. I could practice with both feet; straight on or at an angle knowing the ball would always come back in my general direction. The same applied to bowling at the wicket with a tennis ball or throwing the ball at the wall and hitting the rebound with a cricket bat. Tennis was straightforward and long rallies could be played. The garage at this point was deserted so no one was affected by the sound of a ball on the wall. I could fantasise that I was scoring the winning goal for England, bowling out a top batsman or winning Wimbledon. That wall still exists; the building is now used as changing rooms for football matches in Red House Park.

Despite all the practice with my friend the wall I had the disadvantage of being both a late physical developer as well as a late social developer. I could not get selected for any school team because I was short and fat. I was naturally very self-conscious and managed to get out of PE at Secondary School by taking up the violin. In retrospect I am surprised the teacher put up with me as I couldn't read music and usually mimed in unison with the bow movements of the good players.

One of the reasons I was fat can be attributed in a roundabout way to Adolf Hitler. During World War II food was rationed. The blockade created by German submarines sinking merchant ships in the Atlantic that were carrying food began to have a major effect. Everyone was urged to become self sufficient by keeping livestock and growing crops. My family was fortunate to have a long, narrow stretch of land directly behind our block of cottages. In the area near the cottage vegetables were planted. I had my own patch where I planted carrots, parsnips and lettuces. It was a great learning experience for me. In the middle of the garden my father put up wire netting where fowl, ducks and geese wandered freely. They gave a steady supply of fresh eggs and meat. Every so often a brood of little chicks and ducklings would appear.

At the top of the garden my father built a pigsty. Government rules required that half of the pigs killed should be sold to them, the other half being available for consumption by family and friends. The pigs were always a fascination when family members called; they would always want to see the pig's progress. It became a ritual that always ended in the only joke I can ever recall my father making. As everyone stood around the pigsty in their Sunday best (including hats), someone would always feed my father the question, "Do the pigs have names?" everyone knew the answer, including me. My father would deliver the punchline whilst pointing at me, "Yes, they do have names, the one wearing the cap is called Jim!" After a while I got used to the humiliation.

One problem I did have was being bullied by a cockerel. To take food scraps to be boiled at the pigsty I had to pass through the netted area where the cockerel ruled. Wearing short trousers my bare legs were a target for the cockerel's beak. I think it must have sensed my fear because it didn't attack anyone else.

Naturally I was exposed to the killing ritual of the livestock. Twice a year a licensed butcher would come to shoot two or more of the pigs. When a chicken was needed for roasting my mother had no qualms in wringing its neck. Likewise she had no qualms in drowning unwanted kittens in a bucket of water. Attempts were always made first to find a home for the kittens before such action was taken.

My family lived better than most in terms of fresh meat, bacon, chicken, eggs etc. Sides of bacon would hang from the ceiling in the only living room; pieces were cut as and when required. The strange thing was my father was overweight but my mother was as thin as a rake. My dinner plate was always piled high as I was expected to clear my plate hence my fatness as a child.

It was a family tradition at that time to name a son after the father. Although we were both christened James no one from a working class background would use the name James by way of introduction. It was always Jim. This often led to feelings of inferiority as we were always "Big Jim" and "Little Jim". As a child it wasn't a problem but as an adult I felt little compared to my father even though we were the same height.

When I left school at 15 my father had a job lined up for me in a bicycle/radio repair shop because of my success in building crystal sets at school. On arrival at the shop I was told that I was unsuitable for the job as I was too small and wouldn't be able to stack the cycles in the window displays. My first job lasted less than five minutes.

What happened next turned out to be the best thing my mother ever did for me. As we walked out of the bicycle shop she marched me down to ICI which had a great reputation for engineering apprenticeships. There was usually a one-year waiting list and the new Course had already been running for four weeks. We waited to see the Personnel Manager for about an hour and finally when invited into his office my mother started extolling my modest achievements at Pelsall Secondary Modern School. I still cringe when I remember her words; "He's good with his hands". As it happened one of the new intake had already dropped out. Purely on my mothers enthusiasm I was offered an immediate trial. Six years later I emerged a fully qualified Production Engineer before disappearing into the RAF to do my National Service.

Not only did I emerge from ICI as a skilled craftsman but also as a sportsman in demand thanks in part to Charles Atlas. When I was 17 I was 4ft 9 inches tall and weighed 10 stone and seven pounds therefore still short and fat. At that time there was three other apprentices working with me in the Tool Room. One of the adults also in that workshop was a Polish refugee who had previously escaped from Hitler's Germany. He was very well built, bristling with muscles. His secret was having enrolled on the world famous Charles Atlas Course. It was a correspondence course consisting of a series of separate exercises. He offered to sell the package so the four of us clubbed together to raise the asking price. We agreed that we would share the instruction sheets equally between us, and, at the end of each month we would rotate one of the sheets so we could concentrate on a different part of our body. At the end of twelve months I emerged as having achieved the greatest progress. My height had increased from 4ft 9inches to 5ft 10 inches whilst my weight of 10stone 7pounds remained the same. Fat Jim had become Slim Jim. Probably because I had the training module on leg muscles first and therefore practised longer than the others, I finished up with legs like tree trunks - fifty years later they are still like tree trunks and carry me around football pitches as a referee, onto cricket pitches as an umpire and around Boldmere Golf Course come rain or shine.

Many of my friends and colleagues have tried to rationalise my good fortune whilst travelling abroad. Some describe it as luck, others as fate or having the support of a "Guardian Angel". Whatever it is it also applied to two events in England. Had the outcome of two road accidents been more serious none of the previously listed events would ever have taken place.

The first accident involved a motorbike. Whilst doing National Service in the RAF I had bought a 150cc Velocette, a water-cooled "Silent Ghost", favoured by the police at that time because of its silent approach. (An identical model can be seen in the Birmingham Motor Cycle Museum). I was travelling down Chapel Lane from the top of Barr Beacon when I misjudged a left-hand bend and careered into a brick wall hitting it headfirst. At that time crash helmets were not compulsory. Fortunately I was wearing a helmet; my life could have ended at 23.

The second crash involved my first four-wheel vehicle; A40 Austin open backed pick-up truck. I had attended a Youth Leader's Training Conference in Blackpool and was returning home. I recall going into a bend at 50mph, braking on approach. The next thing I remember was waking up in hospital. I had a head injury and a broken collarbone. On release from hospital I went to the scene of the accident to find the truck wrapped around a tree, a write off except for the radio. At that time seat belts were not fitted so increasing the chances of being killed. Once again I had been spared. It had happened just a few months after my first trip across the English Channel. Instead of visiting 100 plus countries I could have finished with just one visit.

The good fortune I enjoyed in surviving those two accidents has also extended to the young people who took part in the international exchanges I organised. As you progress through the essays featuring the Duke of Edinburgh's Award Exchanges to Nova Scotia and Kenya you will first read of the girl who collapsed into a coma as a result of hypothermia and the boy who was carried unconscious off Mount Kenya suffering from mountain sickness. Both only survived because of the skill of the leaders I selected to deal with such eventualities. More than thirty-five years after these events the consequences on the careers of someone involved in similar situations could be catastrophic, as we have entered the blame culture era.

Sadly one young person died during a training programme I organised on behalf of the Award Scheme in Birmingham in 1980. At that time I was trying to develop Award activities within the inner city. Initially there was a lack of volunteers with the necessary skills to teach the basics of camp craft, country code, self-catering etc. This problem was overcome by bussing 80 young people every weekend to the LEA's Sharpress Outdoor Centre.

I always worked on the principle that only qualified instructors are used for such training. As I did not hold such qualifications my role was back in Birmingham and assessable by telephone. Early one Sunday morning I was shattered to hear the news from the Centre warden that one of the girls had died a few minutes earlier. Having gained a description of the circumstances of her death I phoned her parents. Their reaction came as a surprise; they were calm, almost as though they had been expecting the news. She had collapsed whilst getting out of her bunk bed in the dormitory. The post mortem revealed she had a brain tumour and could have died at any moment. Her parents knew this but had not put this on her medical records. The tragedy of her death made me even more resolved to ensure that everyone in my care would continue to receive the highest level of supervision from adults with the necessary skills to cope with any emergency.

Although there is nothing in my family background to explain my love of travel I can nominate at least two youth workers who helped widen my horizons beyond Great Barr. They are acknowledged in the following essay.

2

The Journey begins in Weston-Super-Mare

Colliding with a police van in Paris
Arrested by the Russians in East Germany
Driving an ambulance across Russia

My international adventures were inspired at the Allen Memorial Youth Fellowship in Great Barr, Birmingham. It was this youth club, under the inspired leadership of Geoff Robinson, which raised my sights beyond the boundaries of Birmingham.

My first ever day away from home was on a Youth Club coach trip to Weston-Super-Mare. I was 18. My parents never had a holiday in their lifetime. The thrill of that trip to Weston led to a week with a friend from the Youth Club on my first holiday at the age of 19 to the Isle of Man. It would be two years later, at 21 and doing two years of National Service with the RAF, that I would spend more time out of England. Three months stationed at Cairnryan in Scotland loading cargo boats for journeys to and from St Kilda in the Outer Hebrides.

I had savoured leadership responsibility as a senior member of the Allen Memorial Youth Fellowship prior to joining the RAF. Having enjoyed the experience so much I decided to enrol on a part time Youth Leadership Course when I was demobbed from the RAF in 1959. The tutor was an exceptional man called John Parr who was to prove my other major role model. Practical training saw me assigned to Hamstead Youth Club and I chose to continue working at the Allen Memorial Youth Fellowship as a volunteer.

In November 1960 I founded the Twenty-Two Club. It had a single material challenge - to build a youth centre in Great Barr that would be independent of any particular religious faith, political party or Local Authority. The first meeting of the twenty two founding members was held in a telephone box, as a publicity gimmick, as we had no base to call our own. The publicity this generated led to an offer of the use of a tin hut as a starting point. The hut, a redundant classroom on the site of St Margaret's C of E Primary School was a single storey wooden structure with corrugated metal sheets on the outside. It felt like coming home to me as I had attended my first primary schooling there and it was from that hut that the adventures started.

The first international experience took place in Easter 1961. It was decided that the Club's football team would travel to Paris in a hired mini bus for a five-day break. A mini bus was booked but unknown to me, for insurance reasons, the driver had to be over 21. My assistant Terry Hall had a driving licence but was only 20. By sheer coincidence I was taking my driving test the day before the scheduled departure. If I passed we could go; fail and the trip would be cancelled. Despite the pressure I passed and France was to be country number 1 of the 100 plus I was eventually to visit.

Anyone who has driven in Paris will know the reputation of French drivers. Imagine after just one day as a qualified driver, trying to navigate the centre of Paris, searching for a pre-booked hotel. Having negotiated the Champs Elysee and passed the Eiffel Tower, the next stage was to travel down a road resembling a racetrack that ran parallel with the River Seine. There were five lanes of traffic and every set of traffic lights was like the start of a Grand Prix race. Unless you made a racing start and maintained 50 mph you would be subjected to blaring horns and irate Frenchmen cutting in front from left and right. After what seemed like hours we finally found the bridge over the Seine that would lead towards our hotel.

The road leading to the Hotel Pension Des Grandes Scales was quite narrow and had cars parked on both sides so there was barely room for vehicles to pass. By now I was really stressed out. We had set off from Birmingham on Friday night, travelled on the ferry from Dover to Boulogne in the early hours of the morning and then driven on the unfamiliar right hand side of the road across France. Half way along the road a black van headed toward me, the space was minimal and as we passed there was a loud metallic sound. We had collided. The excited chatter in the minibus stopped as the black van stopped, the rear doors opened and out jumped ten burly armed gendarmes all dressed in riot gear. None of the gendarmes spoke English and only Alan Green spoke a few words of French. After inspections, and a lot of arm waving and shouting it was decided that only the wing mirrors of both vehicles had connected and we were sent on our way, with no charges made.

On arrival at the hotel I was mentally drained from the journey and settled for an early night but the rest of the group, mainly in the 18 to 20 year old range headed off to explore the local nightlife. At breakfast the next morning there was much giggling and whispering and I eventually pieced together that three of the young men had been picked up by "ladies of the night". They were taken to a place of ill repute, introduced to the delights of sexual intercourse and relieved of most of their money. The three lads entertained their friends by describing the proceedings starting with their private parts being thoroughly washed. More than forty years later would such activities have to be covered by the Safety of Young Peoples Act, under EEC regulations, requiring that such establishments be registered and their staff accredited for "Youth Work Skills?"

The economics of that trip are fascinating today. Expenditure included the cost of petrol of £11, the hotel bill for twelve was £43 and the mini bus hire for 5 days was £15. My first international adventure had cost the grand total of £143, fourteen shillings and six pence!

The Paris trip had been a massive learning curve for me. Never again would the fine print in travel and vehicle hire documents be overlooked and the preparation time before future trips would be greater. A wider awareness of the less desirable opportunities available to impressionable youths had been overlooked too. Should I have ranted and raved or offered counselling to the three who sampled Paris' delights? In 1961 HIV and AIDS was unheard of in Europe but other sexual diseases were prevalent.

In terms of personal development I discovered that a residential experience, particularly abroad, was the most effective and successful teaching aid for young people. In those five days I could literally see them growing up. Their parents commented later on their more responsible attitudes. They were more willing to accept leadership roles in the youth club for the benefit of younger members.

Another valuable learning experience, for the young people and myself was the exposure to poverty. Although France's level of poverty was low, witnessing the homeless sleeping rough and lying over metal grills above kitchen cellars to capture the rising heat was a shock to all of us. Stepping around them as though they were lepers was a new experience to the young people away from the leafy suburbs of Great Barr.

Over the next ten years an International Visits Plan was followed. Every Easter and Whitsun break at least one mini-bus would take a group across the English Channel for a five day adventure. In July and August more ambitious two/three week ventures involving International Work Camps were undertaken. The distances travelled increased with trips to Russia, Italy and Portugal.

The value of these trips had a positive effect, as club members became more concerned with environmental issues outside Europe. A member spotted the following newspaper article, *"Adopt a thirsty elephant. 3,000 elephants in Tsavo, Kenya need a drink. For 36 shillings you can keep an elephant in drinks for a year. Baby elephants half price"*. The members rallied around to adopt "their elephant". Many years later I took a group to Kenya on a Duke of Edinburgh's Award Exchange.

Every time I saw an elephant I was reminded of that article and wondered if that was the elephant that we had supported.

In Easter 1962 a mini-bus group went to Ostend. A sad story relates to a young man called Trevor who tragically died in his late 20s. Trevor had special needs and his social life revolved around the youth club. As the mini-bus set off everyone was asked to check that their passports were with them. On arrival at Dover we were about to board the ferry when Trevor confessed that he didn't have a passport, didn't know how to get one and had been too embarrassed to tell anyone. There was nothing we could do so regrettably we had to leave Trevor on the Dover beach. I had failed Trevor by not checking that he had a passport weeks prior to the trip and in not helping him to obtain one. It's a mistake I vowed never to do again.

There are two nice postscripts to Trevor being left behind. Firstly the Club Members' Committee raised money to support a National Association of Youth Club's programme to send two underprivileged children in Hong Kong on their first holiday. Trevor was chosen to present the money raised. Secondly, Trevor and his brand new passport went on the 1963 Easter trip to Holland.

The summer of 1962 saw the Club's first involvement in an International Work Camp. A group of five, including myself, travelled 3,116 miles on a round trip to San Pedro De Muel in Portugal. The three-week venture cost us the princely sum of £13 each. Transport was my small Ford 10 van. It had been converted with bench seats and windows in the back to accommodate three people and equipment.

The day before our departure the van became part of a world record during the Club's fund raising Carnival Day. The record involved packing 28 young people into the small van and closing the doors. To protect the springs on the van bricks were placed under the axles. The record attempt was successful and all 28 were counted out by a large crowd and recorded on 8mm film.

The Work Camp in Portugal was based in an area where a forest was to be established. There were 40 young people, mainly students from all over Europe taking part. The task for Club members Barry Birch, Cliff Stevenson and myself was to prune the Birch tree saplings that had not grown at least 5ft high. Any that had not grown to this height were to be chopped down so that the most successful could flourish. Each day we held a competition to see which group could chop down the highest number of trees. The Brit's always won! More than forty years later I was visiting Lisbon and asked a travel guide if she knew of the progress of the trees in the North West of Portugal. You can imagine my pride when she told me that the area of saplings had grown into a forest with thousands of tall adult Birch trees.

There were two others in our party but they had not signed up to the work group. They were members of the Youth Wing of Oswald Mosley's Blackshirts, a fascist group that had risen at the time of Hitler. As our Club was independent of politics they were free to take part in any of the activities on offer. Their adventure was to spend the whole time camping on the beach, talking politics with the local youths. Whatever was said had a dramatic effect as the two youths returned to England as converts to a more main stream brand of politics. Mosley had lost two recruits.

The international ethos of the club continued to have many positive influences on the members. Funds were raised for the World Hunger Fund and the World Wildlife Fund. The minutes of a club meeting held in October 1962 read as follows:

"A debate focused on whether the Club should continue to support the World Wildlife Fund as its President, The Duke of Edinburgh, had been involved in tiger and stag hunting. The conclusion was that Prince Philip was bound by society and tradition to take part in these activities and had been put in an embarrassing position by the Fund". Our committee agreed to continue to support the WWF but also to send a letter of protest to the Trustees. Unknown at the time, Prince Philip had feigned an injury to a finger to avoid going on a tiger hunt in Nepal. Ironically the Duke of Edinburgh became my boss years later when I was appointed the Midland Regional Officer for the Duke of Edinburgh Award Scheme.

In 1963 the Easter trip was to Holland. You could never be sure what aspects of the trip the young people would remember. Sometimes they are quite trivial matters such as those mentioned in a report written by Ann MacDonald (nee Bruton):

"I would like to mention the food, chocolate on bread or sweets on bread rate highly in Holland. Breakfast consists of bread and jam. The chips are so hard they fly across the room when you stab them and the meat is transparent. The Dutch seem very fond of spinach, horrible wet grey soggy spinach". No doubt Ann would be slightly embarrassed now by her assessment but it didn't blunt her taste for international cuisine. She has lived in Mallorca for many years.

In July 1963, a group undertook a groundbreaking adventure travelling across Russian controlled East Germany during the Cold War. By now I had acquired my own mini bus so 12 set off across the Channel, through Belgium and into Germany. All 12 were taking part in International Youth Work Camps that were organised by UNESCO in conjunction with the International Jugendgemeinschaft Drenste. Three groups of three were dropped off in West Germany. One group was working in an old people's home in Delmenhorit, another undertaking forestry work in Westertede, and the third group doing conservation work in Oldenburg.

Two others and myself were to travel across East Germany to West Berlin, a city divided by the infamous Berlin Wall. We were based at Waldsehulallee in a forest lodge. The work was to be at Teufelsberg (Devils Mountain). The mountain was in fact the highest point in Berlin and was man made. All the rubble from buildings damaged during the war had been used to create the mountain. The rubble had been covered with thousands of tons of soil. Our task was to dig narrow trenches along the mountainside where the trees would be planted. Forty years later there is a thriving forest and a ski run. In acknowledgement of our work the Lord Mayor of Wilmersdorf invited us to tea in his luxurious parlour and presented signed booklets featuring Berlin.

The highlight of the visit was a drive through Checkpoint Charlie, controlled by British and American troops and into Russian controlled East Berlin. When I returned to West Berlin I wrote the following in my logbook.

"On entering East Berlin I was immediately aware of the stillness after the hustle and bustle of the West. The streets were almost deserted of traffic, trams speed past with only one or two passengers. The footpaths were bare, traffic lights no longer in use. It was a ghost town.

There were big expanses of levelled ground where houses once stood. Bombs had destroyed many and some had been demolished as they were too close to the Wall that divides Berlin. This levelled ground in now guarded by searchlights. Church ruins are frequent, grim reminders of war.

A trip to the Brandenburg Gate told the same story as when viewed from the West. Soldiers of the East and West gazed suspiciously at each other over a distance of 100 yards. The Russian soldiers were on the top of high pillars with binoculars and the usual crowd of bystanders leaning on the barricades. Some like vultures waiting for a possible escape attempt, others with a longing look in their eyes for the freedom of West Berlin. We were fortunate to meet two East Berlin youths that spoke a little English. They joined us in the minibus and gave us a guided tour. We thanked them with cigarettes.

Their tour included the building from where Hitler addressed mass audiences at the height of his reign. It was now a courtyard covered in a mass of weeds. Across from there was a new grandstand, the home of the traditional May Day salutes. Next we went to the Gestapo headquarters with its eight floors below ground consisting of mainly cells and torture chambers, now also overgrown with weeds. On we went to a huge new building under construction that was to house the Mayor.

Our young guides told us that 80% of East Berlin people want to escape to the West. In the winter many starve to death or freeze due to the lack of food and coal. In primary schools Russian is taught and cinemas screen films that contain inserted propaganda. The quality of clothes is poor and dull in design. The imported West German shirts our guides wore cost 80 marks each (£7). For a weeks work they could buy one shirt and nothing else.

It was with regret that we finally had to say goodbye to our guides. It felt sad, as though we were leaving someone in prison whose only crime was to be born on the wrong side of a wall".

Another memory of West Berlin was meeting A. Langhammer (he never used his first name). As a young man he was a top athlete who represented Germany as a sprinter in the 1920s Olympic games. He had also been a Scout Leader during Hitler's reign. He refused to align his Scout Troop with the Hitler Nazi Youth Movement so was imprisoned in 1938. Once the war had swung against the Germans Langhammer and other prisoners were drafted as paratroopers. He survived the retreat from Moscow and claimed to have destroyed the first Russian tank to enter Berlin. He was captured by the Russians and made a prisoner of war. He escaped only to be recaptured by the British.

He was a friend of the father of Baden-Powell, the founder of the Scout Movement. He had Baden-Powell's signature on a German State flag. When I met him he was 70 years old, he lived in a hut in the forest where we were working and was still involved in the Wood Scouts. His wife had been killed in the blitz of Berlin and his other relatives were in East Berlin separated from him by the Berlin wall. My last correspondence with him was a Christmas card in 1964, which said, *"Send my love to Christine, (the princess) and to Mick. In our spirit of real comradeship, yours A. Langhammer".*

At the end of our time at the Berlin International Work Camp we had to cross Russian controlled East Germany to collect our other three groups from West Germany. There were three autobahns linking West Berlin with West Germany. The autobahns were strictly controlled by Russian troops. It was illegal to leave an autobahn after going through a checkpoint. Half an hour into the journey the fan belt broke and I had to wait an hour for a garage to send a mechanic. A further half-hour into the journey I was flagged down by Russian troops. I got out of the mini bus to be surrounded by armed troops. They had stopped me because a car had broken down and the driver needed our help. None of us could speak German and they couldn't speak English. After much arm waving and shouting a rope was attached to our mini bus and we towed the car to the next checkpoint. Initially it was a relief to be travelling along at 50 mph, but I decided it was probably a bad idea as I was towing a car so I slowed down to 30mph. This series of events would lead to my arrest.

On arrival at the checkpoint we presented our passports. When the officer checked my passport I saw him looking at the clock before he disappeared into the office. On his return we were ordered to bring our entire luggage into a holding cell with iron bars at the windows. I was worried, as there were two suspicious items in my luggage. Firstly I had an 8mm camera that I had used to film whilst in East Berlin. Secondly I had collected political leaflets from members of the Work Camp who had come from all over Europe. These leaflets were at the bottom of my case. Just as the search began I remembered the officer looking at my passport and at the clock. I concluded that when I left West Berlin the time had been recorded on the passport stamp. I showed the garage repair bill and after a lot of sketches and sign language the officers understood why we had taken so long to travel to the checkpoint. It had been suspected that we had left the autobahn on a spying expedition. The letter of thanks from the Mayor of Wilmersdorf confirmed our respectability. Had they continued their search of my case I'm sure the outcome would have been arrest and custody.

The next groundbreaking trip was driving a converted ambulance to Moscow in July 1965. At the time we were *"Britain's only Mobile Youth Club"*, a title that was ratified by the Department of Education and Science. The reason for the change of status was due to the loss of our beloved tin hut HQ. *"Premises gutted in raging inferno"* headlined the papers on 14th April 1964. Unable to find alternative accommodation while battling with the Local Authority for a site to build our own premises we resorted to a mobile existence. A Bedford ambulance was obtained from Staffordshire County Council for £35. Parents helped to strip the back of the ambulance and fit coach seats. Fans of the TV show "The Royal" can see a similar ambulance in the opening credits.

Members held a competition to name the ambulance and the winner was "Moby Jim", slang for mobile Jim. The ambulance was christened with a cheap bottle of wine smashed across the bonnet by County Councillor Dorothy Wynne, one of our most loyal supporters.

The 1965 journey to Moscow was a logistical challenge. The local press reported, *"Twenty-four hours before departure the club leader was engaged in a 100mph sports car journey down the M1 to collect delayed Russian and Polish visas"*. This was the time before 70mph speed limits on motorways.

The trip through France, Belgium, Germany, Poland and Russia had a shaky start with "Moby Jim" breaking down twice on the way to Dover due to a puncture and blown core plug. We ended up missing the ferry and enduring a six-hour wait for the next boat.

Three of the group were dropped at an International Work Camp in Braunschweig, West Germany, to spend three weeks working in an asylum. Another three were dropped off in West Berlin. Mike Jenks was the leader supported by Ann MacDonald (nee Bruton) and Linda Birch. Mike was visiting West Berlin for the second time, having been on the 1963 trip. The young women helped on the wards in a hospital, cleaning and giving drinks to the patients. The young men helped in the garden and emptied the bins.

Mike wrote of his experiences in the 2004 magazine "Brummagem", a local history magazine produced by Professor Carl Chinn. *"It was an amazing sight three weeks later seeing Moby the ambulance chugging up the streets of Berlin after its tour of Russia. We remembered the breakdowns and journey out of England and thought it would never get back to Berlin"*.

How true that could have been. Club members Christine Moore, (who later became my wife), Cliff Ellsom, who now lives in Canada and myself could have been killed. I was driving from Minsk to Smolensk during a storm. The road was elevated about 4ft above surrounding fields and was just wide enough for one line of traffic in each direction and space to allow one vehicle at a time to overtake. I was stuck in a line of heavy lorries; travelling at 50mph, faster than I wanted to be but the lorry behind was tailgating me so I had to continue. It was late in the evening and the combination of darkness, no street lighting and heavy rain that created a sense of danger.

What happened next is etched deep in my memory. The lorry in front suddenly braked. I instinctively braked and in the space of a few seconds the ambulance skidded 45 degrees in one direction, then in the opposite direction. This happened at least six times as I tried to straighten up the ambulance to avoid hitting vehicles coming in the opposite direction and to avoid hitting the lorry in front. I knew that if we left the road we would have rolled over down the bank and the consequences quite obvious.

While I struggled with the wheel these elements of our plight were racing through my head. Suddenly my life flashed before my eyes. I saw my mother as a young woman with her hair flowing onto her shoulders. I must have been a baby at the time as I can only ever recall her hair tied back in a bun. She stood tall and straight, all my memories were of a bent figure as she spent all her life as a charwoman cleaning floors. It was an incredible experience. I often wonder if that fleeting experience gave me the strength and skill to straighten up the ambulance and to continue the journey. Neither of my companions said a word. In a state of shock, I drove on without speaking. On arrival at the campsite not a word was exchanged about the incident.

In 2004 Cliff Ellsom traced me through the Internet. I finally asked him about the events of that night. He had no recollection of the near crash and we could only conclude that it was locked away in his memory or he had been asleep in the back of the ambulance and oblivious to what was happening!

The main reason to visit Russia was to see how much of the Government propaganda put out by the British press about Communism was true. On my return to England I wrote a newspaper article on my experiences. Looking back at the article 40 years on, my evaluation seems simplistic but none the less accurate. Read for yourself what I wrote back in 1965, at the height of the Cold War between America and Russia and just months after the Cuban Missile crisis that nearly started World War III.

"Having now visited thirteen European countries I can say without reservation that the Russian working people are the friendliest and most helpful that I have ever encountered; and that includes the English too.

Whenever our vehicle stopped on the roadway, whether it was because of a puncture or having got lost, within a minute a vehicle would stop to see if they could help. They didn't even have to be signalled to stop".

One example was the driver of a milk lorry who took a punctured tyre and myself 20 miles into Brest at the Russian border and then spent an hour going from garage to garage to find one open on a Sunday. Another example was when helped by a taxi driver. On returning with a repaired tyre and after settling the fare, the taxi driver got his jacket off and proceeded to change the wheel for us. It took nearly 45 minutes and the sweat poured off him. Another time a garage repair unit travelled 25 miles to assist with our puncture, and after being unable to supply a new inner tube, fitted a second hand tube without accepting a penny for labour or materials, despite two hours work.

Although the basis of Communism is one of equal shares for all with no class distinction, there is no doubt in my mind that social barriers are still created between "us and them". One of our guides was quite ignorant of the working conditions of the 'workers' and another ended a tour having refused a tip by dramatically saying, *"In our country we do not accept tips"*. The ironic thing was that our guide spoke with a heavy American accent. He had learnt to speak English by watching black market American films that were in fact illegal in Russia.

It is the more educated Russians, the army of civil servants and the military who are the ones subjected to the mass Russian propaganda and thus affected by it. All the Russian press anti-American propaganda was way over the heads of the working classes. For example the Russian press were full of stories of American atrocities in Vietnam, of hospitals bombed, of heavy losses of American troops, claims of 400 planes shot down, all to give the impression of victory for the 'free people of Vietnam over the Capitalist slave drivers'.

Big posters were everywhere calling for World Peace with the Russians appearing to be leading the way. Educated Russians who have never been out of Russia or are unable to receive outside world publications are thus justified to a certain degree in thinking Communism is the be all and end all and that America is the aggressor. To that extent the British people are also brainwashed into thinking the Russians are a bunch of barbarians when in fact the mass of the people are just the same as in England.

I had never before realised the extent the Russians had suffered at the hands of the Nazis. Towns were completely destroyed but, as is the case with Minsk, they have been restored into beautiful cities with big apartment blocks and wide streets. To this end the Russians owe a great deal to women. On building sites women have taken their place alongside male labourers, carrying bricks and mixing cement. On new road developments women could be seen spreading tar and driving steamrollers alongside men, in fact many jobs that might be classified as semi skilled or that of a labourer in the UK would be shared by women in Russia.

If you were politically active in the 1960s were you afraid of Russia /Communism? Have you been surprised to read my simplistic views of 1965 and now think that Russia did not receive a good press in the UK? Did the stories of Russian oppression of Eastern Block countries or the Siberian Work Camps justify the fear of Russia by the West? Did the Russian people have the most to fear from Communism? Prior to Stalin's death in 1953 it is claimed he had overseen the killing of 30 million Russians and a further 30 million had starved in Soviet Work Camps.

One reason for recording my experiences is to encourage others to see for themselves what life is like in other countries and to consider travelling to more emotive areas of our planet.

The return journey from Moscow was not only plagued with breakdowns and punctures. Christine, who had celebrated her 21st birthday at a forest campsite on the edge of the city, had been bitten by mosquitoes and was given tablets that left her weak. It was agreed that we should use the ambulance as it had been originally intended and she was stretched out over three seats as we drove across Russia and Poland.

Poland was a very depressing country, totally under Russian control, people fearful of speaking openly in case they were heard by the Secret Police. The Russians had built a beautiful opera house in Warsaw. The Poles hated this building as it represented their slavery to Russia.

On the final morning I left Warsaw at 5.30am to travel to the Polish border to make up for lost time due to breakdowns. Club members back in West Berlin and West Germany would be stranded not knowing what was happening. Driving a high-sided vehicle on the right hand side of the road meant that because of the camber on right hand bends it felt as though the ambulance would topple over. Therefore I drove in the centre of the deserted roads when on bends. I came out of one bend only to see a police motorcyclist approaching from the opposite direction. He stopped me. Due to language problems I finished up producing my wallet from which he emptied half the contents before waving me on. This was my first experience of official corruption.

Having finally reached West Berlin a new drama was to unfold, leading to our arrest in East Germany by Russian troops. Here is Mike Jenks account from the "Brummagen" magazine, *"Berlin was stuck 110 miles inside the Soviet zone with 3 road, rail and air Corridors administered by Russians and East Germans. They were strict to check out for escapees from East Germany. Half way along the corridor a sudden hiss and a bang and "Moby" blew up! We all got out; poor old Jim removed the engine cover and found a hose had gone. He did a repair but a few minutes later it blew again. We were stuck on the corridor in "no mans land". In a few minutes Border Police came and started shouting but quickly saw we were going nowhere. They gave Jim a piece of paper that saved our lives later on. We were told a repairman was on his way. In half an hour he turned up, tried his hoses but they would not fit. He said he would be back in twenty minutes with the right hose.*

In typical German fashion he did return twenty minutes later with the right hose. Half an hour later with the radiator topped up we were on our way. "Moby" went like a bomb and we were soon at the checkpoint at Helmstadt. This was a fortified checkpoint with a barbed wire fence that stretched for miles. There were Machine gun towers surrounding us and the area was riddled with minefields.

We got our passports and went to queue. Jim was taken away first followed by the other four club members and me. We were all held in a windowless room. Into the room burst three East German officers. They hurled abuse at us in German for about an hour, my German O level was no help. They eventually got fed up and left the room. All I could work out was that it had something to do with time. An hour later a Russian officer and soldiers walked in.

We were very worried now. He informed us that the American checkpoint had been notified of a party of English youths that had been detained for border problems between Berlin and Helmstadt. His English was perfect as he explained that he had been to Oxford and loved it there. He went into details of the charges and said we were two hours late from the Berlin checkpoint and wanted to know what we had been doing along the corridor. Jim explained that "Moby" had broken down twice and was repaired. He showed the initial paper from Border Control officers and the receipt from the breakdown guy.

The officer left with our paperwork. He returned with our passports and said the repairman should have notified the border checkpoint when the repair was completed, but he went to another job and forgot. He confirmed the times so we were free to go. We went through quickly and at the American Checkpoint a Yank said, "I see you Limeys had a bit of trouble, we were just about to send some troops to get you out". Well we were happy to get back home. Well done Jim and "Moby".

Mike Jenks was one of many success stories involving club members whose lives were enriched by international experiences. He subsequently became a youth leader at the Ernest Mason Boys Club in Birmingham and took a number of groups to Berlin to take part in International Work Camps. It would be nice to know how many of those young people passed on their experiences and inspired others to be involved in voluntary work. Mike concludes by saying, *"Later journeys by air and rail to Berlin were never as exciting as dear old Moby. All aircraft were escorted into Templehof by Russian Mig fighters; you could see the pilots they were that close. Rail journeys were long and arduous, imagine the hundreds of Visas' that have to be bought and Border guards with dogs hunting for escapees. Once in West Berlin the place rang with freedom"*.

A recent sad occasion was the funeral of Bill Taylor, who was on the West German leg of our trip to Russia. Bill, Tony Forde and Graham Fisher had worked in the asylum. The Minister describing Bill's life mentioned that Bill's international experiences with the Twenty-Two Club had inspired him and his family to frequently travel abroad and to have a deeper understanding of other lifestyles.

As a tribute to Bill Taylor an extract from his logbook on working in the asylum is as follows, *"It was certainly a very demanding experience. On arrival at Braunsweig we tried to find which bus would take us to the asylum. Too tired to argue we caught a taxi and arrived in style. A few days before we arrived, a patient had escaped and killed a taxi driver with a knife, welcoming news for us. We started to walk up the driveway when suddenly we heard a woman screaming. We Twenty-Two Club members fear nothing and we continued into battle. Further along the driveway more screams were heard. Glancing to our left we saw a group of around forty women. There was a wire fence around the compound to keep them in, or us out. We carried on further to be stopped in our tracks by a large group of male patients, we turned around and they were behind us too. We did not know what to do, whether to laugh, cry, or sit down and pretend to be dead. In the end we were rescued by a kitchen maid who explained to the patients who we were and they started shaking our hands, removing their hats and bowing. They repeated this performance every day of our stay. Although some of them could not read or write, and in some cases not speak, they certainly knew how to welcome us. They were good fun, hard working and went out of their way to help us whenever we needed it"*.

New countries were explored as the three trips a year pattern continued. Two more of note were Greece and Italy. Drama and danger remained a pre-requisite. An extract from my 1969 logbook reads,

"There are different things you associate with every country. For Greece it was tomatoes and the standard of driving. The Greeks are the worst drivers I have encountered. Outside Athens traffic signs are mainly ignored. One of my favourite pastimes was to stand near a "No entry" or "Stop" sign just to see how many times the signs would be violated. Sounding a horn is supposed to be illegal but I was on a coach that passed a policeman booking a motorist. The coach driver showed his disapproval by blowing a raspberry on his horn".

The expression "On a wing and a prayer" that applied to British fighter pilots in the Battle of Britain also applied to Greek coach drivers. Some fellow travellers were on a coach that narrowly missed colliding with a lorry which came round a mountain bend on the wrong side of the road. To mark his appreciation for not crashing the driver stopped for two minutes of prayer.

In England one reads of political unrest in Greece but after ten days I was prepared to write this off as "paper talk". On the 11th day a bomb explosion injured ten and damaged the Olympic Airways office in Athens that we had just visited. The day after I had arrived home the Olympic Airlines plane I had travelled on was hijacked and flown to Albania!

The trip to Italy remains in everyone's mind because it was in the summer of 1966. The ambulance and a hired minibus carried a group of twenty across the English Channel. Six of the group was to be dropped off in France at an International Work Camp. The assignment was to help with the wine harvesting. The rest of the group were to camp out on the beach at Alassio. The memorable highlight was of course watching England defeat Germany in the World Cup Final at a beachside café surrounded by hundreds of German holidaymakers. Despite their disappointment there was no trouble.

Not every club member could cope with the demands of international travel so international issues were brought to them. One such issue was to involve Chairman Mao and his little red book.

In March 1968 I entered into correspondence with Chairman Mao via the Chinese embassy in Peking and with the editor of the Peking Review, China's leading newspaper. Chairman Mao's little red book had become world famous and I was seeking a copy and an interview with Chairman Mao as the editor of the Twenty-Two Club magazine "Yung Tung". The youth club's magazine title was no coincidence. It was a play on the words "Young Tongue" - the voice of young people. A few months later it became necessary to change the name of the club magazine because of a report that appeared in the Peking Review. Chinese children were taught to spy on their parents. One young girl called Tung had a row with her mother over pigs and reported her mother to the police for having more than the allowed number of pigs. The result was the mother was imprisoned without trial. In the Peking Review Chairman Mao praised "Young Tung" for her actions. Changing the name of the magazine was our mini protest against the doctrines of Chairman Mao.

When I received my book from Chairman Mao I wrote the following in the Club magazine, *"I feel the Little Red Book is really an "I'm backing China" gimmick. Two extracts from the book are as follows. At no time and in no circumstances should a Communist place his personal interests first; he should subordinate them to the interests of the nation and the masses. Hence, selfishness, slacking, corruption, seeking the limelight, and so on, are most contemptible, while selflessly working with all ones energy, whole hearted devotion to public duty and quiet hard work will command respect"*.

A quote from the book on the subject of women. *"A man in China is usually subjected to the domination of three systems of authority, (political authority, clan authority and religious authority). As for women, in addition to being dominated by these three systems of authority, men dominate them, (the authority of the husband").*

The thoughts of Chairman Mao were written prior to 1968. By 2005 China has become one of the strongest economies in the world and the Chinese have asserted their physical and sporting superiority by dominating the 2004 Olympics. Does Chairman Mao deserve the credit or do the negative effects of his often-brutal regime cancel out these achievements?

A second example of how the Club brought members in touch with international contacts is as follows. In October 1968 there were flood disasters in Southeast England. In previous years Club members had undertaken voluntary work in Germany through the Internationale Jugendgemeinschaft Drenste. On this occasion they were offering to send young people to England to help with the rescue operations. The letter offering help was sent to the Prime Minister for action. It was accepted as a great compliment that a West German Government sponsored programme would send a letter of help via the Club. The famous quote by US President, John F Kennedy, was most apt. "Ask not what your country can do for you, ask what you can do for your country".

One of the final trips during my time with the Twenty-Two Club was a modest affair to Scotland but never the less it made history. I took the Club Football Team on an Easter tour in 1970 to play three matches. At the time the Club's Under 16 team were mid-table in the Walsall Junior Youth League. Due to a misunderstanding our hosts thought we were representing Birmingham City Football Club and were a top Club. On arrival in Glasgow a Glasgow Select XI was waiting at Lochburn Park Stadium in Maryhill with at least 5,000 people present. The Glasgow Select XI was unique for it was the first time that Rangers and Celtic had ever agreed to field a combined team. It was so "political" that to allow this to happen the teams would change their kit at half time so that they played in Celtic colours for the first half and Rangers colours for the second half. Needless to say the result was a forgone conclusion. The only reason the score was restricted to 17-0 was that every time a goal was scored there was a minor pitch invasion involving hundreds of young children. The time to clear the pitch after each goal meant there was less time for them to score even more goals. The Glasgow Weekly News did a full page on the match focusing on George Stein the son of the Celtic manager Jock Stein and the historic nature of the match. The Club regained some pride in the next two games with credible performances against St Mirren Boys and Vale of Leven, only losing 3-1 on each occasion.

The Twenty-Two Club's international adventures continued until the end of 1970. By then we had raised the funding and physically built a Youth Centre in Great Barr with a floodlit play area. "Moby Jim" had been scrapped, having become beyond the skills of mechanics to keep it on the road. Travel abroad had become cheaper as the flight market expanded. The legacy of driving the ambulance stayed with me for many years. Every so often I would have a nightmare involving driving "Moby" across Russia. It was such a relief to wake up knowing it had only been a dream.

I now needed a new challenge. That challenge was through the Duke of Edinburgh's Award Scheme. The visit of Jimmy Savile in December 1970 to open the club building and launch a "Vanishing Tea Party" fund raising event was to be a fitting conclusion to my time creating the Club. It had taken 9 years and 222 days to achieve the ambition of building an independent Youth Centre in Great Barr.

Perhaps just as significantly, during that period of time, more than 300 young people had taken part in 30 overseas events to sixteen different countries. It had been a small but positive first hand opportunity for those young people to start gaining a whole world perspective of life. It is extremely moving to receive the growing number of messages through the Internet from former Club members from the 1960s who now live and work abroad.

It really had been the "Swinging Sixties" for the Twenty Two Club members. Although the membership was only between 22 and 45 at any one time the Club was never out of the headlines in its aim to raise money to build a youth centre in Great Barr and to have fun. Headline grabbing events included 22 in a phone box, 28 in a Ford 10 van. World record attempts and records broken involved piano smashing, crisp eating and handshaking. Climbing Everest in a day without leaving Birmingham, ambulance pushing, the first car boot sale, a popular music outdoor concert and the booking of Kenny Ball at the Birmingham Town Hall on the night his first hit "Midnight in Moscow" was top of the hit parade, he had been booked four months in advance at the time Trad Jazz was becoming popular. Sponsored animal walks, silences, "Slave for a Day", walking around the Outer Circle in the middle of the night. Christmas carols with a pop group backing recorded in a former piggery in Shenstone a few days after a performance there by Acker Bill. Food parcels for the elderly, a drink drive rescue service on Christmas night. Street parades with a marching jazz band. A company formed that produced the "Short Cut" consumer magazine. During the period when the Club were "Britain's only Mobile Youth Club" there were weekly trips in the ambulance and in a contract hire coach from Central Travel to youth clubs all over the Midlands. A 200 Club with the prize a Mini. The cost of a Mini at the time was £500.

I stayed as leader of the Twenty-Two Club until the end of 1971 to ensure a new leadership team was in place. In the latter months a Duke of Edinburgh's Award group was established at the Club that gave me a valuable insight into what the Award could offer young people in terms of a personal challenge. I would put that knowledge to good use over the next 25 years.

3

Travelling by Royal Appointment

King Asantehene wants the Crown Jewels back
Celebrity Pied Pipers promote the Duke of Edinburgh's Award
Hypothermia drama in Canada and vampire bats attack in the Caribbean

The second stage of my international adventures involved HRH Prince Philip, patron of the Duke of Edinburgh's Award. I needed a new challenge after achieving my ambition of building the Twenty-Two Club so in November 1971 I became the Part Time Co-ordinator for the Duke of Edinburgh Award in the Aldridge/Brownhills area of Staffordshire. The initial brief involved supporting schools and youth organisations in operating the Award Scheme. At that time I was employed as a lecturer in engineering at the Walsall College of Technology.

In 1973 the Award Scheme in Staffordshire set up an International Exchange with an African country as a way of capitalising on the "D of E" having spread to more than 60 countries world wide. Ghana responded and a programme was drawn up that would involve a two-way exchange of Award candidates. In April 1974 the first leg of the exchange involved a group from Staffordshire visiting Accra in Ghana. My involvement was in the recruitment, selection and provision of fund raising support on behalf of Paul Taylor from Pelsall who was to be the Aldridge and Brownhills representative.

The first group from Ghana arrived in Staffordshire in August 1974. One of the Award participants was Ernest Safo Ababio who I was to meet many years later in his capacity as the Executive Secretary of the Head of State Award Scheme, Ghana. Ernest met me at Accra Airport in 2004 when I arrived as voluntary adviser for the "D of E" This 30 year relationship with Ernest is explored further in the essay devoted to West Africa.

Although I was not on the 1974 trip to Ghana, the log book impression of Paul Taylor alerted me to the great potential in entering into International Exchanges with other member countries of the D of E. Three key elements of the exchange were identified, each of which would have a lasting effect on Paul and other members of the group. The first was the Community Service Project in a tribal village whereby they would help in building a school and an irrigation channel to improve crop production. Secondly, the home stay element where the hosts shared their homes with overseas guests. Thirdly, to gain an understanding of the poverty of village people, the lack of clean piped water, no electricity, primitive sanitary facilities, inadequate amounts of wholesome food, poor health care provision and limited educational opportunities.

The Staffordshire group returned to England with a request from the King of the Asante Tribe to Prince Philip: *"Please return the gold and silver relics stolen in 1874 that are currently displayed in the British Museum"*. An extract from Paul Taylor's' log explains the meeting with the King, *"Today we attended a reception at King Asantehene's Palace. Asantehene is a tribal King who still exercises considerable traditional control over an ancient tribe of three million Asante subjects. He received us with great enthusiasm and spoke to us directly. This surprised all present as he normally speaks through a mediator, not a translator, due to his "Godly" status. He gave us drinks and talked informally to us about our stay. He was intrigued by our efforts to see Ghana. "Why Ghana?" he asked. He jokingly threatened to keep us captive until the celebrated Regalia captured by the British during the Sargrenti War in 1874 were returned safely to his care. He gave to each of us a copy of a booklet that explained his Cause. He urged us to contact our Prime Minister and Prince Philip to press for the rightful return of his tribe's heirlooms"*. Ten years after the king's request a number of gold and silver Regalia were returned to Ghana. The Staffordshire group had been successful ambassadors on behalf of King Asantehene.

On evaluating the enormous success of the Ghana visit I was to organise a series of other Exchange Programmes including trips to India, Kenya, Egypt, Canada, Trinidad, Tobago, Hong Kong and China.

In April 1974 there was a series of boundary changes when Aldridge and Brownhills amalgamated with Walsall Council. I was transferred to the enlarged Authority and continued as a Part Time Award Co-ordinator.

One of my first targets was to establish an International Exchange Programme on behalf of Award candidates in Walsall. The first suggestion was a link with a school in Ethiopia but it was ruled out at the Award HQ because of political unrest in that country. St Lucia was the second choice but was ruled out because of travel costs. Third time lucky and an exchange with the Cobequid Educational Centre in Truro, Nova Scotia was arranged. The exchange brought me into contact with two exceptional people, Mrs Judy Chambers, Award Leader at the Centre and Mr Phil Bishop, the Award Officer for Nova Scotia. Judy Chambers went on to receive the Queens Medal during the Silver Jubilee celebrations in recognition of her work in the community.

A group from Canada arrived in Walsall in 1978 with the return visit to Nova Scotia in 1979. The success of the Canadians visit to England is best summed up by young Canadian Patti Rushton who wrote:*"The best experience of my life. The exchange was a wonderful experience for the other "Dukes" and me. After three wonderful weeks in our Queen's homeland, we headed back to our own homes and families with lots to tell them all. About the week spent in Wales where Dukes learned to canoe and rock climb. The mountain was hard walking and climbing, but it was worth it. When we reached the top it was breathtaking"*.

Canadian Colin Kent wrote: *"To me not one day was wasted. It seemed that every effort was made to see that we Canadians were shown all there was to see. The Wedgewood Pottery Company was great. I had heard of Wedgewood pottery and it was neat to watch the demonstration, the throwing of dishes and the women painting the saucers. These three weeks were the best three weeks I have ever known and I would like to go back to England sometime again soon"*.

The Canadian Co Leader Phil Bishop wrote: *"I feel the most important aspects of this exchange were the sharing of feelings and emotions as the activities unfolded. To see, talk and live with other people of another country, to experience your own personal feelings as each day passes is indeed a wonderful thing, one which this type of visit can only afford. To the Canadians who had the privilege of attending, it will be a lifetime memory. Barriers were crossed, although in most cases not that great, they were still there. New friends were made and a better understanding of the way other people think and live was experienced"*.

The second leg of the 1979 Exchange visit to Nova Scotia gave me an even greater insight into group dynamics of Exchange work. It has strange how casual remarks remain in my memory years later. The first example was an instruction to all visitors to a National Park. No trace camping - leave only footprints, take only memories. The second is advice if confronted by a bear. Don't try to escape by climbing a tree - bears can climb faster than you can! Just walk slowly backward talking in a low calm voice. Janet Stokes of Walsall wrote, *"The most memorable part of the trip was the time spent at the National Park Kejimkujik. The actual expedition was really worthwhile, the fact that you could canoe all day without meeting any other human beings and across the still lake view the wildlife, such as deer, porcupine, birds and many others. It was a different world"*.

Heather Evans of Walsall wrote about a visit to a former British Fort in Canada. *"The visit to Fort Louisbourg was the most worthwhile, as you could get a fairly accurate picture of the people and their lifestyle instead of a vague idea gained from textbooks. On television you only see the various enactment's of battles which had occurred but hardly anything on the everyday lives of ordinary folk.*

Canadian Andrea McCallum concluded, *"I value friendship even more since this exchange. It's given me a greater insight of the lives of the people we met and how much they now mean to me. Our dream of a Canada/England Exchange has been fulfilled"*.

At the conclusion of this Exchange Programme I was appointed as a full time Youth Worker in Walsall with a special responsibility for the Award Scheme. It was a major decision to give up twelve weeks a year holiday as a College Lecturer for a more modest three weeks and no extra pay. However I had become mentally drained after lecturing for twelve years and the thought of repeating the same lectures year after year had no appeal to me. The move was to pay off handsomely a year later when I was appointed as the Award Officer for Birmingham, a newly created post to promote the Award Scheme in the Inner City Area.

During the previous ten years as a part time Co-ordinator I had been comfortable with the image of the Award and how attractive it was to young people. It had been easy to maintain a successful programme with highly motivated young people. The Inner City area of Birmingham was totally different. My initial research showed the central area of the City was a desert as far as the Award was concerned. A map of the city on my office wall showed an outer circle of Award groups that corresponded to white middle class family areas. I had taken on a four-year contract to make the Award attractive and appealing to an audience that could not see any relevance in it to them as either Award candidates or Award leaders. In the Inner City of Birmingham, as in other cities, the Award was perceived as white, middle class and elitist. My work over the next three years as an Inner City Development Officer and subsequently for a further 14 years as a Regional Award Officer for the Midlands would destroy that image and International Award Exchanges would help achieve that image change.

The perception that the Award was only for white youngsters was overcome by three methods. The first was to convince the Award Directorate to provide funds to allow me to appoint part time sporting celebrities to act as role models for the Afro Caribbean and Asian communities. My first recruit was Tessa Sanderson, fresh from winning a gold medal in the Los Angeles Olympics. Tessa was followed by other Olympic Stars, Judy Simpson, Phylis Smith, Sonia Lanaman and Phil Brown. These International stars, all Midland based successful role models, were to act as Pied Pipers to the ethnic minority communities. In subsequent years this approach was adopted nationally with the appointment of Kris Akabusi. The second method to overcome exclusion was to produce Award promotional literature in several languages to represent the multi cultural diversity of the community. By showing respect to their language and culture, parents were more encouraging when their sons and daughters expressed an interest in the Award scheme. The third method was to organise International Exchanges to the countries of origin of immigrant families living in the Midlands. It gave young people born in England the opportunity to explore their roots in the Caribbean, Africa, Asia and the Far East.

I was fortunate to receive the support of like-minded visionaries who could see beyond the white/elitist image the Award had developed. The two principal supporters in Birmingham were the late Albert Weedall and Gordon Philpott. The Award Directors during my term of office to whom I have the greatest respect were Robert Heron and Sir Michael Hobbs. Without the backing of these four powerful people the Award would not be so vibrant and diverse today.

In addition to providing ethnic role models to inspire young people to join the Award and to encourage adults to offer their voluntary services the next stage was to introduce Adventure Role Models. One of the first was Lord Hunt, the leader of the team that conquered Everest for the first time. I conducted a videotaped interview with Lord Hunt in Henley on Thames just a few months before he died. Lord Hunt was the first ever Director of the Award Scheme. I suggested to him that he was the Award's first "Pied Piper" and that he had helped to inspire young people to climb their own Everest. Modestly he acknowledged his contribution and endorsed my plans to introduce modern day adventurers to the Award.

During the fourteen-year tenure as the Regional Award officer the following adventurers shared a Conference platform with me. Lisa Clayton (now Lady Cobham), the first woman to sail around the world single-handed. David Hempleman-Adams, Everest climber, the first person to climb the seven highest peaks on all seven Continents, first solo unsupported expedition to the magnetic North Pole and first Briton to walk solo to the South Pole. Dame Mary Peters, 1972 Olympic Gold Medal winner of the Pentathlon. The respect Dame Mary commands in Belfast is reflected in an incident during her visit to the Birmingham Award Conference. There are two airports in Belfast, normally Mary travels from the one that connects with Heathrow. On this occasion the flight to Birmingham was from the other airport. When Mary turned up at the wrong Belfast airport telephone calls to the other airport were made, the flight delayed, and a car provided to take her at top speed to catch the delayed flight. Under normal circumstances members of the public would complain but Mary was applauded as she stepped on the plane, a mark of respect to a Liverpool born woman who was an icon on both sides of the religious divide in trouble torn Northern Ireland in the early 1990s.

Rebecca Stephens the first woman to climb Everest, was a "Pied Piper" for young Midland women. Rebecca undertook two major engagements. The first was during the 40th Anniversary Celebration of the Award with a promotional talk in a building that was originally Lincoln Prison. The second talk was at my final Regional Conference at Fairfax School when she shared the platform with David Hempleman-Adams, Rickii Hunt, another conqueror of Everest and TV Gladiator Judy Simpson. Rebecca was so moved by the whole proceedings that at the point of saying goodbye she asked if she could kiss me! On recovering from the shock I happily obliged. The Conference was so special that the only regret was that it was not possible to bottle the euphoria present in that Hall packed with 600 plus Award supporters. It would have been worth a fortune.

Sir Chris Bonington was also a conqueror of Everest, the President of the British Mountaineering Council and prolific writer. He was another to generously devote his time as was Professor David Bellamy, Botanist, writer and broadcaster. He is also one of the world's great conservationists and one of the few experts to dismiss the threat of global warming as a myth. He says it has occurred on other occasions in the past and it is an entirely natural phenomenon. Glaciers have melted and the ice caps have retreated before.

The final adventurous celebrity and role model was Robert Swan. He first came to prominence when he recreated the "Footsteps of the Scott Antarctic Expedition" and arrived at the South Pole in 1986 with two colleagues on the longest unassisted march in history. He became the first person to walk to both Poles when he reached the North Pole in 1989. 200,000 children who followed his progress on the Internet supported the "Ice Walk". Robert Swan became a UN Goodwill Ambassador for Youth. Surprisingly Robert hates the cold and won't walk anywhere unless he's got a "darn good reason!"

Not all the celebrity "Pied Piper's" were climbers, walkers or athletes. Two of the great names in football, Sir Stanley Matthews and Brian Clough combined to help me launch the concept of Open Award Centres linked to community based sporting facilities. In the early 1980s, football stadiums, like other sporting facilities, were only accessed fortnightly on a Saturday afternoon for so many months of the year. Young people idolised their local star players but their only contact was via the terraces. I persuaded Sir Stanley to give his name to a promotional event staged at the Stoke City ground where I outlined the concept of Open Award Centres. The Clubs were urged to open up their facilities on midweek evenings so that their supporters could use the training facilities, receive coaching from qualified coaches and to meet the players informally. Brian Clough was one of the first to respond by setting up an Open Award Centre at Nottingham Forest. Supporters of the Club who had previously never considered enrolling as Award participants now did so. Thanks to the support of Andrew Messenger and Paul Turner, I persuaded West Bromwich Building Society to sponsor an Open Award Centre at West Bromwich Albion. One of the highlights was the annual presentation of Award Certificates to the participants on the pitch at half time by one of the star players in front of 30,000 spectators. Once this concept of sporting links with football was established I opened similar Centres linked to Rugby Union, Cricket, Athletics, Rowing etc. Without realising it Brian Clough had become a "Pied Piper" for the Award.

I had the pleasure of acting as Master of Ceremonies when Brian Clough presented Awards in Nottinghamshire. I related a story told to me by Sir Michael Hobbs, former Director of the D of E, which reflects the generosity of spirit of Brian. During his time as a Major General Sir Michael was the Commanding Officer of a Guards Regiment based in West Berlin. Nottingham Forest was playing a European Cup match in the former Olympic Stadium behind the Berlin Wall in East Berlin. Sir Michael marched his regiment through Checkpoint Charlie in the Berlin Wall to the stadium to cheer on the Forest team. They were the only British supporters there. Brian remembered this support and when later approached by Sir Michael agreed to send four of his star players to visit a badly burnt soldier in hospital who was on the critical list. Support from the Forest players continued back in England and eventually the soldier recovered and attended a Forest home game as guest of honour. He attributed his recovery to the inspiration provided by the players.

The support from members of the Royal Family in promoting the Award Scheme cannot be underestimated. Since 1971 I can vividly recall Royal visits, firstly from Prince Philip and subsequently Prince Edward. On one of the visits by Prince Philip the final engagement in Birmingham was to visit Fairfax School. The school was acknowledged as the most successful Award Unit in the world, having achieved the most Awards. The pioneering Head Teacher at that time was Gordon Philpott. Normally the back up by Royal staff was impeccable, however they had misread the weather forecast and it started to rain as Prince Philip arrived. They had forgotten to pack umbrellas, fortunately I came to the rescue producing two large green and yellow umbrellas bearing Prince Philip's personal cipher. I had acquired these at a celebrity golf competition at Wentworth where Prince Philip had opened the new third course and named it the Edinburgh Course. Peter Allis was the Master of Ceremonies and golf stars Gary Charles and Peter Thompson were the first to drive from the first tee.

A postscript reinforcing Prince Philip as a "Pied Piper" concerns the umbrella. At the following Regional Conference the umbrella Prince Philip carried and featured in numerous newspapers was raffled. The winner was Wolf Zeuner of Hannibal fame. He organised Ian Botham's sponsored walk with elephants across the Alps recreating the journey of Hannibal. Wolf was such a Royalist that I had to write an official letter confirming that Prince Philip had actually used the umbrella. Apparently Wolf displayed the framed letter next to the umbrella in his home.

One of the Birmingham tours undertaken by Prince Edward involved a visit to Sparkhill to one of the most successful Open Award Centres in the country catering for unemployed young people whose family roots were in the Caribbean. The inspirational leader of the inner city group was Mrs Jean Parry. When Prince Edward entered the Job Preparation Unit, he was greeted by the "ugly sisters" enacting a scene from Cinderella. The three sisters were in fact 6ft tall black young men wearing women's clothing and extravagant make up in the traditional pantomime style. Without a trace of reverence they rushed to welcome Prince Edward, gushingly chanting, "Welcome your Majesty" and giving elaborate curtsies. One of the "sisters" pointed to the Gold Duke of Edinburgh Award badge the Prince was wearing and said, "Oh he's wearing his daddies badge". Prince Edward responded well, giving as good as he received.

After the initial frivolity they got down to important issues such as how ethnic minorities viewed the Award as a "white" programme. They suggested a need for more black role models to promote the Award nationally. An example was given of how publicists ignore black issues concerns BMW cars. In Sparkhill these cars were known as "Black Men's Wagons". They posed the question, "Do you ever see black men driving cars in TV commercials. In the 1980s the answer was a definite no, things have certainly changed in recent years.

Prince Charles inadvertently became a pied piper for the Award when visiting Handsworth in Birmingham just after the mid 1980s riots. My office building was on the Soho Road, and at the very centre of the riots. The Scout Association and the Princes Trust shared the building. Prince Charles had come to praise the work of his Trust's volunteers under the exceptional leadership of the Midland Director, Dave Parker, also a tireless supporter of the Award Scheme.

The reason Prince Charles was able to visit an undamaged building was attributed to information provided to me by a West Indian Community Leader. The work being undertaken by the Award in Handsworth and Sparkhill had been recognised. The projects linked to the unemployed, young offenders, those with Special Needs and targeted at Caribbean families had been accepted as being of great value. On the stretch of Soho Road where we were based three buildings were undamaged. One was a social club, the second Rustie Lee's restaurant, (she was one of the early TV chefs) and thirdly the Award Office. Apparently on the night of the riots when shops were being looted and properties set on fire, there were bouncers from the social club guarding the three properties. It was a major sign that my campaign to destroy the "white middle class" label of the Award was working.

International Exchanges continued to involve ethnic minorities in the Award Scheme. One of the earliest was a revolving Triangular Exchange Programme between Trinidad, Tobago, Canada and Birmingham. The three-year programme ran from 1982-4. Candidates from the Caribbean and Canada visited Birmingham in the first year for a four-week programme involving a foot expedition, community service project and home stays. In year two the Canadians were the hosts to the other two countries and in the third year Canadian and English candidates visited the Caribbean.

It will become apparent from reading the impressions of the visits by candidates that there were massive examples of personal development taking place that would have a lasting impact. A total of 180 young people took part in at least one of the three visits and many more were involved in social events linked to the visiting groups.

The level of responsibility accepted by leaders was extremely high. It always seemed a flippant remark but "Bring them back alive and well" was the bottom line. On five occasions that aim was almost not achieved and could have led to a loss of life. Two such incidents occurred during the Triangular Exchange.

The first example occurred in Nova Scotia, Canada when one of the Birmingham group, Elizabeth Whalley, went into a coma following a water based incident. It followed an afternoon of water skiing on a lake. The light went quickly in the early evening with a corresponding drop in temperature. Elizabeth collapsed as she left the water suffering from the effects of hypothermia. She was carried unconscious to the log cabin where a fire was already roaring. The Canadian First Aiders removed her wet clothes, wrapping her in blankets in front of the fire. Concern was shown when Elizabeth remained in a coma. As a last resort the biggest person present, a 6ft plus tall West Indian lad was stripped off and he and unconscious Elizabeth were zipped into a double sleeping bag to capitalise on his body heat. The relief was immense when Elizabeth regained consciousness. Elizabeth was not the only one who suffered from hypothermia. The log cabin kitchen resembled a casualty station as others were wrapped in blankets and plied with hot drinks and warm clothes. At breakfast the next morning a minute's silence was devoted to give thanks and reflect on the need for constant vigil by leaders and candidates alike when engaged in outdoor pursuits.

Elizabeth frankly recorded her memories, "*I don't remember much about it. I woke up the morning after just happy to be alive and I noticed things I had always taken for granted before. Life meant so much more to me that day, and that was probably the most important lesson I learnt in Canada. At any time I could lose everything I have, so its up to me to make the best of what I have now. I'm not a religious person, but for a few hours that day I believed in God and believed that He had made it happen to prove to me how very lucky I am to be alive and fit and the person that I am*".

Lyn Jordan also wrote about that night, *"The night that will stay in all our minds is when a few participants got hypothermia. To see those people we knew so well, sitting, looking straight ahead with hands as cold as ice was a frightening experience. That night showed how close we all were and how much we cared for each other"*.

Elizabeth made a full recovery and years later I read an article about her in the Daily News headed, *"Rugby Star Liz gets her England Chance"*. She had been selected to play in the first ever Women's Rugby International between England and Wales. The Canadian First Aider, Miss Blanche Gibbs, who helped Elizabeth, reflected with pride as I passed on this news. Blanche was also on hand when candidates showed signs of hypothermia, hallucinations and distress while passing through a swamp area during the expedition. All recovered fully thanks to Blanche.

One of the new experiences in Nova Scotia for British and Caribbean participants was "tubing" on the Gasperaux River. This involved one or two people sitting in an inflated inner tube and being carried a mile down a fast flowing river. An exhilarating experience.

The programme concluded with Civic events with Government leaders. Had the trip been a success? Here are the views of two of the British group;
Steven Richardson wrote, *"The friendship of the Trinidadians and the Canadians was outstanding. Colour, culture or country didn't matter and were not thought about-we were one big family. If only the World leaders and society in general could feel the same the world would be a happier place"*.

Deborah French continued, *"When I think of Canada I remember the sea, the unforgettable expedition, lovely wooden houses, the warmth and friendliness of the Canadians who made us feel welcome wherever we went. The music is my lasting memory of the Trinidadians - singing and dancing wherever we went and giving everyone a good time even in difficult situations. An unforgettable experience, always a joy to look back on. I got a lot out of the Exchange - I hope I put something back in too! It's given me more self-confidence to overcome difficult challenges and to mix with other people. In a world troubled by relationships between nations we should take notice of one of the "theme songs" of the Exchange "Ebony and Ivory". I am proud to have taken part in such a successful Exchange. Thank you"*.

The third leg of the Exchange revolved around the islands of Trinidad, Tobago and Nelson. It was whilst on the island of Nelson that a major medical crisis occurred. The three key elements of the visit included an expedition having to use machetes in the jungle to cut through the undergrowth whilst looking out for rattlesnakes. A community service project planting trees and home stays with host families. Birmingham Co-leader Sue Clegg describes her home stay experience, *"Up to much noise at 7.00am. It sounded like chickens and a puppy whining somewhere. A machine of some sort starts up. The chickens squawk and scream in an awful crescendo.*

Sounds like a massacre, and it was! The family industry is slaughtering, plucking and selling chickens. I ventured down to watch on invitation of the mother. The chickens for sale are picked by the customer, slaughtered with their heads chopped off and plucked by a machine".

It was decided early in the planning phase that I would visit Trinidad in advance of the main party so that I could fully brief the participants, leaders and parents on my return. My visit coincided with the annual Trinidad Carnival, a great musical/dance extravaganza. I picnicked with my host Lt. Colonel William Henry, the Award Officer for Trinidad and Tobago and his family in the grandstand for ten hours as over 10,000 dancers and musicians paraded past. The music blasted from giant speakers mounted on flat-topped lorries, which also housed the musicians. Hundreds of dancers in vivid coloured costumes danced behind each float. A tape recording of the top ten calypsos of that 1984 visit remains one of my prized possessions.

The second death defying experience occurred on Nelson Island, a small island off the coast of Trinidad. It had been a former prison and was now overgrown with wild vegetation. During the first day the group had been cutting down weeds as part of a programme to convert the island to a nature reserve. On the first evening everyone was issued with mosquito nets with strict instructions that they must be used. The next morning one of the Canadian young men was missing at breakfast time. Two of the leaders went to look for him. As they entered his room they found him lying in bed covered in blood with blood splattered on the walls and ceiling. He was not in his mosquito net. What happened was linked to vampire bats, the bats had been disturbed during the days work. The bats had flown through the window and attacked the Canadian. Their bite contained venom, which sedated their victim. They had drunk his blood and spread the blood around the room by flapping their wings. He was taken to hospital and given blood transfusions and antibiotics. The prompt action saved his life. Although he recovered fully from a physical point of view I often wonder if he ever wakes up during a nightmare that repeats the vampire attack. He may live with the memory of that attack for the rest of his life.

The jungle expedition was considered so dangerous that a small squad of soldiers were assigned to shadow the groups. Dressed in camouflaged uniforms the soldiers could not be detected against the dense jungle backcloth. Each evening the soldiers' would report to the expedition supervisors at the camp fire site. Although it was reassuring to know that emergency help was always available it did prove a problem to the girls as reported by Rebecca Harris nee Paske.

"Going to the toilet in the jungle was a major issue because although you could seek out a dense area of vegetation you did not know if it was occupied by one of the camouflaged soldiers!".

Brummie Jane Dolling provides closing thoughts on the Trinidad visit, *"The month was a great experience and I would certainly do it all again. I remember the great fun we had and the new friends we made. To meet and dine with the President of Trinidad and to swim amongst gorgeous coloured fish are events most people only dream about"*. Linda Frew concludes, *"My suntan may fade but my memories never will"*.

On returning home the parents of the Birmingham Award candidates combined to offer a surprise thank you party for the opportunities their children experienced. John Sims organised the party at his home and invited Prince Philip to attend. Although Prince Philip was unable to join us he sent a personal letter which was framed and presented to me. The letter, reproduced here, remains a treasured memento of a successful Exchange Programme that could have ended in tragedy on two occasions:

Buckingham Palace

Over the years one of the many pleasurable aspects of the Award Scheme has been the opportunity provided for young people to meet their counterparts from other countries through Exchange Visits and Projects.

Such experiences are of great value to those fortunate enough to take part, and the successful outcome is always related to the hard work and planning which the Scheme's leaders subscribe to these events.

I am aware that Mr Jim Parkes, as the Scheme's Development Officer in Birmingham, has been responsible for arranging visits between Award participants in the Midlands and those in Trinidad, Nova Scotia and India.

I know also that a tribute is being made to Mr Parkes by participants involved in the various exchanges and by the parents. In consequence, I am pleased to add my own congratulations to him and to all concerned with these splendid and worthwhile International Exchange Visits,

Philip

In accepting the above praise I have to acknowledge the contribution made by my Personal assistant Mrs Gillian Watson who was exceptional in her work at the Birmingham Inner City Award Office. Gillian was also part of the Award Scheme's history as one of the first girls to ever achieve the Gold Award. Subsequently her sister Mrs Margaret Pearce joined the Award Office team and also gave first class support. Mrs Hazel Corden continued that quality of work on moving to the Outward Bound Trust. One of the first boys to gain the Gold Award was Tony Mullins who has been a major supporter of the Award in Birmingham for many years.

4

Punishments that fit the crime - A World Wide Perspective

The loss of a limb or Community Service?
The unequal treatment of women – "Honour Killings"
Justification of the death penalty?

Two questions that arouse great passion are; what constitutes a crime? What is the appropriate level of punishment? The answers to both questions can depend on where you live in the world, what religion is predominant, if it is a democracy or a dictatorship, whether people steal for survival or for greed and whether the death penalty is an option.

Consider the following questions, which are based on actual Court cases that I have encountered while travelling the world. Should someone convicted of killing a child or a pensioner receive the death penalty? Should a householder who kills a burglar be given a custodial sentence? Should women who commit adultery be stoned to death? Should persistent rapists be castrated? Should drug smugglers receive the death penalty? Is it a crime to steal paperclips from your employer or for a starving person to take food from a dustbin? What sentence should a drunken driver who kills other road users or pedestrians receive?

Many countries respect the UK criminal justice system and have adopted its principles and procedures that have stood the test of time. In recent times two major changes in cultural and political circumstances have impacted on the deliberations of Judges and Magistrates in the UK. The first is the influx of immigrants who have brought in practices acceptable in their country but are contrary to those in the UK. An example is an arranged marriage against the bride's wishes. The second is the Human Rights Act that applies to all members of the European Economic Community. A whole industry has evolved within which the rights of defendants have become enshrined in British law. Legal supporters of the Act claim that without a written constitution, which the UK has never had, their client's human rights have not been fully protected. Cynics may say the Act is a rogue's charter that can be used to avoid a just sentence.

How much of your thinking on what constitutes a crime and what constitutes the appropriate punishment is coloured by the newspapers that you read? The tabloids have been criticised for undermining the work of the Courts by their emotive headlines that describe apparent miscarriages of justice and apparent inadequate sentencing. As the reports unfold readers are asking themselves how Judges and Magistrates have concluded their decisions. It is often the final paragraph of the newspaper report that states the perimeters of the sentencing guidelines as defined by Acts of Parliament and the mitigation of the offence/offender. Whilst the report of the case may bring you to the view that the offender should be locked up and the key thrown away, the sentencing guidelines may not permit such action.

The most negative excesses of media privilege often occur when trials last more than one day. Each day a headline blares out an accusation, which, in subsequent days prove to be untrue. Such sound bites can condemn the defendant in the eyes of the readers and if they are subsequently found to be innocent the papers concerned build another storyline so undermining the justice system. That literary legend, "Disgruntled of Tunbridge Wells" has a field day in the letters page of the tabloids.

The next time you feel disgruntled by a sentencing decision consider the legal practices in other countries and the sentences handed out. As a Justice of the Peace I have had an advantage over none magistrates in gaining access to some overseas Courts but nevertheless tourists are welcome to sit in the public gallery of courts in many countries. Half a day off the beach somewhere abroad can prove informative, enlightening and, considering the sentences for similar offences in the UK, sometimes mildly entertaining.

I have attended Courts as an observer in more than 40 countries. These include Magistrates Courts in Capetown, Port of Spain (Trinidad) and Barbados. Supreme Courts in Singapore, Kabul (Afghanistan), Accra (Ghana), Sydney, Jerusalem, Dublin, Caracus, Mexico City, Istanbul and South Africa's Constitutional Court in Johannesburg. Criminal Courts in Los Angeles, Tel Aviv, New York, Damascus, Beirut, Nashville, Amman, Gaborone (Botswana), Dar es Salaam, Harare (Zimbabwe) and Phnom Penh, (Cambodia). The Palace of Justice in Rio de Janeiro, Buenos Aires and Lima (Peru). High Courts in Karachi and Toronto. The Halls of Justice in San Francisco and District Courts in Tokyo and Lanaka (Cyprus). A Municipal Tribunal in Havana. Youth Courts in New Orleans and Colombo. Municipal Courts in Bangkok, Ho Chi Min and the Court of Justice in Tehran. A Mobile Court in Abuji (Nigeria). I have visited prisons in Winson Green (Birmingham), Grahamstown and Cape Town in South Africa and the redundant Alcatraz in America.

Drink driving is a major problem in the UK and Europe but let us start our world tour in Jordan where it is a minor issue as it is a predominantly Muslim country. Police have no breathalyser kits and if someone is suspected of drink driving they are taken to hospital for confirmation of their alcohol level. A sheet of paper is rolled into a tube and the driver has to blow into the tube. The doctor makes a value judgement on how strong the smell of alcohol is. A weak smell warrants a small fine, 10-dinar (£10) and a Court visit. A strong smell has the person kept in hospital overnight, taken to Court the next morning and sentenced to a 100-dinar (£100) fine and jailed for 7 days. There is no disqualification or points on the licence for either sentence. Speeding used to attract a fine and points but from November 2001 points were scrapped and the fines doubled. It appears that no one will ever be disqualified from driving in Jordan for such offences.

Drivers over the legal limit are treated more severely in other countries. Research conducted in 1987 showed the following; (some of these laws may have been scrapped due to the Human Relations Act). In Malaya the driver is jailed and if he is married his wife is jailed too. In Finland and Switzerland a one-year sentence with hard labour is given and in Russia the driver is banned for life. In Bulgaria a second conviction results in execution whilst in El Salvador the first offence is the last as they are executed by firing squad.

A sobering, self-inflicted drink driving punishment befell American Richard Harris. Twenty-seven years ago he parked his Jaguar in a multi-storey car park. After a night of heavy drinking, he could not remember where he had parked his car. Recently, in a New York garage, the car was discovered. Mr Harris has received a £300,000 parking bill from the car park managers!

In Jordan the King has absolute power over the Courts. Sentences such as hanging for murder, treason or child rape have to be approved by the King. The King, who also has the power to overrule any decision taken by Jordan's Parliament, can also overrule these Court sentences. How would you feel if the British Monarchy held such power from the throne?

The equal treatment of women is one battle that has been fought and won within the British Judicial system but the fight for equality still continues in many countries. At a conference I attended in Amman entitled "Cleanse the laws, not false honour"; I heard a typical example of the different treatment given to men and women. A man was released from prison within six months after stabbing his pregnant sister 13 times until she died. It was done to cleanse family honour. The unmarried sister wanted to marry the father of the child and her parents had given permission. The brother disagreed. Had the roles been reversed and the sister had killed her brother, she would have been sentenced to be stoned to death.

A delegate told the Conference, *"My husband always beats me and I think it is normal because if he did not beat me, he would not be a real man"*. Another delegate told of the inhumane treatment of women in the Sudan where the barbaric practice of female circumcision continues. Courts in the Sudan also consider it "scandalous conduct", punishable by 40 lashes for wearing make up, pants, or for acting in an "indecent manner". The definition of such behaviour is purely subjective, not defined in law. What will it take before men and women in Sudan are treated equally and fairly?

The Buenos Aires Palace of Justice (Supreme Court), in Argentina is most unusual. The nine judges who preside over appeals against a sentence receive only written submissions with no formal representation. All reference books are based on US case studies. Appeals against the Court's decisions can be made to the International Court in Puerto Rico. In the courtroom and the retiring room there is a large crucifix and Bible emphasising the influence of the Catholic Church. Ninety nine per cent of judges are Catholics. Appointments are also based on political support. Occasionally a judge is appointed without any legal knowledge, the person having been rewarded for supporting the Government in some way. In Criminal Courts one Judge presides, there are no Lay Magistrates. Is it healthy for the Church to be in control of decisions of justice? The same question applies to countries whose legal system is based on Islam.

Laws in Brazil are based on compromise with Courts in Rio de Janeiro taking a pragmatic view of minor issues, a policy that is mirrored by the police. A typical example relates to car parking. A law was passed to stop cars parking on pavements which was welcomed by pedestrians. However there weren't enough car parks so cars parked on the road caused major traffic jams bringing the city to a virtual standstill. Compromise kicked in, the law was ignored; cars were parked on the pavement, the police took no action. Red traffic lights at night are ignored to avoid drivers being robbed at deserted junctions. Police allow red light jumping to keep traffic flowing and avoid crime. It is claimed the compromise works as Brazil is the only major country in the world never to have had a bloodletting revolution in its history. Would the "compromise" approach work here in the UK? Would you run a red light or park on the pavement?

The Magistrate's Court in Bridgetown, Barbados, is based on the British system although they have dispensed with lay persons as Magistrates; Magistrates now have to be trained lawyers. The maximum sentencing powers in a Magistrates Court is a custodial sentence of three years for drug offences and two years for other minor offences. Serious crimes such as murder are transferred to a Judge in the Assizes Court, which meets quarterly. Barbados has the death penalty of hanging. Appeals against this sentence on behalf of a defendant have to go to the Appeals Court in England. As England does not recognise the death penalty the appeal against the sentence is always successful. All the islands in the Caribbean are trying to free themselves from this restriction and wish to have their own Appeals Court. At the time of my visit in 1988, 20 people were on death row.

During my visit to the Bridgetown Court there was a British couple in the dock. They had been caught with marijuana cigarettes in their hotel room. They were fined $750 with the alternative of seven months in custody on default. Once paid they would be on the next plane out. On relating this case to English cricket fans staying in my hotel, there was immediate panic and the disposal of items down the toilet! The sound of flushing toilets all over the hotel must have aroused the curiosity of hotel staff. Had all the guests come down with a stomach bug? Is the Barbados approach of heavy fines or an alternative prison sentence a sound policy?

My visit to Cambodia in December 1999, just days before the world would be celebrating the millennium, was one of the greatest cultural shocks I have ever experienced. As the world moved towards the 21st century the majority of Cambodians were trapped in the nineteenth century, particularly those living in villages. An example was in a Police Report I acquired featuring a man accused of witchcraft. The village elders sentenced him to death; his liver was removed, cooked and eaten by the elders to cleanse the body of evil spirits. His wife and children were banished from the village. The man's crime that led to his death was for dispensing herbal remedies so successfully that they thought he was working with the devil. The local police chief claimed that nothing could be done and that he received similar reports of tribal justice on an average of ten times a month. Investigations were always met with a wall of silence.

Primitive justice is not only restricted to villages. Another police report showed that people are taking the law into their own hands in the capital Phnom Penh by hanging known criminals in the street from lampposts. This follows reports that Court Officials have been accepting bribes to drop charges against criminals before a trial to avoid long prison sentences. A prison governor had been charged with receiving bribes to release prisoners early. The Prime Minister had intervened and ordered the re-arrest of all released criminals. The Prime Minister has now been criticised for interfering with the justice system even though it is known to be corrupt. Was the Prime Minister justified in taking such actions? Should politicians be allowed to interfere with the judicial system?

People power in isolated rural communities not only occurs in Cambodia but in countries such as India and Tanzania. In a reported incident in 2005 a mob of 150 women in Muddireddypalli, Southern India, decided the village barber was engaged in black magic. The mob beat up Mr Parvathalu, locked him in his barber's shop and then set the shop on fire burning him alive. Unlike the police in Cambodia the Indian police have taken action and immediately arrested 67 of the women. The other 83 had run away. The local court will have a difficult job if all 67 appear charged with murder, even more so if the other 83 are captured. Is it feasible that the court could sentence all 150 defendants to death?

In the village of Nyabugombe in Tanzania, Gesala Mibubo was accused of using witchcraft to stop rain falling on the village. He was taken before the local vigilante leader where the villagers convened a kangaroo court that swiftly passed a guilty verdict. The sentence was for a mob to kick and punch Mibubo. The punishment only stopped when it was realised that he was seriously injured. He was taken to hospital where he died. The local police chief admitted there had been numerous incidents of this nature and that the answer was to educate the people on such matters as weather conditions. There was no indication from the police chief that any other action would be taken against the kangaroo court or the mob.

During my visit to Kabul in Afghanistan in 2004 a unique opportunity presented itself that allowed me to attend the Kabul Supreme Court. The trial taking place was to become International news because the three defendants were American civilians charged with kidnapping and falsely imprisoning Afghanistan citizens. It was the first time that TV cameras operated by Afghanistan or International TV stations had been allowed into a Court hearing. It was also the first time that foreigners, (including myself), had been allowed to attend as observers.

The defendants claimed that they were operating on behalf of the USA and Afghanistan Governments in tracking down Osama Bin Laden. They were rounding up alleged Taliban fighters, torturing them for information on the whereabouts of Bin Laden and when they failed to get the information they imprisoned them in houses they had converted into secure prisons. The Judge and two Clerics found them guilty and sentenced them to 10 years imprisonment. They were branded as mercenaries seeking to claim the millions of dollars reward that are on offer for capturing Bin Laden. The American and the Afghanistan government had disowned them. Highlights of the trial were shown on BBC World that evening but CNN did not carry the pictures or a single detail of the trial-one assumes that these three "mercenaries" embarrassed the US.

The leader of the American group was "Tora Bora" Jack Idema, a former Green Beret. He still claims that he was working on behalf of the American government and under orders from US Defence Secretary Donald Rumsfield. The so-called "counter terrorism" mission would have rewarded his team with $25 million if it had led to the capture of Bin Laden. There may have been some truth in the claims as his sentence has subsequently been reduced on appeal to five years, a comparatively light sentence for kidnapping and torturing Afghans. He even has his own website that he posts to from the Pul-e-Charki prison on the outskirts of Kabul.

Should TV cameras be allowed into British courts? Could live coverage undermine the form of censorship imposed by the tabloid press who only report the most sensationalised elements to the proceedings?

The start of criminal proceedings was observed in an interesting case in the Provincial Court in Vancouver, Canada. The event that led to a woman defendant appearing in Court started as a motoring accident but ended up as a murder charge. The woman defendant was driving alone along a dark country road when she hit a pedestrian. The man smashed through her windscreen becoming trapped in the process, his head and shoulders in the car and his legs outside on the bonnet. He was still alive and the woman tried to free him but was not strong enough. Instead of calling for an ambulance or the police she drove home with the man still stuck in the windscreen. When she got home she parked the car in the garage and shut the door. On a couple of occasions in the night she checked on him to see if he was still alive and to say she was sorry. She still did not telephone for the police or an ambulance. She went to work on the bus the next morning. Three days later she checked the car again. The man had since died. The police were called and she was charged with murder.

The woman driver pleaded not guilty to murder. The case went through a series of legal processes before coming to trial and it was not until early in 2003 that a jury found her guilty of murder. She was sentenced to 50 years imprisonment.

Fans of the TV show CSI: Las Vegas may recall this story line that was revamped and relocated to Las Vegas. In this version of the story the driver was a man and the body was extracted from the windscreen and dumped on wasteground. The damaged car was repaired overnight by a criminal contact of the driver. The twist in the story was although the CSI team traced the car and driver they could only charge him with minor offences as it turned out that the victim was trying to commit suicide and had deliberately stepped in front of the car. If you were a juror at the trial of the Vancouver woman would you have found her guilty of murder or manslaughter or could she be innocent on the grounds of temporary insanity?

The justice system and the press in China were still under government control in 2004 despite China's emergence as a leading international trading partner. I was in Peking, (now Beijing), in 1988, just a month before the Tiananmen Square massacre when tanks drove over protesting students. News of the massacre was suppressed across China. People living in Shanghai only learned of the massacre years later. An international report published in 2004 described the media as a "feeble controlled press with a deep fear of offending authority". China executes 15,000 people a year after minimal trials, sometimes televised, and imprisons more than 300,000 in labour camps.

One dangerous act of theft occurred during my visit to Beijing. More than 500 manhole covers were stolen in the night. The covers were offered back to the Authorities the next day for ransom. There were numerous accidents involving early morning cyclists and open man holes. Knowing the brutality of the Chinese Authorities at that time it seemed to be not only a stupid crime to commit in endangering innocent workers but also for exposing themselves to the Authorities during ransom negotiations. Retribution would likely to have been swift.

My visit to the Accra Supreme Court in Ghana gave me the opportunity to use my skills as a mitigator - usually I am on the receiving end of such an address. A notice in the Court entrance stated that the use of mobile phones in Court was a criminal offence. My guide had been so engrossed in explaining the Court proceedings that he had forgotten to switch off his phone. During the Judge's summing up my guide's phone rang. The Judge responded, "Bailiff arrest that man!" I immediately stood up and introduced myself as a Magistrate from England and apologised on behalf of my colleague. I explained how he had been so engrossed in explaining the workings of the Court to me that he had overlooked switching off his phone. The Judge welcomed me and accepted the explanation, giving a warning to my colleague as to his future conduct!

In another Courtroom a trial was taking place concerning a vicar accused of taking $3,500 from a church member on the pretence of securing a visa for her to study in the USA. He had promised to help by praying for her. He had pleaded guilty and so far had repaid $1,000. Sentence was deferred.

Iran frequently hits the headlines for its political ideology that influences and fuels unrest in the Middle East. The treatment of its own citizens under the banner "the punishment fits the crime" remains brutal. On my visit to Tehran in 2000 I was fortunate to gain access to the Tehran Court of Justice. A single Judge was presiding; there are no juries. All Judges and Clerics are government appointed and must be followers of the Muslim faith; the laws of the country are based on the Koran. The death penalty exists for murder, arson, rape and political activity. Fines are used extensively to raise revenue for public services.

The Judge who was dealing with four men convicted of being drunk in public showed a sense of humour. Drinking alcohol or smoking in public is not permitted in Iran. The men were given a heavy fine and ordered to ride donkeys through the streets where they lived, but sitting facing the donkeys tail. This was an example of public humiliation to reinforce the law.

A more brutal public event occurred during my stay in Tehran. A woman was stoned to death in a public execution for murdering her husband. She was buried up to her neck so that her breasts were not hit. The spectators nearest to the victim then bombarded her with stones until she was dead. Her lover was hung from a large crane so that his dangling body could be seen up to a mile away. At another "event" more than 20,000 attended a public execution to witness the death of a man convicted of murder and rape. He received 214 lashes before being hung from a crane in front of a cheering crowd.

Brutality linked to death sentences can be traced back for centuries. Roman trials around 80 BC had a death sentence that involved the convicted criminal being flayed, then sown into a sack with a dog, a monkey, a cockerel and a snake, and then thrown into the River Tiber.

Do you believe a Holy book can be the sole source of reference when convicting and sentencing criminals? Could the Bible be used in such a way? What do you think about sentencing criminals to death? Would you ever attend a public execution?

Japan also has the death penalty but only for extreme crimes such as those committed by serial killers. I visited Tokyo's District Court and the Supreme Court. By a coincidence both Courts had cases dealing with terrorists involved in Sarin gas attacks back in 1994. Members of the Aum Shinrikyo Terrorist Group were involved in releasing nerve gas into the Kasumigaseki Station on the Hiblya Line. Co-incidentally I had passed through that station on the way to Court. The Sarin gas subway attack had been an event that had rocked the world in which twelve people had died and thousands suffered sickness. Three people were being sentenced in the District Court. Toshiyasu Ouchi was found guilty of being involved in the hanging one of the Cult members. He claimed he was only involved with cremating the body in a microwave charged incinerator.

In the Supreme Court Kozo Fjinaga had his ten-year sentence upheld for helping the Cult build the Sarin gas spraying truck used in the attack. The Aum Shinrikyo Terrorist deserter Kazaaki Okazaki was sentenced to death for killing four errant Cultists in 1989. One of those murdered was a lawyer trying to help parents free their children from the Aum Cult. Can you imagine the panic that would be created if Sarin gas were released into the London underground? If you are opposed to the death penalty would it make you reconsider your position, particularly since the London underground bomb attacks in July 2005?

In Malaysia, Islamic law and Parliamentary law are inter-linked. A case was in progress concerning a man who was challenging the interpretation of the Koran in respect of the number of wives he's allowed. His argument is that the Koran says a man may have one, two, three or four wives His interpretation is that he can take one wife, then in a separate ceremony take two more, then three more and finally four more making a total of ten wives rather than four! The man already had fifty-two children from his ten wives! If his appeal fails he will be sentenced for bigamy. In normal circumstances a husband needs consent from any existing wives before entering into a new marriage.

Consider the above case, if you are a man living in the UK not bound by the Koran. Would you want four wives? Could you cope with the physical and mental demands of four wives? If you are a woman would you want to share your husband with three other wives? Under the rules of multiple marriages a husband must treat all wives equally. If he "visits" the bed of one wife during the week he has to "visit" all the other wives too. If he buys one wife a present he must buy the others a gift of equal value.

Female Malaysian High Court Judges are in a minority; there are only four out of the 74 Judges. Under Islamic law a woman is not allowed to sit in judgement of a man so the range of work undertaken by women Judges is very limited.

The death sentence remains in Malaysia. Hanging is the sentence for murder, drug selling and carrying, armed robbery and kidnapping. Drug smugglers are using young children to smuggle drugs, as children under 10 cannot be charged for such an offence. A sixteen-year-old had recently been sentenced to hang for drug offences; the sentence was being appealed. A twelve-year-old had been charged with murdering a five-year-old. The case is to be heard in the High Court not the Juvenile court. The prosecution will be asking for the death penalty if the youth is found guilty. Could you sentence a youth to death if you were a Malaysian? Should the death penalty be returned to the UK? If so what offences deserve a death sentence?

Another of the trials I observed whilst in Malaysia involved a slightly built woman, barely 5ft tall, who was accused of assaulting six large police officers. Apparently she had gone to the Police station to complain about an incident for a second time after getting no satisfaction the first time. She got angry and allegedly assaulted the six officers. The evidence against her was very strong as the six officers collaborated their own stories. She had no witnesses. It seemed incredible that such a small woman could beat up six officers, particularly as there was no evidence of any injuries to the officers. The defence suggested malicious accusations were being made. The judge adjourned for a month to consider her decision so I do not know the outcome. Sworn evidence suggests she is guilty, logic suggests she is being framed. What do you think, is she guilty?

Community service orders are extremely common in the UK and have also been used for many years as a punishment in Singapore. Orders are made for minor offences such as dropping litter on the street. In addition to a fine the offenders undertake twelve hours of litter collection wearing brightly coloured smocks to draw attention to their offences. Singapore has since been voted the cleanest city in the world.

Does this Singapore punishment fit the crime? The police in Singapore also impose on the spot fines for pedestrians who cross the road against a red signal. Would you support the introduction of such an offence in the UK?

Serious offences committed by young people are a growing problem throughout the world. A typical example was that of a trial attended in Christchurch, New Zealand. It involved a group of 12 and 14 year olds. The two principals were the 14 year old girls who, aided by others, battered a man to death and then drove around in his 4x4 wagon until arrested. Apparently the gang of six were known to the police and lived rough in alleyways. The police had ignored them despite their potential for causing trouble.

A New Zealand Youth Aid Report showed that more offenders are committing serious offences at a younger age. Youths cannot be charged until they are 14, except for murder and manslaughter, where the lowest age is 10. Earlier in the year a gang of nine young people, 12-20 year olds, were charged with the murder of a pizza deliveryman.

The above incident could have occurred in the UK just as easily as in New Zealand. What are the factors that lead young people to commit such crimes? Is TV and cinema violence a contributing factor? Is it due to the decline of the number of marriages with more single woman bringing up children without the support of a positive male role model?

Nigeria is considered to be the third most corrupt administration in the world according to a recent report from Transparency International. A visit to the Abuja Supreme Court provided a concrete example. There is an African adage which says "Every day for the thief, one day for the owner". The current example featured six policemen on trial for the extortion of N100, 000 at gunpoint from a medicine dealer.

Another case held in the Military Court saw three senior Naval Officers charged with stealing the Merchant Tanker "MT African Pride". It has not been recovered – where do you dispose of such a large ship? If the idea catches on will Army Officers start selling tanks and Air Force Officer's selling aeroplanes to the highest bidder?

The Nigerian Supreme Court is looking to revise the guidelines originally introduced by the British in an attempt to speed up justice. It is proposed to remove the principle of "Beyond reasonable doubt" because it has allowed "many that have committed grave crimes to delay the process of justice and waste the time of the Courts".

An unusual initiative encountered in Nigeria was a Mobile Court in the grounds of a football stadium. I found the Magistrate sitting at a table under a canvas sheet to protect him from the sun. He was working alone with no Court Clerk or police officers present. The defendant standing before the Magistrate had that morning received a summons for street trading without a licence. He had been told to report immediately to the Mobile Court to face an on the spot fine. In light of claims of corruption by police and the judiciary is it wise for a single Magistrate to work alone? How would you feel living in the UK if trust in the police, the courts and the government became as low as it is in some African countries? Consider the effect on your day to day life.

Visits were made to the Supreme Courts in Karachi and Faislabad in Pakistan. They retain some of the traditions of former British rule including the quaint 1900 style uniforms and plumed turbans worn by the Court Ushers. Although the Court's library is stocked with Commonwealth case law, the majority of the sentences imposed bear no resemblance to those given out in UK courts.

The limited role of women in public life in Pakistan remains a potential flash point. The Courts have been criticised for treating them unequally in respect of "Crimes of Honour". Under normal circumstances the death penalty would be enforced for murder. If, however, a husband murders his wife because she has committed adultery the death is excused as a matter of family honour. If a wife were to murder her husband for committing adultery she is sentenced to death.

Traditionally, if a wife commits adultery, she is banished from her home never to see her family again. The man she was having an affair with can stay but has to pay compensation to the husband. This method of "honour" doesn't reach the Court and is considered local justice. Former Prime Minister Benazir Bhutto reported 240 "Crimes of Honour" deaths in the first nine months of 2000. The majority of "Honour" sentences imposed on women are now confined to rural communities. A more enlightened view is being adopted by the educated classes in the cities.

There are no separate Courts for juveniles; they also share the same prisons as adults. In the year 2000 there were 20,000 under 16s in prison, with larger numbers of under 18s. In a leaked report I read of the horrendous conditions inmates suffered and the abuse of their human rights. People on remand who have not been convicted of any crime are held in custody in the same conditions as convicted prisoners. Some may spend months or even years on remand. Even when acquitted honourably there is no compensation. Jail inmates are often herded into over-crowded halls and barracks. Most sleep on bare floors. Food has no nutritional value. Prisoners who can afford it cook food brought in by relatives. Personal property of prisoners goes astray, taken by prison staff. Prisoners are charged for privileged light work. Visitors have to pay guards for allowing food to be brought in. Drug trafficking is permitted for the staff's own consumption and they share in the profits of selling the drugs to prisoners. The increase in the number of prison riots confirms that things are getting worse and hopes that the recently elected Military Government would root out the corruption and improve living conditions are fading.

The death penalty in Pakistan is hanging and it is used for offences of murder, terrorism, blasphemy and drug running. A trial I attended involving blasphemy featured a fourteen-year-old illiterate boy who was accused of writing slogans on a Mosque. Although there was no evidence that he could read or write, or any evidence of what was written on the Mosque, the youth was sentenced to hang. After the trial an appeal was launched and despite death threats to the Defence lawyer and his family the sentence was overturned. Irrespective of the merits of the case, to commit a fourteen-year old to hang for writing on a wall is barbaric.

Religious Islamic law and politics are linked. In 1984 General Zia decreed the Hudood Ordinance under which elements of the Islamic codes called Shariah were incorporated into Pakistani law for crimes such as drinking, theft and adultery if committed by a Muslim. Shariah punishes theft with amputation and adultery with stoning. In 1986 a law was passed which makes blaspheming the Prophet Muhammed punishable by death. In the year 2000 some 2,500 people are said to be in jail convicted of blasphemy charges. Do you ever have meaningful conversations about the role of women? Do you believe religion and politics can be combined in devising a punishment regime?

Saudi Arabia remains one of the countries I most want to visit, Iraq being the other. I have made numerous unsuccessful applications for a visa. Unless I receive a personal invitation from someone in authority in Saudi Arabia or convert to Islam I've got no chance. Even the British Council could not help based on my request that I wanted to study the Saudi legal system in my capacity as a Magistrate. Their response was that even they couldn't get access to Saudi courts so I haven't got a hope!

Allowing a man to have four wives can turn out to be an advantage to the wives as can be seen in the following arrangement from Saudi Arabia where women are not allowed to drive. Four women who teach in a remote village had to hire a driver to take them on a lengthy and tiring journey every day. After a while the four teachers formed an opinion that the man had "good morals" and had confidence in him. Another key factor was that the driver lived in the village where the school was situated. It was then decided that the four women would marry the driver and live in his house in the village next to the school. They pay their driver/husband a share of their monthly salaries to make up for his loss of earnings from taking them to school. An example of a marriage of "conveyance" rather than "convenience"?

Based on the experiences of a colleague, who has worked in Saudi Arabia, I established that the country claims not to have a policy of religious discrimination. However, there are no Christian Churches, Jewish Synagogues or Buddhist, Hindu or Shinto Temples. The legal system is based on laws written 1400 years ago. The laws have not been updated to cover "new" offences such as those linked to cars, the Internet, cloning technology or television. Courts are not open to the public and the proceedings are never reported.

Public executions take place after Friday prayers in the main square outside the central Mosque. Officials lay out large plastic sheets to collect any blood. If relatives of the victim shout for their release the prisoner pays with blood money instead of their life. Drug dealers who cannot "buy the blindness" of customs officers or the police are eventually beheaded. This suggests that bribery and corruption exists amongst Government staff.

Women must be completely covered in black clothes, they must not drive a car, have no beach wear, must not enter a bar and must not attend any entertainment or sporting events such as the cinema, football, golf and tennis tournaments, etc.

During a visit to South Africa in 1993 I was able to visit two prisons, a privilege not experienced by many foreigners under the Government's Apartheid regime. The first visit was to Grahamstown Youth Prison where I gave a lecture to staff on my work with young offenders in and out of custody in the UK. Nelson Mandela, President of Gold Shield Award, (their equivalent to the Duke of Edinburgh's Award Scheme), praised the growth of the initiative I had introduced. One of my prized possessions is a framed letter of thanks from Nelson Mandela.

The second prison I visited was in Cape Town. Whereas Grahamstown had a modern prison, Cape Town's prison was old and rundown. Children and adults mixed freely in the prison. Children were used as "runners" for drug barons who controlled the prisons and were sexually abused. Three gangs dominated the prison; every prisoner was expected to join one of the gangs and came out of prison with that gang's tattoo.

Children as young as eight were locked up with adults, their only crime was defined as "loitering". They had been abandoned by their parents and were living rough on the streets before they were sent to prison.

A visit to the Colombo Magistrates Court in Sri Lanka was very interesting. The legal system is based on the British system with Juvenile, Adult Magistrate

Courts and High Courts. The actual operation of the Courts has adapted to the cultural differences between Britain and Sri Lanka. An example was the case witnessed in the Juvenile Court. Twelve years ago five children were orphaned when their Tamil parents were killed in the fighting in the North of the country. The soldier who discovered the children living rough found them homes but all five went to different families across Sri Lanka. Twelve years later two of the brothers and a sister were reunited through a media campaign. All three had been with good families who had provided a proper education and all now had good jobs. They had located their younger sister who was the subject of Court proceedings. She had not been so fortunate and had been treated as a slave by her adoptive family. Now 18 she had never had a day's education, had not been allowed out the house alone, had no friends, never been to the cinema or to any entertainment events. She had cooked, cleaned and looked after the children of the family. She received no payment for this work.

The proceedings in Court were to grant custody of the girl to her older brothers. The mother of the family that had enslaved the girl was in Court. The only sentence available to the Court was to order the woman's family to pay compensation of 2000 Rupees a month (£17) into a Trust Fund in the girl's name for the next twelve years – the period that the girl had been a slave. I spoke with the reunited family members who were overjoyed to have gained the freedom of their sister. Their next task was now to locate the fifth member of their family. All they knew was that a priest had been given custody of their sister. They had traced the priest to India and were awaiting his arrival. Hopefully the priest would know which family the fifth child was placed with.

The relatively happy ending to this case highlights the difference between Court systems and lifestyle. It is a regular practice in Sri Lanka for poor families to sell their children to wealthy families where they are used as servants. Cases only emerge like the one described when a child has been found never to be sent to school. It is only because of the efforts of the other three members of the girl's family that the case ever came before the Court. Thousand of others are not so fortunate. Can you ever imagine any circumstances or being so uncaring that you would sell one of your children into slavery?

A return visit was made to South Africa in 2005. In terms of crime I discovered that Johannesburg had gained a reputation as one of the most dangerous cities in the world. The Citizen, one of South Africa's leading newspapers, carried the headline "Heisteria" to describe the 20 heists that had taken place in November alone. The South Africa Sun newspaper carried the headline "Bullets, Bullets, Bullets" as six are killed and 30 injured in a month of mayhem. Bank managers are predicting that robberies from security vehicles will total 400 for the year – an average of more than one a day. With the World Football Cup due to be held in South Africa in 2010 the authorities are desperate to overcome the violence.

Analysts believe that the military precision behind the raids on banks and shopping mall security vans points to former South African Defence force personnel or former soldiers from Mozambique or Zimbabwe. Groups of ten carrying AK-47 weapons ambush armoured vehicles, running them off the road before blasting away with their automatic weapons to break in. They show no fear of security guards or police who turn up at the scene, and will engage in a shoot out, killing anyone that gets in their way.

A new tip for tourists. If you see an armoured vehicle turn up at a bank or shopping mall then beat a hasty retreat so as not to get caught up in a gun battle between the robbers and the police.

Another example of the scale of danger to tourists is reflected in the closure of the 200 bed Carlton Hotel in the city centre. The building stands empty because residents were getting mugged as they entered or exited the building. Gangs were lying in wait for the unsuspecting hotel guests.

An interesting place to visit is the Constitutional Court in Johannesburg, the most senior court in South Africa. Its role is similar to the House of Lords in the UK, dealing with major issues submitted by the lower courts across South Africa and parliament. The public is welcome and there are guided tours of the whole site.

During my visit a landmark ruling by the Constitutional Court gave the green light to same sex unions. The Court found that the current common law definitions of marriage and the Marriage Act were unconstitutional and has now referred its judgement to Parliament to change the Act within one year. Same sex couples will have to wait until then to have their marriages legally registered.

The review by the court has lasted nearly 12 months. Those for the change in the Marriage Act were the African National Congress, Gay and Lesbian organisations and the Centre for Applied Legal Studies. Opposing the changes were the African Christian Democratic Party, Doctors for Life and Jamiatul Ullama, the Council of Muslim Theologians. Archbishop Desmond Tutu commented "I would prefer they were called same sex unions because using the name marriage raises too many hackles. I support the right of all people regardless of their sexual orientation".

Another major reason to visit Constitutional Hill is that it reflects the fight for freedom of black Africans and traces the overthrow of apartheid. The Constitutional Court is situated in the heart of the infamous Number 4 Prison that housed freedom fighters such as Mahatma Ghandi, Nelson Mandela, Oliver Tambo and Robert Sobukwe. In the Women's jail inmates included

Winnie Madikizela-Mandela and Albertina Sisulu. Some of the original cells have been retained which reflect the inhuman conditions in which prisoners were kept.

There is a large foyer in the main court building that can be used for holding the traditional People's Council. The Councils are used to settle issues involving individuals in a village. Jurisdiction is awarded to the King of the Kingdom covered by the village concerned. Nearly all cases are settled within the village and the foyer in the Johannesburg Court is purely symbolic. The Council's currency is a cow so if someone commits a crime such as theft their punishment would be in cows. The victim would be awarded a number of cows from the family of the thief. If there were a dispute about the exchange of a dowry between families the King would set a number of cows to be exchanged.

If a family does not meet its responsibility in supplying the labola (dowry), the other family can withdraw from the agreement, the consequences of which can escalate as seen from the following report. Jack Chitoto came home to find his wife had been taken away by her parents because the labola had not been paid in full. Mr Chitoto, armed with an axe, seriously injured his wife and in-laws before committing suicide by drinking pesticide. How many cows are you or your spouse worth?

Another form of "Honour" killing was encountered during a visit to the High Court in Dar es Salaam in Tanzania where a murder case was progressing. Whilst murder means the same throughout the world the circumstances leading to such a crime are coloured by tradition and local circumstances. In terms of a label the background to the case would be described as "domestic".

The defendant was accused of battering his wife to death after accusing her of selling a hen without consent. The husband had returned home from the pub and demanded an explanation from his wife for her selling the hen. He had accused his wife of insubordination. Witnesses reported that the woman tried in vain to explain to her husband that she had sold the hen for 2,000 shillings, (about £1.50), because she had not been given any money to buy food. The case was adjourned for sentence. What could be said in mitigation? He is likely to get a light sentence as the victim was his wife and the tradition of wife beating is common in most tribal villages.

When is murder not murder? If you live in Botswana the answer is, when it is a "Passion" killing. A rare case was heard in Francistown High Court. Normally if a husband kills his wife over a domestic issue he is not charged. Likewise if a man kills his girlfriend for breaking off a relationship the matter would not go to court. The inference being that a person is in such a state of passion that they are not acting rationally. The Judge, Justice Lelsididi, caused shock by sentencing the defendant to a 12-year jail sentence. This in itself seemed light as it was a brutal murder with the victim stabbed 18 times. Never the less this was a landmark case in Botswana. "Passion" or provocation cannot be accepted as an excuse for murder.

As the previous cases have been drawn from Asia and Africa it does not mean that "honour" killings do not take place in the UK. A Bangladeshi father ordered his two sons to murder an Iran-Muslim student for getting their sister pregnant was sentenced to life imprisonment in London in 2005. The sister had been subject to a family arranged marriage that she didn't want. In sentencing the Judge, Mr Justice Gross, said the term honour killing was a "grotesque misnomer". The action of the three men had "permanently dishonoured their family with the stain of murder".

A new debate to commence in the UK concerns the interpretation of murder. The Government law reform officers suggest that some murders should be re-classified as manslaughter creating an American style system. "Murder One" and "Murder Two" have become an established method of separating deaths into different categories. Was there an intention to kill? Did death occur during a fight that went wrong? Is there an element of "mercy" in the killing? Such a change would bring to an end the mandatory life sentence for murder in the UK. What do you think? Should killing another person be re-classified in line with the American system?

Human trafficking remains a major issue in Mozambique and South Africa according to the Southern African Counter-Trafficking Programme. Although some Mozambique women and children have been rescued from sexual exploitation in South Africa the authorities have difficulty in bringing prosecutions to court, as there are no laws to prosecute human traffickers. Mozambique women and children are sold in South Africa to miners on the West Rand for about R500 (£70) each. Other are sold to brothels in Johannesburg for R1000. Zambia is also battling against the slave trade. Their government is currently amending the Penal Code and the Immigration Act to include human trafficking as a specific offence.

Travelling across Africa by road at night along unlit country roads can be extremely dangerous. One such tragedy was recorded in the Gaborone Coroners Court in Botswana. The victim was the Chairman of the local Council. His car was found upside down in the road, he was dead, as was a donkey at the side of the road. Although there were no witnesses it was concluded that the driver had collided with the donkey during a lapse in concentration. Farmers allow their cattle to wander around the countryside looking for food because they cannot afford to buy cattle food.

This world tour of criminal justice concludes in America. In January 1995, on a return trip from Australia, I had a stop over in Los Angeles. It was the first day of the OJ Simpson trial, the footballer and film star accused of killing his wife. I went straight to the Court and identified myself as a magistrate. All the seats in the public gallery had been allocated months ago following a lottery but I was allowed to sit in adjacent room and watch proceedings on a monitor in the company of a Court Clerk.

There had been no problem in finding volunteers to sit on this trial. Over 5,000 applied for jury service with 24 selected. The trial lasted almost eight months. I followed its progress back in England on TV every Sunday evening. A quote from a juror released after 117 days was, "It was like being in the most expensive prison in the world". Jurors were dropping out at regular intervals; there was a fear of miss-trial if they were to run out of jurors. It is believed that jurors were displaying symptoms of the "Stockholm Syndrome" where hostages came to identify with their captors, subconsciously believing they were as much on trial as OJ Simpson. Tension developed between African Americans, Whites and Latinos, which led to fights amongst the jurors.

On the night of the trial verdict riot police were on the streets of Los Angeles, as it was believed that a guilty verdict would start mass riots. It may have been a factor in the jury's "not guilty" verdict for the charge of murdering his wife. Although OJ Simpson was found not guilty a civil case subsequently found him guilty and he was ordered to pay nearly £20 million to the victim's families. It is not known if it was ever paid in full. Did you follow the OJ Simpson trial? Do you think he was guilty or did the juries' fear of a racial riot influence their decision to find him not guilty? Do you think he was innocent based on the defence evidence?

During a visit to the Hall of Justice in San Francisco in March 2000 I was mistakenly given a higher profile than I deserved as a Lay Magistrate. As a result I was given a half-hour interview with the District Attorney Terence Hallinon. He was second in seniority to the Governor of California. Both are elected by the people and can serve for a maximum of two terms of four years. Terence Hallinon, a Democrat, accepted Clinton's weakness for women. In his own election fight for office he discovered his main rival had been caught by the police with a prostitute but had not been charged. Hallinon made this public and it affected public opinion in his favour and Hallinon was elected for another four years. He showed me a framed press cutting on his wall featuring the downfall of his rival. He showed no remorse for his tactics in a climate of "dog eats dog".

Crime at that time was down in San Francisco, particularly serious crime. His policy of "three strikes and you're out" appeared to be working. After three serious offences there is an automatic twenty-five year jail sentence with no remission. Fifty per cent of crimes were drug related. Plea–bargaining is encouraged. A trial by jury follows if all other options are exhausted. Unlike the UK, the US Probation Service frequently recommends imprisonment.

Would you support the "three strikes and you're out" policy? Do you find merit in plea bargaining which usually diminishes the severity of the charges and subsequently a reduced sentence? Should the British Probation Service remain positive when preparing reports looking for mitigating factors that will keep a client out of custody?

During a visit to the New Orleans Juvenile Court in 1999 it was reported that there had been a small decline in the amount of youth drug taking. The number of murders had also fallen, attributed to a move away from Crack Cocaine to Heroin use. Users of Crack tend to be violent whereas those on Heroin tend to be sleepy and keep to themselves.

The Juvenile Court operates a Victim's Charter. It spells out the rights of victims of crime. Adult victims can sit in when the offender is in Court and they are able to tell the Judge what they think the sentence should be. They can also ask for retribution, e.g. payment to cover damage to property. If the offender and their parents cannot pay, the Judge will order the offender to take an after-school job to pay the fine, costs or compensation. The judge has a list of job opportunities available. This sounds ideal providing you can find enough employers to take on young offenders.

The enlightened approach to sentencing young offenders for murder in New Orleans is the opposite to the rest of America. Amnesty International and Human Rights Watch has compiled a report that shows that America's record of sentencing children to life in prison without parole violates the United Nations Convention on the rights of a child. The 2005 Report shows that 2,225 children are in prison for life, some as young as 10. The report says that 59% were given a life sentence for their first conviction and 29% did not kill anyone but were part of the crime linked to murder.

The report "The Rest of Their Lives. Life Without Parole for Child Offenders in the US" states, "Criminals to young to vote are being transferred instantly into adults for justice purposes. Criminal punishment in the US can serve four goals: Rehabilitation, Retribution, Deterrence and Incapacitation. Sentencing children for life without parole fails to measure up to all four accounts".

Do you believe that children aged 10 and upwards can never have their lives redirected from negative influences that caused them to be involved in murder? Without the incentive of parole what have they to look forward to? However low the success rate, surely, in a humane society, we are obliged to seek to rehabilitate young offenders and not just lock them away for life?

Another difference between the USA and UK was found in the New Orleans Adult Court is in the use of Probation. An adult offender in the USA can be sentenced to 12 years Probation; the normal maximum in the UK is 2 years. They might also have a sentence such as 3 years in prison and 9 years on Probation or some other combination. The cost of introducing this system to the UK would be enormous, it would take millions of pounds to recruit and train extra Probation Officers to cover the increase in the number of clients.

During a visit to the Nashville County Criminal Court, I was introduced to the Senior Judge and the District Attorney. We discussed trends in crime in the UK and USA. My hosts agreed there is still a great deal of male dominated crime in the Deep South, but not so much in the North (New York.) The laddish behaviour of girls in the UK had not yet reached Nashville hence there is less juvenile crime amongst girls. This is changing according to research from Little Rock. The population of woman prisoners has increased. Many are single mothers who tend to be drug dealers using the sale of drugs to support their children. The police have targeted women in particular as part of an anti drugs campaign.

The right of a citizen to carry arms under the American Constitution remains a major issue despite recent mass shootings and the increase in gun crime. An example of the hunting mentality was noted that on the first weekend of the Deer shooting season 200,000 men would be out hunting and would kill in the order of 100,000 animals. If that is the first day total what will it be by the end of the season? Perhaps the increase in Virtual Reality hunting and fishing via computer will eventually decrease these killings. At least no animal ever dies although there will be an increase in American couch potatoes. Which would you prefer? – couch potatoes or macho Americans?

The world tour of crime and punishment is concluded. Based on what you have read, would you say you are a member of the "Flog em and hang em" brigade? When the question of sentencing is raised are you "up front" or "sideways" in your opinion. In other words do you have a clear view about sentencing options or do you sit on the fence?

Are the people of Cambodia justified in hanging criminals from lampposts because they have no faith in their judicial system? How could the treatment of children in South Africa and Sri Lanka have continued for so long? How can the continuing abuse of women's rights as described in Pakistan, Jordan, Sudan, Saudi Arabia and Iran be tolerated in the 21st century?

Citizens in the UK enjoy many rights denied to those in other countries. Free democratic elections, a free press, equal opportunities for men and women, an independent judicial system and legislation to protect children. These rights have been gained over many years at great cost and should be protected.

When I was in Cuba I saw a reverse image of what the UK enjoys. The Courts are known as Tribunals manned by Government appointed officials therefore having no independence. People trying to flee Cuba who have opposed the Castro administration face death by a Military firing squad. The press has no freedom. Child prostitution is prominent. Castro rules–ok?

The people of the UK should treasure their rights; every citizen has the responsibility to vote in both Council and Government elections. Citizens called for jury service should not seek excuses not to do their duty. If approached by colleagues or friends to apply to serve as a Magistrate you should give such invitations the greatest consideration.

You have been on a quick tour of the world's criminal justice systems. It is time for you to be the Judge. Do you need to sentence yourself to be a more responsible citizen or are you already such a person?

5

Spiritual Enlightenment in India

Stalked by a Tiger
Removed from a train at gunpoint
Working with Mother Teresa - Reception at her home

Afour way Duke of Edinburgh's Award Exchange commenced in December 1980 with a visit to India, and concluded with a second Indian group coming to England in 1983. The three year programme involved more than 150 Indian and British Award candidates. The programme co-incided with my move from Walsall as a Youth and Community Worker to the post of Award Development Officer for the Inner City of Birmingham. This meant that Walsall and Birmingham were both co-hosts and providers of Award candidates to visit India. The second of our two groups were truly international with half being drawn from multi-racial communities in Birmingham having Asian, African, or West Indian origin. For some it was an opportunity to explore their roots.

The programme proved so successful and ground breaking in its design that HRH Prince Philip wrote a foreword to the Evaluation Report covering stages 1 and 2 of the four way Exchange.

Buckingham Palace

There may be many differences in life styles, in customs and in cultural activities among the people of the world but all human communities share a common responsibility for the upbringing of their future generations. The Award Scheme, which is designed as a means of helping adults to meet this responsibility also provides a useful link between all those who are concerned about the welfare and development of the young.

Nothing brings people together more easily than sharing a common interest. In this case the Award Scheme provided the reason for the exchange of young people between Walsall and Bombay but I hope that there will be a much wider spin off from this enterprising project.

The exchange between Walsall and Bombay was a great success as this account makes clear and I very much hope that this example will inspire many other similar projects with equally rewarding results.

Philip

On the 15th December 1980 a party of 22 from Walsall left Heathrow Airport on a 6000-mile journey to Bombay, (recently renamed Mumbai). They were to be the first ever group of British Award Scheme candidates to visit India while undertaking Award activities. What they experienced while in India is best summarised through the eyes of the British participants.

Helen Titley starts our story as the plane has come in to land at Bombay Airport, *"As the plane doors slid open, it suddenly hit me. I was in another continent. Standing there waiting to set foot on Indian soil I suddenly felt very alone and quite frightened. What was in store for myself and the rest of the party in the next thirty-one days? My mind buzzed with a thousand questions - all of that had one thing in common - the answer - wait and see".*

The group did not have long to wait before the fascination of Bombay opened before them. The journey from the airport was quite eventful with the bus breaking down and the journey completed in a fleet of taxis, all with "Kamikaze" drivers. These first few hours posed the group with their first challenge. Jolanta Cichosz describes the journey and the challenge. *"As we travelled into Bombay from the suburbs, shacks were situated alongside the road, housing thousands of families. Beggars became part of our everyday life. When we travelled in taxis and stopped at traffic lights children, mothers with babies, the elderly and some disabled people, would come up to the windows and ask for money or food. The most distressing moment that I have ever experienced was when someone behind me called out and I turned around and to my horror saw a young girl, without an arm from the elbow downwards, presenting herself to me. I looked away immediately with tears in my eyes, I felt sorry for the girl, for her disability, but more so for the fact that she had to beg to survive".*

How do you prepare young people for such an experience? Robert Deeley sums up the problem. *"Despite the monthly meetings I attended where films were shown and various speakers invited to give the group some kind of impression of what India was really like, I was still surprised to see crudely constructed buildings of tin or wood and straw just erected anywhere at the side of a road, that people had made their home".*

Paul Tunnicliffe remembers the street dwellers. *"The poor lived on street corners with their few belongings scattered about them on the pavement with the crowds of people in the rush hour walking through their living room. Here they lived through summer, winter and monsoon with the natural air conditioning of warm fronts, cold fronts, high-pressure zones, and low-pressure zones, as God decided what to do next with the weather. These people had a hard carpet of flagstones and cobblestones, strewn with a mixture of rotting food and cow dung. They share their homes with mice, rats, discarded cats and half starved dogs".*

Within the first hour we had to come to terms with a lifestyle totally alien to our own. Horror stories were related of the way in which village children were brought into the city by "Fagin's". Limbs were intentionally broken and left in grotesque positions to exact the greatest amount of sympathy. Beggars with no legs propelled themselves on flat trolleys as they weaved up and down the streets looking for tourists. When travelling in taxis it was wise to have the window up despite the heat. It was not just the problem of begging hands being thrust into the taxi but on one occasion a beggar thrust the head of an enormous snake towards my face, the snake being coiled about his body. The tactic was that if you gave him some coins, he would remove the snake, which was only inches from my face. Almost rigid with fear I groped for some money from my pocket. At that point the lights changed and my driver roared off as the snake was quickly removed from the taxi.

I don't know if the next incident was related but when we passed the next Hindu Temple the driver, without stopping, put both his hands in the prayer position and bowed his head for a few seconds, leaving the taxi completely out of control. I have been to India three times and I am still not sure if they are meant to drive on the left or right side of the road. A fact noted by the late, great, cricket commentator Brian Johnston.

The first stage of our visit was to involve staying in the homes of our Indian hosts. No one was going to live in a roadside cardboard shack but in comfortable high rise accommodation blocks. The Indian Award participants were in full time education and therefore language was not going to be an issue. The opportunity to live with an Indian family and to share their lifestyle was to be one of the most rewarding educational aspects of the visit. Here's Gail Lycett's description,

"The Indian people are the kindest, warmest people I have ever met. Their sincerity is something special that cannot be put into words. Everything they said came from the heart".

During the home stay period in Bombay the group engaged in many study tours. Jill Deeley tried to come to terms with the role of the religion and the lifestyle of the street dwellers. She wrote, *"I was confused by the lifestyle, for example the Mosques. Yes, so grand and majestic they stand decorated with gold leaf, diamonds and marble worth millions of pounds. But less than 20ft away people are living in squalor. Sacks were rolled and unrolled daily on the pavements, these were people's "homes". I realised how desperate and piteous the lives of street dwellers were, it made me feel spoilt and gluttonous. The only explanation my Indian host could offer was that religion was the only thing in life to motivate them, the promise that the next life will be better".*

International agencies such as Oxfam can be seen across the City trying to improve the quality of life for the most deprived families. One of their ventures featured mobile crèches. When a new high rise building is to be constructed the builder recruits an army of construction workers from drought hit areas like Andhra and Maharashtra. The migrant workers live on site in simple constructions made from paper, cardboard and straw. The men are paid 7 Rupees a day (42 pence) and the women, (who do the same amount of work), receive 5 Rupees a day (30 pence). The children are left to run wild on the site, receiving no education. Once the first floor is completed the Oxfam mobile crèches move in with the reluctant approval of the builders. They provide educational facilities and as the rest of the building rises they expand upwards, up to 150 children are catered for. Trained workers ensure the babies are fed and cleaned, younger children organised for play and creative activities and older children introduced to the disciplines of regular study. A doctor calls for a weekly health check and a daily midday meal is prepared. Volunteers work from 8am to 4.30pm, helping in any way they can. Walls become blackboards and slates and chalks are used for writing. A piece of cloth tied to a stick is a paintbrush. Civic Authorities accept no responsibility for the children and they do not interest politicians, thus they belong nowhere and to nobody. Visiting the crèche made me appreciate how lucky we are to have an education system that caters for all children and that they are not left to wander the streets or be used as child labour.

The second stage of the programme was undertaking an Exploration Project at the Matheran Hill Station. It was a beautifully quiet location 2,500ft above the plains with breathtaking scenery, and an abundance of wild life including panthers, poisonous snakes and tribes of monkeys. It was situated 60 miles from Bombay and was reached via an old steam engine drawn train. The train was crammed full with up to a hundred in each of the carriages that had no doors, just an opening in the sides at both ends. The train stopped for about 30 seconds so if you wanted to embark you had to push through the crowd. If you don't want to get off be careful you're not pushed off! I witnessed a man carrying a baby trying to get off at three consecutive stations without success.

The dormitory accommodation at the Hill Station was basic and nature provided its own alarm clock to ensure we got up early with monkeys jumping on the tin roof at 6.30am. The Exploration involved studying the wildlife. Everything seemed so much bigger than anything we had experienced before, ants an inch long, lizards and scorpions that looked like plastic toys, giant butterflies, cork trees, vultures, eagles and bats as big as seagulls were all observed.

The visit to Matheran coincided with Christmas Day; it was to be a Christmas like no other. Here's Rachel Bush's thoughts, *"This Christmas meant more to me than all the ones before and those likely to follow. We had a few streamers and balloons provided by our Indian friends and our Christmas tree was a sprayed branch. On Christmas morning we opened the cards and presents we had brought from home. As a surprise we had a magic show by a wandering magician who amazed us by levitating his assistant 5ft into the air. This was amazing and took our minds off Christmas at home. A snake charmer was part of the performance. Robert Deeley volunteered to play the bean pipe as the cobra rose swaying from the basket, a great photo opportunity. We cooked our own dinner that was topped off with Christmas puddings we had brought from England. The most memorable part was going to a small chapel for a service. Everybody took part; all denominations and religions were there yet everyone praised the Lord for his wonderful birth. As the service wore on it hit me that this was the real Christmas-no television, snow, a little food (although it was sufficient). The whole service was too much for me and many others; we were all deeply moved especially watching the children joining in. Never again will I eat too much at Christmas. I will think of the people who starve and to them Dec 25th is just another day".*

I can concur that the service was exceptional. I had not spoken from a pulpit before and the combination of events and the surroundings proved too much for me as I began to cry. Here were Christians, Muslims, Hindus, Parses and a few without a religion, all sharing a mystical moment. The sky was pitch black, stars sparkling like diamonds, the only sounds were the movements in the undergrowth as wildlife passing on their way. Samantha Bell summed up the evening; *"I discovered the true meaning of Christmas".*

Here is a view of India not seen by a tourist and described by my wife Christine as to what makes these kind of adventures so worthwhile; *"A group of us set off from Matheran to a small village of mud huts known as the "Village of Hope". As we descended the freshly hewn steps of the mountain path, which the villagers had recently completed, we seemed to enter another world. In appearance it was like the opening scene of "The Sound of Music", - rolling hills with a few goats scattered here and there. The lower we went the warmer the temperature. In the distance was a primitive school room constructed of corrugated sheets. The village itself was in an idyllic spot, nestling in the valley and comprising of 10 huts. It seemed a healthier alternative to City life, but the people still had a physically hard life, selling firewood to survive by carrying it up the mountain to the town. They were able to grow a little rice each year although the ground was mainly infertile. We were invited into a mud hut, which was well constructed consisting of a timber frame with a thatch on corrugated sheet roof. The hut was spatial, clean and cool. As we climbed back up the mountain we felt like "Jack" climbing the "Beanstalk", because the two worlds, one at the bottom of the mountain and one at the top, were so different".*

The third stage of our programme was a week long Community Service Project in an isolated village. Our base camp consisted of two brick built rooms, one being a kitchen and the other a communal bedroom. It was located 5 miles from the village we had adopted back in England. I had anticipated that this project would be the ultimate test of character for the group. You can only prepare to a small extent with the aid of films, photographs and magazine articles. How would the group respond to a journey back in time? Could they cope, would they respond to the conditions and physical demands? I had no need to worry, they were magnificent.

The work included constructing a road, clearing a site for a hospital, white washing houses, constructing homes, making clothes for village children, organising sports afternoons for children, playing a cricket match against a village team, singing and dancing for villagers and assisting doctors at a clinic. Just listing the work does not do justice to the groups efforts. They worked in temperatures in the 90s, walked up to 10 miles a day to and from the base camp, did physical work in the morning, organised social events for the children in the afternoon and entertained villagers at night.

At the base camp washing facilities were a bucket from the well, beds were sleeping bags on a hard floor with lizards on the walls in the girls quarters and rats running over the boys sleeping outside on the porch. A single toilet served thirty people; food was short on occasions. By 10pm each night everyone was asleep, oblivious of rats and lizards, just content with a good days work.

I have the utmost admiration for the group. At one stage we had three stretched out from exhaustion, others had sore eyes and skin from using primitive whitewashing equipment that covered them from top to bottom. Most of the group suffered from sickness and diarrhoea. Despite these hardships they fulfilled the whole programme thanks to the support of the Indian Award group members and the kindness and touching gratitude from the villagers. You could feel the group grow in stature. Village life had taught us to think more of others than ourselves. We began to question what was right or wrong with our society. It was extremely satisfying to have made a contribution to the village whether it be in the form of a £300 water pump we had donated, the slates, chalks, sweets and toys to village children or the hours of pleasure sports afternoons and evening dances gave. Before the group left England I predicted that they would come home with a new philosophy of life. If I am proved right it will be the village project that will have had the greatest influence.

The major material contribution to the village was of course the provision of the water pump. Prior to the installation of the pump the women villagers had a mile round trip fetching water from a well and carrying water jars on their head, journeys often made four times a day. It was not only physically demanding but took a large proportion of their day. The provision and installation of the pump in the heart of the village was to be a legacy of our visit.

Although not of material value we did contribute to the folklore of the village through participation in a cricket match against the villagers. Picture the scene, the ground was an area totally devoid of grass in the middle of a village surrounded by mud huts. The wicket was cow dung smoothed by many hands and baked hard under the sun. There was just one bat that had been carved from a tree branch that had to be dropped every time a run was attempted. There were no pads or gloves, just sticks from a tree as wickets. It was agreed with their captain that as I was the only person who played cricket regularly that every member of our party of 18 would field and bat to try and make the game more equal.

They won the toss and batted. It was just after midday and the temperature was in the 90s. The villagers hit a quick fire 200 plus before declaring having realised that we weren't very good as we wilted in the sun. I opened the batting and was scoring well as the wickets tumbled at the other end. A half a century was scored before I was caught on the boundary; we were 10 wickets down for just 66 runs. Up to this point the village adults were going about their normal tasks. The men were wandering across the outfield with cows and goats and the women carried bundles of firewood on their heads. The girls in our team had tried to dress as sensitively as possible not to offend the older members of the village; however, it was impossible to disguise the physical characteristics of one of our girls. Jane, (her name has been changed to avoid embarrassment), was well proportioned compared to the women villagers who were slightly built because of the limited supply of food. As Jane strode to the wicket there was an immediate reaction. Jane had good eye/ball co-ordination and gave the first ball a massive swipe. I shouted, "Run Jane" and she ran. There was an amazing silence for a few seconds as she ran. The players stood in awe as she thundered down the wicket with her bosom heaving. For the next 20 minutes the bowlers sent down long hops and full tosses allowing Jane to hit the ball and run. As we were shouting her to run so were the villagers! Catches were deliberately dropped; no one wanted the wondrous sight of Jane running to end. As our score rose over a hundred and Jane scored 50 she accidentally trod on her wicket, not only snapping two of the stumps but also ending our innings and the entertainment of the villagers. Initially there was an air of gloom before everyone joined in the applause as Jane walked off the field. The result was an easy win for the villagers but the star was Jane.

Our departure was extremely emotional. Co-leader Dennis Parker summed up his feelings, *"For a month I was able to be myself. Never a harsh word. I said to Giresh only a few days before leaving that it was a dream. He said "No Dennis, this is reality". I realise now what I really meant. It was the totally unselfish caring by our hosts, forming bonds of affection. Ideals in practice making life as if in a dream".*

Before the group had set off for India I said it would be the trip of a lifetime and it was. I said it would change them – and it has. I said they would step back in time and they did! The flight back to England had a dramatic moment. One of our group was ill on the plane. It appeared to be so serious that the plane made an unscheduled stop over in Rome because of the fear of Cholera. Fortunately it proved to be a false alarm. Once again I was to get everyone home safe and well.

The second leg of the Exchange Programme saw a group of 24 from India arriving in Walsall on the 18th July for a four-week visit. The Walsall group that had visited India earlier that year may have been apprehensive but so were the Indian visitors. Mehejabeen Kazi felt very unsure, *"For a long time I've read Indian newspaper reports about racial riots and the skin heads in the UK. I needn't have worried, there was only excitement and wonder, a month of fun and laughter"*. Shirin Darbary's thoughts were on the British weather, *"I stepped off the plane at Heathrow and the chill wind froze me to the bone. How would I survive four weeks in this weather?"* Shirin was describing a British Summer.

The visitors undertook a parallel programme of home stay, an Exploration project of restoring a stretch of the Cromford Canal at Matlock, a Community Service project in Pembrokeshire, South Wales, that involved working with a National Trust team on coastal reclamation and an Expedition in the Derbyshire Peak District. There were Civic Receptions and a grand finale at the home of Mr and Mrs Botterill at Gould Firm House near the top of Barr Beacon. The outdoor party was like being back in India; our visitors in beautifully coloured clothes, Indian food, music and dancing. Mrs Bapsy Chubb, Chair of Trustees and group leader echoed Prince Philip's words, *"Exchanges such as this one help bring the world closer together"*.

The third stage of the Exchange Programme proved to be the most dramatic and dangerous of the four stages. As I was now working in the Inner City of Birmingham, I recruited a group of Gold Award Holders from there as well as a smaller contingent from Walsall. What I had in mind needed an older group in the 18-21 range. The unique feature of the group was the number drawn from ethnic minority families who would be exploring their family roots whilst abroad.

The first major element of the visit was a conservation project in the Corbett National Park. It was called "Operation Tiger". The park had been designated as an Animal Sanctuary and we were to monitor the movements of the resident tigers.

A briefing session was held in the Warden's office amongst his collection of animal trophies, the centrepiece of which was a 400lb stuffed tiger. There was a skin taken from a tiger that had been killed by a panther that in turn had been killed by an elephant. The elephant's tusks were on display; it had been killed by a falling tree!

On the first morning we were roused at sunrise, 5am. We rode on elephants, four to a saddle, through grass "as high as an elephant's eye" as the song goes. We were looking for the spoor of the tigers and signs of any of their kills. It was a wonderful experience splashing across rivers even though we did not catch a glimpse of a tiger at the time. Later that day we set off in two mini buses towards the river. The vehicles were parked up and we all entered straw covered hides on a high bank overlooking the river. From there we could spy on a host of animals at the water's edge. The description of Corbett Park is a "zoo in reverse", where animals watch humans. Little did we know that 20 yards behind was an 18 stone tiger watching us! Fortunately it was not hungry and wandered off. We quickly returned to the mini bus to view the enormous paw marks left by the tiger as it had circled our vehicle. We had had a lucky escape.

At the completion of our stay in the National Park we returned to Delhi. Our next visit was to be to Agra and the white marbled Taj Mahal, one of the 'Seven Wonders Of The World'. It must be one of the most photographed buildings in the world and is quite breathtaking. It is strange that many people don't visit the black Taj Mahal just across the river. Apparently the King hadn't intended for people other than himself to visit the white Taj, which was a memorial to his wife. The Black Taj was intended for visitors. Depending on which guide you speak with you will get a different version of events regarding its completion. To ensure another building of its beauty and design could not be built again, the King ordered that the architect is blinded and his thumbs chopped off say one story. Alternatively, you may be told that all 22,000 slaves, who helped build the memorial, had their hands chopped off so that they could never build anything so beautiful again. The second version sounds too incredible to be true.

Balbir Singh, a member of the Birmingham group, went on an adventure of his own choice, supported by Keith Brant. Balbir chose to visit Dhandwar in the Punjab, a village where he was born and had left aged 7 to live in England. He had many relatives who still live in the village including his grandmother who was nearly 100. They also visited the Golden Temple at Amritsar, the major centre of the Sikh religion. Balbir describes his pilgrimage to the village, *"My family were waiting for me and for the first time in my life I cried because I was so happy, it was a dream come true. There were a lot of relatives I remembered"* Keith also commented on the welcome, *"I was the first white person to visit the village. When I first appeared children ran away from me or stood and stared from a safe distance"*. The postscript to Balbir's visit was his admittance that he was too "Westernised" and couldn't return to live permanently in the village. The only modern facility was a loud speaker system that aroused everyone at dawn to go to prayers.

Back in Agra four of the girls had their own drama when a drunken man got into their hostel room. Fortunately one of our group, Mohamed, heard the disturbance and called the Manager. The man was dragged out by four members of staff and beaten with bamboo sticks. Instant justice, Indian style.

The journey from the hostel to the railway station presented a personal challenge to Ian Mailes. Ian was a member of St John's Ambulance Brigade. Our coach approached the scene of a road accident; here Ian describes what he saw, *"The man lay in the middle of the road marked with a circle of bricks. I've seen dead bodies before but none that shocked me as much as this one. It affected everyone in the coach too. There was silence for the next hour"*. Ian got off the coach to see if he could help but left his passport in full view on the back seat. No one noticed the quick hand that reached in and took it. It took me two days to get a replacement from the British Embassy to get Ian out of the country.

The train journey from Delhi to Calcutta via Varanasi took 44 hours and would involve the military. I had purchased tickets in advance for five compartments. Although the compartments were like miniature cells, dirty with iron bars across open windows, at least we felt secure as we travelled to the Holy City of Varanasi. It is claimed that Varanasi is the oldest living city in the world. It has been the Hindu Spiritual Home for India for 3,000 years. There are thousands of temples and shrines in the streets and alleyways. Many Hindus travel hundreds of miles by foot to be cleansed at the stepped bathing ghats that line the Holy River Ganges. They come to wash away their sins, to offer prayers and flowers and to sprinkle the ashes of the dead on the sacred waters. Some pilgrims come to die, their bodies are burnt at the river edge and their ashes scattered on the water. Sometimes the cremation was not completed before the remains were thrown into the water. As we travelled down the river in rowing boats our oars would become entangled with partly burned arms and legs. We arrived in Varanasi on Christmas Eve. On Christmas morning some of the group including my wife Christine, travelled in boats on the river as the sun rose, a wonderful experience I was told.

The train journey to Calcutta on Christmas Day proved to be one of the most traumatic journeys ever experienced. I had booked five compartments for the second stage of the journey. Unfortunately, due to corrupt rail officials the tickets had been sold five times over. When we got on the train our five compartments were already overflowing with almost 18 people crammed in each. We all camped out in the corridor with our luggage. Protests to the inspector were fruitless; our four native speaking members tried to reason with the inspector in his language without success. Three stations later we were greeted by armed police and ordered off the train at gunpoint. Apparently word had been forwarded that troublesome British passengers were clogging up the corridors. Once again we protested showing our travel documents. Passengers on the stationary train looked on as if watching a play unfold. A senior officer who spoke English appeared so I took over. The outcome was that passengers in one compartment were removed, our entire luggage placed in it and our group allowed to stand in the corridor. My son

James, who was seven at the time, was placed on the roof rack for safety. The irony was we were removed for safety reasons, (clogging up the corridor), whilst there were people travelling outside on the roof of the carriages and on the buffers. They had disappeared as the train had pulled into the station but as soon as the train started to move they jumped back on to continue their free ride.

At the completion of the 15-hour journey we went to the YWCA International Hostel in Calcutta which was to be our base for the next week. The hostel was a magnet for the beggar children, some of whom lived and slept on the entrance steps. Snehdeep Ahluwalia was naturally making comparisons between her life in Birmingham and that of these children. *"The children were just like ordinary children, (a lot sweeter as a matter of fact), the only difference being that they did not know who their parents were. One of them, disabled, without legs, was said to be the best pickpocket in Calcutta, but to us he was just a sweet lad"*.

The group was to take part in a Community Service Project at the village of Khareberia, 15 miles South of Calcutta. It had been set up in 1943 by the YWCA at the time of the Great Bengal Famine to help the starving and dying. Tremendous progress had been made with the establishment of a school, clinic, immunisation programme, maternity hospital, tube well, weaving centre and a girls club. During the stay at the Khareberia, our group were able to help with potato planting, spinning and weaving, (the products of which were sold in the local market to bring in valuable revenue), nursing duties in the maternity hospital and at the weekly clinic. One of my favourite photographs is of my daughter Leigh, 10 years old at the time, weaving on an old style loom, sitting on the grass next to her Indian tutor, a skill handed down for centuries.

One of the greatest culture shocks whilst working in the village occurred at the weekly clinic. Our girls, 18-20 year olds, were confronted by a 14-year-old girl with a baby who was a widow. She had been subjected to an arranged marriage at the age of 12 to a man 25 years old. Her husband had subsequently been killed in an inter village dispute. Could there have been anything more dramatic to bring home to the girls the quality of life they enjoyed compared to the girl with the baby?

During the time at Khareberia Clinic and the Children in Need Clinic at Cini we had worked alongside members of Mother Teresa's Religious Order. At the completion of our stay Mother Teresa invited us all to her home in Calcutta to say "Thank you". The group gathered expectantly in a small sunlit courtyard for one of the greatest moments of our lives. Suddenly a small figure stepped from the shadows and said "God Bless you all". For ten minutes she chatted with every young person asking about his or her aspirations in life, signed autographs and posed for pictures. Finally she blessed the group before disappearing back into the shadows. Many had tears in their eyes and were too choked to speak as Mother Teresa left. A truly memorable experience heightened by the group spontaneously singing a Christmas carol. Just recalling this has brought tears to my eyes.

I was subsequently to have further contact with Mother Teresa. By amazing coincidence Mother Teresa visited Bombay during our final home stay period. She was to lay the foundation stone for SCOPE, India's national Institute for Research. When she stood up to make her address she looked tired and frail. The first few words were very subdued but suddenly, as if charged by some outside force, she literally glowed and gave an uplifting address. Many years later I visited Albania where Mother Teresa was born and also attended the Notre Dame De Lourdes Cathedral, in Casablanca, which is dedicated to her and to the cause of Sainthood.

The lives of three of the young men in our group have been changed dramatically because of the work of Mother Teresa. The first was Robert Deeley who also went on the first India Exchange of 1980/81. He was so moved by the plight of so many deprived people that he and Ian Henry ran a number of fund raising slide shows in the Walsall area prior to this second visit, this time as Gold Award Holders. They raised £2,800, which was presented to the Erdington, Birmingham branch of the Co-workers of Mother Teresa. After our group had completed the one-week project at the YWCA village, Robert stayed on for a further week forgoing the trip to Goa with other group members. During this extra week he worked in the Titogaila Leper Colony. Robert describes his work treating a man with Leprosy.

"I was asked to help one of the Australian nurses to treat a man that had been living rough on the street. There appeared to be a large sore that covered about half his foot. Annetta, the nurse, started by piercing the sore and drained off a white coloured liquid mixed with some blood. She then removed a large area of surface skin that came away easily. I held the man's foot steady as she operated. Underneath the skin was a large hole full of puss. After cleaning the wound it was dressed. A very strange thing happened later when I was asked to help carry what I thought were patients to the ambulance ready for transferring to Prem Dan. I only realised they were dead bodies when I saw them being thrown into the back of the ambulance. It was a shock as I'd carefully carried an old man who had his eyes fixed on me thinking he was in a trance when he was in fact dead!"

The second young person to have been influenced by Mother Teresa features in a strange story. The responsibility of taking a group of young people abroad is greater today than in the 1980s but nevertheless I always saw my first priority as getting everyone back alive, fit and injury free. For the first time ever I failed as far as one person was concerned. For the sake of anonymity we'll call him John. John, 18 years of age was about to start college/university but became infatuated with Mother Teresa and refused to return home with the rest of the group. He stayed on to work on the projects in Calcutta. John turned up in Bombay on the final night at a farewell party organised by one of the host families with nearly 100 present. I was angry with John as he had an infectious disease. I could accept his decision to stay but not his irresponsibility in putting everyone at the party at risk.

On arrival in England, I tried to explain to his parents that he had refused to come home and I was unable to change his mind. About eight months later, I heard that he had arrived back in England and taken up his studies again. However, 15 years later, when sitting in the Magistrates Court as a JP, I saw the defendants solicitor pass a note to the Court Clerk who then asked the bench to retire. I looked carefully at the defendant, in his late 30s, but he did not seem familiar. In the retiring room the Clerk read the note which said, *"Please congratulate Mr Parkes on his MBE. In view of our past history would he stand down as I don't want my client to be compromised by our previous relationship"*. The solicitor was John and although I had not recognised him, was greatly offended at the suggestion that I might be prejudiced toward his client, so I switched the case to another courtroom.

The third and most wonderful example of a life changing experience is that of Paul Hackwood. On meeting Mother Teresa he wrote, *"It was a wonderful experience. The place was alive with the spirit of God. It was an intensely moving experience seeing the actual faith of all the Brothers and Sisters of Charity. The atmosphere at the Mother.House was filled with love, a quality that's needed to work with those in need"*. At that time the company he was working for went into liquidation. After the trip to India he entered into Further and Higher Education and achieved a degree and a place at a College of Theology. Around eight years after the trip to India I received an invitation to his ordination into the Priesthood. Paul later returned to India as a Missionary. I cannot begin to explain this wonderful transformation and how proud I am of Paul.

The Calcutta programme completed we set off by a train to Bombay. Thanks to the influence of a YWCA senior manager we had five compartments and travelled in comparative luxury compared to previous journeys. This comfort did not however put an end to the drama of travel. Whilst waiting for the train to depart an Indian beggar woman with a baby came to our open window and thrust the baby into the arms of one of the girls and ran off. A porter, seeing the episode ran after the woman and dragged her back and returned the baby to her. The porter explained that the woman believed her baby would have a better life brought up in England.

The journey across India took 42 hours. There were numerous stops where we took the opportunity to stretch our legs along the platform. Inevitably beggars approached us. Marian Singh gives her reaction; *"I never ceased to be shocked by what*

I've seen, a little girl about 7, carrying a baby came up and was begging for food and money. While she followed me the baby stopped crying so the girl smacked its legs and the baby started crying again. I was shocked and angry. The girl, although young, knew how to gain sympathy from tourists".

Mohamed Mukadam had a similar experience. He and his family came to England as refugees from Uganda at the time of Idi Amin and his brutal regime. *"I was staring out of the train window when a beggar came up to me, looked me straight in the eyes with an appealing look. I was stunned by a sudden force, my mind flashed back to Uganda. I didn't know what to do. The beggar looked at my food so I gave it to him. He thanked and praised me before walking away into a corner to eat. For the next few hours I was in an unfinished nightmare".*

The final stage was a boat journey from Bombay to Goa. It was to be an exploration of the influence of the Portuguese who arrived 400 years ago and an opportunity to recuperate. Some of the group visited the Tomb of St Francis, Keith Brant irreverently said, *"We saw St Francis' body still undecayed after 400 years. Every 10 years they open his tomb and people can kiss his feet. Awful isn't it?"*

The programme concluded with a return to Bombay to the homes of the host families. Sheryl Stonehouse concludes, *"I remember sitting at home in England feeling scared about coming here, it was a fear of the unknown. However, the past month has been one of the greatest of my life. I've been totally drawn into a new culture".*

The final leg of the four way Exchange took place in May 1983 when the Indian group shared a programme at Hereford Wake House in Northampton, the National Trust Base Camp at Hawkeshead in the Lake District and in the homes of Award participants in Birmingham. There were numerous Civic Receptions and the Indian leaders were invited to a Gold Award Presentation at Buckingham Palace. The only blip in the programme was that the rainfall in the first part of May was twice the norm.

Fund raising is a key component to ensure that people from disadvantaged homes can take part in International Exchanges. Many ingenious ways have been found of funding such enterprises, of which a recipe book is a successful example. The recipe book in question featured the favourite recipe of the Prime Minister at that time, Mrs Margaret Thatcher. It was called "Coronation Chicken" and had been a family favourite since 1953. The choice was no doubt also influenced by the marriage of the Prince of Wales and Lady Diana Spencer which took place in the same month as the Indian visit.

The Award Director at that time, Robert Heron wrote, *"Exchange visits between groups of Award holders and their leaders from many different lands has done much to widen International understanding, not only in the varied fabric of the Award Programme, but also of the ways of life and thought of those who dwell in countries outside their own".*

6

Climbing the Great Wall of China

The pre-Tiananmen Square Massacre Meeting
The surrender of Hong Kong
The Chinese Refugee Dilemma

Election time in the UK raises the perennial question of how to involve young people in politics. The Duke of Edinburgh's Award Midland Regional International Programme to China and Hong Kong at Christmas/New Year 1987/88 provided an answer in the form of a continuous four-week political experience. Britain was preparing to hand over Hong Kong to the Chinese in 1997 yet Chinese Refugees were still making life threatening escapes over the border into Hong Kong to enjoy the freedom of a democracy and escape the tyranny of Communism. The refugees were voting with their feet to enjoy the freedom of the ballot box in advance of the hand over.

The Hong Kong Chinese were the most competitive society I have ever encountered. Virtually everything was treated as a competition, even the D of E Award. The Chinese refugees were despised and if encountered would be handed over to the police for deportation back to China, to face the death penalty. They had no compassion for the plight of the oppressed working class Chinese. A prime example is featured later.

In terms of our Hong Kong hosts and their welcome of Award participants from England I described their efforts on our behalf in 10 words - generous, meticulous, efficient, professional, competitive, flexible, hospitable, humorous, caring and challenging. The Chairman of the Award, Mr J. P. Lee, the Executive Chair, Mrs Maria Ting and the Assistant Award Officer, Mr Ringo Wong, were quite exceptional people.

Hong Kong airport at that time was considered one of the most dangerous in the world. The planes had to sweep down between skyscrapers and when landing be able to stop before finishing up in the bay.

The first stage of the programme was based at the Award Training Centre in the Northern Terrorties. The purpose built centre was opened by Prince Philip in 1986 and funded by Hong Kong's Royal Jockey Club. More than 30 Hong Kong Award participants shared the dormitory facilities with 16 British candidates.

The early part of the programme allowed our group to acclimatise to the lifestyle and climate. One of the first places visited was Ocean Park that housed a water theatre where whales and dolphins performed amazing tricks. The show concluded with a thrilling display of high board diving by Hong Kong's Olympic team who were warming up for the Seoul Olympics.

At the Award Centre the skills of the martial art Tai Chi were practised. Art activities included making Chinese lanterns, producing key rings featuring Chinese knot tying and developing the skill of paper cutting. As a warm up for the expedition the group travelled on the ferryboat from Kowloon Island to Cheung Chan Island for a treasure hunt. A sad sight was a former Japanese Army Officer marching up and down the edge of the sea, shouting out commands as if he was in front of an army of men. Obviously a shell-shocked victim of World War II.

One evening the group dispersed across Hong Kong to share an evening meal with the families of Award participants. Staying in their homes was out of the question due to the limited space in the high rise blocks. Dominic Stewart described his experiences; *"Out of all the visits undertaken in Hong Kong the one that brought everything alight was the visit to the home of an Award candidate. It gave me an insight into the limited space available to Hong Kong residents. The family of five seemed well off, the father had a good job in the Police force but they still only had three rooms. The set up was like a theatre performance. Once we finished the meal, the dinner table and chairs were folded down, packed away and moved aside, which gave enough space to move the television in and move the settee to an accessible position, almost like on a conveyor belt. It was amazing to see how they kept it clean and clutter free in such a small space with so many in the family. Even though my stay with the family was just for a few hours I learnt about their fears of the hand-over of Hong Kong to China and how nearby countries like China and Japan are taking away their trade by making goods better and cheaper"*.

The programme followed was extremely varied. It included a community service project where the group spent time at the Tai Po Work Activity Centre and the Shatin Lek Yeun Sheltered Workshop for the disabled. A few days before Christmas Eve the group staged a concert to highlight the entertainment culture of the two countries. My son James, the youngest of the group, dressed up as Father Christmas and presented small gifts to our hosts.

The first major example of the competitiveness of the Hong Kong Chinese was reflected in a Dragon Boat race. None of our group had ever paddled in a

Dragon Boat and with TV cameras present we expected a massive defeat. To everyone's surprise we won, the superior weight and strength of the Brits overcame the boat skills of our hosts. As the British group passed the winning post the Hong Kong boat sank. Karl Hallam ungraciously wrote, *"We English like to rise to a challenge no matter how great. The odds of us being more skilful and dextrous were poor, but English grit won through and we triumphed, a great feeling was felt by all. The Hong Kong people sinking and then being saved was the icing on the cake!"*

A more gracious account of the joint activities was provided by my daughter Leigh, *"The skills and recreation day was great. Although I didn't manage to do any Chinese knots, my lantern fell apart, my paper cutting went wrong and I couldn't do Tai Chi it was a great success. I made a lot of friends and have a lot of happy memories"*.

Christmas Day in Hong Kong was a marvellous experience. We travelled to Kowloon for informal sightseeing in the morning with a rendezvous at the Floating Restaurant at lunchtime for a Christmas meal celebration. Although turkey wasn't on the menu a great time was had eating a wide selection of Chinese delicacies. In the evening a Barbecue was held at the Training Camp with many of the Hong Kong Residential Project participants returning to the Camp to celebrate with their new friends. A Christmas never to be forgotten.

The four-day Gold Qualifying Expedition in the Northern Territories was to be the most dramatic period of the stay. The groups of six, three participants from each country, would trek for 50 miles in the mountainous terrain close to the Chinese border. One participant would be rescued by launch after a rock fall and a group of six had to decide the fate of a Chinese refugee.

On the first evening concern was felt as one of the groups had not reached their checkpoint and were still missing 24 hours later. A full-scale search was launched with 100 volunteers from the Police, Marines, Fire Service and Award Assessment Staff. The problem had been created when Elizabeth Pattison was injured in a fall. Dominic Stewart and Hong Kong participant Joseph Law went for help but were defeated by darkness and the dense forest. An uncomfortable night was spent propped vertically against a rock face with the sound of lapping water below. The next day they were spotted and Elizabeth was taken off the rocks by launch to hospital. Dominic describes his experience, *"It was dark, we weren't sure of our location and Elizabeth was unable to move her right arm as she had fallen off a rock. I found myself making decisions I never thought possible. I had to find help, but not alone because the terrain was rocky and extremely steep with dense forest totally surrounding us. Joseph and I progressed through the forest only to find our sense of direction rapidly disappearing. We had only one aim, to get Liz off the mountain safely. Although something inside told me to keep going we were only getting further out of the way. Slowly we made our way back to the girls to find them lying almost vertically against a flat rock. I slept for six hours balancing on two large rocks, one of the most difficult night's sleep I'd ever had! The feeling of being enclosed made me feel like an animal in a cage, made worse by seeing the sea below. The relief I felt when we were finally rescued will never be forgotten".*

There is a sad postscript to this event. A short while after returning to England Dominic was killed in a climbing accident. The loss of such a dynamic, fun loving and caring person was greatly felt by his family and by everyone who knew him.

A different type of drama was unfolding within the second group. They came across a refugee who had escaped across the Chinese border. It was an event to personalise a political experience in a practical way. The two main characters in the plight of the refugee were Janet Millard from England and Ada from Hong Kong. They were locked in a verbal battle that would decide the refugee's fate, whether he would reach safety or be arrested, returned to China and be executed. I was not present during this stand off so here's Janet's report; *"It was nearly two o'clock as we walked steadily up the peak when out of the bushes appeared a young man with his arms outstretched holding a map of China. Ada, our Hong Kong companion immediately panicked and shouted "We must go, we must go". I looked at Ada as the refugee remained rooted to the spot. Our refugee was miming to us that he had swam across the border and gone three days without food or water. "We must go, it is dangerous here", said Ada. I could not understand her attitude and refused to move. She whispered to us that because he was a refugee we must not help him. My emotions were stirred; Ada shocked me. I looked at my team-mates for support, but they looked as bewildered as I was. Ada continued to try to get us to move on. "It is dangerous for he may have a gun or a knife, please hurry". She then said that we could give him some bread, he bowed his head continually thanking us for the little food we had given him. I so desperately wanted to give him my water bottle, but at the same time felt torn. I was staring into the faces of Hong Kong and China and experiencing the fear that they held. I had a gut feeling of fear, but not for me, for our refugee. I had tears in my heart because I could not understand what he must have been going through. I refused to do any more map work and handed the map over. I no longer wanted to be part of the D of E or part of Ada. I walked away from this man, to us a solitary representative of China, for all I knew he could be dead by the end of the day. My last look at our refugee was to see his frail figure come together with much thankfulness at receiving just four pieces of bread. It was as if I was seeing it in slow motion. I was silent for a long time after searching inside for an answer to my own actions and to know why Ada had such fear in her. I began to question her, and she explained "Many Chinese people come over to hurt us, we do not want them here". I made the assumption that Ada had a great dislike for China and was talking about the China/ Hong Kong situation. She was very withdrawn and appeared not to want to answer any questions. I needed to know more. Ada responded, "Many of the Chinese come over here thinking that they can get rich and instead of working like we do in Hong Kong, they rob jewellery shops and banks". There was much bitterness in her voice. I so much wanted to understand and appreciate her point of view. Ada said, "I am very scared because there may be more of them watching us, and we have no way of protecting ourselves, we must move quickly to the campsite". My experience was not over, we were a mile from camp when I glanced down at the stream below and standing by a tree looking in our direction was our refugee. I said nothing in case Ada changed our route. We arrived at the stream and filled our water bottles. We were preparing to leave when the refugee appeared. He stood looking at us and pointed at a sign in Chinese. He appeared to be asking which way to go. Then he muttered a few words and Ada reluctantly answered him. He had asked the way to an urban area as he had friends there who could help him. "I'm afraid he will be caught by police as he has no identity card", Ada said. I feared that Ada had given him false directions. As we arrived at the campsite my last thoughts were with the refugee, praying that he made it. I'll remember our refugee and many thousands like him, who are struggling uphill for one thing - survival".*

I was proud of the stance of Janet and her team-mates Peter Jackson, Teresa Ronan and Imogen Collins. They had shown compassion against the rigid political dogma expressed by the Hong Kong members. Their powers of persuasion had given the refugee the chance to seek a better life. Had you been a member of the group would you have given the refugee food and water? Would you have directed him towards an area where he was likely to get arrested? Who made the correct decision, Ada or Janet?

Chinese refugees were not the only problem at that time. The "boat people", refugees from Vietnam, were still being housed in refugee camps in Hong Kong. During a later visit to Vietnam I encountered a man who had attempted to flee the country only to be thwarted three times, captured and imprisoned in Vietnam. Hong Kong political writer Kevin Sinclair summed up the main attitude towards Vietnam refugees in a report. *"Lets be clear about this; every person in the refugee camps - with the exception of those born there - is told when they first arrive in Hong Kong waters that they are not wanted, that their chances of resettlement elsewhere are slim and if they choose to stay in Hong Kong they will be locked up and held behind barbed wire indefinitely. These people are not our responsibility. They should not be a burden borne by the tax payers of Hong Kong".* No doubt readers will be as shocked as I was at the lack of compassion for the Vietnamese refugees.

It is ironic to hear similar comments being expressed in England nearly 20 years later during the 2005 Election campaign. The racist remarks of Kevin Sinclair must have been particularly painful to the members of our group who were of mixed race parentage. Their parents had been previously welcomed into the UK as political and economic refugees.

The use of heroin by young people was becoming a major issue at that time. Hong Kong had become a world trading port for drugs grown in the "Golden Triangle" (Thailand, Burma and Laos) and the "Golden Crescent", (Pakistan, Afghanistan and Iran). A great deal of attention was being given to ensure young people do not become hooked on drugs.

When a young person appears in court for drug related offences there are a number of courses of action. There may be a fine for the first offence; subsequent offences bring into play the Social Services with rehabilitation programmes. Serious offenders are placed in residential camps for a period ranging from 6-12 months. The camps are situated in isolated areas including uninhabited islands. A rigid programme of activities is undertaken including opportunities to continue educational studies leading to exams and the learning of trade skills. Perhaps similar camps could be established on deserted islands in the Outer Hebrides to help some of the young criminals in the UK, who are dependent on drugs, to receive medical treatment in a drug free environment. Nearly 50% of young people who commit crimes in England are taking illegal drugs. They are caught in a vicious circle, stealing to feed their habit.

The second stage of our programme involved a flight from Hong Kong to Beijing (formerly known as Peking). During the flight the group were able to reflect on their time in Hong Kong. Elizabeth Richard's opinions were confirmed by others.

"After experiencing a trip of a lifetime to what must be one of the most exciting places in the world, I will never forget the warmth and hospitality shown by the Hong Kong people. Although there are many cultural differences between our races, particularly their highly competitive attitude to life, there was an incredible strong feeling of friendship which developed between the Hong Kong/UK candidates".

The opportunity to undertake a cultural study tour of China was the icing on the cake for the whole exchange programme. It gave the participants the chance to see for themselves the difference in political ideologies between what they know of Western politics and to compare them with the Communist style of government. It was even more important to view this first hand with the forthcoming Chinese take-over of Hong Kong from the British.

The group departed from Hong Kong in the early afternoon with temperatures in the near 80s. Their arrival in Beijing via Tianjin was in darkness with temperatures of minus 9. The CAAC flight was one hour late in departing which gave us an immediate comparison of attitudes towards the general public because there was no comment or apology from the Captain. It was treated as if it didn't matter and was of no consequence. The service on the plane was extremely austere and the in-flight food basic. There was instantly a change in atmosphere and the feeling of oppression was felt on the plane. This was heightened with the appearance of a mass of forms that had to be completed in triplicate before arrival in Tianjin. The landing was most eerie; our plane was the only one in sight. It was dark with a light covering of snow as a bitterly cold wind blew across the airfield. There were hardly any lights and the airport building 200 yards away looked particularly forbidding. It was like part of a film set trying to portray a cloak and dagger scene of intrigue. The Customs officers presented an equally grim welcome as Passports and documents were checked. The group was quiet at this stage as the excited chatter of Hong Kong disappeared from their thoughts.

As the plane took off from Tianjin for Beijing the mood was still sober. Everyone was naturally apprehensive on what they would encounter, particularly in respect to the accommodation and transport. There is always a doubt when corresponding with unknown personalities and the danger that words have different meanings when translated. The first doubt was quickly overcome when the group were greeted by a friendly English speaking guide who escorted us to an extremely comfortable coach that was blasting out heat to combat the freezing temperatures. The Airport was situated approximately 15 miles outside the City and the drive to the Hotel was totally absorbing and fascinating. Everyone was obviously aware of China's reputation for being a country of bicycles but to see thousands ten abreast across the road was overwhelming. There was an eerie silence due to the few forms of motorised transport; there was just a gentle swishing of tyres as the mass of cyclists travelled in both directions.

As the coach got nearer the hotel doubts by the group on their accommodation rose again. The reality was unbelievable as we pulled into the Park Hotel, a luxury five star Hotel that had only been open to the public for a month. As we entered the deserted, mirrored walled lobby, a grand piano played in the bar area. It was quite overwhelming and the group dispersed to their rooms with excited chatter as they passed the Disco and Restaurants to their rooms with colour TV and a refrigerated drink cabinet. Although we were surrounded by luxury there was still a feeling of being under constant observation. Although the coach had an extensive boot our luggage was transported separately from the Airport. This may have meant our luggage was screened before our arrival at the hotel. That is something we shall never know.

The All Chinese Youth Federation had arranged the programme for the visit and included visits to major historical sites, the highlight being the Great Wall of China. Prior to the visit I was on the NHS waiting list for a hip replacement operation for 3 years. I was determined not to miss out so had a cortisone injection, a steroid hormone, to ease the pain. It proved to be a waste of time and money but with the aid of a stick I "walked the walk".

The group climbed the Wall at the same point as the Queen during her visit in 1986. At that point the Wall rises steeply to the East and more gently to the West. The Western journey is now called "The Queen's Walk" and although a gentle slope at first it became quite severe the further you travelled from that point. The walking wounded among the group progressed as far as they could soaking up the atmosphere and taking photographs. The mountainside surrounding the Wall was covered in snow and there was a biting wind but nothing could take away the excitement and memory of this experience. We all bought Certificates and T-shirts proclaiming "I climbed the Great Wall".

During the next five days the group were closely chaperoned by our guides. Despite close supervision and the guide's reluctance to discuss politics or lifestyles we were able to wallow in history. The main places visited were the Ming Tombs, Tiananmen Square, Chairman Mao's Memorial Hall and the Forbidden City, (filming of the "Last Emperor" had recently been completed and was due for release in the UK). At the Memorial Hall we joined a small queue to visit Mao's Tomb. A large sign proclaimed that visitors were not allowed to make any noise or spit in the building. The presence of armed soldiers reinforced the feeling that if someone digressed they would be shot! Mao's illuminated tomb was an eerie sight and posed the question as to how much longer the State display of the body would continue.

The Summer Palace gave our Chinese guide the opportunity to remind us that the original Palace had been burnt down by the British-French Allied Forces in 1860. The Palace Lake was covered with hundreds of people skating in the sunlight. At Beilhai Park our guide remarked that Buddhist Temples were no longer in use as *"religion is irrelevant and banned by our previous beloved Chairman Mao"*.

All our visits were rigidly marshalled, only being able to visit "tourist" parts of the City. The hosts provided a coach to ensure we were under their control. Never-the-less the journeys were exciting, as there was so much to see. The chaos of cyclists weaving between occasional motorised vehicles led to the start of a competition that scored five points for a near miss and ten points for a direct hit. Every day the total was well into three figures. Even our coach was involved when it removed someone from their bike.

The meals in Beijing provided another opportunity for interesting comparisons. Breakfast western style was taken at the Hotel and the other two meals a day at seven different restaurants around the City. The restaurants were extremely basic, sufficiently cold to require diners to wear their coats during the meal. A steady stream of dishes was delivered to the table, much of the meat was of unknown origin but many were keen to sample everything from snake to animal eyes.

An exciting evening activity was a visit to a Chinese theatre that involved walking through narrow side streets, which in itself was a memorable experience. The theatre was very basic with hard wooden seats mainly occupied by business people and tourists.

The main entertainment themes in the theatre were acrobatics and magic. Most acts involve live animals, which would shock animal reformers in the UK. One magician walked from the stage into the auditorium apparently carrying nothing. He walked up to Joanna, one of our participants and produced a foot long fish from her lap, which splattered water everywhere. The fish was then deposited in a large tank of water on the stage.

The main shopping opportunity was at the Friendship Shops provided by the Government to attract foreign currency from tourists. Admission was closely controlled and although the majority of Chinese could not afford the prices anyway any visitor who was apparently Chinese had to produce evidence at the entrance to prove they were a tourist before being allowed in. There was a wide range of tourist items such as mechanical pandas, Chinese clothing, footwear, fur hats, etc. The staff was disinterested in providing service, unlike Hong Kong where they came onto the streets to persuade you to come in and look around. The most significant action by assistants was when a mother and toddler came in. Assistants fussed over the child, as Government policy limits each family to one child, children are fawned over. This policy has produced alarming trends because if the first child is a girl she may be killed as the family is considered a failure if there is not a male to continue the family name. During Chairman Mao's 40 year reign China's population doubled so the one child policy came in 1979 in a Government attempt to control the population explosion. There are many Government restrictions on families with more than one child. The family are fined, the second child is denied free education and pregnant women are put under pressure by Social Workers to have a termination. Despite this extreme policy China's population is 1.1 billion, a fifth of the world's population. China has only 7% of the world's arable land to cope with this enormous population.

Injuries sustained on their Gold Expedition led to a hospital visit for Elizabeth and Jocelyn for check-ups on their elbow and ankle respectively. They were treated in a large room where everyone waiting could see others being treated. A x-ray machine in the corner of the room had no shields so that everyone in the room received a small dose of radiation when Elizabeth's elbow was x-rayed. A standard treatment for joint injuries involved putting on a mud like substance and a bandage. The Doctors wore bloodstained overalls and did not give the impression of confidence. Can you imagine the field day lawyers in the UK would have in our compensation culture?

During free time in the evening our group went in twos or threes exploring in the vicinity of the hotel. They had to sneak out the back of the hotel to avoid our minders. The use of rickshaws provided an important form of transport as they wound their way around the back streets of Beijing. Visits to dodgy cafés provided an exciting background and a source of fascination for the locals. Our guide was coerced into an impromptu meeting in one of the bedrooms to discover what life was really like in China.

An objective of mine was to encourage links between the D of E Award and the All China Youth Federation in the hope of developing an Exchange programme. Prior to our meeting with the Federation I telephoned the British Embassy regarding exit Visa's for the Federation's young people. There was a recorded message that abruptly said, *"It is not possible to ring this number"*. I quickly hung up fearing my call was being traced to the hotel by Secret Police. Seventeen years later China have relaxed their travel rules and the first package holiday came to London in July 2005.

We spent a day at the Federation headquarters. There was the traditional exchange of gifts and greetings on behalf of the Lord Mayor's of the Cities represented by our group. In return we received books featuring art works produced during the Chinese International Year of Youth.

Following the formal input the Chinese young people representing Colleges, Universities, Trade Unions and political parties split into groups so that everyone could explore each others attitudes to a wide range of issues. Sir Robin Day would have been impressed by the interview techniques of the British participants who gave their Chinese hosts a severe testing of their personal ideologies. Although the majority of the sensitive questions were unanswered the loyalty of the Chinese young people was tested to the full. It must be extremely difficult to justify a political system that, irrespective of your trade or profession, you only earn £15 a month. Factory workers, shop assistants, office workers and doctors all receive the same salary. Even university lecturers and professors receive £15 although they do get free accommodation, holidays and transport is provided. There is no incentive to work hard or for promotion. There are severe unemployment problems. The Government solution of job sharing reduces unemployment figures but the amount of work done is no greater.

As the group sessions continued it became apparent that there were Communist Party members present making notes on any Chinese delegates making anti-Government remarks. In my group two Chinese girls were reduced to tears when comparisons were made between the freedom of the British group and their own situation. Issues of freedom of speech, rights to follow religion, choice of political ideologies at Election time, gender equalities in education and employment, social freedom etc.

At this time, in January 1988, student unrest was rising against the tyranny of Communist rule. Just weeks after our visit the Tiananmen Square Massacre took place. Hundreds of peacefully parading students died under the tank tracks of the Chinese Army. Although news of the massacre was suppressed across China scenes of crushed bodies were transmitted across the world. I often wonder if any of the students we met at the Youth Federation died on that tragic day.

Although none of our group was harassed personally during the stay we were aware of the atmosphere of intimidation imposed by the Police and Military. They have instant powers to fine offenders and confiscate bicycles or other forms of transport. Our coach was stopped as the driver had allegedly gone against a signal from the officer on point duty. The driver and guide received a public reprimand in the street. Despite this humiliation the driver was relieved not to be fined.

The final highlight of the stay in Beijing was a visit to the Zoo to see the world famous Giant Pandas. The Pandas would eventually become a way of breaking down international barriers when they were allowed to mate with Pandas in England and America. After many photographs the group bought clockwork Pandas as souvenirs.

We said goodbye to our hosts to fly back to Hong Kong via Tianjin. The visit to China had been a truly memorable experience. On arrival in Hong Kong there was a large group of young people from the Award Scheme waiting to meet us. We all went to the Harbour for a ferry boat across to Kowloon for the last time. We shared a meal before an emotional farewell at the airport as we headed home.

Snippets from the logbooks of the UK participants entitled, *"My View of China"* makes interesting reading nearly 20 years later. Robert Firkin, *"I came to the conclusion that China is a country about to undergo dramatic, (even if slow), change and with more democracy being introduced people are becoming more important than politics"*.

Elizabeth Pattison, *"I didn't know what to expect in China. I knew it would be different from anywhere I'd ever been. I asked friends who'd been to the USSR what a Communist country was like but this didn't prepare me for what I saw in China. The first thing that struck me was the people. The weather was freezing but even so they all looked so cold and anonymous. They seemed to be minding their own business as though they were scared to look round and talk. They all cycled at the same speed in similar clothes, mechanically functioning. I didn't expect everything to be so dull and dirty. I later watched the film "1984" and it was so similar to China, the machinery was old fashioned and things were left unfinished like buildings etc. So many soldiers and police standing around made me feel uncomfortable like I was being watched, it was unnerving"*.

Mark Woodhouse, *"How can I explain China? The people are stern faced, robotic and cycling their life away on the one hand but showing warmth and kindness on the other once you got to know them"*.

Karl Hallam, *"I had a great time saying Ni How (hello) out the window. The response was incredible and made me feel I had made their day by giving them attention and recognising their individuality, something the Government obviously does not do"*.

Jocelyn Hyland, *"When we landed in China there was an awful atmosphere. I felt like a convict and was treated like one. It was made worse as none of the security people smiled or laughed which put hostility in the air"*.

Dominic Stewart, *"Our visit to the Great Wall made me feel privileged to be on the journey. When I walked along the Wall I could easily have been dreaming and only now has it sunk in where I've actually been. A journey and experience never to forget"*.

The 1997 take-over of Hong Kong has of course happened and a form of local Elections have taken place. China itself has changed and the fears of the Hong Kong and Chinese people have not materialised. Hong Kong continues to be highly successful as a staging post for world goods. China is being wooed by the Western World as it represents the biggest market in the world. Along with co-leaders Alan and Maureen Cleasby and my wife Christine we survived many adventures alongside our young people as history was made. Once again we had *"brought them back alive"*, with the added bonus that we are all now more politically aware and more understanding of the needs of others.

The contribution being made to international understanding was recognised in 2001 by Commander Loftus Peyton Jones, Overseas Director of the Duke of Edinburgh's Award. In a personal note to his book "Challenge and Opportunity - The story of the Duke of Edinburgh's Award Worldwide" he wrote the following. *"With kind regards and much admiration for your enterprising international spirit"*. Being Acknowledged along side Lord Hunt, the first Director of the Award and leader of the team that climbed Everest, was a great honour.

7

Serving the Community in Nairobi

Arrested In Uganda and Kenya
Near death experience on Mount Kenya
On Safari in Amboseli

The third stage of the adventures linked to the Duke of Edinburgh's Award Exchange Programme involved Uganda, Kenya and Egypt. Kenya was the principal destination. The young people were to experience levels of poverty that they had only previously encountered on a superficial level in newspaper reports and on television. They were to be challenged physically and mentally in ways difficult to imagine in advance.

The Christmas/New Year period of 1989/90, when the trip took place, co-incided with my time as the Duke of Edinburgh's Award Regional Officer for the Midlands. Award candidates from all walks of life jostled for places through a rigorous selection process and a series of fund raising events spanning 12 months. By the time of their departure from England they had developed a strong team spirit which would help them to overcome many demanding events and challenges. I set off from England two days ahead of the main party to ensure that the arrangements made by our hosts were adequate and to make any necessary adjustments. Although this plan was sound, in reality it turned out to be a bad idea as I was arrested twice before the group had even arrived in Kenya.

The first arrest happened in Entebbe, Uganda. Entebbe airport had been the centre of international news a few months earlier during the terrorist hijacking of a passenger jet. My plan was to stay overnight in Entebbe, do some sight seeing, before catching a flight to Nairobi the following day. The only sights of Entebbe I saw however were the walls of an overnight cell.

As I got off the flight from London, along with all the other passengers, I was herded towards the medical area where compulsory injections against Yellow Fever were being administered. This posed two problems, one was that I had received all the necessary injections back in England, including Yellow Fever, and secondly, the actual life threatening inoculation process. Medical staff were using the same needles on groups of 10 or more, making the possibility of picking up an infection, such as Aids. I produced my inoculation certificate, refusing to have any more injections. This caused quite a scene as other passengers started refusing their jabs and so I found myself quickly marched away and put in a cell where I spent the night. The next morning it was suggested that I could catch my flight to Nairobi on payment of a "fine" of £50. No charge papers or receipts were involved; it became apparent that the "fine" was really a bribe.

Relieved to have been put on the flight to Nairobi I settled down not knowing that in a few hours time I would be in another cell, this time in Kenya. On arrival I was greeted by the Warden from St John's Church where the group would undertake a Community Service Project. We drove off in a battered old car only to be stopped at a checkpoint manned by a solitary police officer. This turned out to be another scam. The officer circled the car pointing out a number of dents and scratches on the bodywork. Addressing me he said, "*I haven't had any breakfast this morning*". So what I thought, what's going on? In effect he was asking for "Tea money" that I was expected to pay even though it wasn't my car. The first problem was that I had no Kenyan money, not having had enough time to change money at the airport. Secondly, he didn't understand the value of the English currency offered. On reaching an impasse, despite the Warden's intervention, the police officer got into the car and we were told to drive to the police station where I was placed in a cell. An hour later, after the Warden had finally confronted a Senior Officer I was released. Apparently the Warden had convinced the Senior Official that I was a VIP and a personal friend of the Duke of Edinburgh!

The main group arrived the next day via Cairo. They had encountered a different type of problem. During the baggage transfer in Cairo six sets of luggage were incorrectly labelled for Karachi. For nearly two weeks six members of the group had to borrow clothes from other members whilst waiting for their luggage to arrive from Pakistan.

On arrival at St John's Church the group were asked to sum up their initial feelings. Trudy Pritchard proved to have second sight, "*My fears concerned forgetting important things; I had made a checklist so this fear wasn't too great. I was naturally concerned about mountain sickness when climbing Mount Kenya. My other main fear was losing part or all of my luggage, (a fear I had joked about on a number of occasions). I'd kept quoting the joke advert about BA: breakfast in London, lunch in New York, dinner in LA and luggage in Bombay. I suppose I had been tempting fate*".

My daughter Leigh, a Gold Award participant wrote, "*We were to work together, despite any trivial differences this month, as one family. We were to share our problems, happiness and tears but we would all support each other no matter what happened*".

St John's Church was situated in Pumwani, on the outskirts of Nairobi. The Reverend John Ndung'u was an exceptional and compassionate person. The church site consisted of a hostel for the elderly, a school, craft training centre, vicarage and the main church building. The group was to spend their time working at these community facilities. The whole compound was a Christian oasis surrounded by the most distressing poverty one could find anywhere in the world. The church provided the salvation to people living in shacks, sharing open community toilets and a standpipe for water.

The qualifying Gold Expedition to climb Mount Kenya was to be a highpoint for a number of reasons, and least of which was the near death experience of Andrew Cartwright when he was carried off the mountain unconscious on a stretcher. But for the skill of the Kenyan supervisors Andrew would have returned to England in a coffin and my career in youth work would have been over.

The recruitment of the Kenyan expedition supervisors and climbers had started with a chance conversation with Robert Swan, the intrepid Arctic explorer. During the Ice Walk venture a number of Gold Award Holders from all over the world took part including Kenyan Stanley Gauthui. Through Stanley I recruited Joseph Muteroh, an absolutely brilliant supervisor of the climb and Joseph Kingala of Starehe Boys School who included a number of Award participants from his school on the climb.

The five-hour journey from Nairobi to the base camp at 10,000ft was by mini-bus and Land Rovers. It was complicated by a heavy storm that turned the mountain tracks into a quagmire. Supported by English co-leaders Alan and Maureen Cleasby, we were to set up an emergency camp using a log cabin as a base. This proved to be a sound decision as three members of the group returned after two days suffering from hypothermia and mountain sickness. Breathlessness, nausea, headaches and a desire not to eat became apparent. It was difficult to sleep due to the lack of air. My son James, then 14, also returned after successfully completing his two-day bronze Award Expedition in the foothills of Mount Kenya.

Prior to the arrival of the three who had correctly aborted their climb our time was spent exploring the area around the base camp. We were to record a host of wild life including Monkeys, Rock Hydra, Elephants, Elands, lizards, Chameleons, Gazelles and the animals feared by the Kenyans, Buffaloes. At night they would disturb our sleep as they sharpened their horns on the side of the log cabin.

While we were exploring the real drama occurred much higher up the mountain. Monica Phokela was one of the group who decided to abort the climb and complete her expedition at a lower level on the mountain. This was both brave and sensible. Monica wrote, "*Memories? Illness! Being sick, feeling dizzy, headache, stomach-ache, tiredness and breathlessness. Sounds good eh? Why did I choose to virtually kill myself for some medal? We didn't know whether we were going to live or die. The worst part was making the vital decision of going up or down. If I went up things could have been worse but going down meant I'd failed my quest to climb Mount Kenya. I now believe I made the right decision, although I still feel guilty and unable".*

One of the group who made the wrong decision to continue was Andrew Cartwright. Trudy Pritchard gave a first hand impression of the difficulties faced by Andrew. *"At the end of the third day all my feelings of excitement dramatically changed to those of fear and fright. Andrew sat down on a rock unaware of everything around him. His face had changed, his eyes glazed as Tracey and I started to put a waterproof jacket on him he started shaking. I had never been so scared in my life".*

At 6am on December 21st eight of the group made the last hundred feet to Point Lenana at the top of the mountain. The views were breathtaking as the sun rose. They looked down on clouds and saw a passing plane below. Everyone shook hands and congratulated each other. Andrew was not able to make that final climb. As he drifted in and out of consciousness the Kenyan leaders Joseph and Stanley carried him down the mountain. Back in Andrew's hometown of Lincoln his mother had a premonition that he was close to death. There was no logical explanation for this premonition as she didn't know the actual dates of his expedition but sensed he was in danger. Andrew made front-page news in Lincoln as he slowly recovered. The immediate effects were deafness in one ear and the loss of feeling in one foot. Also badly affected was Daniel Coulson, fortunately over the next two weeks they both recovered completely. A reflection on how tough the conditions were is demonstrated that two of our experienced Kenyan leaders also experienced difficulties. Joseph had frost bite on his tongue and Moses had frostbite on his fingers. To relieve the pain he put his fingers into hot cups of tea.

Andrew's near death experience had a profound effect on everyone. Here's Andrew's account, *"What an experience! One I'm never likely to forget the events of, or the effects on me as a person. It's not until a situation like that occurs that you realise the extent a team can pull together and literally save lives. The climb itself was straight forward, the only way I could tell the height of the mountain, besides the obvious, was the devastating effect on my health by the altitude. I had to decide whether to carry on up the mountain or make my way down. I now know I made the wrong decision. I was being stubborn and I hate anything beating me so I thought I should battle on. In fact as team leader I ended up endangering the rest of the team. For me to live now is something special, I didn't realise how close to death it was possible to come but now to live is to push to the ultimate limit but to always keep in mind the lives of others with you".*

To celebrate Andrew's recovery and climbing Mount Kenya the group signed an Award T-shirt and hung it over the bar at the Naro Mor lodge. It joined other T-shirts from all over the world. The celebrations were completed with a short drive to the Equator for a mass photo session.

Two days after the group's climb there was a double tragedy on Mount Kenya. Two Kenyan porters had died and the tourist they accompanied was missing, feared dead. There is a fine line between success and failure. The entire group recognised the massive contribution made by their supervisors Joseph Muteroh, Stanley Gauthui and Joseph Kingala, plus the Kenyan Award participants.

The group returned to Nairobi and St John's church on Christmas Eve. Not only was this an opportunity to celebrate Christmas but to give thanks for the recovery of Andrew and Daniel. The service began at 10pm, concluding at midnight. Our group contributed to a packed Church with five musical offerings and readings. The atmosphere was electric, as the midnight bells rang out there was a mass conga around the church with people singing and clapping. The few hand made streamers that decorated the church were taken down and used to decorate their homes.

At the Christmas morning Service the vicar announced, "*At the end of last night's service a child, around 3 years old, was found in the Church. Will the parents please collect the child after the service from the vicarage*". It's alarming to think a family could misplace a child. The vicar also remarked that he hoped that the people who had helped themselves to the Christmas decorations had made a good job of decorating their homes. There was just one balloon left to decorate the church.

During our stay at St John's Church every opportunity was made to converse with other church users and visitors during the free time between working in the old people's home, the school and the craft centre. There were restrictions on such talks as the boys could only speak with the Men's Union and the girls at the Mother's Union. This segregation was based on the traditional male/female relationships of native Kenyans. Women are treated as servants, undertaking heavy manual work, having a large number of children and with all family decisions being made by the husband. This sounded like the relationship between my grandparents in the early 1900s.

A walking tour with Kenyan teenagers through the slums of Nairobi was fascinating. The sad fact was that even when families had been moved out of their corrugated shacks into concrete structures they took their old habits with them. An education programme aimed at hygienic living conditions was obviously needed. Otherwise slum living conditions were transferred from one slum building to another. On one estate a group of Kenyan teenagers cynically called out, "*Welcome to our concentration camp*".

One of the visitors to the church was a teacher from Northern Ireland who taught at a Masai Mara village. The Masai are the most underprivileged tribe in Kenya. One of the stories she told showed our group how fortunate they were to live in England. *"Each year the young men of the tribe go into the bush armed only with a spear on a traditional ritual to prove their manhood. When they track down a lion they form a circle around it and start a strange throat warbling sound that induces a hypnotic state in them. The lion isn't happy with this sound and attacks one of the youths in the circle. This is the moment of truth. In a split second, the youth chosen by the lion realises that their hope has been recognised. The Masai has to plunge his spear into the lion or die. No one else can react until the first spear has landed, then they can all join in and kill the lion. If the first Masai survives he leads the march triumphantly to the village. The bushy part of the lion's tail is tied to the spear and the victor becomes a hero in the community".*

One distressing feature of the Masai tribe is that some children are married at 8 years old. Arranged marriages in rural countries involve dowries. A son is worth 100 goats and a daughter 90 goats. Sexual matters are discussed only between children and grandparents. The ritual of circumcision for men and women still dominates family life. The gradual reduction in the birth rate, greater educational and career opportunities and the introduction of labour saving devices in the home will eventually free Kenyan women from their manual bondage. It is already happening in cities, it may take another 50 years for rural communities.

Our stay at St John's coincided with the Archbishop of Kenya's visit. To mark his visit there was a marathon service including a mass confirmation, induction into the Mother's Union, communion, the blessing of our group and a wedding. At the concluding meal our group sang "Kum Ba Ya" and "The whole world in his hands" two very appropriate choices. Helen Hancox mesmerised the Kenyans with her rendition of "Albert the lion".

The third element of our programme was to explore the wildlife and the conservation work undertaken in one of Kenya's leading National Parks. Our journey to the Amboseli Game Reserve near the border of Tanzania was extremely difficult due to heavy rain. Dirt tracks were treacherous with the mini buses bogged down and needing tractors to pull them clear. The group was rewarded with incredible close ups of wild life thanks to the skill of Masai tribesmen. There was a stand-off with an enormous rhino just 20 yards away and an elephant with a broken tusk with a reputation for charging cars. We saw a wrecked car covered in blood that had been a victim of that elephant the previous night. We parked in the middle of a herd of grazing elephants. A baby elephant, just a week old, was an amazing sight, as were two young elephants practising tusk fighting. We saw a troop of baboons, a cheetah and a lioness with their young cubs, all so close that even without telescopic lenses our cameras captured amazing close-ups.

New Year's Eve in a hunting lodge was celebrated with freshly cooked suckling pig, turkey and Impala. Some of the group celebrated the New Year twice, once at midnight African time and three hour later at British time. No wonder they were tired the next morning!

On returning to St John's we found that abnormal rain for that time of year, two and a half inches had fallen in one night, had taken its toll on the hostel. The ceiling and walls were dripping with water, the floor inches deep in water and the clothing and bedding left behind was soaked. It was little consolation to hear that it hadn't rained in December or January for 11 years!

Once we had dried and cleaned the hostel there were still encounters with wildlife. We were warned to always put our shoes on before getting out of bed in the middle of the night. The crunching of large cockroaches underfoot was a familiar sound from the darkened corridors leading to the toilets. Lizards also appeared on the walls at regular intervals and occasionally mosquitoes were heard. This was no holiday trip!

The Old People's Home, part of the Community Service programme was a fascination for both our young men and women. The occupants were former prostitutes whose ages ranged from 65-92. The women came to Nairobi when they were young from the country. As they aged and lost their appeal they became outcasts with no family to care for them so the St John's Church took on that role.

Although I was the only member of the group to be exposed to corruption I thought it important that every member should be aware of the problems faced by the majority of Kenyans, problems that they had been sheltered from up to now. Information provided included details of President Moi's New Year message attacking bribery and corruption. He said to the nation: *"It (bribery) corrupts and totally seals off the mind from truth and fairness. Bribery allows chang'aa in the market, issues a driving licence to unqualified persons, appoints a job seeker to the wrong job, and worst of all, it frustrates and kills the morale of people in the task of nation building"*.

Chairman Moi was also highly critical of members of the police and youthwingers. When checking overloaded or unroadworthy vehicles a few days before Christmas they let off drivers from being prosecuted by accepting a bribe. This corruption by police was confirmed by a recent survey undertaken in the Pumwani area and brought to our attention by the vicar. The public rated Youthwingers public enemy number one, the police second, robbers and thieves third and solicitors and lawyers fifth. Youthwingers are young people recruited by the government from the ranks of delinquents on the assumption that responsibility will change their ways. They are issued with a uniform including a distinctive red shirt and black beret and have powers of arrest. Many complaints have been made that they abuse power by stealing property from people on the streets and from homes on the pretext of investigating alleged crimes.

Road accidents resulting from poor driving and vehicles in a dangerous condition are common across the whole of Kenya. Efforts to overcome the problems once again have been blocked. It was announced by President Moi that one of the major measures to reduce road accidents has had to be withdrawn for the fifth year running. It had been proposed that all public service vehicles were to have a regulator fitted to prevent them from travelling at more than 80km per hour (50 mph). No one has taken any notice of the regulation; hence it has been withdrawn again. Road deaths are running at an all time high with 57 killed in one road accident. "Sleeping policeman" are already prominent on most main roads and particularly outside schools, hospitals, police stations etc. These special ramps are also at the approach to villages on the main roads. Speed is not the only problem. Many of the vehicles are not roadworthy and would certainly fail a UK MOT. It is not uncommon to find more than 100 people packed into a 50-seater bus. People also hang out from the sides of mini buses in an alarming manner. There are enormous potholes in many of the outer city roads and vehicles have to move in and out to miss them, causing more risk of accidents.

The third major issue brought to the group's attention was the subject of Aids. Doctors and missionaries recuperating at St John's Church told of their experiences in the Lake Victoria area of Uganda and Kenya. Whole villages have been wiped out by Aids. Voluntary groups are running camps consisting of thousands of orphaned children, many with Aids. A clinic in the area reported that 60% of the people who attend for treatment for Cholera, Typhoid, snakebites etc are found to be carrying Aids following a blood test. It was fortunate that issues of corruption, transport and Aids did not impact upon the group to their detriment. Thanks to the skill of the Kenyan expedition leaders, I was able to bring everyone back to England alive, my prime objective. The young people themselves had changed beyond recognition.

Helen Hancox wrote; *"My education is more important to me than ever and I realise just how lucky I am in so many ways and how much we generally abuse our benefits and blessings, everyone not just me".*

Charlotte Ducker wrote; *"Whilst the expedition stretched us physically, it was the people of Kenya themselves who had the greatest impact on me. It is their simplistic lifestyle, their selflessness and strength of character, which will leave an everlasting impression. They are good people although many live under conditions of extreme poverty; yet they always manage to smile and welcome strangers. For many, it is their strong belief in God, which manages to sustain true happiness and a meaning in life, as seen in Pumwani. The special people we met, the Vicar, his wife, the members of the Mothers and Fathers Unions, and many others, work so hard to bring their community together and provide much happiness and hope to such a poor area. Our group was filled with admiration and respect for these wonderful people".*

Simon Ingyon wrote, *"They are a very friendly society. Whenever we return or leave the compound the children are always waving which makes you feel good inside. I learnt not to take things for granted as the Kenyans have a lot less than we do but they are always happy and smiling. I think the Kenyan people and society is how Britain should be. It would be much nicer than everyone rushing around with no time to spare. I wish people in England would say "hello" in the street as they do here. A quote from a magazine sums it up, "Europeans have the watches but Africans have the time".*

I knew from past experience that the group would need to unwind and talk about the trip before returning home. Some needed counselling after the trauma of working in the slums and the experiences on Mount Kenya. One unexpected question I received was, *"Why did you select me for this trip?"* I responded by saying that during the selection and interview process they had showed leadership potential that I believed could be harnessed for the benefit of their local community in the future. What I did not say was I was disappointed in their lack of motivation to work without supervision during the community service project at St. John's Church. It would be interesting know if 17 years down the line if that potential has been realised.

We chose Cairo in Egypt to debrief. As it was their winter season and the low tourist season it was possible to get good quality hotel rooms at a reasonable price. Highlights of the stay in respect to the history and culture of the country were visits to the Pyramids of Giza, one of the seven wonders of the world, Cheops and Chephron, the Sphinx and the Egyptian Museum to marvel at the treasures discovered in Tutankhamun's Tomb. Riding camels at the foot of the pyramids proved very exciting.

This short break ensured plenty of rest; time to sleep, lots of food to replace some of the weight lost and time for everyone to put their adventures into perspective. It had been one of the hardest international experiences I had supervised. My end report reads as follows, *"The highest praise must go to our Kenyan hosts. The British group was an exceptional cross section of young people that would be difficult to duplicate in respect of temperament and attitude. The support of my wife Christine and Alan and Maureen Cleasby ensured that everyone returned safe, well and enriched in spirit".*

8

To fly or not to fly - Terrorists rule OK?

Chinese oppression of Buddhist Tibetans
State of emergency in Nepal
Kashmiri terrorist attack on the Indian Parliament

The pressure and responsibility of taking groups of young people abroad finally became too great. The "Blame Culture" spreading from America linked to the growing number of "Politically Correct" regulations led me to retire from personally leading groups abroad after the 1990 Kenya programme. In my new role as the Midland Regional Officer of the Duke of Edinburgh's Award and later, as the Development Manager of the Outward Bound Trust Bursary Programme, I adopted the role of adviser to other groups. My personal circumstances had also changed with my daughter Leigh and son James fleeing the coup to establish their own careers. That meant I was free to travel independently, to go to places that the average tourist would not visit, to see for myself what it was like to live in the countries that were considered dangerous, physically and politically and where history was being made.

As an independent traveller my only consideration when planning to go abroad is now self-preservation. No longer am I bearing the responsibility of bringing the young people in my care home safely. As previously described I had many narrow escapes in terms of bringing everyone home alive. It was time to quit while I was ahead.

Irrespective of being a single or group traveller there needs to be a good preparation time, at least 6 months before a trip. Since my first group led programme to Paris in 1961 the world has, in many areas, become a more dangerous place. The decision to continue with a planned visit to a country prone to terrorist activities becomes more demanding.

The most shocking terrorist attack is of course the attack on the twin towers in New York on September 11th 2001. It is the kind of atrocity that is ingrained in people's minds. *"Where were you when the planes flew into the twin towers?"* A question that attracts an immediate answer. I was in a lunch meeting with officers of the Hilton Foundation in the restaurant on the top floor of the Hilton Hotel in London, one of the tallest buildings in the city. The fear that the terrorist attacks in New York were to be duplicated in other major cities led to the spontaneous mass evacuation of employees from the Canary Wharf building, the tallest occupied building in London. In a state of shock, or perhaps with a touch of bravado, we continued with our meeting.

The September terrorist attacks created a dilemma for me. In October I had air tickets and a plan to visit Jordan which not only borders Israel, Saudi Arabia, Iraq and Syria but was on the flight path of the retaliatory strikes on Afghanistan by Allied Forces in search of Osama Bin Laden's Al Qaeda who had claimed responsibility for the New York attack. A month later in December 2001 I also had air tickets to visit India, Nepal, Tibet and Kuwait. To fly or not to fly – Terrorists rule ok? Not as far as I was concerned. I was not going to give in to terrorists. History was being made and I wanted to be a witness.

This is the story of my December 2001 visit to India, Nepal, Tibet and Kuwait. The visit to Jordan in October 2001, referred to above, is included in the "Cradle of Civilisation" essay. Did you give in and change your travel plans after September 11th? Have you put off travelling abroad? If so, think again and enjoy new adventures.

I arrived in Nepal via Delhi before taking the short flight from Kathmandu to the Holy City of Lhasa in Tibet. Lhasa is 13,000ft above sea level. People with heart conditions or high blood pressure are advised not to visit because of the dangers of altitude sickness, which cause nausea and breathing difficulties due to the reduction in oxygen levels. It can take two or three days to acclimatise and the weather in the winter months can be bitterly cold. Among the recommended travel items are a hot water bottle and a portable oxygen producer. I had neither.

Contrary to my expectations Lhasa had many modern buildings, wide smooth roads, was litter free and with unpolluted air. There were of course Yaks, butter tea, prayer flags, prayer wheels and Buddhist monks in orange robes chanting "Om Mani Padme Hum". Altogether a more traditional image of Tibet.

Public toilets rarely feature in third world travel books mainly because they don't exist, men and women relieving themselves in full view can be disconcerting at first. There is a story involving a tourist that has entered the folklore of toilet humour. Readers with a sensitive stomach should skip the next few paragraphs. It started with a tourist being refused access to the Lhasa Hotel (formerly the Holiday Inn), to use its facilities, as he wasn't a resident. The hotel receptionist pointed out some dubious looking public toilets across the road. Aware of the reputation of public toilets in terms of hygiene the tourist looked through one of two open doorways to see a dimly lit area of dirty, smelly water. Holding his nose he walked in only to fall into a 5ft deep cesspool. What he had thought was just surface water on the floor was in fact the surface of human waste. Fortunately he was tall enough to push his head above the surface and scramble out. He had entered the service entrance, not the customer entrance.

The tourist staggered into the street choking on excrement. A hotel employee, seeing his plight connected a water hose to spray him down. An ambulance was called and he was rushed to hospital to have his stomach pumped and to be plied with salt tablets to make him sick and finally receive a series of injections to combat any infections.

The tourist survived. His clothes were destroyed and replacements obtained. Over the next few days he would have to re-live the experience when trying to explain at border crossings why his passport and money were brown coloured.

One of my reasons for visiting Tibet was to see what impact Chinese rule had on the local people and their Buddhist religion. Buddhist priests as a theocracy had ruled Tibet for much of its history although from 1720 to 1911 it was under Chinese administration. China formally took charge in 1950 when their forces moved in and eventually renamed Tibet "an Autonomous Region of China" It was a brutal take-over.

In 1961 a report of the International Commission of Jurists accused China of genocide. During the Cultural Revolution (1966-76), led by Chairman Mao, many Tibetan shrines and monasteries were destroyed. Surprisingly the Palace of the Dalai Lama in Lhasa was spared despite Mao's wish that it should be destroyed, (it is now a museum). The Dalai Lama fled to India in 1959 and was followed by 100,000 refugees, he has never returned. I went to such a camp in Nepal where residents earn a living making carpets. After Mao's death in 1976, liberalisation policies led to monasteries being rebuilt and a massive increase in Chinese immigrants. There are now equal numbers of Chinese and Tibetans living in Tibet.

No doubt the Chinese will say that the means have justified the ends. In reality the Tibetans never had a chance in defending their country against the Chinese in military terms because their weaponry was so out of date and the nomadic nature of their existence. This was shown in 1903 when a British military force of 10,000 based in India, which mainly included servants carrying equipment, was able to capture Lhasa in a few days. The reason for the incursion was to establish a treaty with Tibet/China to protect India's border from attack by Russia. Do you agree with the Chinese occupation of Tibet that their means justified the ends?

The Tibetan people appear to have finally come to terms with the Chinese occupation of their country. A mixture of communism and commercialism in terms of business opportunities, improved living conditions, an improved infrastructure which includes the building of many roads, have brought about this change of heart. A major railway is under construction that will link Tibet with Beijing for the 2008 Olympics to be hosted by China.

Readers with an interest in religious comparisons might wish to compare the Ten Commandments handed down by Moses with the Ten Meritorious Deeds of Buddhism. Do not kill, do not steal, restrain from inappropriate sexual activity, lying, gossiping, cursing, sowing discord, envy, malice and opinionatedness.

Flights from Lhasa to Kathmandu ran only twice weekly so a 4x4 Landrover provided an exciting journey through mountain passes flanked by snow covered mountains for the return to Nepal. The Nyalam Pass, 16,000ft high provided stunning views despite feelings of nausea and headaches due to the high altitude. Numerous checkpoints were encountered but there were no corrupt practices being undertaken by guards. A far cry from my experiences in India where palms need to be greased to ensure safe passage. My journey concluded with the drive over the Friendship Bridge into Nepal.

The departure from Tibet, a former war zone, into Nepal in the middle of a civil war against the Maoists was reflected by the headlines in the "Kathmandu Post". *"Army repulses attack, over 60 terrorists killed"*. *"700 Maoists surrender in four districts"*. *"Terrorists shoot one dead"*. *"Fourth blast in Kathmandu"*. *"Army foils terrorist attacks in Kathmandu"*. As part of the State of Emergency a night curfew had to be observed and I.D cards/passports were to be carried at all times.

The Nepal Communist Party Maoist's had been waging a war against the existing constitutional, monarchical, democratic system since 1996. They shunned their chance to make a case by not taking part in the 1999 elections. The events of June 2001, when Prince Dipendra killed eight members of his family, including his father King Birendra, fuelled claims that the monarchy and the government were corrupt.

Nepal is the birthplace of Lord Buddha who was born 2500 years ago. It is also the home of the Sherpas of Everest fame and the hill tribesmen who have earned fame in the British Gurkha regiments.

Accommodation was soon booked at the Hotel Marshyangdi as there were very few tourists because of the fighting in Afghanistan. There are a number of impressive national heritage sites to see including Patan, the city of fine arts. E. A.Powell described the city of Bhaktapur in his book "The Last Home of Mystery", *"Were there nothing else in Nepal, save the Durbar Square of Bhahtapur, it would still be amply worth making a journey halfway round the globe to see. Also known as the City of Devotees it displays elegant art, fabulous culture and colourful festivals".*

In light of the recent massacre of eight members of the Royal Family I was interested in visiting their open-air cremation site. The concrete slab where their bodies were burnt in the Hindu tradition lies on the bank of a river and adjacent to a hospice. It is considered unlucky to die at home so sick relatives are moved to the hospice to die. Bodies are carried outside and burnt on the slab and the ashes are scattered onto the river. Only the wealthy can afford this kind of ritual. Children can be seen searching the riverbed for material remains, such as gold teeth.

The level of poverty in Nepal is extreme as is highlighted by this report of twelve year-old Ramu Mandal. Ramu supports his two younger brothers and a baby sister; their parents have died. Everyday the twelve-year-old pulls a rickshaw on the streets to earn money to feed them. It can take 12 hours to earn between 90-120 rupees, the equivalent £1. Ramu pays 20 rupees a day to hire the riskshaw, 10 rupees goes on milk for his sister and the rest goes to feed his brothers living in a cardboard shack. Asked about his life where education will never be an option, Ramu replied, *"My parents left me with the responsibility of looking after my younger brothers and sister. I have no other option but to work, it is a sin to steal and I could never force myself to beg".* Ramu, at the age of twelve, has become an adult long before his time.

Poverty is not just restricted to urban areas. Whilst on a jungle safari in the Royal Chitwan National Park I saw poverty in the villages on the outskirts of the park. It is a small consolation to know that my financial contribution to join the safari will help improve their standard of living. The safari involved riding an elephant through the jungle searching for the famous Bengal tigers, one horned Rhino, wild elephants and leopards. A canoe trip brought close contact with crocodiles and many species of birds. The most fascinating experience was visiting an elephant nursery and feeding the baby elephants.

One evening was spent in the village where I met the villagers and watched their traditional Tharu dancing. Before the night was out I was on stage joining in! On the second evening I attended a multi-religious meeting and finished up being the guest speaker at five minutes notice. The content of my talk can be found in the essay devoted to an alien visitor from Space who encounters different religions.

The Himalayas and Mount Everest dominate the Nepal/Tibet border. As a teenager I remember the celebrations on the Queen's Coronation Day in 1953 in praise of the British led team that climbed Mount Everest for the first time. Although I never attempted to climb Everest I took a flight in a small plane from

Kathmandu around the top of the mountain. Snow whipped up in gale force winds as we looked for any climbers on the mountain side. A photograph taken in the cockpit and a certificate are reminders of the experience.

The final highlight of my Nepal trip was a visit to a Tibetan Refugee camp in Kathmandu. Fronted by a Tibetan Handicraft Emporium the site embraces the message of Lord Buddha who preached peace and compassion for all living beings. There were many fine examples of handicrafts including woodcarvings, carpets, incense, prayer flags and herbal products. I was able to see refugees making carpets, one of their best sellers. Proceeds from the Emporium support thousands of Tibetan refugees living in Nepal.

The third leg of this tour was to India. A flight was booked to Ahmedabad arriving in time for second cricket Test between India and England. This was my third visit to India; the previous two involved leading groups of young people undertaking their Duke of Edinburgh's Award as previously described. The first visit had been the most spiritually uplifting international experience of my life. This time I was frustrated by the lack of progress in improving the quality of life of the poverty stricken masses. Billions of Rupees have been spent on a space programme while millions still sleep on the streets of the major cities.

There are a number of memorable experiences whilst in Ahmedabad that are covered more fully in the essay on religion. The Test match had moments of high drama but the match ended in a draw as India refused to take up the challenge set by the English captain Hussain. Anticipating this negative response I left Ahmedabad after four days to fly to Delhi, a decision that could have proved disastrous.

On arrival in Delhi I booked into a reasonably priced hotel which was situated just half a mile from the Indian Parliament building. Within minutes of my arrival the hotel was rocked by sounds of gunfire and explosions from grenades. Parliament was under attack from terrorists. For the next 45 minutes the sounds of battle continued, accompanied by police sirens and the sounds of fire engines.

The terrorists were Kashmiri Separatists. At the conclusion of the suicide attacks the five terrorists and six security guards had been killed. The 200 members of Parliament present were unharmed. During the next few days India and Pakistan were on a war footing. The "Hindustan Times" read *"Democracy Attacked. PM vows do-or-die battle against terror". "India calls on Pakistan to close down Kashmiri Terror groups". "Pakistan on top alert as India vows retaliation" "Pakistan President Musharrat warns India against precipitous action".* I had inadvertently left a state of emergency in Nepal for another in India.

During the next few days India and Pakistan sought to defuse the possibility of an all out war. The big international concern was that both countries had nuclear weapons. Do you think that atomic weapons will ever be used in battle again? Do you understand why people become suicide bombers? While mulling over such questions life in Delhi carried on as normal. I looked for inspiration as I re-visited the Taj Mahal, the Red Fort, the Kutab Minor and the funeral site of Mahatma Ghandi, (Raj Ghat).

The final stage of my tour should have been a routine flight from Delhi to London with a brief fuel stop in Kuwait. Due to the terrorist alert in Delhi all flights were delayed. This proved to be a stroke of good fortune for me as by the time the plane arrived in Kuwait City the connecting flight to London had departed. At no cost the airline provided accommodation at the Safir Hotel. With a little "persuasion" I was able to convince the Hotel Management that I was a businessman and secured a visa that enabled me to tour the city.

Kuwait City had been re-built after the Gulf War attack by Saddam Hussein on the 2nd August 1990. Iraq was given a deadline by the Allied Forces to leave by the 15th January 1991. When Saddam Hussein refused the Gulf War began with Allied bombing raids on Kuwait and Iraq. The offensive only lasted 100 hours and Allied Forces had liberated Kuwait City completely by the 26th February. The first task was to put out the fires at hundreds of oil wells that had been set alight by the retreating Iraqis. There were no signs today of war damage within the city but a short journey into the desert showed burnt out tanks and other wrecked military vehicles. The re-building of Kuwait City had not been a problem to the oil rich country that had also received a large sum of money from the Iraq government in compensation.

It was quite a relief to arrive back home in England. In a month I had sampled Chinese oppression of Buddhist Tibetans, survived a State of Emergency in Nepal, a Kashmiri Terrorist attack on the Indian Parliament, the threat of nuclear war between India and Pakistan and seen the effects of Saddam Hussein's attack on Kuwait City. At the same time I was following the liberation of Afghanistan through the media. My media tag "Lucky Jim" had proved true once more. Terrorists rule ok? - Not this time.

9

Dodging rockets in the "Cradle of Civilisation"

Life in Israel, Syria, Lebanon and Jordan
Surviving the "Jerusalem Syndrome"
Encounter with Hizbullah terrorists

In the fifty plus years that I have been following world politics four of the most featured Middle East countries have been Israel, Syria, Lebanon and Jordan. Despite being involved in armed conflicts Jordan has still been able to attract tourists whilst Lebanon and Syria have become virtual no-go areas, only the most adventurous exploring their borders. Israel, despite the almost weekly conflicts with Palestinians, remains a magnet to people from all over the world because of its unique place in world religion.

The first of three visits to the area was to Israel in January 1996, a few months after the start of a series of Palestine suicide terrorist attacks. It appeared that I was the only non-Jewish male passenger on a packed flight as mine was the only head uncovered. A storm was raging over Tel Aviv causing the plane to sway dramatically as we made our descent. Spontaneously copies of the Torah emerged and everyone started to pray loudly. Although I was not part of the prayers I felt reassured that I was in safe hands and the plane did land safely. The dual aims of this visit were to understand the pressure the Israelis were living under and to visit many of the places in the Bible where Jesus Christ had travelled.

1996 was the fifth anniversary of the Gulf War. One of the lessons learnt from that war was the need for all new housing to have a "protected room" that could withstand bomb blasts and seal out gas. Each block of four apartments must have such a room. Families were issued protective suits and masks for their children. The Jerusalem Post of the 12th January 1996 marked the anniversary with the headline, *"Our homes in the front line"*. Included was a photograph of one of Saddam's Scud missiles being tracked by an Israeli Patriot missile over Tel Aviv taken in 1991.

Young people are conscripted into the army at 17. It was very disconcerting to see the fresh faced teenage soldiers socialising in McDonalds whilst carrying their automatic weapons. The fear was that a disagreement over a girlfriend or verbal abuse between youths could seriously escalate with such weapons readily available.

A novel conservation initiative attracted my attention. I visited the Modin Forest near Tel Aviv where you could plant a tree and dedicate it to someone special. A tag is placed on the sapling so a note can be made on its progress. My tree bears my late parents names and by now should be well established.

At a beach side café in Tel Aviv I assessed the safety of visiting Jerusalem with Israel's Director of the Duke of Edinburgh's Award Scheme. He encouraged me not to give in to those trying to destroy Israel's "Promised Land". The Award Scheme's only concession to terrorists was to allow groups out on expeditions to be shadowed by the military when in isolated, rural or mountainous areas.

Jerusalem proved to be an extremely moving experience. The sense of history in being able to walk the path of the cross Jesus carried on the way to be crucified on Calvary and to visit the Church of the Holy Sepulchre where Jesus was laid to rest was overwhelming. The Western Wall, the holy place for Jews, seen many times on television took on a new meaning in terms of understanding the passion of those praying there. To observe the Dome of the Rock, where Mohammed made his ascent to heaven, the most revered Islamic holy place, highlights the difficulties in securing a political settlement that will satisfy Jews, Christians and Moslems. In the week spent in Jerusalem Palestinian suicide bombers killed 46 Israelis, 19 were killed and many injured in a bomb blast on a bus. The Jerusalem Post headline read, "*Death leads public to avoid buses*". Undeterred by these attacks I joined a series of tours that took me to Bethlehem, the church of the Nativity and Capernaum, the fishing village where Jesus first taught. I floated on the Dead Sea, climbed to the top of the fort at Masda, overlooked the Golan Heights, (not knowing that one day I would be looking in the opposite direction from the Syrian border), had tea overlooking the Sea of Galilee and visited Joseph's workshop in Nazareth. There were constant reminders of the danger of terrorist attacks such as roadblocks on the road to Jaffa where a car bomb had exploded. Danger was only a heartbeat away.

I usually write my journal at the end of each day. However when writing this essay I found no record of my visit to the Holocaust Memorial. All I can remember is darkness; candles and the gentle voice of a woman giving the names of the children whom were Holocaust victims. It had been such a dramatic and moving moment that I had blocked out parts of the experience from my memory. I couldn't even remember which town the Memorial was based and had to consult a guidebook to relive what I had seen. The following describes what I had blacked out.

The Yad Vashem in Jerusalem houses the Holocaust Memorial to the Jews murdered by the Nazis. The approach to the Memorial is called the Avenue of the Righteous, which commemorates non-Jews who risked their lives to save Jews, (as featured in the film "Schindlers List"). Israel bestows the honorary title "Righteous among the Gentiles" and the right to plant a carob tree bearing their name. The Hall of Remembrance is a spacious, windowless interior with the names of the Nazi death camps set in the floor in Hebrew and Latin. An eternal flame burns in memory of the dead. The place that moved me the most was the Children's memorial set in an underground room with glass walls reflecting five candle flames, creating the effect of countless flames each symbolising a child's soul. A woman's voice reads the names of the dead children, their ages and place of birth. Near the entrance to the site stands a six-branched candlestick, the symbol of Yad Yashem. Its six arms symbolise the six million Jews who perished at the hands of the Nazis.

On my departure from Israel there was much to reflect on, not least how fortunate I had been to avoid direct contact with terrorist activities. Unknowingly I had also avoided what some tourists know as "Jerusalem Syndrome", a psychological reaction experienced by some tourists. The condition can lead seemingly stable people into believing that their arrival in Jerusalem is the result of some Divine calling. Those badly affected can be seen walking aimlessly around the streets, bearded and wearing long robes. They tend to be male, unmarried, in their early 20s, from Western Europe and North America, Jews and Christians from homes with a religious upbringing. It is believed that some of those affected have travelled to Israel to escape some form of turmoil in their lives. Unfortunately, with all the terrorist attacks in Israel, they are escaping one form of turmoil for another resulting for some in a psychological breakdown.

The second visit to the "Cradle of Civilisation" was to Syria in February 1999. Using Larnaka in Cyprus as a base I flew to Damascus then travelled overland to Beirut in Lebanon, concluding with a flight back to Cyprus to recover! A number of excursions across Syria and Lebanon were undertaken including a visit to the Iraq border. Before this trip I had to surrender my passport despite it being valid for four more years. As I had an Israeli stamp in my passport it would have prevented me from entering Syria and Lebanon, two of the countries in conflict with Israel.

Syria has been dominant in its position and role in the current problems faced in finding solutions to the establishment of Independent States for Israel and

Palestine. In the 12th century Syria was a major force led by Saladin who, in 1187, crushed the Crusaders in the Battle of Hittin and stormed Jerusalem. Saladin's success led to the Third Crusade under the leadership of Richard the Lionheart. After a series of battles a peace deal was signed that left the Crusaders in control of the coastal area and Muslims in control of the interior.

In modern times Syria fought alongside Egypt, Lebanon and Jordan against Israel in the six-day war of 1967 resulting in Israel taking over Golan Heights from Syria and Jerusalem's old city from Jordan. In 1973 Syria again supported Egypt in attacking Israel and again they were defeated. Israel's control of the Golan Heights proving decisive.

In 1982 Israel invaded Lebanon in retaliation to border raids, not withdrawing until 1985. Lebanon itself was involved in 15 years of civil wars fuelled by interventions by the USA, UK, France, Iran and Syria. Fighting eventually ended in 1990 when Syria, with approval of the USA moved in.

On arriving in Damascus I found a suitable hotel in the centre of the city without much difficulty. I never saw another tourist the whole time I was in the city, the only foreigners were there on business. I settled down for what I was hoping would be a good nights sleep. At 2am I was woken by the sound of planes overhead. The noise was deafening and not knowing what was going on was frightening. Were Israel launching one of its retaliatory attacks, had I arrived at the start of a new war? Whatever was going on lasted nearly an hour; the only reassurance was that there were no sounds of explosions so Damascus was not the target. I enquired the next morning about what had happened but no one would explain. I found the answers in the English language paper "The Syria Times" that reported on the Israeli bombardment of towns in the Al-Qeseyeh Valley. They also reported that American F-115 aircraft had dropped tons of laser-guided bombs on Iraqi targets in the heaviest air strikes since Desert Fox. They also reported that British planes had bombarded positions near Baghdad. I had inadvertently placed myself on the flight path of Israeli, American and British aircraft-welcome to Damascus!

Undeterred by a lack of sleep I was quickly off on a tour of Damascus. It is claimed that Syria is the "Cradle of Civilisation" and that advanced methods of Agriculture and Metallurgy were developed here as well as the first alphabet. Religions, philosophies, the language of trade, systems of urban development, diplomatic and cultural exchange, all have their roots in Syria.

Damascus, for its part, claims to be the world's oldest inhabited city. The most significant religious building in Damascus is the Omayyed Mosque which dates back to 705 AD. The Mosque was formally a Christian cathedral which itself was built on the site of a Roman temple. In a city whose population is 86% Muslim, one of the most revered Christian sites can be found inside the Mosque, the domed shrine containing the Tomb of St John the Baptist. Nearby is St Paul's Church named in memory of St Paul's life changing religious experience on the road to Damascus.

A full day was spent on a 95-mile trek across the desert to Palmyra. This is a remarkable site, a crossroads where East and West met over the centuries, an oasis set in the middle of hundreds of miles of desert. The site is mentioned in stone tablets dating back to the 19th century BC. In the first century BC the Romans came and built many of the structures that still stand and gave Palmyra the name "A city of a thousand columns". Palmyra is close to the Iraqi border so I persuaded the driver to take me as close as possible in the hope of seeing some evidence of last nights military events. All we found was a brick built building on the Syrian side with a large sign that read "Baghdad Café". Unfortunately it was closed.

Heading back toward Damascus we came upon a Bedouin camp. Dotted across the countryside small flocks of sheep and goats were tended. Although there were a few camels on view the main form of transport seemed to be the 4 by 4 Landrover. The camel has been relegated to providing meat, leather, milk and wool. One tradition that remains however was the famed hospitality of the Bedouins. The family provided small cups of tea and coffee as we sat in their camel skin tents, a humbling experience given their limited resources.

The next stage of my exploration involved hiring a car and driver to take me from Damascus to Beirut in Lebanon via the ancient Phoenician City of Byblos in the north of Lebanon. Once over the border into Lebanon progress became very slow and fraught with danger. Every few miles a roadblock would be encountered, those manned by Lebanese or Syrian troops were not a problem but those manned by the Hizbullah or Palestinian guerrillas were scary. Heavily armed they demanded payment of a toll before allowing us to pass. The money was no doubt being used in the fight against Israel but no matter how offensive that may be it would have been life threatening to refuse to pay.

It was a quite a relief to eventually arrive in Byblos. Arabs, the Crusaders and the Romans had occupied this 7000-year-old town. The historic sites are well maintained and protected. Excavations have unearthed large pottery jars from 3,000/4,000 years BC. These pots were early "coffins" where the deceased and all their earthly possessions were placed and then buried. In 1200 BC the scribes had developed an alphabetical script, the precursor to our modern alphabet.

Baalbek, 55 miles north of Beirut lived up to its name as one of the Middle East's most spectacular archaeological sites. The town has numerous claims to religious fame; it started as a monument to the Phoenician god Baal, the Greeks renamed it Heliopolis, City of the Sun. The Romans used the site to worship their god Jupiter. Roman heritage can be seen at the Acropolis, Jupiter Temple, Bacchus Temple and the Temple of Venus.

Feeling adventurous I took a trip along the south coast to Sidan and Tyre. Due to their strategic position Alexander the Great, Crusader Baldwin, Salidan, the Crusader Templars and the Babylonian King Nebuchadnezzer have conquered them. Now in 1999 the area is a war zone again with Palestinian guerrillas exchanging rocket fire with Israelis. Tension was particularly high as 1,000 unarmed students marched from Beirut to the border village of Arnoun tearing down barbed wire fences to liberate the village from Israeli control.

The following day Hizabullah guerrillas, no doubt inspired by the students, started firing rockets into Western Galilee killing Israel's most senior Commander in South Lebanon. All commercial flights were cancelled as Israel replied with rocket attacks on Hizbullah campsites and I was stranded in Beirut. The United States, France and Syria worked together to defuse the situation from becoming a full-scale war. The Lebanon Daily Star headline read, *"Israel plans massive air, land and sea offensive"*. The fears of an all out war re-surfaced again as they had while I was in Syria.

Back in Beirut I occupied my time by reflecting on the previous plight of John McCarthy, Terry Waite and Brian Keenan who had spent years chained to the walls of Lebanese cellars during a hostage crisis. At the end of the Civil War in 1991 there had been a massive rebuilding programme in the attempt to restore Beirut to its previous title of the "Paris of the Middle-East". There were still large areas of damaged buildings showing scorched brickwork and twisted metal girders that had melted in the heat of explosions and gunfire. I walked along the beach and despite stepping over assorted mounds of rubbish I was able to relax. It was quite a surprise to find a McDonalds restaurant, which seemed out of place in war torn Beirut and which provided thoughts of home. This was the area of Beirut that in 2005 the President of Lebanon was killed by a car bomb. Diplomatic negotiations eventually succeeded and flights from Beirut were resumed so I was able to return to Cyprus and unwind before returning to England a few days later.

My third visit to the "Cradle of Civilisation" was to Jordan in October 2001. The timing of the visit has to be put in context with the events in New York on the 11th September, just a month earlier. Since September 11th, the number of tourists visiting Jordan had dropped by 50%. American tourists visiting the UK had dropped by 48%. There was also a major impact on the tourist trade in countries blameless of terrorist activity.

In evaluating whether to continue with my trip I considered three major factors. One was statistical. There are billions of ordinary citizens and only hundreds of people prepared to commit suicide for their cause. The second factor was being "ordinary". There is no credit in killing ordinary people. The rise in the level of security offers reassurance for travellers. The sense of outrage against the Twin Towers attackers has unified more countries against terrorists than any other act of war in modern times. Thirdly, the only way to show terrorists they cannot win is for ordinary people to continue doing ordinary things. That same spirit emerged during terrorist attacks in London in July 2005.

Now is the time to solve many on-going conflicts. Countries of wealth and power should re-distribute some of their wealth to the poorer, deprived countries. The gap between the wealth of the Western world and the poverty of the Middle East, parts of Asia, Africa and South America has grown to massive proportions. The uniting of World Leaders can end many territorial disputes. Ceasing the oppression of citizens, particularly the women of Afghanistan, would be a positive outcome of the September 11th tragedy. There are also many other major issues to be resolved such as the creation of peaceful co-existence between Palestine and Israel. The problems of Kashmir disputed by India and Pakistan and the claims of the people in the Philippines, Sri Lanka, Iran, Northern Ireland, Sudan etc. "Life will never be the same", lets hope it is for good not evil.

The original plan for this visit was to use Jordan as a base and then visit Iraq, Saudi Arabia and Kuwait. Due to Allied attacks on Afghanistan the opportunity to obtain visas for Iraq and Saudi Arabia became impossible. My flight to Amman via Paris was disrupted due to restricted air space over London, again one of the consequences of the September 11th attacks. After a two-hour delay in Birmingham my connection from Paris had left. Air France provided free accommodation until another flight to Jordan could be found. After two days in Paris a flight to Beirut in Lebanon was provided.

Two days were spent in Lebanon again at the expense of Air France. The stop over in Beirut was an unplanned bonus. Beirut had barely changed since my visit in 1999 in terms of conflict. During the two days three major incidents took place. At Batroun arsonists set fire to a Lebanese Mosque, the latest in a series of attacks on places of worship by Israeli sympathisers. Previously attacks had been made against the Saint Elias Church and a Greek Orthodox Church in Tripoli. At Haltax Israeli warplanes attacked Hizbullah positions after resistance fighters had fired rockets and mortars at Israeli outposts. A parade of open top cars raced through the centre of Beirut that night firing automatic weapons in the air. No one attempted to halt the parade as members of Hizbollah made a show of force.

Beirut airport was a ghost town. Only three planes were due in or out that day, such is the scale of Lebanon's isolation. It was a relief to depart safely to Amman for the final leg of my journey to Jordan.

The warmth of my welcome in Jordan astounded me. Strangers approached me in the street and asked where I was from and welcomed me. The authorities had taken great efforts to reassure tourists. Their borders link with Syria, Saudi Arabia, Iraq and the Palestine townships adjacent to Israel. Three million Palestine refugees are now valued citizens of Jordan and the country is a long-standing friend of the UK. The precautions taken include the positioning of tanks in front of the British, American and Israeli embassies. All tourist coaches and mini-buses carry a police officer as reassurance. Only two small protest marches against the attacks on Afghanistan were reported, undertaken by university students. Jordan is predominantly a Muslim country and co-exists with ease with the small Christian churches. Any anger is directed at Israel for its failure to establish the State of Palestine.

The only other example of tension whilst in Jordan occurred in Petra. I was in a shop when I heard gunfire outside. Seeing my reaction the shopkeeper reassured me that it was traditional for guns to be fired in the air during a wedding parade.

The most convenient and instructive way of getting around Jordan was to hire a car and English-speaking driver. It was interesting to learn the thoughts of a Jordanian. One of my drivers told how he had been affected by the 11th September attack in New York. The post office had notified him that there were five letters from America waiting for collection. He was expecting letters from friends but refused to collect the letters in case they contained Anthrax. He told the post office to destroy the letters.

My travels took me through the Jordan valley, which was once one of the great land trade routes. Many castles still exist to record the strategic value of the country to many great and powerful nations. Many of the places and events that took place there are recorded in the Bible. The most impressive of Jordan's historical sites is the World heritage town of Petra, a city carved from red stone. The Treasury was the focal point in the film, "Indiana Jones and the Last Crusade". The results of earthquakes millions of years ago have created a landscape unrivalled anywhere else in the world. So dramatic is the landscape that the film "Mission to Mars" was also filmed there. One of my personal highlights of Petra was a horse ride through the red rock city. Other places of historical interest visited were Madaba (City of Mosaics), Mount Nebo (where Moses died and is buried), The Dead Sea, Lot's Sanctuary, Jerash (Northern Jordan), an ancient city of unbroken human habitation since Neolithic times,

Ajloun (the castle where Salidian defeated the Crusaders in 1189) and the Crusader Castle at Kerak.

There are only six cinema screens in Amman, a city the size of Birmingham. Cinema going had collapsed since the recent introduction of satellite television. I saw the film "Snow over Cedars"; there was only one other person there. The film featured America's internment of all people living in America who were Japanese. This followed the attack on Pearl Harbour by the Japanese in World War II in 1941.

An interesting postscript to the internment of the Japanese. Following the attack on Pearl Harbour all Americans of Japanese descent were ineligible for the draft. It was not until 1943 that an All-American born Japanese army unit was established. They fought with great passion in Italy and Southern France against the Italians and Germans earning great respect. Their regiment became the most decorated of its size, not only in World War II but also in the entire history of the US Army. Many of the medals were awarded posthumously reflecting their bravery under fire. How can you reconcile the loyalty of the American Japanese with the aims of their Japan based countrymen who were waging war against American forces in the Pacific?

Two other interesting experiences in Amman were linked to sport and justice. A summary of the differences in the sentencing of criminals between Jordan and the UK are featured in the essay on Crime and Punishment. Contact with the King of Jordan was at a football match. I visited the National Stadium for the Premier league match between Faisaili and Jazira. Faisaili were top of the league and won 2-0. The price of admission was very low compared with other forms of entertainment, only 75 dinars (75 pence). Before the game a cheerleader orchestrated clapping and cheering. This continued throughout the game supported by a man with a big drum. Apart from the referee I was the only one watching the game, not the cheerleaders. The only time the crowd ignored the cheerleaders was when a goal was scored.

The King of Jordan is a fanatical supporter. Television highlights from an Asian Football Competition showed the King wearing a football shirt sitting in the grandstand with his wife. All his male relatives had shirts too, numbered 99. During the penalty shoot-out the King leapt to his feet as the winning goal was scored embracing his male relations in an unashamed display of public delight. I can't recall the Queen or Prince Philip engaging in a similar public display of emotion when England won the World Cup in 1966.

Reading the January 2006 edition of National Geographic magazine I encountered two new terms – happenstance salvation and happenstance death. The writer, Frank Viviano, drew a distinction between the fine line between death and starvation in a country like Iraq. By arriving a minute early or late could be the difference between being an observer of the consequences of the work of a suicide bomber or being their victim.

In 2005 I was reminded of my stay in Amman by the report that Al Queda had used a husband and wife as suicide bombers in attacks on three wedding parties in which 57 were killed. One of the hotels was the Days Inn Hotel, where I had stayed. The scenes of devastation reminded me of my frailty and good fortune in avoiding such happenings on my travels around the world.

On my departure from Jordan I reflected on a poster seen in a Travel agents in Amman.
"There are three kinds of people...
There are those who make things happen
There are those who watch things happen.
There are those who wonder what happened".

Hopefully people who know me recognise that the first two represent my aims in life and my love of travel. Which statement applies to you?

10

The event that killed Apartheid

Meeting Nelson Mandela and Desmond Tutu
Cape Town Cathedral riot
The Garden of Eden for UK Wrinklies
Transformation of Soweto
Deported from Mozambique in the back of a lorry

The 1993 visit to South Africa started as a cricket tour but ended in one of the defining moments of world history - the end of apartheid. Two of the principals involved in this historic event were Nelson Mandela and Desmond Tutu. I was to meet both as apartheid unravelled before my very eyes. I am content to be called an opportunist because that state of mind put me in the front stalls of the audience for the final act… Although I was criticised at the time and put myself in dangerous situations I would still do it all again.

In 2004 I returned to Africa this time to The Gambia and Senegal. With a predominantly black government in power in South Africa I was particularly interested in how other African countries were responding to their own freedom and self-rule. Purely by chance I came across the growing tourist trade involving UK Wrinklies and young Gambian men and women.

In April 1993 I visited South Africa as a member of the Warwickshire County Cricket Club's Supporters Tour led by the former Sussex and England Test Player Alan Oakman. The players were undertaking pre season training and playing a number of games against South African teams in the Cape Town area. My plan was to enjoy the cricket, tour the wine growing regions around Stellenbosch and to travel independently along the Garden Route via Port Elizabeth to Grahamstown to offer advice as a volunteer to the South African version of the Duke of Edinburgh's Award.

The Warwickshire team and supporters were staying at a hotel near the Newlands Cricket Ground where England and South Africa play in the Test series. Racial tension was high at the time as the fight against apartheid was reaching a climax. Within minutes of arriving at my hotel one of the elderly women supporters was mugged. She had just stepped outside the hotel foyer with her bag around her neck when two men on a motorcycle raced up. The passenger wrenched the bag off the victim bringing her crashing to the ground before racing off. A broken arm and the loss of her passport, credit cards and cash were the consequences. The attack left everyone in shock. What had we let ourselves in for travelling to South Africa at this time? Little did we know that events over the next three weeks would lead to the end of apartheid and that we were to witness a major historical event.

Apartheid has its roots in the Dutch Reform Church in the 19th Century when white members of the church said, *"We will no longer drink with these slaves and former slaves out of one common cup and not share bread in the church"*. The majority of the government at that time was members of the Dutch Reform Church and so it followed that church policy became government policy.

The first settlement in Cape Town was established by the Dutch India Company in 1652 and was intended as a staging post for providing fresh fruit and vegetables. Settlers from England and Holland were encouraged to establish farms. In effect the settlers were used to drive out the native Hottentots. The natives were also ravaged by exposure to European diseases such as smallpox. Ten years after the establishment of the Dutch settlement they started to bring in slaves from East and West Africa as cheap labour to farm the land. It was not until 1834 that slavery was to be abolished by the British. Although apartheid was officially ended with the first free elections in 1994 there are still many examples in 2005 where economic apartheid still exists more than three hundred years after the first settlers from Holland imposed themselves on to the native Africans.

In a society so divided along ethnic lines it was refreshing to visit Grahamstown and witness a multi-racial youth programme in action. I was following in the footsteps of Nelson Mandela who was the President of the Gold Shield Award, South Africa's title for the Duke of Edinburgh's Award. Nelson Mandela had been presenting Bronze, Silver and Gold Awards. I was there to meet Craig Andrew the National Director for the Award in South Africa and to share the results of initiatives that I had piloted in England. These were to be taken up with great success.

The main success was to be developing the Award within youth prisons. A talk was given to staff in the Grahamstown Prison on how the Award could be broken down into modules representing the four sections of the Award, sport, community service, skills and expedition. Modular certificates were introduced for each section to encourage and reward young people of low motivation to strive to complete all four sections. As a result of the initial presentation the National Director of the Award started a pilot scheme in 1994. Eleven years later HRH The Earl of Wessex visited South Africa to join in the celebrations of the success of that pilot programme. The Award now operates in 40 prisons across Africa, so far 21,000 young people at risk have been challenged by voluntarily taking part in the programme. One of the Gold Award Holders, Alfonso Van Heerden, told how he had changed, *"I was an active prison gangster and was sentenced for a very bad crime but then the Gold Shield Award crossed my path and changed my life for ever"*. The success of that initial presentation back in 1993 is my legacy to South Africa.

I was privileged to have contact with Nelson Mandela on two occasions. The first was prior to the memorial Service at Cape Town Cathedral and the second at the International Convention Centre in Birmingham where we briefly chatted following his election as the President of South Africa.

A few weeks after my first contact with Nelson Mandela I received a letter dated 21/04/1993 from him that included the following.

"For me, one of the most pleasurable tasks amongst the many that I am asked to perform is certainly that of meeting children and applauding them for their efforts and excellence in all fields.

In South Africa it is of particular importance to advance work amongst children of all races to ensure, especially for the black youngsters who have so much to catch up on after the years of apartheid, that those of us who can should assist in this work".
With best wishes for your work.

Nelson R Mandela, President, African National Congress.

On my return from Grahamstown I rejoined the Warwickshire touring party back in Newlands. I joined in some of the activities whilst still going off on mini adventures trying to assess the full impact of apartheid. A visit was made to the home of Mick Dunwell, a white British passport holder who served in the Rhodesian Airforce prior to Rhodesia becoming independent. He had been a resident of South Africa for 12 years. His home was set in a comfortable white residential area where the residents employ private armed guards and have roadblocks at all entrances to the estate. Mick Dunwell always carried a revolver and had a Bull Terrier as an additional house guard. Although not a resident in South Africa at the time of the Governments Sharpeville Massacre in 1960 or the shooting of the children in Soweto in 1976, he still felt a sense of responsibility for these tragic events. Mick Dunwell lived in constant fear that the ANC campaign of non-violence would be over ruled by extremists who were getting more vociferous by the day. That fear was to be tested a few days later.

During my time at the Youth Prison in Grahamstown I had heard of the exceptional work being undertaken by the Church led Child Charity, NICRO, in prisons in Cape Town. Children were being kept in prison in the same cells as adults and many were brutally treated. NICRO was leading the fight for segregated areas for children. The NICRO office was in Woodstock that could only be reached by public transport. It was a no go area as far as taxis were concerned. As the only white person on the bus I obviously felt very conspicuous and was starting to have doubts about whether I was being sensible. The landmark where I was to get off was not known to the bus driver so I took his advice and got off outside a police station. A young black man got off the bus at the same time and asked where I wanted to go. It turned out that the Inspector at the bus station had put me on the wrong bus and it was a two-mile walk to the NICRO office in an area known for muggings of unwary visitors even in daylight. Sensing my concern he volunteered to guide me there even though it was totally away from where he wanted to go. Thanks to his considerable intervention I arrived safely at the NICRO office and so did not become another victim statistic.

The work of NICRO was not only to ensure that young children were not locked up with adults but also to prevent them being imprisoned in the first place. Most of the children had never committed any crime other than loitering. They were homeless and living rough in alleyways. These street children survived by begging and scavenging food from dustbins. They are rejected by their parents and get no form of education. They form gangs and as they grow older get more into serious criminal activity. The police would round them up and have them imprisoned without trial. By combining the efforts of all churches the children were being taken off the streets and cared for. They had been so successful that the number of young children, some as young as eight, in the Cape Town Prison had dropped from 1500 to 15. An impressive achievement. At the conclusion of my fact finding visit, one of the members of staff drove me back to my hotel to ensure a safe return.

The stay in Cape Town coincided with the Easter celebrations. I attended the Easter Sunday Service that was conducted by the Reverend Christopher Ahrends, assistant to Bishop Desmond Tutu. The Reverend Ahrends had previously been exiled to Zambia and whilst living there was the victim of a parcel bomb that was allegedly sent by the South African police. He lost both hands and an eye in the explosion. Despite this atrocity and the murder of Chris Hani a few days earlier his sermon was based on restraint and moderation.

At the conclusion of the service I was able to obtain the signature of Bishop Desmond Tutu in the book "Crucible of Fire – The church Confronts Apartheid". The book features sermons and interviews given by the Bishop and other preachers of non-violence including Alan Boesak, Jim Wallis, Frank Chikane and Joyce Holiday.

A few days before the Easter Sunday Service on the 10th April 1993, Chris Hani, leader of the Communist party and a former ANC member had been assassinated at Boksburg, a town between Cape Town and Stellenbosch. I was in the Warwickshire coach coming back from Worcester at that time and had to travel through Boksburg on the way back to our hotel. A small petrol bomb was thrown at the coach but caused no damage. The tension in Cape Town and the rest of South Africa was electric. Was this to be the final atrocity that would lead to a mass uprising against apartheid?

Nelson Mandela and Desmond Tutu were battling frantically to prevent the black townships from erupting into violence. In an attempt to defuse the situation they declared a day of prayer to commemorate the life and work of Chris Hani. A commemorative service was to be held in St George's Cathedral. The evening before the service Nelson Mandela appeared on television to urge a peaceful celebration at the cathedral. He called on blacks and whites to combine together on the streets in a peaceful assembly to show those responsible for killing Chris Hani that apartheid will only be defeated by non–violent means. This was a massive gamble being made by Nelson Mandela and the ANC Leadership. The alleged assassin was Janus Waluz, an immigrant from Poland in 1981. He was a member of the Afrikaner Weerstandsbeweging, the leader of which was the notorious Eugene Terre Blanche. Blanche had changed the spelling of his name so that when translated the last two names mean "white land".

I was inspired by the appeal for a non violent celebration of the life of Chris Hani, so asked all the members of the tour party if they would come with me to the service in Cape Town the next day. There was not a single volunteer. Later that evening Andy Mole and two other members of the team came and suggested it would be too dangerous to go and that they were concerned for my safety. I thanked them but was not deterred. I sensed that one of the great events in world history would be the result of this Commemorative service, the end of apartheid in South Africa.

The next morning after a hearty breakfast, armed with my camera and dressed in my oldest clothes I caught a train from Newlands toward Cape Town. My plan was to assess the situation station by station. If everything seemed calm and orderly I would stay on the train. If not I would get off and return to my hotel. I later realised that I had gained a false sense of security as there were no shanty towns on the line from Newlands to Cape Town. Station after station passed with no sign of trouble but as the train pulled into the main station in Cape Town everything changed. Trains commandeered by the ANC were pulling into adjacent platforms packed solid with people from the townships. People were hanging on the roofs and the sides of the carriages. As the trains pulled in there was a great roar as they poured onto the platform. Thousands converged from the different platforms chanting nationalist freedom songs and high stepping in a giant mass of humanity toward the cathedral. The sounds reverberated off the glass ceiling of the station; they were certainly celebrating.

Violence Erupts in Cape Town, the End of Apartheid.

Petrol Bombs explode and people are thrown through shop windows by looters.

I

Bin Laden's HQ prior to the liberation of Afghanistan.

Addressing the Conference at Abuja in Nigeria on World Aids Day.

The first of a number of breakdowns as Moby Jim travels to and from Moscow.

The Twenty Two Club L/R - Cliff Ellsom, Christine Moore, Tony Forde, Jim Parkes, Graham Fisher, Linda Birch, Michael Jenks, Anna Bruton and Bill Taylor.

Promoting the Duke of Edinburgh's Award in Bombay.

Baghdad Café on the border of Syria and Iraq - closed for business.

Ready to board the flight around the top of Mount Everest from an airstrip in Nepal.

Telecom engineers monitor the bugging devices during the Japanese Embassy hostage crisis in Lima, Peru.

Enjoying the Test Match in Faisalabad, Pakistan with members of the "Barmy Army".

A thank you gift from HRH Prince Philip on retirement from the Duke of Edinburgh's Award Scheme.

Armed Troop carriers on guard in Kabul in Afghanistan as a new mosque is built.

Walking the Great Wall Of China.

Instructions to prisoners at the infamous Khmer Rouge Detention Centre in Cambodia under the leadership of Pol Pot.

A traditional African welcome at the Abuja airport in Nigeria with musicians bearing gifts and playing welcome songs.

Meeting Mother Teresa with my wife Christine, my daughter Leigh, my son James and other members of the group.

The Parkes Family in front of the Taj Mahal with Birmingham Gold Award participants, Ian Mailes, Marion Singh, Salim Mulla and Gene McLeod.

Planting a tree in memory of my parents in the new Modin Forest near Tel Aviv.

Desmond Tutu preaching in Cape Town Cathedral.

Gaining a B. Ed. Honours degree the hard way by evening and weekend study.

Sir Trevor Brooking presents the Gold Award Certificate to my daughter Leigh at St. Jame's Palace.

Riding a horse through Petra in Jordan.

The first sight of the Treasury in Petra, Jordan.

Geisha girls prepare for the annual street parade through Kyoto in Japan.

The massive Iguacu Falls on the border of Brazil, Paraguay and Argentina.

Preparing to fly over the Nazca Lines in the Peru desert.

Receiving the MBE from Her Majesty The Queen.

*My son James shares the proudest material moment of my life receiving the MBE at
Buckingham Palace.*

I decided to remain cautious and waited a few minutes before following the end of the parade toward the Cathedral. On leaving the station I spoke with an international monitor wearing a plastic I.D. smock. He and his colleagues were there to observe the behaviour of the police, the army and the demonstrators. Despite Mandela's appeal for white South Africans to join the celebration I saw barely a dozen on the road, except for members of the army and police, amongst the 100,000 moving through the city. The small number of white South Africans were mainly ministers and priests trying to ensure that their congregations behaved.

There were other white South Africans on the balconies of their shops that flanked both sides of the main road. From their perspective they were watching street theatre and being entertained as thousands Toyi Toyied and sang as they passed beneath them. A car cavalcade came through with international statesmen and celebrities including Mohammed Ali, the former heavyweight boxing champion. I moved along taking photographs as I went, figuring I might be protected if mistaken for a press photographer, as protesters for and against the parade would want their message relayed around the world. Eventually I could travel no further as the crowd came to a standstill in front of the cathedral. Not being able to hear the relayed proceedings I decided not to push my luck and so started back toward the station. Inevitably a minority took advantage of the peaceful celebration by looting some of the big department stores. The first sign of trouble was the noise of petrol bombs exploding in one of the side streets. A crowd fleeing the violence was running toward me so I also ran to find cover in the doorway of a supermarket. I could see people inside the store packing the entrance, securing the doors making it impossible for anyone else to get in. In the distance I could see people being thrown through plate glass windows and electrical goods and furniture being looted. The people on the balconies started to panic and reinforce the ground floors of their stores; it was no longer street theatre to them but self-preservation. The police responded with tear gas and rubber bullets. Army personnel carriers moved in to protect property.

Having failed to gain entrance to any building I started running toward the railway station. It was virtually deserted at this time and I quickly found a stationary train that was due to travel toward Newlands. The next ten minutes seemed to be the longest of my life. I had visions of thousands of people pouring into the station either to wreck the place or attack any lone travellers, particularly white ones. The train eventually departed and I settled to reflect on what had happened and what might have happened. On arrival in Newlands I made a beeline to the nearest photo store to get my film developed. After another anxious wait the film was developed and all was well. On arrival back in England the local press featured photographs of exploding petrol bombs under the heading, "Local Man Escapes Violent Mayhem". Lucky Jim had survived again while watching history evolve. Within weeks apartheid was scrapped, the first free and democratic elections would take place within months and in 1994 Nelson Mandela became the President of South Africa.

Nelson Mandela and his supporters Desmond Tutu, Allan Boesak, Frank Chikane, Steve Biko and others had succeeded because they had led a campaign of non-violence inspired by Mahatma Gandi. It was Gandi who had led one of the first campaigns against the South African government in 1891 highlighting the discrimination directed at the Indian community. The experience Gandi gained in South Africa eventually led to the success of the campaign he inspired to gain independence for India from the British.

Nelson Mandela can be justly proud of his election. It had been a long and difficult road since he had been arrested in the 1960s and imprisoned on Robben Island for 27 years.

While in Cape Town I had been receiving airmail copies of the Birmingham Evening Mail and one report mentioned that an England and Nottingham cricketer had failed to attend a court hearing for motoring offences in Birmingham and a warrant had been issued for his arrest. It was a pure coincidence that as I was entering the hotel lift to the restaurant the cricketer concerned stepped in as well. Nottinghamshire County Cricket Club was also sharing the same hotel and you can imagine his surprise to be confronted with a newspaper report that he was to be arrested on his return to England. All thoughts of his meal were gone and the player frantically telephoned his solicitor back in England to sort out the problem.

The day after the service of celebration it was time to depart for England. There was to be one last scare as on the way to the airport our coach was hit by a petrol bomb. Thankfully it was quickly extinguished.

On the flight home a number of unrelated issues were being recalled as I made my notes of the visit. The conscription of all white males at the age of 18 for a years service into the army. Wife beating, a black South African tradition that was adopted in modified form by the white Afrikaans. The cost of petrol included third party insurance so that motorists only have to pay an additional premium if they want fully comprehensive cover. The Scout Association did not admit girls. This decision was based on culture. It was believed that males would dominate decisions and therefore defeat the objectives of integration.

I had noted a number of examples of political graffiti on my travels. A notice seen outside a factory said, "*Rottweilers patrolling day and night - Please make their day*". The only problem being that the Rottweilers were fast asleep under the sign. Three examples of graffiti that focussed on political ideology:

The ANC slogan *"One person one vote"*. The black terrorist group APLA slogan was "One bullet, one settler". The Afrikaan AWB slogan was *"One bomb, many Kaafa"*.

To conclude on a lighter note a piece of poetry by an unnamed African UDF poet. It begins, *"In order to ensure absolute national security, the government has passed the Animal and Insect Emergency Control and Discipline Act…*

It outlines the new regulations: buffaloes, cows and goats are henceforth prohibited from grazing in herds of more than three; birds can no longer flock, nor bees swarm, for such constitutes unlawful assembly; penguins and zebras are ordered to discard their non regulation uniforms; and under no circumstances are elephants to break wind between the hours of 6pm and 6am, for such could easily be interpreted as gunshot and might spark off a riot".

The first of two visits to West Africa was in February 2004. It was 11 years since my visit to South Africa and I was interested to see to what extent the ending of apartheid in South Africa had impacted on other parts of Africa. The first stop was Bangul in The Gambia which I was to use as a base when touring, including a visit to Senegal. It was a short ride from the airport to the Campo Beach Hotel that I used to acclimatise. I had been warned about being hassled if I went out of the hotel onto the beach but that did not deter me. True enough, I had barely walked ten yards when I was approached by two youths about 17/18 years of age. They greeted me like a long lost brother and invited me to their home to meet their sister who was *"good marriage material"*. Out hustling the hustlers can be fun. Releasing a load of fictitious information and providing plausible reasons for not accompanying them to meet people who would give *"a good deal"* in the market or to go to their bar. I escaped on the basis that I would meet them later at their bar to meet their sister. They would be in for a big disappointment when I did not turn up.

The experience reminded me of a former colleague who was to be married in Guyana to a Princess while on a community service project with a group from Birmingham. In his late fifties he was no doubt flattered by the approach of this beautiful young women even though he must have known that he was being used to get her into England with a British passport. Because it was not possible to complete all the formalities of marriage and citizenship while in Guyana he returned to England. On hearing of his intentions, his brothers and other members of his family tried to talk some sense in to him. Eventually they succeeded when he realised he was being conned. I still have the vision of my friend walking through the streets of Erdington with a stunningly beautiful Guyana Princess on his arm. The dream would probably only last a short time before she would disappear, perhaps emptying his bank account as others have done with gullible elderly tourists. Had it been genuine, perhaps he would have returned to Guyana as the village chief on the death of the Princess's father.

After just one night in The Gambia it was off to Senegal across the Gambia River by car ferry. Vehicles were given first priority including open top lorries full of live animals such as sheep and goats. Native foot travellers were the last to get on, herded into a shed with massive steel gates on the dockside. Hundreds of people could be seen looking through the grills waiting for the gates to be thrown open. When released they made a mad dash to find a space between the lorries, cars and coaches. During the 45 minute 17 mile crossing the passengers busy themselves preparing fruit and vegetables for sale. Unsuspecting tourists find their shoes have been whipped off and someone polishing them for a price still to be agreed. Women display lengths of cloth for sale, boxes of cigarettes are available at a special price, money dealer's flash handfuls of notes wanting sterling or dollars to exchange. As the ferry docks they all dash away to harass the passengers waiting to make the return journey.

The road from the ferry to the Senegal border is horrendous, even where Tarmac exists there are enormous potholes. Vehicles move across the width of the road seeking the smoothest route, which is often on the wrong side of the road. Once through the border from the The Gambia there is a stretch of smooth road in Senegal that stretches approximately 20 miles before it becomes a rutted track. Eventually we set off at right angles towards the coast and the hotel accommodation. The beach side hotel was miles from anywhere and extremely calm and relaxed. Although the site was only 120 miles from the capital Dakar it would take six hours to travel there as the roads are so bad. This was the same length of time it took to fly from London to Dakar.

One of the highlights of the brief stay was to attend a tea ceremony at a school in the village of Toubaeouth. The school had been built with funds from the hotel. The children 3/6 year olds, were so unspoilt and charming. Within seconds every visitor had a child clutching their hands as they walked through the village. Three rounds of tea were consumed each getting progressively sweeter that caused a head to form on top of the tea. Freshly caught fish and rice were prepared and cooked whilst we toured the village, so that we could sit down and talk to the teachers over a meal.

Late in the afternoon a youths football match took place against another village. There was not a trace of grass on the pitch and clouds of dust rose as they ran around. Most of the players did not have boots or matching shirts, the cross bar was a rope stretched across the top of two goal posts and there were no line markings. The village elder who was to referee the game didn't have a whistle. To award a free kick he would have to clap two pieces of wood together. I volunteered to referee the game as I had my whistle with me. The players were suitably impressed, as they had never played in a match before with a qualified referee or someone who owned a whistle.

The most difficult part of the game was to judge which direction to award a free kick because of the lack of matching shirts. In terms of judging whether the ball was out of play or not was based on whether the ball had disappeared into the surrounding jungle and was unplayable. The game ended in handshakes all round. No doubt the event has entered into the village folklore, the day a referee from England took part in their annual match. Due to the dust that rose from the grassless pitch, I had developed an even deeper tan-dust coloured.

Another interesting visit was to a local fishing village that had previously been sponsored by the Japanese. Unfortunately their motives had been purely economic. They did build a number of structures that still served a purpose but they had over fished with their factory ships and when the fish stocks declined they went back to Japan leaving the villagers to face the consequences of low catches for many years to come. Even some of the small engine driven fishing boats they had left behind were useless because the villagers could not afford the cost of repairing them when they eventually wore out.

The third trip from the hotel was by speed boat around the coast to an island that was a bird sanctuary. The idea was that we could relax by the pool at a sister hotel until 6pm when the birds would be returning to nest for the night. The only problem was that the hotel was totally deserted. Not a single employee or guest. Apparently the hotel and the island were so isolated that no guests were attracted so all the staff had been laid off. Our group consisted of a Belgian family of three, the guide, the boatman and myself. It was like a plot of a murder mystery that only the Belgian detective Hercule Poirot could solve. The trip finished well once it was time to sail around the island to see the many species of birds at close quarters - herons, pelicans, cormorants, etc.

After three days in Senegal it was time to return to The Gambia via the car ferry in a battered jeep plus driver and guide. I secured accommodation at the African Village Hotel in Bakau. The hotel was very basic with frequent power and water cuts, no radio or TV, but in a good beachside location with good food. It was fascinating to observe the numerous black and white relationships that were taking place in the hotel and on the street. The fascination was to observe white women, well past their prime with young Gambian escorts in their mid twenties. Likewise there were white males past their sell by date with stunning young black women. It would be interesting to know if these were just holiday fantasies being relived by grateful wrinklies or whether it was providing an escape route to the UK for young Gambians.

One of the Gambian highlights was to spend a full day on St James Island, and to retrace the roots of the slave trade as researched by Alex Hayley in his book "Roots". The book tells the story of the journey of one of the slaves taken from the village opposite St James Island to a slave plantation in America. At the village the oldest descendent of that slave's family aged 92 was the centre of attention. She was seven generations down the line since the taking of her descendants and the eventual abolition of the slave trade, first in England and later in America after a bitter North v South war in the 1800s. The full horror of the capture and treatment of the slaves was featured in the village museum. The ruins of the fort and the holding cells captured the degradation and despair of the people who were treated like animals.

A second full day tour was made to the National Park at Makasutu. The park was set up to protect the animals, reptiles and birds from extinction. It also featured forestation work and crop development. Bird watchers were in their element as the expert guide identified numerous species. A canoe ride through the Mango swamps proved to be something I would never do again. The canoes were carved from tree trunks and therefore had no flat bottoms. Eight people sat directly behind each other with a boatman at the back paddling and steering the canoe. The slightest sideways movement by any of the eight passengers would set the canoe rocking from side to side dramatically. I was expecting to be tipped overboard at any moment, the fact that I am a poor swimmer added to the level of fear. The 30 minute journey seemed to last an hour and the pain from cramped muscles was excruciating. Landing was an enormous relief – never again. A buffet lunch plus entertainment of music and dance helped everyone recover. A passing troop of baboons reminded everyone we were in Africa.

By prior arrangement half a day was spent at the Presidents Award Skills Centre in Bakau, (The Gambian D of E Award Scheme). A training session was run for the benefit of Gambian Award leaders that focussed on initiatives I pioneered in the Midlands when I was the Regional Officer. The centre is twinned with the D of E Award in Scotland and has benefited by receiving containers packed with surplus equipment such as sewing machines and an electric generator. The containers have been retained and used as storage facilities. It was great to see young people learning basic skills in Information Technology, motor maintenance, carpentry and dress making. The traditional Gambian skills were reflected in the colour and design of the dresses being made and also in the furniture designs. The young people not only leave the skills centre with Bronze, Silver or Gold Awards but more importantly the skills to gain employment. This is a prime example where equipment rather than money from the UK are being put to such good use.

An insight into the reliance of tourists to support the economy was highlighted by an incident involving taxi drivers outside my hotel. I asked for a taxi to the skills centre and agreed a one way price of £3. It appeared that the taxi I was assigned to had jumped the queue. A big row involving eight drivers started as I sat in the taxi and watched the drama unfold. They knew I would eventually travel back to the hotel so they were interested in another £3 fare even though I couldn't give them a time for the return journey. Once the right driver was identified I was away, the meeting lasted four hours and the taxi driver was still waiting for me. A guaranteed return fare of £3 was his priority as other fares would be unlikely. Certainly not the situation with UK taxis.

There were two touching scenes on my departure from The Gambia. A white, middle aged, plain looking woman was saying farewell to her Gambian lover. She got on and off the coach outside the hotel at least six times to embrace the man with tears streaming down her face. She thrust a handful of notes into his hands apologising for not having more. At the airport a similar scene involved a grossly overweight middle aged white woman and her Gambian toy boy. They were kissing and cuddling in the middle of the airport before she dissolved in tears as her flight was called and she had to leave her lover behind. Based on the above relationships I coined a new marketing slogan for the Gambian Tourist Board, *"Gambia - The Garden of Eden for UK Wrinklies, male or female"*.

On the flight home I reflected on my original question prior to arriving in West Africa - what had been the effect on The Gambia and Senegal as a result of the end of apartheid in South Africa? There appeared to be no racially motivated unrest. White residents were still present in a business capacity and were working in partnership with Africans, rather than treating them as economic slaves. Village communities were stable but still lacking basic amenities. They were earning a modest living through collective enterprises such as food, textiles and handicrafts. They appeared to enjoy a greater level of self-government and democracy than their South African neighbours. I certainly felt safer in West Africa than I had in South Africa twelve years earlier.

In November 2005 I returned to Africa, principally to compare South African lifestyles now with those encountered in 1993. A second objective was to explore Botswana, Zambia, Zimbabwe, Tanzania, Mozambique and Zanzibar. Perhaps it was age taking its toll but there were a number of occasions during the four weeks that I thought I had made a big mistake to undertake such a venture and that I might die.

One massive success story since 1993 has been the transformation of Soweto. During the apartheid era Soweto was one of the worst examples of a slum township for black citizens. Every property was a shack made from any scrap materials such as wood, sun dried mud bricks, cardboard, scrap wood, etc. The thousands of dwellers did not have adequate sanitation or clean drinking water. Virtually everybody was unemployed and the mortality rate high.

Today Soweto is emerging as a model town where 90% live in degrees of comfort based on their occupations. The guide for my visit was very class conscious and as we drove around he would point out the "upper class" houses with their security systems, well laid out gardens, etc. Like wise he identified the "middle class" houses with the cars parked on the drive and the more modest "working class" purpose built properties, all of which reflected a quality of life unparalleled to the apartheid days. Ten per cent of the original shacks remain as a reminder of life prior to 1993. These shacks are progressively being bulldozed and replaced with brick built structures complete with water, electricity and sanitation. In the meantime life for the shack dwellers remains fraught with danger and presents a reminder of the deprivation previously experienced by everyone in Soweto. During the previous weekend hundreds were left homeless as fire swept through one of the areas killing six people and injuring many more. It was believed that a candle or a paraffin lamp had started the fire.

In the centre of Soweto is one of the biggest hospitals in the country. It is named after Chris Hani. Earlier in this essay I referred to the assassination of Chris Hani during my 1993 visit to Cape Town, the service of Commemoration at the cathedral, the riots after the event and the subsequent scrapping of apartheid. The hospital is a fitting tribute to his memory.

Perhaps the most surprising landmark in Soweto is an 18-hole golf course. Back in 1993 no one could have believed a golf course could ever be found in the heart of a township.

The tour of Soweto concluded with a visit to the street on which the separate homes of Desmond Tutu, Nelson Mandela and Winnie Mandikizela – Mandela are to be found. The street has become a pilgrimage site to recognise those who led the fight for democracy although one of these, Winnie Mandela, is awaiting sentence having been convicted of criminal offences. Nelson Mandela's home has been turned into a museum and features awards such as the Nobel Peace Prize. A more unusual trophy is the World Boxing Championship Belt that Sugar Ray Leonard presented to Nelson Mandela as a mark of respect for what he had achieved The house is very small and modestly furnished, reflecting the basic lifestyle of a hero of the people.

In a neighbouring street was the memorial to the school children who were shot and killed by soldiers in 1976 whilst holding a peaceful march against the restrictions of apartheid. It was such a shocking event that it triggered international condemnation.

Having completed my review of the changes in Soweto during the period 1983 to 2005 I set off to explore the countries in Central and East Africa previously listed. It was the visit to Mozambique that really put me in fear of losing my life. Whilst in Dar es Salaam I contacted all the airlines that flew into Mozambique. Although I could get a flight into the country I could not get a connection to get me back again in time to fly back to England. Not to be defeated I booked a flight to Mtwara on the Tanzania side of the border. The plan was to travel by bush taxi from the airport to the village of Kilambo, to pass through the border controls and then cross the Rovuma River to Namoto in Mozambique. What I had not bargained for was having to travel nearly 100 miles on dirt roads with not a yard of tarmac. The potholed roads made travelling the most dangerous I have ever experienced. The vehicles accessed were wrecks compared to what we are used to in the UK. It is claimed that as a result of the poor road network some people in rural areas starve because of a lack of food while in other areas crops are left to rot because there is no way of getting them to market. Conditions are even worse in the rainy season when roads become impassable. Journeys that normally take a matter of hours can take several days.

Within hour of hitching my first lift I was already regretting my decision to travel overland. I was in the back of a lorry with at least 20 other people hanging on for dear life every time the truck hit a major pothole and took off. After a two-hour journey to the first border I was already bruised on my back, legs, and arms from being thrown around. Having passed through the Tanzania border office I was faced with the Rovuma River which is the border with Mozambique. To get across the river I had to put my safety in the hands of four native river men who assured me that they could get me across the mile wide river for $10. What they did not tell me was that the water level was dropping and most of the journey would involve walking over sandbanks. We set off in a canoe for the first few hundred yards before stepping out onto a sandbank. After half a mile I became a passenger on the back of one of the river men as he walked through thigh high water before depositing me into another canoe that had set off to meet us from the other side of the river.

Once on dry land there was another one-hour nightmare journey in the back of a lorry across Mozambique. I was told by the only other English speaking person in the truck that one of the worst accidents to occur on this stretch of road had involved a bus that had attempted to cross a flooded bridge but had been swept into a river, killing the 70 people aboard. A report on road traffic casualties produced by the World Bank has described the roads I was travelling on as some of the most unsafe in the world.

On arrival at the village of Namoto all the passengers were herded into the ramshackle Immigration Office. As the only white person I posed a talking point for the villagers. My intention had been to travel along the coast to Palma but that plan was aborted when my visa was not accepted. Had a sum of money changed hands I would have been allowed to continue. It was now late in the afternoon and there was no way for me to return to Tanzania that day so I was put in a small bamboo shack inside a 20ft high stockade. There was just a mattress on the floor and a candle for light. A guard slept outside the door to the hut.

The woman who ran the village shop/bar was very kind. She prepared an evening meal of rice and fish and a bowl of spaghetti for breakfast. Asked how much I owed her, she said just $2 so I gave $10 in appreciation.

I tried to settle down to get some sleep but there were numerous skirmishes. The first involved the discovery of a 6ft long poisonous snake that had crawled into the stockade. It was attacked by a spade-wielding villager who eventually killed it, then paraded his kill around the stockade before adding it to a cooking pot. The second skirmish occurred in the middle of the night when four wild elephants raided the village to eat the fruit off the trees. The villagers rushed out banging drums and hitting the elephants with sticks to drive them away.

At 5am a combination of cockerels crowing and the need to go to the toilet in the bush was to be the start of another hectic day as I was about to be deported. Going to the toilet is itself a dangerous exercise because of land mines. Thousands remain buried near the Mozambique border, relics of a previous colonial war. However desperate you are, do not venture more than a few yards into the bush. One farmer did not follow the advice to give mines a wide berth as he tried to protect his crops from elephant raids. The farmer dug up a landmine and buried it near the spot where the elephant normally travelled. Unfortunately the farmer forgot where he had planted the land mine and was killed hen he accidentally stood on it.

The driver of the first truck to pass through the checkpoint that morning was told to ensure that I was returned to Tanzania. The whole nightmare journey along pitted roads and across the river was to be repeated. As I clung onto the side of the lorry I vowed that if I survived this journey I would never attempt such a venture again. It was not a question of age but of fear for my life.

On arrival back in Mtwara I booked into a guesthouse for the princely sum of $5 a night. You can probably work out that it was pretty grotty place but I at least felt safe compared with my previous accommodation. The next day I was to fly back to Dar es Salaam.

I later discovered that my flight via Tanzania Airlines had also been a dangerous undertaking. The Director of Airspace Security reported that the age of the planes and obsolete instruments put passengers at risk. The period of my stay in Africa had been a bad one for flight passengers in other parts of the world with a plane crashing into a housing area in Tehran, a plane over shooting the runway in Chicago hitting cars on a freeway and a flight from Abuja in Nigeria crashing and killing more than 100 passengers. Having previously flown out of all three airports, it focussed my mind as I prepared to fly back to Dar es Salaam which was to be my final base before returning to England.

In terms of expectations the nearest I came to being disappointed while in East Africa was during the visit to Livingstone in Zambia to see Victoria Falls. The journey from the airport to the falls was promising; we stopped to allow two elephants to cross the road in front of us. The driver said it was a good sign to see the elephants on the move as it signalled the start of the rainy season and that the elephants were moving towards fresh feeding grounds.

Accommodation was secured at the Zambezi Sun Hotel, pricey but perfectly situated for walking along the top of Victoria Falls. A bronze life size statue of David Livingstone is at the commencement of the path to the Falls. As the rainy season had only just commenced the Zambezi River was not anywhere near its full width as it reached the top of the falls. In a few weeks time water would be cascading over the rock face for the full length of half a mile, sending spray high above the falls in a crescendo of sound. I had to settle for a trickle and a gentle murmur. A large video screen in the dining room showing the falls in all its glory was a small consolation.

There was some interesting wild life in the hotel grounds as well as along the Falls. Residents were advised to give a wide berth to a crocodile that comes out of the river to bask on the lawn. Each afternoon a troop of moneys with their tiny offspring would cavort about the lawns, also keeping a close eye on the crocodile.

During the stay in Dar es Salaam there was an earth tremor in the city at 3.20pm. At that time I was on the 9th floor of the New Africa Hotel having afternoon tea when the whole building started to sway backwards and forwards. Naturally there was panic as everyone ran out of the building. The tremor was caused by an earthquake in Lake Tanganyika where a reading of 6.8 on the Richter Scale was recorded. Neighbouring countries also felt the effects. The ground shook in Nairobi and Mombasa but the worst hit area was Kigoma in the Congo where homes were toppled and some killed. Also affected were border towns in Zambia and Malawi. Fortunately there were no deaths, injuries or damage to buildings where I was although some people who had been on the top of a 15th storey building were treated for shock.

There were other memorable events recorded during my tour of East Africa. They are featured in the essays based on specific issues. Essay 4, Crime and

Punishment, includes references to high crime levels in Johannesburg, "Passion Killings" in Botswana, "Honour Killings" and kangaroo courts in Tanzania. Zimbabwe's "Drive out Trash" and other draconian measures under President Mugabe can be found in essay 11, Government Propaganda. Football World Cup black magic in Africa features in essay 17, which covers sport.

The final excursion of this tour was to Zanzibar Island off the coast of Tanzania. It was a two-hour ferry ride across the Indian Ocean from Dar es Salaam. The management of boarding and embarking the ferry boat was chaotic reflecting the difference between the order and discipline of queuing in the UK and the free for all mentality of East Africa.

As the ferry pulls into port the hundreds on board swarm towards the gang plank that was wide enough to allow people two abreast to pass along and get off. A similar number on the quay try to get on at the same time instead of allowing the ship to empty. The situation is made more farcical as many of the passengers carry luggage or products for sale. Boxes of all shapes and sizes are carried on their heads. Large items such as mattresses, tables and chairs are carried in the same manner. A lone police officer attempted to keep order, lashing out with his truncheon every so often when he got riled. If passengers left first in an orderly fashion followed by those wishing to board it would end the chaos, speed up the loading process and allow ferries to arrive and depart on time. I wonder how many centuries it took before the British embraced the concept of queuing?

Although Zanzibar comes under Tanzania's governance it maintains an unnecessary Immigration and Customs system with subsequent delays in form filling and passport checking. Zanzibar has a rich history of sultans, slaves and spices. Dr David Livingstone set off from Zanzibar for his first trip into Africa. Arab traders and the British have left their mark on the architecture of Stone Town, the heart of the island. Despite the ferry chaos it was an interesting day and a highly recommended trip.

It was with great relief when I finally took off from Dar es Salaam for my flight home. It had been an exciting tour with many memorable moments. Although I would not attempt it again don't be put off. Africa needs you. Take the comfortable and safe option of a guided group tour if you are not feeling adventurous.

11

Evaluation of Government Propaganda

Manipulation of the Press
The Suppression of the Facts - The role of the Media
The justification of travel
Operation "Drive Out Trash" in Zimbabwe

This essay is a mixed bag of mini events across a wide area that may interest, amuse, inform or challenge. As a general policy I do not visit the same place twice, preferring to explore new destinations. New countries are emerging all the time as people struggle and succeed in establishing independent states. Examples of this are the new Baltic States of Estonia, Latvia and Lithuania. One exception has been America because of its size and diversity. Although I have visited America five times I am still to visit Boston and Washington.

Two of the countries previously featured that had a major impact on my world knowledge and understanding were Russia and China. As previously described I visited Russia in the 1960s, just after the Cuban Missile Crisis, and at the height of the cold war. It was during that visit that I first encountered the extent to which the people of Great Britain were being subjected to a campaign of Government censorship. The media played a supporting role depending on the political leanings of its owners. Socialism was either being glamorised or demonised. The reality was that both Russia and the countries they ruthlessly controlled such as Poland and East Germany, were in the grip of the 10% of the population that were Communist Party Members. I had discovered for myself that the average Russian was kind, warm and friendly. They were just as much victims of the Party Members as the people of Poland and East Germany. The Russian government was engaged in the same ideological propaganda as the British and American Governments - Communism v Capitalism.

In 1998 I made a stopover in Moscow hoping to see that the softening of the Communist doctrine was working for the benefit of its own people. There was little change. The mainstream Russians were still kind, warm and welcoming. The officials employed by the State were surly and appeared depressed. Although the main airport now looked modern and clean its management and service was poor. Very few people were arriving and tourism was still minimal. The modern shops in the airport were now stocked with top international products but no one was buying. Perhaps the biggest changes were that the majority of airport staff were women and that there were no longer armed soldiers on duty as if expecting a military invasion at any moment. Hopefully by 2005 the picture is now more positive.

The second major country to be re-evaluated has been China. There have been two previous references to China in this book. One involved obtaining a copy of the Little Red Book whilst editor of the Twenty Two Club magazine "Yung Tung". The second was taking a Duke of Edinburgh's Award group to Beijing on a cultural exchange visit in 1988. In the mid 1960s Mao Tse Tung was portrayed in the British Media as a heroic figure and the darling of left wing socialism. What the British government and the media did not report was that Mao was responsible for the deaths of 70 million Chinese people, during his drive to become party chairman and the ultimate leader of a brutal Communist regime. The tally of 70 million deaths was greater than the combined losses of the military and civilians in the two world wars. This figure includes those killed in Stalin's Gulags or during Hitler's genocide of the Jews. Mao ruled by terror, murder and torture were his tools. The 6,000-mile Long March became glamorised as the people's struggle against a corrupt Nationalist Government when it was in fact a journey encouraged and funded by Stalin. It was Stalin who engineered Mao's appointment as leader of China's first Red State.

The first Communist Party Conference took place in 1945 following America's intervention when they ordered the Nationalist Party to call a cease-fire against Mao's depleted troops. This decision allowed Stalin and Mao to form a massive Communist partnership. By 1949 Mao was the absolute ruler of China and free to instigate a series of programmes that would enhance his personality cult but would be disastrous for the people of China.

First came the industrial programme of 1958 – "The Great Leap Forward". This programme created a famine as the farm collectives failed and 38 million starved to death. In 1966 came the Cultural Revolution that involved removing all the educated classes from society. Teachers were killed and books burned. It was a policy that would be copied by the Khmer Rouge in Cambodia. Then came the creation of teenage Red Guards waving their Little Red Books, who were taught to denounce their parents and to report them to the authorities if they acted against the state.

As I reflect back to the mid sixties I feel ashamed that I was sucked in to the cult following of Mao Tse Tung. I believed in the media reports that glamorised the people's struggle for freedom. I believed that the struggle was just and fair because the British Government, like America, was silent on what was really going on in China. I am still ashamed that I reproduced extracts from the "Little Red Book" of Mao. It was only when the story of the girl named Tung appeared being praised for reporting her parents to the authorities, leading to their imprisonment that a glimmer of truth started to emerge of what life was really like in China at that time. Readers of a certain age may recall the exploits of Mao Tse Tung in the 1960s and how his "heroic" exploits were liberating China from a corrupt Nationalist Government. Do you, like me feel cheated that the British Government suppressed the truth about what Mao was really doing to his people? Do you really believe the British media did not know what was happening in China nor did the government, for political reasons, suppress the British media?

In 1988 when leading the Award group on the Cultural visit to Beijing, I was still not fully aware of the true scale of terror that Mao Tse Tung had inflicted on his people. People were still filing past his embalmed body showing their respects. An enormous picture of Mao still dominated Tiananmen Square. It was only a few weeks later when Chinese Tanks were crushing protesting students under their tracks that the brutality of the Long march, the Great Leap Forward and the Cultural Revolution, started to emerge. Although the Tiananmen Square massacre was featured world wide it would be years later that the rest of China would learn officially what had happened.

The British Government's suppression of the truth about China under Mao Tse Tung reinforces my belief of the importance of international travel. The more you travel the greater will be your understanding of the plight of people who live under a dictatorship. Hitler, Stalin and Mao Tse Tung were eventually overthrown at enormous cost. An earlier intervention in Iraq could well have saved the lives of many citizens of that country and particularly the thousands of Kurds who were gassed by Saddam Hussein. The evidence of the mass graves proved that this was not a propaganda exercise and was a justification to overthrow Saddam Hussein. I am looking forward to the day when it is safe to travel to Iraq to experience the new found freedom of the people following the success of their first free elections. A separate treat will be to visit the Hanging Gardens of Babylon, one of the Seven Wonders of the ancient World.

There are many examples of the positive or negative influence of the media on world events in other essays. Vietnam, for example, it was only when CBS TV News began featuring the weekly arrival of body bags containing American troops that the public opinion changed against the war. Media pressure helped overthrow the apartheid government in South Africa. Editors opposed to Iran's government have been jailed. The Sri Lanka press were prevented from publishing reports of Tamil terrorist attacks until months after the attack. Editors in Pakistan have led the fight to expose injustices of the treatment of women, administrative corruption and child labour. The press are not allowed to report the proceedings in Law Courts in Saudi Arabia.

The UK's media generally acts as the conscience of the public. It probes and presents information that may be politically biased but hopefully readers, listeners and watchers are aware of such bias and are brought closer to the truth and are able to form their own opinions of issues such as Iraq, Iran, Afghanistan, Palestine etc.

The only alternative to gain a wider world perspective is to travel and see for yourself. It may prove expensive but with the growth of Internet information costs can be trimmed. During the 45 years of visiting the countries featured there has been only one freebie; I have never got around to calculating the cost of visiting 100 countries. The freebie occurred during my time as the Midland Regional Officer for the Duke of Edinburgh's Award. All the nine regional officers were attending a quarterly meeting when the director of the day, Major General Michael Hobbs (later Sir Michael Hobbs), announced that he had to turn down an invitation from one of the Award sponsors, Mars, to attend a social function in Monaco and the football World Cup Finals in Italy. He asked if there was a volunteer to represent the Award. Naturally I jumped at the chance, as did one of my colleagues Paul Redrup. A draw was made which Paul won. On reflection I still do not know why but he decided to step down in my favour. Perhaps it was because of my continued involvement in football and other sports with young people. It was to be my reward.

The Mars sponsored trip was to involve 100 of their best customers. It was a way of saying thank you to them. The whole group was flown out to Monaco where we were to share a 5 star hotel. The hotel was situated above the subway where the Formula One cars roared through during the Annual Monte Carlo Grand Prix. The hotel was also part of one of the major Casinos. There was a roof top swimming pool for those more interested in a tan than winning or losing a packet on the card tables. On the first evening there was to be a major dinner and an International Cabaret Show for our pleasure. On entering the banqueting suite I found I was positioned at the end of a table directly in front of the stage, separated by a small area set aside for dancing. Little did I know that the stage was moveable or that I was to become part of the cabaret.

As the six-course meal progressed the orchestra was playing popular music of the day. The wine was flowing and the chatter got louder when, following a fanfare, the stage started to move toward the tables. As music from "Cats" boomed out a team of topless dancers with sporting cat's tails emerged to entertain. Have you tried eating your dessert whilst gorgeous dancers are cavorting just inches away?

The major act was a juggler of international renown. One part of his act was to involve me; I had no say in the matter as he just firmly led me on to the stage. He was spinning plates on the ends of rods, six at a time. He took my wrist firmly and put the rod in my hand and started rotating my wrist. To my amazement I was able to keep the plate spinning although the longer I did it the tenser I became because I feared I would get tired and drop the plate on to the floor. In the meantime the juggler was keeping the other six plates revolving whilst walking about he stage cracking jokes. After what seemed like an age he took the rod and the revolving the plate off me and invited a large round of applause which duly followed. There was however a sting in the tale of this act. Once the applause for me had ended he stopped spinning the rod and laughter followed because the plate couldn't have fallen off because it was connected to the rod by a wire. All the other plates and rods were genuinely spun. My moment of fame had ended in an anti climax.

The second day saw all the guests being transferred in luxury coaches from Monaco into Italy and to the San Siro Stadium in Milan. The first match of the World Cup was to be Brazil v Scotland. The seated area elevated above the pitch and overlooking the half way line provided a wonderful view of the match. The match itself was disappointing in terms of excitement. Brazil won 1-0 with Scotland seeming more interested in defending than attacking. After the match we returned to Monaco and our luxury hotel.

The final day was spent on the hotel roof enjoying the swimming pool and just relaxing. This had been a wonderful three days thanks to Mars, the Award Director's prior engagement and my colleague, Paul Redrup's kindness. If ever he reads this book he may regret retrospectively not making the trip himself.

The remaining countries featured in this section focus on more social, environmental and cultural issues. In August 2002 I took a tour taking in the Czech Republic, Slovakia, Hungary and Austria. The physical scars of Hitler's campaign to take over the world may have gone but the mental scars of the elderly still remain. Old scores are still being settled as some of the politicians currently holding office are being outed as former Communist puppets of Stalin.

On arrival in Prague, a natural disaster had struck the area. There had been eight consecutive days of rain across Central Europe. The water level of the Vltava River was 20ft higher than normal. In some parts of Prague the rooftops of riverside buildings were all that could be seen. The centre of Prague was initially closed off as volunteers including me, were filling sandbags to protect historic buildings. The floods also created a mini Chernobyl as a chemical plant, damaged by the floodwater was leaking poisonous gas. What a welcome to the Czech Republic. After a further two days of rain the weather changed and the normal hot summer weather returned. Slowly the city returned too normal. Although the cellars of the Opera House were flooded the orchestra were playing impromptu concerts in the Town Square to raise morale. Public transport was still disrupted, as the underground Metro was still flooded.

One of the interesting excursions out of Prague was a half-day visit to Karlstejn Castle. The castle built in 1348 was the home of the Royal treasures for hundreds of years. The main feature was the chapel of the Holy Cross - a Gothic gallery whose beauty is acclaimed worldwide.

Although there was still evidence of the recent floods the roads were passable. The only other occupants of the mini bus were an Asian American couple and a driver/guide. I have to admit I was ashamed of the married American couple. It would be pure speculation but I attributed their behaviour to the twin towers terrorist attack in New York on the 11th September. The couple lived in New York and had been economic refugees welcomed into America over 10 years ago. They both got into a blazing row with the tour guide at the castle because they were not allowed to visit a part affected by the floods. The most arrogant and telling remarks were along the lines of the following *"You need our money, we keep your economy going, you can't manage your economy without us, you rely on us to bail you out, if it wasn't for us you'd be out of a job, etc"*. This behaviour was inexcusable and a bad reflection on the two Americans.

A train journey was to take me from Prague to Budapest via Bratislava in Slovakia. The arrival in Bratislava was initially very depressing. The station was at least a mile out of the city centre. The walk from the railway station towards the city centre was through dingy blocks of flats typical of the conditions of East Germany in the 1960s. On reaching the river Danube there was a massive transformation, like going into another world. The whole central area had been rebuilt and restored to its pre 1939/44 - war condition. Traffic free squares were lightly populated, mainly by tourists. Slovakia was still recovering from Communist rule that ended in a bloodless Revolution in the 1990s. Bratislava is at the centre of the countries recovery but there is massive unemployment, particularly among young people across the country. Fashion wise red streaks were the current hair fashion across central Europe. At least 10% of the female population, young, medium and old had that hair colour. Dress wise, women's tops with one shoulder exposed was the current fashion.

The floods that had affected Prague had subsided by the time I arrived in Bratislava. I was able to sit on the bank of the Danube; sipping tea and enjoying cream cakes watching the day unfold.

The train journey continued to Budapest, the Hungarian capital. Purely by chance my hotel was walking distance from the football stadium where Ferencrarosi played. Just a few days previously they had defeated Manchester United in a European Cup game. The game I was able to watch was a league game against Sopron. Another sporting highlight was to be the Hungarian Formula One Grand Prix. Not having been to a live Grand Prix I thought I would check it out. It turned out to be as boring as the races I had seen on TV. Apart from the scramble at the first bend on the first lap it was the usual procession. The noise was tremendous; the speeds overwhelming at first, but it became boring after a while. At least I have experienced what Grand Prix racing is all about and wouldn't need to go again.

One of the principal dangers walking around Budapest are fake policemen. People posing as police stop lone tourists demanding to see their passports, currency and credit cards. Working in pairs one of them starts berating the target whilst the second person is helping themselves to the cash. They invent some imaginary law that has been broken before walking off leaving a bewildered victim. These types of confrontations take place in quiet side streets, places to avoid. Depending on the nationality of the victim they would also take their passport which could be sold on at a big profit. The victim would be told to report to a police station the next day to collect their passport. It would then be realised that they had been robbed.

Hungary in 2002 was still recovering their self-belief and building up their economy since the end of Communist dictatorship. A number of government ministers are under investigation for corruption during the time they had collaborated with the Russians. I took an open top bus tour of Buda and Pest, the two areas that give the city its name. The guide was proud to identify Heroes Square to mark the fight against the Russians and their Statue of Liberty. The many statues of Communist leaders Stalin, Lenin, Marx and Engels have all been removed from the streets of Budapest.

As a result of the continuing effects of the flooding I decided not to travel to Bucharest in Romania but instead to fly to Vienna in Austria, The floods were flowing North to South, the same route that I was taking, before this change of plan. Vienna like most of Central Europe was rebuilt after the War and buildings accurately restored to their former beauty. Large squares traffic free and lined with street cafes, street entertainers and buskers all added to the atmosphere. The buskers were very talented with string quartets challenging individual musicians and were certainly the most talented buskers encountered to date. Horse drawn carriages added to the colour and moment.

One of my lasting memories of Vienna was a classical concert featuring the works of Johann Strauss and Mozart. As the Opera House was undergoing restoration the Concert, featuring the Wiener Hofburg Orchestra in period costume was staged at the Hofburg Imperial Palace. A wonderful setting, sell out audience and beautiful music and singing, an exceptional evening.

Corfu and Albania were the venues in September 2003. The principal reason for visiting Corfu was to take part in a series of golf days organised by the Solos holiday group. The Calimera beach Hotel and the Corfu Championship Course were the attractions. During a break in the golf I sailed from Kerkyra on Corfu to Saranda on the Albanian coast, a 1.5 hour journey. I caught a coach to Butrinti; a United Nations protected heritage site. Examples of the occupation by the Greeks (4th Century BC), the Romans and the Turks in building design were to be seen. The fortifications were built on the same principles as the pyramids. The Greeks shaped and numbered massive blocks of stone weighing many tons, manhandled them up the mountain and then positioned them accordingly.

There were very few private cars on the roads, probably the lowest of any developed country. A number of expensive Mercedes cars, believed stolen from the UK were seen. During the Communist regime no members of the public owned a car. Only after the overthrow of the government around ten years ago was anyone able to afford a car. During a bloodless coup a new government was formed although many of the Communist leaders re-emerged as elected representatives.

What little savings the general public had were virtually wiped out in a Government pyramid scam. Everyone was urged to invest their savings into a lottery that would guarantee to double their money in 12 months. After 6 months the scheme went bust and everyone lost their savings.

The roads outside the town were appalling. On one country road, due to the narrow width, the bus I travelled on had to reverse three quarters of a mile to allow another bus coming in the opposite direction to pass. The reversing journey was along a winding cliff road with a steep drop down to the sea, a frightening experience that fortunately did not have to be repeated.

Hundreds of partially built hotels can be seen all around the bay. Apparently people who trade in immigrants are laundering their money by buying up prime sites and then leaving the skeleton of the building until more money is raised. The only signs of illegal activity seen were men carrying bundles of bank notes offering special rates. This was done in full view of the police officers sitting in street cafes drinking coffee.

Although I travelled alone from Corfu I took the precaution of booking onto an excursion with an English speaking tour guide. By paying in Corfu there was no hassle with the police at the border whilst other tourists were not so fortunate as they were frequently stopped, passports checked and small fines administered for alleged discrepancies in their visa/passport. An example of the corruption that is still a problem.

The population has dropped from 8 to 6 million over the past 10 years. It started with a "brain drain" with doctors, nurses, teachers, engineers etc emigrating to Greece, Italy, USA, Canada, UK, etc. Then followed the unskilled labour drain and the flood of illegal immigrants across Europe. Unscrupulous crooks became millionaires through this 21st. Century slave trade.

A change of direction and temperature with a visit to Reykjavik in Iceland. It was just a 2.5 hour flight from Birmingham to Keflavik. Iceland is probably the youngest country I have visited as it only emerged from the sea after volcanic activity 3000 years ago. It is not a beautiful country as 80% of the landscape is black volcanic rock. Only 20% of the island supports grass with only 2% of that supporting trees. Evolution can be witnessed today with small areas of moss appearing on rocks. Their economy is suffering as fishing is the only major export and its whaling fleet was at the time banned due to alleged over fishing. The countries main natural asset is an unlimited supply of underground hot water. Water is heated by underground volcanic activity and is piped to every home, school, factory etc. There is no need for gas or electric heating or coal/ wood fires. All the public swimming pools are outdoors despite the cold because the water underground is at 98 degrees Fahrenheit.

Prior to the development of modern houses the design of homes was based on the traditions of those encountered in Indian villages, Animals were kept at ground level with the family living in a single room above to utilise the heat from them. Animal lovers would find Iceland difficult; the only two wild mammals on the island are the Arctic Fox and mice. Residents of Iceland all share the same naming system. Surnames always end in son for men and daughter for women. For example a man called Jonson is the son of Jon. A woman named Smithdaughter is the daughter of Smith.

The terrain, particularly in the North of the island is as close to conditions on the moon as anywhere else on earth. America astronauts trained there prior to Armstrong being the first man to walk on the moon. The people of Iceland experience 24 hours of daylight during the summer while in the winter they receive just 3 hours of daylight per day. Their big claim to fame is that they are considered extremely genetically pure. The country is the centre of world research for cures of many medical conditions. It provides a valuable source of revenue and as there are strict laws on inter family breeding and the lack of cross breeding with other nationalities the result is pure genetic lines that can be traced back over centuries. Family records are so accurate that family members can be traced back to 1704. Hereditary illnesses can also be traced and eradicated in the current population. The same principal applies to animals. Cows, horses and sheep differ from other European animals having been free of cross fertilisation with other breeds. If a racing horse travels abroad it would not be allowed back in to the country because it would have picked up conditions that horses on the island would not be immune to.

My most fascinating experience was to bathe outdoors with the temperature at freezing point in the Blue Lagoon, a geo-thermal pool that harnesses Iceland's natural energy. The Blue Lagoon is a pool of mineral rich seawater that bursts from the ground. Blue green algae and white silicon mud form light natural sediment on the bottom of the lagoon to give a soft milky aqua marine colour. Hundreds of people were sharing the lagoon, the water temperature being between 36 and 39 degrees C. The steam rising from the water surrounded by volcanic rocks gave a surreal experience like nothing I have ever seen. The spa claims many beneficial health treatments, similar to the Dead Sea, which I have also experienced.

Staying in a cold climate, a brief visit was made to Lapland, part of Finland in the Arctic Circle. Although not a fan of snow and ice, the chance to meet Father Christmas just a few days before Christmas was irresistible. The plane from Birmingham to Rovanjemi was packed with excited children and their parents. On landing the temperature was way below zero but everyone was kitted out in a one-piece thermal suit and snow boots. A fleet of coaches took everyone to the Reindeer Park. My first challenge was to ride in a husky drawn sleigh through the snow with the sounds of sleigh bells ringing around the forest. The local children were earning pocket money by dressing as elves carrying lanterns, and waving to the passing sleighs from behind trees.

The highlight for the children was to join the queue to the log cabin where Father Christmas was holding court deep into the forest. It must have been a wondrous moment that they will never forget. Lunch was provided by the local villagers, again bringing valuable trade to their limited home budgets. Hot soup was served from a large pot with bread, cheese, pancakes and hot berry juice. After lunch there was a ceremony to mark crossing the Arctic Circle and the award of a certificate. Heading back to the airport, the coaches stopped off at a large tourist supermarket. The top priority was to buy special stamps and for all my Christmas cards to be franked with the Lapland stamp. I imagine that my Christmas cards, that go to people all over the world, would have raised a few eyebrows bringing greetings from Father Christmas. Although this had all been achieved in a single day it proved a truly memorable experience. Even when on the plane we were treated to seeing the Aurora Borealis as we took off. Some tourists can spend a full week in the area and never see the unique and spectacular Northern Lights. A roast turkey dinner on the plane completed a wonderful day. My only regret was that such an opportunity never existed when my own son and daughter were young children. Perhaps their children may get the opportunity.

Perhaps it is a sign of old age but I decided to take my first and only cruise in November 2003 on the Saga Rose. The Canary Island Reverie Cruise would not only visit the Canary Islands but also take in Morocco, Spain, and Portugal. Apart from two horrendous nights, one going out and one near the end the cruise was excellent value once a few technicalities were ironed out. I had specifically asked for a single cabin in the quietest part of the ship but had been placed near the engine room. After two nights of very little sleep I obtained sleeping tablets from the ships doctor. By a stroke of luck for me but not another passenger, a cabin became available away from the engine room as the occupant had to be ferried away to hospital on the mainland. The worst two nights were during major storms. The ship was rising and falling for two days, passengers clinging to the rails as they moved about the ship. The dining room was barely half full. One night it was so bad I had to grip the sides of the bunk to stop myself being thrown out of bed. I suppose the choice of November for such a trip was taking a chance on the weather.

Apart from the turbulence on these two nights the cruise was excellent, The quality of the food, entertainment and social life was top rate. The principal speaker was Sir Bernard Ingham, former Press Secretary to Margaret Thatcher, with whom I had a row after his talk. The topic that fired me up was the Human Rights Act and his criticism of judges and magistrates. During the question time I argued against his presentation. In a typical politicians response he totally ignored my question and presented a response that he knew would strike a positive chord with an older audience. Whilst he got rapturous applause at the time, he also got an earful from me after the presentation that led to a mumbled apology.

The format of an island a day and a guided tour of each, appealed to me. The order of visits commenced with Funchal on the island of Madeira, known as the "island of eternal spring". Santa Cruz, La Palma was next and the first of the islands dominated by volcanoes. La Palma is known as the steepest island in the world. The Taburiente volcano has formed a gigantic crater soaring up to 7,960ft. There are a number of other volcanoes on the island with Tenegufa last erupting in 1971. The town of Santa Cruz de la Palma perches on the edge of another volcano, La Caldereta.

It was predicted at a conference in London in August 2004 that the Cumbre Vieja, a 6,334ft high volcano could collapse during the next eruption tearing the west side of the mountain free, sending almost half of the island, 500 billion tons of rock, crashing onto the sea bed. It would displace more water than any single event in history. A tidal wave is predicted 300ft high and travelling at 500mph. Within 10hours the wave would stretch 12,500miles from the Caribbean to beyond Boston in America. It is claimed that Boston, New York, Washington DC, and Miami would be wiped off the map. In Britain the tidal wave would be smaller at 40ft high but towns along the south coast would still face awesome devastation. Research and monitoring of the volcano has ended because Spain has withdrawn funding. The volcano last erupted in 1971. Just days after the August 2004 conference the awesome effects of tidal waves were seen in Boscastle in Cornwall. The village was virtually wiped out by a flash flood 12ft high wall of water. Consider the consequences of a predicted 40ft high tidal wave hitting the South Coast of England should the collapse of the Cumbre Viega volcano come true.

Las Palmas, Gran Canaria had contrasting sandy beaches and snow capped mountains. The island introduced me to Cow Houses and to cows who are treated like family members. The main house has an additional room exclusively for the cow. There is so little vegetation because of the volcanic rock and the lack of soil that a traditional straw roof on a separate shed would have been too expensive, hence a tiled roof as part of the house. The farmer takes fresh food into the cow room each day. There is no spare land to allow the cow to graze – if it was let out it would eat the vegetables. Every inch of land is precious for the growing of food to survive. It is more economic to feed the cow waste food and weeds. The milk from the cow helps the family to survive.

Santa Cruz, Tenerife was the next stop. The tour included a visit to the 7000ft volcano that dominates the island. Scientists in 2003 were predicting the volcano would erupt in two years time. The rise in temperature and ground movements has led them to this prediction. Insurance companies are taking the advice seriously, as it is no longer possible to insure property or life on the island. The tourist guide wanting to play down the threat, took us to the restaurant in the crater of the volcano.

The port of Santa Cruz presented an example of how money does not necessarily bring contentment. There are two monasteries just 50 yards apart, one that caters for the children of rich families and the other supporting children from poor homes. The incentive to rich families is that they can be buried inside the monastery rather than in a churchyard. The down side has been the number of outbreaks of plague over the last 200 years caused by decomposing bodies.

The volatile nature of the region was reinforced on the next stop at Fire Mountain in Lanzarote. Fire Mountain was certainly a live volcano as was demonstrated by our guide in four separate tests. Firstly a shovel full of volcanic dust from just 12 inches deep was passed around. The temperature of the dust was at the boiling pint of water. The second test involved dropping a piece of wood into a 4ft deep hole. The temperature at the bottom of the hole was 200 degrees centigrade and within a minute the wood was on fire. The third test involved a pipe set 10ft into the ground. The temperature at the bottom of the pipe was 500 degrees C. A bowl of water was carefully poured down the pipe and within 3 seconds steam gushed out with a loud bang just like an Icelandic geyser. The final test was conducted in the restaurant where a well-shaped hole had been built, 10ft deep above molten lava. A metal grill on the top allowed food to be barbecued. This had been a quality demonstration and showed how science can be made interesting.

Travelling down from the top of the volcano there was a stop at an incredible green lagoon at the volcano's base. It was so colourful and out of character with the rest of the terrain which was black volcanic rock. The unique colour was created by green lichen growing out of the volcanic rock under water. Equally dramatic was the Los Jameos Del Aqua Grotto. It was an enormous cave created by cooling molten lava. An auditorium had been created where concerts were a major attraction. In the centre of the Grotto was a pool that was the home of small Albino crabs that could be seen clambering over the rocks. The unusual thing about these crabs is that they are not normally found at sea level, preferring life at 1000 yards below sea level.

The tour of the island complete, the ship turned toward the African coastline to Agadir in Morocco. The hustle and bustle of the Kasbah and the Berber Markets was in total contrast to life on board the Saga Rose. Casablanca was the next step with two religious buildings having the greatest impact on me. The first was the Notre Dame de Lourdes, the Catholic Cathedral. It was incredibly beautiful with the full length of the side walls covered by coloured glass at least 40 yards high depicting scenes from the Bible. Mother Teresa's pictures and work was featured at the entrance to the Cathedral as part of the movement toward her Sainthood.

The second major structure was the Hassan II Mosque, the second biggest in the world, Mecca in Saudi Arabia being the largest. It was built in 1992 and has a retractable roof like that at the Millennium Stadium in Cardiff. The mosque can hold 100,000 praying simultaneously with the area outside the Mosque able to accommodate a further 80,000 worshippers. The prominent minaret, 230 yards high is the tallest in the Moslem world. At night a laser beam shines out to the east in the direction of Mecca and can be seen 35 miles away. The proximity of the mosque and the Cathedral demonstrate that two religions can live in harmony.

There were just two more ports of call before sailing on to Southampton. Cadiz in Spain and Lisbon in Portugal. Lisbon carried the greatest interest for me having been part of the establishment of a forest on the North Coast as described in a previous essay as leader of the Twenty-Two Club. Lisbon at this time was gearing up to host the European Football Championship, and all the hotels were sold out months ahead. I suspect unwary supporters will finish up camping on the beach. Apart from the initial problems of a cabin over the engine room and the two storms, I really enjoyed my first ever cruise and would certainly recommend it as a safe way to see the world, even if it is just one day at a time.

There is one coincidence to conclude the cruise. The reason I had gone on the cruise was to mark my retirement for the third time, from the Outward Bound Trust. The captain of the Saga Rose was David Warden-Owen. His father was one of the first ever instructors at the first Outward Bound Sea School in Aberdovey, nearly 60 years ago. As a result of this discovery the Captain's father has been added to the Outward Bound's Role of Honour.

Returning to land based adventures one of the triangular visits involved Croatia, Bosnia and Montenegro. Dubrovnik in Croatia was used as a base in 2003. The scars of the many battles that had plagued the area were starting to heal and life was settling back to normal. The walled city of Dubrovnik had been restored and it felt comfortable and relaxed there. Bosnia was much more threatening. I travelled to Mostar Neuma by public transport. There was virtually nothing to see or do other than reflect on the many shell or bullet holes in the side of buildings. Rather than go looking for problems I settled down in a street café and waited for something to come to me. I didn't have to wait long. Three cars containing six tough looking characters encamped in the café opposite. After a while a mobile phone rings, there is a loud conversation and then two of the men jump into a car and drive off at high speed. Ten minutes later they roar back in high spirits with high fives all around. What ever had happened had appeared to be successful. They were in such high spirits that four of the men grabbed the four corners of a car and man handled it into the centre of the road, leaving it there. A little while later a police car came past, the officers eyed the car and the group then drove off. The assumption on my part was that the gangsters were running the town and not the police.

A tour of Montenegro was much more relaxed. Montenegro remains part of Yugoslavia. The markets were buzzing with activity but people encountered in other situations seemed very subdued, almost as if they are still in a state of shock after the many years of fighting, internally along ethnic lies and externally with the invading Germans. Croatia is showing them the way to attract tourists as Dubrovnik seeks to regain its title as the "Jewel in the Crown of the Adriatic".

Tunisia was another of my twin activity tours, on this occasion golf was the main element. My base was to be Hammamet, on the coast with golf tournaments at the Yasmine, la Forel, and Les Olivers Golf Club. The planned trip could have ended in disaster. My flight to Monaster was from Manchester. Soon after take off the alarm was raised because of a problem with the planes rudder, it was necessary to make an emergency landing at Birmingham airport, ironic as I had driven from there the previous evening to catch this early morning flight. Fortunately the plane landed safely and the necessary repairs were completed. Another scare satisfactorily concluded. On one of the free days I caught the train to Tunis and used it as a base to visit the Roman settlement at Dougga and the massive Coliseum at El Jem. Another priority was to visit the Medina Market in the centre of Tunis. It is so large that it dominates the city. Travellers will be familiar with the problem of hustlers who prey on tourists offering to introduce them to relatives who run stores that provide a special price. During my early travels I used to ignore them but now I exploit them.

The example in Tunis was as follows. I started walking down one of the main streets getting my bearings before entering the Medina when I was overtaken by a man who asked if I needed any help. I said no politely and he walked on. Having done a right turn I was suddenly faced with the same man coming from the opposite direction. This time he greeted me like a long lost brother, all very clever if contrived and so I pretended to be taken in by his warmth. Over the next hour we visited a number of stores run by his cousins who were selling carpets, clothing, brass ornaments, shoes, etc. At the same time I was plied with coffee and biscuits. I managed to make plausible excuses for not buying at that time assuring them of a return visit, but not stating when. My guide was getting more exasperated as he was losing out on commission when more gullible victims were wandering the streets. After what had been a guided tour of the Medina I returned to my starting point. In frustration he asked for money to cover his time. I thanked him for his time but said, "No thank you" to this request. The hustler had been out hustled.

This essay is a mopping up exercise as explained earlier; not all 109 countries that I have visited have been featured as nothing of significance may have happened there. For example, I cannot remember anything out of the ordinary happening in Switzerland, Belgium, Holland or Luxembourg. Beautiful scenery, buildings and nice people are my only memories. My memory of Copenhagen revolves around the Little Mermaid and the Tivoli Gardens decked out in Christmas decorations.

Malmo in Sweden only brings back memories of a ferry ride and a tour of the football stadium. Malta reminds me of the cricket match played by the military. Dublin was more memorable as I attended a meeting in the castle and had the most amazing guided tour in an open topped bus. The guide had an amusing anecdote for virtually every landmark we passed. He was so funny that I started writing down some of his quips. Although they are more amusing when spoken I hope you get a flavour from his Irish humour. I likened him to an Irish Ken Dodd, he fired jokes like bullets. As we passed the Royal Oak Pub - *"Two guys search you for weapons when you go in, not to worry if you don't have a gun, they will provide one". "The biggest funeral in Belfast passed this last year; it took 14 men to carry the beer".*

"Two guys in a pub. My wife's is an angel - You're lucky Paddy mines still alive".

In contrast to the humour of the Irish Republic life in the North was tenser. The every first sight of the armoured vehicles patrolling the streets of Belfast came as quite a shock and a reminder that tension was high following IRA attacks. One truly memorable natural sight was the Giants Causeway. The shape of the pillars rising from the ground defy explanation and it is one of my top ten choices of natural wonders of the world.

The first of two dramatic experiences happened to me while in England rather than in a more volatile part of the world. It was in the early hours of the morning on the 23rd September 2002. I was woken by the sound of falling crockery. The whole room was shaking and objects were skidding around the tabletops and the floor. It was as if the building had been rocked by an explosion but without the noise. Gripping the sides of the shaking bed a thousand thoughts flashed through my mind as I attempted to make sense of what was going on. After two minutes the building was still. There had been an earth tremor of 4.8 on the Richter scale, just 10 miles away in Dudley. It had been the fourth biggest tremor to ever strike Britain and was equivalent to 1000 tons of TNT, a small nuclear bomb. The biggest previous tremor of 6.1 had occurred on Dogger Bank in the North Sea in 1931.

The second was on July 28th 2005 at 2.30pm when the biggest tornado to hit the UK struck Birmingham. The wind speed was clocked at 136mph and struck the Kings Heath and Moseley area, eight miles from my home. Roofs blown off and cars were wrecked as they were tossed into the air. Emergency services said it was a "miracle" that none was killed.

What with the emergency plane landing, the Dudley earth tremor and a tornado, I no longer had to travel to find high drama, it could quite easily find me at home.

The two major geographical features of my three-country bus tour of the Baltic States of Estonia, Latvia and Lithuania in September 2005 are trees and town centres. The terrain is as flat as a pancake. There are no mountains and the highest hill; Suur Munamagi in Estonia is only 340 yards high. Mile after mile the only sights are ramrod tall Birch trees flanking both sides of the road. The occasional field with a handful of cattle plus a distant windmill are the only breaks in the monotony. All vehicles use full headlights during the day from September to April. From October 1st until the end of April it is compulsory to fit snow tyres even though there may be no snow. The average temperature from December to March is minus 15-20 C.

On the positive side the town centres are of good taste and design. Tallinn, Parnu, Tartu etc were laid bare by the Nazi and Soviet troops so the town centres were rebuilt and many old buildings restored with wide-open spaces and grassy areas within the shopping and business areas. It felt relaxing and comfortable when wandering around, more so than any city centre I've visited in the world.

By way of diversion from miles of trees I took a ferry day trip from Tallinn in Estonia to Helsinki in Finland. Finland is unique in having 180,000 islands and lakes in such a small land mass. In Helsinki the coast line is so jagged that there are 11 bridges over short stretches of water to avoid winding detours, particularly during the winter snow. The major event in the sporting history of the city was the staging of the Olympic Games in 1952. The stadium remains in use and some of the best views of Helsinki can be seen from the 240ft high stadium tower. The dock side market is a big attraction to the tourists arriving daily on cruise ships. The fur products attract the greatest interest.

Estonia and Latvia provide a number of examples of Government legislation influenced not only by these countries but also by the EU. In some cases the legislation is in conflict. A prime example is Latvia s intention to restrict marriage to heterosexual couples whereas the EU recognises gay partnerships. Commenting on gay marriages being officially recognised across the EU, Inese Slesere, of the Latvia First Party, stated that "I am proud that such marriages are not recognised in Latvia".

Amnesty International have joined the debate by expressing deep concern that leading Latvian politicians have made remarks that may incite verbal and physical attacks. This specifically relates to remarks made by leading politicians in the run up to the first ever "Gay Parade" held in Latvia. Unbowed by this criticism Latvian politicians have called for the Riga Chief Executive and the Mayor to resign for staging the "perversion parade".

Estonia has become a leader in terms of influencing EU legislation in respect to rubbish and could lead the way to the appointment of Police Dustmen. On 1st October 2005 the Packaging Deposit Scheme was introduced. It became compulsory for shop owners to accept the return of packaging such as metal, glass, plastic, milk cartons, yoghurt beakers, etc. A small charge of one Kroon is added to the price of such items at the point of purchase. When the contents have been consumed the buyer is legally required to return the empty containers in exchange for the 1 Kroon deposit back. The government Packaging Act is aimed at protecting the environment. Electrical goods such as television sets and refrigerators are also included in the scheme with higher deposits.

Shopkeepers are against the programme because they have to set up recycling plants to handle all the different materials at their own cost. A number of new companies have been set up to handle and process the returned items and they expect payment to come from the shop keepers. It is claimed that it will be the consumers who will be penalised as the price of goods will go up to cover the cost of recycling.

This government initiative came about when Estonia volunteered to engage in recycling as a reason for being granted membership of the EU. Having secured membership, they are encountering the anger of both sellers and buyers as a result of the Packaging Act. There are a number of possible consequences of such a policy. If it works in Estonia it will encourage the EU to introduce the same policy across all member European Union States. When Finland introduced a similar scheme 10 years ago there was chaos in the first year but gradually it has been accepted. If the policy is to work properly it could lead to the introduction of dustbin inspectors. Householders could be prosecuted if the contents of their bins include cans, glass, plastic bottles, etc. Scavengers could start raiding bins overnight to collect recyclable materials to obtain refunds.

An idea to add to the debate on citizenship in the UK is offered by Estonia. If a refugee wants to become a citizen of Estonia they have to undertake a written test that includes the ability to answer questions involving at least 2000 Estonian words.

The Latvian press is strongly critical about "the army of hedonistic foreign bachelors who are arriving in search of cheap alcohol and sex". This story includes the UK weekend bachelor parties travelling on low cost airlines. The President states "they do not care about anything but satisfying their biological needs". There is however very little debate about limiting the activities or advertising of the Latvian companies that provide sexual services or that these establishments are also frequented by Latvian and Russian men. A blind eye is turned as long as the money keeps rolling in.

The "Lithuanian Left Handers Club" has become a world leader in terms of supporting left-handed people. A virtual shop has been established offering specially designed products such as stationary, household utensils, leisure goods, body care items, school merchandise, etc. It will be interesting to follow the progress of this initiative. Perhaps a reader will take up the challenge of filling a niche in the UK market.

There is another innovative venture taking place in Lithuania with the establishment of the Athletics Party to contest parliamentary seats. The Chairman of the Parliamentary Commission for Youth and Sports Affairs is not impressed; "We already have the left wing, the right wing, and the centre. Initiatives to establish parties based on a profession or hobby are laughable. We should then also create a party of plumbers and one for blacksmiths". It will be interesting to see if the Athletics Party gains any seats in the next election.

The most memorable place I visited was the "Hill of Crosses" just out Siauliai in Lithuania, one of the world's leading pilgrim sites for the Catholic Church. It came about during the 1831 and 1863 rebellions and grew under the brutal regimes of the Germans and Russians in the 20th century. Its popularity for pilgrims was so great that the Russians bulldozed the site repeatedly in the 1960s. Local people responded by recreating the memorial. Pope John Paul II's visit in 1993 brought the site to the world's attention. An estimated 80,000 crosses are placed there, the number growing daily as Catholics from around the world send crosses to commemorate their loved ones. Small metal crosses swing gently in the wind creating a mystical tinkling sound, a spiritual and moving experience.

The three states have been occupied by Sweden, Germany and Russia. During these occupations hundreds of thousands were killed trying to defend their country. The Museum of the Occupation in Riga, Latvia records the occupation by the Nazi's and then Communists from 1940 to 1991. Stalin deported 44,000 Latvians to Siberia, tens of thousands never returned. During the four years of nazi occupation concentration camps were built in Riga and the majority of Jews there were murdered. Touring the museum helped me to understand the nations psyche.

In terms of a Government's military oppression of its people and the control of the media Zimbabwe is the 21st century equivalent of what I had experienced in Russia in the 1960s and in China in the 1980s. During 2005 there have been many references in the UK media to the so called racist attacks on white farmers and abuse of black township settlers. How true were these accusations against President Mugabe and what was life really like in Zimbabwe? To find out the answers I visited Harare in December 2005.

Superficially Harare looks a very modern city with many impressive buildings in the city and a new airport. Major roads in the city are in good condition from a driver's perspective but many pavements are potholed with some dangerous gaps into the drainage system. Beggars are not tolerated and moved on by armed police or army personnel. I was moved on for loitering when I was trying to get my bearings from a street map. A machine gun waved in my face prompted a rapid departure.

Inflation had gone out of control with 112,000 Zimbabwe dollars to the pound. I changed £60 and received nearly seven million dollars, a wad of money I couldn't even hold in one hand. On departure I tried to cash in 3 million dollars but they wouldn't except them. I had the choice of throwing them away as I wasn't allowed to take them out of the country or spending them in the duty free shop. Having my passport withheld until the money was spent focussed my mind. I bought two T-shirts for the 3 million dollars at a price millions in Zimbabwe could never afford.

A more serious consequence of the Mugabe regime involves the country's debt for goods received. During my stay the country ran out of petrol and all flights were cancelled leaving thousands of visitors stranded. Petrol stations were deserted and taxi drivers stranded on the sides of roads with empty tanks. Problems in Zimbabwe are not aired due to the government controlled press. Neighbouring countries had no such restrictions. The South African Star wrote, "the stench of sewage and rotting garbage wafts the homes. Garbage collection is the latest casualty as Zimbabwe's economy crumbles as there isn't any petrol for garbage trucks. There is concern about disease spreading in the city. Health Authorities reported outbreaks of dysentery and food poisoning blamed on frequent water and power cuts". I can confirm this report as I saw piles of rubbish dumped in alleyways and my hotel was without water for a day.

I am in no doubt that many negative reports in the British press about the Mugabe's regime are true. "Operation Drive out Trash" did happen in Harare and thousands of displaced slum dwellers are now living, (and dying) in shanty towns in Bulawayo. The country is running out of anti-retrovival drugs. The Parliamentary Committee on Health admit that only 20,000 Aids patients receive medication whilst 300,000 need them, the government blames a foreign currency shortage.

People queue outside banks for hours to withdraw money, many walk away penniless as money runs out. Another prized commodity is sugar. I passed a grocery store surrounded by hundreds of people. Word was that there had been a delivery of sugar. Security guards tried to control the crowd by letting in one at a time. Every so often guards began hitting the crowd with batons as they surged forward, the police stood by watching.

How does Mugabe survive with life so difficult? There appears to be two main reasons, firstly the continued support from Thabo Mbeki, South Africa's president despite the criticism Zimbabwe receives from other African countries. Secondly the security grip Mugabe has. During my stay Parliament was in session. As I passed the building I was stopped many times by armed police officers who circled the building. Marksmen on high buildings were clearly seen. Leaders of the main opposition have been silenced as Mugabe tightens his grip. Earlier that year it was reported that Mugabe was seriously ill in hospital. His rapid walk to his heavily surrounded security car gave the impression that he was fully recovered and his only health fears would come from a bullet.

The same level of security surrounds the Presidential Palace. I visited the Harare Sports Club, the cricket test venue for the national team, which is opposite the Palace. I was warned by armed soldiers to "Walk on, don't look towards the high barbed wire walls or the watch towers". "You will be shot if seen using a camera".

On the evening of my afternoon visit to watch the proceedings outside Parliament, I was having a meal in the hotel when two men approached me. Even though there were empty tables, they asked if they could join me. After a few minutes of light chatter the alarm bells started to ring in my head when one of them casually remarked "Did I see you outside Parliament this afternoon". A little later I was asked what I thought of the Presidential Palace. It became obvious to me that I was under investigation by members of the secret police. I had not mentioned that I had walked past the Palace during my visit to the Harare Cricket Stadium to watch the Zimbabwe Under 19 Team in action. Eventually I completed my meal and excused myself. The fact that I was able to do this, meant that my guarded answers had satisfied the two men. I was happy to suggest we might meet again the next evening knowing that my flight out of Zimbabwe was the next morning.

During my stay in Harare I visited the Criminal Court to witness Zimbabwe justice in action. Although all the trappings of Colonialism across Zimbabwe have long been stripped away, the judges still retain their wigs and gowns. Court officials are addressed as Comrades, which acts as a reminder that Zimbabwe remains one of the few remaining Communist countries in the world. Although I was allowed to sit in court as an observer, none of the judges would agree to talk to me about the justice system. This is the first time such a courtesy has ever been denied to me in any court worldwide. A Court Clerk, risking his job suggested the judges would have difficulty in explaining to me their lack of judicial freedom, due to government patronage.

Mugabe continues to enrage President Bush, his severest critic. On the State Radio Mugabe said "Zimbabwe will develop power by processing uranium which has recently been found in the country". Mugabe already has close ties with two countries with controversial nuclear programmes, Iran and North Korea. If it is true that uranium has been found, then the world has become a less safe place.

Returning to the question as to how Mugabe survives, the last word is left to the taxi driver who took me back to the airport. His view was that the people of Zimbabwe are so poor that they cannot afford weapons and ammunition to mount a civil war against Mugabe. He appears to hold all the aces as long as he has the support of his senior staff in the army and the police.

The title of this essay referred to Government propaganda and the role of the media. I started with Russia and China and will now finish in Dubai and Kuwait. The English language Gulf News is very popular with 70,000 ex pats who live there. To the casual observer it appears to be a well presented publication. On closer examination it will be seen that 90% of the news comes from around the world and has been censored to match government and religious ideology. The remaining 10% of news featuring Dubai is strictly monitored by the government. The only items on government expenditure that are featured are those that put the government in a good light. Reports on criminal sentences focus on Islamic laws, particularly where foreigners are involved. As Friday is a day for prayer newspapers are even more closely monitored to avoid anti islamic news that could arouse ill feeling. Pictures of scantily dressed women would not be featured.

The minimal role of women in business is highlighted by the lone woman employee of the Gulf News. Her stories are confined to those involving women. A rare opportunity arose following the arrest of two elderly American women, one in her seventies, who were charged with evangelising without government permission. They were arrested for reading from the Bible and distributing copies to interested listeners. The sentencing judge ordered their removal from Dubai as punishment. The women vowed to return next year to continue their attempt to convert Dubai citizens from Islam.

The government monitors meetings between senior sheikhs and visiting world statesmen. Government employed photographers record traditional greetings and approved prints were sent to the newspaper regardless of their quality. Approved captions were also provided allowing sheikhs to gain political advantage.

The closest the British press come to censorship is through the political persuasion of its owners. Are you immune to such persuasion? Do you choose your daily paper on the basis of its pro or anti government stance?

12

A South American Adventure

A car bomb in Argentina
Volcanic eruption in Mexico
Arrests in Ecuador and Columbia and a mugging in Peru
A week in a love hotel

I was due to retire at 60 as the Regional Officer of the Duke of Edinburgh's Award Scheme. Much to my delight I was offered a five year contract as the Bursary Programme Manager for the Outward Bound Trust. Prince Philip was patron of both charities and Sir Michael Hobbs; Director of the Award, became the Director of Outward Bound. To celebrate this new challenge I went backpacking around major cities in South America for six weeks in January and February 1997. Despite careful planning there were numerous logistical problems involving flights to twelve countries, five of which were not on the itinerary. There were three sailing ventures and twenty long distance bus/coach journeys. Visits were made to five Supreme Courts as a visiting Magistrate. The distance walked was at least 150 miles.

The trip began on the 21st January 1997 with a twelve-hour flight from Heathrow via Madrid to Rio de Janeiro. The temperature on arrival at 5am was 82 degrees F. Accommodation booked via the Bureau at the Airport found me in a hotel fifty yards from Copacabana Beach.

A disadvantage of travelling alone is that you often become a target. Whilst dining on the promenade of Copacabana beach an attractive young women sat by me and told me what to see in Rio. I was studying a map at the time and was interested to know how the conversation would end. Finally she asked me to buy her a drink valued at $5 US, the meeting ended with "no". She was obviously more interested in something more expensive than a drink.

Although I didn't experience hostility as an Englishman, history books portray how Britain ruined a major part of their economy. Prior to 1880 Brazil was the world's number one producer of rubber. A British botanist smuggled 1,000 plants out the country to plant at Kew Gardens in England. By 1910 he had developed a disease free rubber plant. This new strain of plant was planted in Malay and Britain became the world controller of rubber production. Meanwhile Brazil's rubber industry collapsed.

I was interested to learn about Brazil's legendary Amazon women. Much to my surprise they are a myth according to Brazilian research, as their existence has never been authenticated. A story that may have started the myth is based on the capture of one male native speaker whose language was similar to the expedition guides. This led to problems with translation so this story cannot be relied on. The native claimed that Amazon women lived in a walled town, were stronger than ten men and that once a year all the fit males from neighbouring villages were ordered to a one day mating ritual. Any female babies resulting from this annual ritual were retained and the boys were returned to the villages. None of this has been authenticated although a deserted walled town was discovered but without evidence of an all-female society. The mystery remains, did they ever exist?

Copacabana Beach is a highlight of Rio. It's floodlit at night with beach bars along the promenade where families have their own concrete cellars to store beach equipment. My visit occurred a week before the annual Carnival. I enjoyed a preview as fourteen Samba schools rehearsed some of their dance routines based on historical events or Indian legends. The floats were hidden away to protect the designs from rival schools.

An interesting sociological fact is that both the black and white populations are in decline due to the popularity of inter-race marriages. Sociologists predict a future generation neither predominately white or black skinned. They define this race as "coffee coloured people". A similar prediction is made for Venezuela's population.

Travelling on a bus in Rio is interesting, you enter at the rear where there is a turnstile with an operator, you pay to be let on and depart from the front. Passengers are packed like sardines along with chickens, parcels etc. Two of the major landmarks in Rio are the Christ Statue and Sugar Loaf Mountain, which are on opposite sides of the city. A cable car is the method of getting to the top of the Sugar Loaf Mountain whilst a cable rail car is the method of reaching the Christ Statue that overlooks the city. The massive statue has a small chapel set in its base that can accommodate approximately ten worshippers at once.

As previously mentioned something dramatic usually happens whilst I'm visiting a country for the first time. In Brazil there was an unnaturally ferocious tropical storm on the very edge of Rio with torrential rain and lightening. There were massive floods in the surrounding areas and a stretch of beach was totally washed away. Fortunately there was still time to repair the damage before the thousands of international visitors were to flock in to the Carnival the following week.

My next stop was Buenos Aires in Argentina. After a three hour flight I sought a hotel at the airport information desk. I wanted something central and reasonably priced. The receptionist said she knew of an ideal hotel and provided free transport to the Hotel Lisboa. The street on which the hotel stood was very drab with an adult cinema opposite. The entrance to the hotel was clean and tidy although there was no sign of occupants or staff. After banging the desk bell a receptionist arrived looking surprised to see me. On being told that I had been sent from the airport information desk she gave me a knowing look and showed me to a room on the third floor. The room was spotless and very cheap and after the rigours of the journey I wanted an early night and so had settled down by 10pm. However, I hadn't noticed that the room was next to the lift and was to spend a very disturbed night for every hour on the hour the lift would come up and down. It was puzzling as well as disruptive.

The next morning I went down to breakfast and I was the only guest there. Apparently they had booked someone to come in just to prepare my breakfast of fresh pineapple, eggs and toast. Wanting to ensure a decent night sleep in the future I went back to reception and eventually found someone to serve me. I explained about the noise of the lift and was shown to another bedroom at the bottom end of the corridor away from the lift that would hopefully solve the problem. As the day wore on there were still no other guests so I began to make enquiries and it turned out that I was booked into a Love Hotel, a fancy name for a brothel. Love Hotels are allowed to operate providing they also accommodate people not interested in sex. That week I was the nominal guest who helped meet the requirements of the hotel licence. Businessmen would have a regular booking, same woman, same room, and same time every week. Because of my importance to the hotel I was never approached once with offers of sexual favours.

On the second day I was exploring the city centre when a car bomb exploded in the next street. Fortunately my only discomfort was to be covered in dust. The next day there was a protest march following the murder in the blast of the country's top reporter/photographer Joze Cadezas. The protesters claimed that his assassination was an attack on democracy and that it was a move back to the 1970s when thousands were killed by police death squads. The media claimed the investigation by Cadezas exposed police officers with links to the Mafia.

A visit was undertaken to the English Club in the city; the first problem was that the receptionist didn't speak English. There was a picture on the wall showing that Prince Philip signed the visitor's book in 1956. I was allowed to speak to the Club Secretary over the intercom and his first question "Am I wearing a coat and tie?" As the answer was no he refused to let me in. I mentioned the fact that I worked for Prince Philip but he was not impressed so the whole visit turned out to be a waste of time.

The next day involved coach, rail and boat trips to Tigre and the Delta basin, the entrance to the Amazon Jungle. The rail link consisted of just eleven stations on Argentina's only privatised railway that had been funded by the residents. They pay an annual subscription to maintain the electric carriages and eleven modern stations and shopping malls they had built. The journey was luxurious compared with the rest of the rail system run by the government.

The boat tour of the Islands in the Delta portrayed high-income families living in modern homes on stilts with their own jetty and speedboats tied alongside. They also operate a water taxi service with its own petrol station and have a junior school on one of the islands. There was a major problem with river pollution, as there is in the whole of Brazil. Debris floated down river including bottles, boxes, mattresses etc. The water was dirty brown but people still swam among the rubbish, they must have built a strong immune system to combat water borne diseases.

Very few people spoke English so negotiations proved difficult. I tried the local barbers and was supposed to get a ten dollar haircut but finished up with a twenty dollar designer cut, another example of exploiting tourists. Admittedly the barber took a long time cutting it and it looked good. The same cannot be said of my haircut in Mexico City. The barber assured me he could speak English. I asked for a medium short, back and sides with a little off the top. He placed the electric clippers at the bottom of my neck and zoomed up in a single movement. Realising I was about to become a skinhead I shouted at him to stop. He stopped just in time and I ended up looking like a skinhead with a flat cap!

A bonus was the English newspaper The Herald that has a circulation of only 4,500 and costs $1. After a week in Brazil with no UK news it was great to read the Herald every day. The main news item that caught my attention was that Argentina was benefiting from the British beef crises by selling beef to Russia. The orders totalled 3.4 billion dollars, which of course was a loss to the UK and Europe. The Argentine government was calling for a referendum on the Falkland Islands and was proposing joint sovereignty with Britain to solve the oil problem. The issue of sovereignty has been unresolved for the past 160 years. Although the Argentinian's are still anti-British about the Falklands I was never hassled about it. The only sign of the recent war was a damaged destroyer rusting away in the Amazon Delta Basin.

One of the natural wonders of the world is the Iguazu Falls near Puerto Iguazu. It is a one-hour flight from Buenos Aires. The airport was a collection of old shacks, an old bus took passenger's thirty miles to Iguazu that resembled a one-horse town in the Wild West. It was raining on arrival but the bus had no window wipers and there was a dramatic moment when a large bird crashed into the windscreen leaving six large feathers stuck in blood on the glass for the rest of the journey. A second bus was taken deep into the Brazilian Rainforest to the National Park on the border of Brazil, Paraguay and Argentina.

River's flow from the three countries into the horseshoe shaped falls that extends more than seven miles before cascading down hundreds of feet. I was able to walk over the falls on narrow walkways, an incredible experience. It was also possible to take a motorised rubber dingy and sail up the waterfalls. The dinghies bounced in the massive waves, to the sound of roaring water. There were colourful butterflies and birds in abundance. The whole experience gave me a real understanding of the Brazilian Rainforests and the Amazon. There was even the bonus of a plate of chips and a glass of beer on the balcony overlooking the falls as I marvelled at the scene below.

The journey back to Buenos Aires involved two more journeys in the rickety buses back to the ramshackle airport. It was so lacking in facilities that we had to walk across the runway to the plane. As it was raining we were all issued with large umbrellas that had to be brought back every so often until everyone was aboard.

A day trip to the Gaucho Festival at a cattle farm known as Estancia was another highlight. On the way the coach stopped at a massive flea market renowned for antiques. In the square were musicians, dancers and artists. After looking around I relaxed in a chair on the sidewalk with a cup of tea reading the English football results in the Herald. The tango dancers attracted a large audience so I stopped to admire their skill. This was a mistake as I was soon led to the centre by a beautiful dancer. Despite my protests of never dancing the tango I was soon gently but firmly guided across the flagstones roughly in time with the music.

On arrival at the festival we had a meat pie known as Empanada and a glass of red wine. Lunch was in a large wooden structure, open at the sides, with long tables at the front of the stage. Barbecued meat cooked on enormous outdoor barbecue at least 40 yards long. The first course consisted of a black sausage; the second course something like a stick of black pudding. The third course was a beefsteak the size of a plate one inch thick which was delicious and the fourth course was chunks of chicken. After an hour of eating it was show time. There were musicians and tango dancers in brightly coloured dresses. Originally tango dancing was only for men and was introduced in the early 1900s for the upper classes who didn't agree with men and women making physical contact in public. Eventually attitudes changed and women were allowed to tango.

After the musical entertainment we went outside for a display of horsemanship, you could ride a horse or go on a sulky carriage. The highlight was the Sortija races where horsemen raced at top speed in twos to try and spear a ring above head height, dangling on a rope using only a wooden stake. The hole was no more than an inch in diameter and the stake was half an inch diameter and nine inches long. It was incredibly skilful and whenever a ring was speared a Gaucho would present it to a lady guest in return for a kiss.

The next stage of my tour was to fly to Lima in Peru. I was to land as shooting was heard from the Japanese Embassy as the hostage siege that had been running for some weeks continued. There was no information desk to seek accommodation, so I was just wandering around when a woman approached and enquired if I was looking for a hotel. A second woman arrived on the scene and they started to row as to who had seen me first and who was going to provide accommodation. I decided to go with the first woman who was at least wearing a badge and who claimed to have her own travel agency and was put into a taxi and despatched to the Boliva Hotel in the San Martin Plaza. It was an incredible building that looked like a palace in India in the 1900s with enormous stone columns. There were waiters in white jackets, black trousers and bow ties with chamber music wafting gently on the air. The only disconcerting feature was the number of bullet holes in the outside of the building! I told the agent, whose name was Theresa, that I wanted budget accommodation and she suggested something at $120 US per night; my budget was nearer to $20 US. We came to a compromise so I was booked into the hotel whose normal charge was $120 yet paid only $30.

The arrangement was that Theresa would come to the hotel that evening with details of trips and help me change my traveller's cheques into Peruvian currency. Well that was the start of another adventure when she turned up in a typical wreck of a Lima taxi. It was like being in a stock car race as we drove across Lima late at night with everyone tooting their horns and cutting each other up. The roads in the suburbs were in poor condition, there were cars without lights and police roadblocks every so often. Eventually we pulled up outside a dinghy building with two gangster figures at the door and two molls on either side. Theresa took me up stairs to a large room with about seventy people sitting in rows. She marched straight to the front and into another room to see the money dealer. There were two gangster types on the balcony surveying the street. I don't know how much they thought I would change but the intention was that there would be only a 2% charge instead of the 10% charge made back at the hotel. Having changed a small amount of money it was back to the hotel on another mad drive during which we collided with another taxi. On arrival back at the hotel Theresa produced a 3 day package of events that would cost $500, which I rejected pleading poverty. She then came up with a $180 three-day tour that would include additional visits to the Inca Museum and sights around the city. By 11pm the deal was struck, one great adventure had ended but the questions were 'What had I let myself in for'? and 'had I been ripped off'?

The first port of call on the tour was to be the Japanese Embassy where the hostage siege continued. The area around the Embassy was very attractive but there were enormous slums on the outskirts of the city. The siege had commenced before Christmas but was still going on in February. Manhole covers were open and there were telephone engineers listening in on telephone calls and bugging devices that had obviously been planted in the Embassy. The siege eventually ended on the 23 rd April when the Embassy was stormed and all the rebels and one hostage killed. Twenty-five hostages were also slightly injured.

The main part of the day was to be devoted to studying the Inca Civilisation with visits to museums sprinkled with little adventures. Theresa provided a car and a guide, which I shared with two Americans, we spent the morning at the National Museum. There are massive collections of gold and silver items of the Inca civilisation era. The Incas only reigned for 100 years which surprised me as some of their pottery design and art work was not as good or as elaborate as produced by tribes who they conquered, some of whom would have gone back a thousand years.

In the afternoon we visited a major Inca site known as Pachacamac, an Inca fortress thirty miles south of Lima. The fortress was set in an area that looked like a moonscape with no trace of vegetation. There has been no rain for years on the coastline of Peru. There was one interesting scene where a witch doctor was conducting a ceremony involving eight natives. A native was writhing on the ground as if possessed. The witchdoctor placed his hands on his head to exorcise the man and calm him down.

The Gold Museum at Alonso featured a collection of pre Inca and Inca items. There was an example on show of a skull that had been smashed with a club, where a piece of the skull had been cut away and replaced with a piece of sheet gold. Records showed that 60% of people injured in battles who received this treatment recovered from the operation.

One of the important lessons of survival as a tourist is the need for patience and here is a typical example. The two Americans who shared the morning tour with me had been met in the foyer after breakfast. They were very full of themselves, offering hospitality to anyone who cared to visit them back in the USA. They were bragging about how good it was in America and generally being jolly good fellows. That evening I met them again at the travel agents collecting my programme for the next three days. By now the Americans were fuming and getting angrier by the minute as they waited for their own programme. The problem was that their Visa card could not be acknowledged. There were many telephone calls and long gaps in waiting for replies. Apparently they had been there for four hours and they were in a state of absolute desperation. So much for American tolerance and composure.

It was necessary to make a major decision as to whether to travel inland to Machu Picchu or along the coast to Pisco, Ica and the Nazca Lines. My rough timetable would not allow me to do both and so I decided that the coastal road and the lure of the runways in the desert that were claimed to have been carved by visitors from space to be of the greater appeal.

The journey to Pisco involved travelling on a typical South American bus with no air conditioning, packed with people, livestock and vegetables. There were numerous stops and whenever there was a stop traders would come onto the bus with fruit and drinks. In some instances sellers would get on at one village, move up and down the bus selling their wares then get off at he next village. They would then return on the next bus repeating the exercise. There was one interesting guy that came on with a case of religious books, he gave a 10 minute speech with such passion that you would think he were Billy Graham. I didn't understand what he was saying and obviously didn't buy anything. Having survived the three-hour journey to Pisco, I booked into a hostel and spent a pleasant hour walking around the main Plaza taking in the sights.

The next morning there was a 30 minute drive to the Bay of Paracs, a wildlife reserve full of the white flamingos that feature on the flag of Peru. There was a small boat to take tourists to Ballestas Island. Sealions, seals, penguins, Guano birds, turtles, albatrosses, pelicans and seagulls were the only occupants on the island. As we arrived there were two bulls fighting in the middle of the sealions. As the boat passes along the coastline there is an enormous candelabra engraved into the Paracs desert. Apparently this was carved more than a thousand years ago and it is at least 100 yards in length. Scientists think it corresponds to the Southern Cross constellation, others say it is a stylised drawing of a cactus, a symbol of the power of the Charvian culture.

Ballestas Island was important during the last century because of Guano; a mineral consisting of bird droppings used as fertilisers in Europe. It was the number one exported item and slaves were used to mine it. Many deaths occurred from the fertiliser fumes. The mining operations jetty still remains; it was used in a James Bond film.

Following the morning sail I caught a bus to Nazca via Ica, a journey inland into the Andes. Ica was an oasis within a desert and a wine-growing region. As the bus completed its journey a gang of pick pockets who were already aboard moved into action. I was at the back of the bus with four American and German students. Their cases and rucksacks were in the bus hold. I never let my luggage out of sight and kept it with me under the seat. Five minutes from Ica the Peruvians started a well-rehearsed strategy. The person opposite started a conversation and I tried to dismiss him by answering *"do not understand"*. A second man stood up and tried to engage my attention to a newspaper article featuring attractive women with an invitation to meet them, again I declined. As the bus stopped the first person pointed to the floor where I'd been sitting displaying a coin as if to say he had dropped one on the floor. He got down on all fours so I was stranded behind him with a queue building up behind me. Suddenly I felt a hand in my back pocket. It was a deep pocket, with no wallet, but had about fifty dollars in notes. I grabbed the wrist of the person behind me and dug my nails into his skin. He pushed me over the top of the person still crawling on the floor looking for imaginary money and rushed off the bus. I chased after him. Meanwhile the driver had opened the hold and as the thief ran off the bus he grabbed two large items of luggage. They turned out to belong to the American students. Obviously the tactic was to steal our money and the entire luggage before we got off. I got off lightly in thwarting that attack. The Americans, a brother and sister were shattered at the loss of their entire luggage. They had been in Peru for five days and intended to hike for another five weeks. The Police were called but there was no sign of the thieves. It was believed that the bus driver was part of the scam but we had no proof. I had survived my first mugging.

The final stage of the journey to Nazca was a three-hour journey across the Andes Mountain range. It was an incredible journey with mountainous winding roads with massive drops on either side of the road. There were little crosses set on the side of the road where accidents had occurred before and people lost their lives.

On arrival at Nazca I booked into La Borda Motel which was about a 20-minute drive out of the little run down shanty town. It was an incredible Motel at the end of a long winding drive, miles from anywhere. There were Spanish style lodges, two swimming pools, (one without water), and an outside restaurant with palm trees. There seemed to be only one other guest there at the time. Having written up my notes of my lucky escape I enjoyed a peppered steak and a Pisco sour. This is a national drink and consists of Pisco, lemon juice, egg white, sugar, syrup plus a touch of Argentinean butters, it was a powerful drink.

After breakfast I set off for the flight over the Nazca Lines in a small plane that seated just four passengers plus the pilot. The lines in the desert are quite incredible but the flight was painful for me, I felt sick, my shirt was soaking wet and sweat was pouring down my face. The plane, swooping low over the desert had proved to be a strong laxative and it was an incredible relief to land and lie down for an hour to recover.

The Nazca Indians etched giant images on the desert surface by brushing away the surface soil 2,000 years ago. The images included birds, 60 yards across, a killer whale, a 90 yards wide monkey and a 40 yards wide spider. There are also straight lines and a trapezoid that were constructed a few hundred years later. Some theorists suggest aliens did this work, others suggest that it represents an astronomical calendar and some believe they represent fertility rites. These lines and objects can only be viewed from the air because you need to be high for the shapes to be recognised. It poses the question as to how those who carved the shapes and lines would know that they were drawing in such accurate proportions because they would never have seen the results of their work at ground level? Having recovered from the flight I then caught the bus for the eight-hour journey to Lima back across the mountains and deserts.

The next stage of the journey was to fly to Venezuela but there was a problem. Visvas Airline with whom I had booked had gone bust. After much negotiation another airline was persuaded to pick up the responsibility for my ticket. Little did I know that the flight via Ecuador and Columbia to Caracas would lead to my arrest in both countries. On arrival in Quito in Ecuador I found that martial law had been declared. We were all marched off the plane at gunpoint. Most of the passengers getting off the plane were press, radio and TV reporters, who had come to record the crisis. I was mistaken for a reporter and escorted to a cell along with the others. In the cells we met other members of the media, who told me that soldiers were out on the street, there was street fighting and civil war was a strong possibility. The problems occurred when Parliament impeached the President because they claimed he was insane. He refused to resign. The Vice-President claimed the presidency as his successor. The Leader of the parliament also claimed the presidency hence three Presidents at the same time. The Generals then declared martial law and took over the country.

Eventually we were all marched out of the cells and back onto the plane to Bogata, Columbia. The same routine occurred there as we were marched under armed guard to the cells, by now I was the only non-media person under arrest. There had also been a military coup in Columbia but for no apparent reason. All the public service workers had gone on strike in response. The Military had taken over running the airport so I was concerned about whether the soldiers knew what they were doing, even in simple terms of refuelling the plane. After lengthy questioning I was released and put on a plane to Caracas in Venezuela.

On arrival in Caracus I left the plane and immediately attempted to re-confirm my next flight, which was to Mexico City. When I asked for directions to the airline office my request was met with great merriment as the airline had gone bust. Some seats had been transferred to a new airline but not mine. I had to go on a waiting list so I wasn't sure when I would fly out, whether it be this week or next.

The hotel bureau at the airport identified a reasonably priced hotel called Colisso. It happened to be a Bank Holiday and the annual National Carnival was in full swing. The parades were near my hotel on the Plaza Venezuela. There was a mass of people and samba bands parading along the plaza. The carnival was a magnet to tourists and on a par with the carnivals in Brazil, Chile and Trinidad. After the excitement of the carnival I then hired a car and driver for a day tour of Caracas and the neighbouring towns. It was extremely hot so we had the windows open. We travelled roughly a mile when a water bomb was thrown threw the window and exploded in my face and soaked me. Apparently it is a quaint custom for local youths to take advantage of the Carnival to abuse people.

The tour of Caracas included the Simon Bolivia Square; Bolivia was the apparent saviour of the country, his statues are everywhere. The guide took me to Bolivia's former home, the Parliament building, the football and baseball stadium, the bullring, a glass factory, craft markets in local villages and finished up with a drive into the National Park, a forested area overlooking Caracas. The driver introduced me to a traditional lunch consisting of a fifteen-inch diameter maze pancake, cooked on a large flat stove with three slices of cheese added and folded like a pancake, which was extremely filling.

My priority after four days of sightseeing was to confirm my next flight. Finally a package was agreed taking me to Panama City in Panama, San Jose in Costa Rica and my next destination Mexico City. My South American adventure was moving into Central America, but not before a big scare in Caracas.

As I came out of the travel agents I was suddenly engulfed by a mass of people running down the street. Rather than getting knocked to the floor I ran with them. I had accidentally joined a rally of university professors on strike. Police were using their batons and beating everyone in reaching distance. Eventually I managed to dodge into an alleyway to escape the mayhem. There's never a dull moment in South America!

My flight to Mexico City went reasonably smoothly and allowed a brief look around Panama City and San Jose while waiting for connecting flights. The arrival in Mexico City was far from smooth with a volcano in the east of the city erupting and sending clouds of ash over the city. Mexicans live in fear of major eruptions. There are four volcanoes in the area including, Popocatepeth, the

"Smoking Mountain". Eleven years previously there had been an earthquake linked to a volcanic eruption that destroyed many buildings and killed hundreds of people in the city. Since that event the southern town of Puebla's population had increased from one to two million as people left Mexico City for fear of more earthquakes.

Mexico City is 6,000ft above sea level and the low oxygen levels combined with the polluted air caused by excess traffic left my eyes stinging and running for most of the day. By the second day my eyes were getting used to the pollution and I started a series of walking tours. The first stop was the Basilica De Guadalupe, the holiest place in Mexico. Its fame matches that of the Fatima site in Portugal where the Virgin Mary was said to have appeared, a site I have also visited. In 1531 a native boy out in the fields saw the vision of the Virgin Mary. He was told to build a church, and so he ran to the city and told the Bishop. The Bishop however wanted proof and so the vision appeared to the boy again and told him to gather roses, put them in his cloak and take them to the Bishop. When he opened the cloak in front of the Bishop, a beautiful image of a dark skinned woman believed to be the Virgin Mary was imprinted on the cloak. The cloak now hangs on the wall on the site where the original church was built. Many years later the church started sinking into the subsoil and so a new Basilica was built and opened by the Pope in 1987.

The Pope visited again five years later when there were 4 million people in the grounds of the Basilica. The new church is also starting to lean because of the poor subsoil and scientists are trying to correct the movement. They are the same team of experts who are working on the Leaning Tower of Pisa. Pilgrims walk hundreds of miles across Mexico to pray at the Basilica in front of the cloak depicting the Virgin Mary.

The second major site visited that day was the Pyramids of the Moon and Sun at Teotihuacan, built 100 years BC. The Aztecs were in control of the Pyramids from 1400AD. It was the Aztec capital in 1519 when Cortez led 500 Spaniards and 60 horses to attack the 300,000 inhabitants. Cortez recruited natives from neighbouring tribes and with their help achieved a stunning victory. I climbed the Sun Pyramid which was very steep in places. This completed my set of Pyramids climbed along with those in Egypt and Peru. The climb was helped by my first lengthy conversation in four weeks shared with an English tourist from Kent who ran a youth cricket team. We had a great two-hour chat as we climbed the Pyramids sharing anecdotes about the great Kent and England cricketer Derek Underwood who had run a coaching session for my youth team at Four Oaks CC.

Sunday is a special day for leisure and religious events in Mexico. Places and events that caught my attention were the Ballet Folk Law De Mexico at the

Palcio de Belles Artes, the floating gardens at Xochimilco, and the main cathedral where services continued despite the building being supported by scaffolding to stop it from sinking into the ground. All this subsidence is the result of the whole of Mexico City being built over an underground lake.

On day two a full day bus tour was made to Taxco and Cuernauaca, the City of Eternal Spring. The Woolworth's heiress, Barbara Hutton, commissioned a two year survey to find the perfect place to build her home and chose a long green valley, totally enclosed by mountains which block the rain clouds. It has pure mountain water, clean air and a consistent climate. The rainwater from the mountains irrigate the valley making it lush for growing crops. The mansion she built was turned into a five star hotel after her death.

Taxco is high on the mountainside and is known as the Silver City. The Spaniards discovered silver in 1525 and used local Indians as slaves in the mines. In the early 1800s a French prospector found a rich new strain and Taxco is now the countries centre for silver smiths. During a tour of the Taxco market the guide showed a plastic bag containing live beetles about half an inch long which were on sale. On the first Monday of November the Bishop leads all the able bodied people to the top of the mountain for prayer. On returning they eat these beetles raw or fried. They continue to eat beetles from November to March. No one knew for centuries why this tradition had started. Scientists eventually discovered that the minerals in the silver mines exposed the natives to radiation. As the beetles were rich in iodine, this counteracted the effects of the radiation, a cure the locals discovered by chance.

Another important tradition of the City of Taxco was a 2,000-year-old ballgame and religious ritual known as Tlachtli. Players using their hips, elbows or knees kept a solid rubber ball in the air. The spectators would gamble on the result and the loser of the final game was gruesomely decapitated and his head used as a ball, or he was tortured to death and his body trussed up into the shape of a ball and bounced through the town. The game is still played today but without the gambling or the human sacrifice!

The next coach tour took me towards Texas. The news that morning of a transport strike meant food shortages at the weekend. Even more disconcerting was a report of an accident involving a tourist coach and lorry where eleven people were killed, mainly from the resulting fire. Only half an hour into my journey to Tula, the coach, while travelling at 60mph in the middle lane, braked as a lorry started to pull out. The coach went into a skid and bounced off the side of the lorry and back into the outside lane. The side of the coach was damaged but no one was injured. The coach driver didn't even stop to check for injuries, shock or damage; he drove on as if nothing had happened, as did the lorry driver.

An hour later the coach had to make a detour due to the driver's strike. They were blockading the road in protest at police corruption at night. Apparently police cars stop lorries on isolated roads and demand a toll before they pass. After a long detour we arrived in Tula, the centre of the cement industry. Whole sides of mountains have been removed and no doubt all the mountains in the area will disappear in time as cement is mined and exported around the world. Tula is the former capital of the Taltec Indians who abandoned the town in 1168AD. They also had a special ball game similar to the one in Taxco. The difference was the winner would be the human sacrifice, as they believed it was a great honour to die as they went to a higher place.

My return to Mexico City was hampered by the biggest traffic jam I've ever encountered. 600 riot police were removing 1,500 Tabasco Indians from the Main Square in the City. The Indians were protesting that Pemex, the National Oil Company, had stolen their land. They claimed the Company was polluting the land and they hadn't been paid compensation for their loss. The seven–lane highway leading to the city came to a standstill for two hours. The next day the Indians were back in the main square so it had all been a waste of time.

Recovering from the journey I visited a local restaurant and entered into a fascinating conversation with a former Iraqi pilot who, at the age of 21, had flown Russian Mig Jets in the Gulf War for Saddam Hussein. After the war he defected, escaping through Turkey with false documents and claimed political asylum in Sweden. While in the Iraq Airforce he had trained Saddam's nephew who proved to be a useless pilot. On a training flight the trainee panicked and fired the ejector seat. He was too near the ground, the parachute did not open and he was killed on impact. An enquiry found the trainer blameless but he feared his chances of progress in the airforce were limited and he feared retribution from Saddam Hussein.

My dinner partner had another interesting story to tell as he had just been on tour in Guatemala. Whilst walking through a zoo with some friends they saw crowds of people running in the same direction. They thought some animals must have escaped and the people were running for safety. In fact they were running to the Leopards Pit where a man intent on committing suicide had jumped into the pit. The two leopards started to tear the man to pieces as members of the public tried to keep them off him by throwing drinks cans and sticks. Eventually the leopards started to fight each other over the man's remains. The fire brigade had to use hoses to drive off the leopards and recover the remains of the body.

The next tour took in Puebla, the site of the Napoleon's Mexican defeat in 1862 and to Cholula to see the largest pyramid in the world in terms of circumference. When the Spanish invaded they built a church at the top level rather than destroying the pyramid. As there was a dust storm raging I took shelter by walking through a network of tunnels underneath the pyramid.

The final day in Mexico was marked with the news that a Senior General had been arrested due to links with drug barons. He had been appointed to track down drug traffickers but was charged with receiving money to protect the traffickers from arrest.

The South American adventure ended on my departure to Miami. I unwound from the trauma of the past six weeks by relaxing in a small apartment on the edge of Miami beach. I reflected on how fortunate I was to live in England. Corruption, oppression and poverty are evident throughout South America. The "ordinary" people I came into contact with were so kind, friendly and charming. They deserved better. It was within the Government, Civil Service and the police that examples of corruption were found. The frustration of having to live in a climate of fear must be demoralising.

I met two fascinating characters in Miami. The first was a 97-year old lady known as a "Snow Bird" who was staying at my apartment block. Every winter her relatives put her on plane in New York to spend three months in the Miami sun to avoid the harsh North American winter. She was the oldest person I've ever met and intellectually was exceptional for her age. She described the effects the Wall Street Crash had on her family and the protest rallies led by Dr Martin Luther King as black Americans sought racial equality.

The second personality I encountered during a round of golf at the North Shore Golf Club. He was a former US Army Officer who was stationed in England during the War and had been a member of Glen Miller's US Military Band. On demob he continued his career as a musician and writer and worked for many years at the nightclubs in Las Vegas. He played with many of the musical greats including Frank Sinatra and Dean Martin.

In keeping with the rest of my tour there was a dramatic send off as I flew out of Miami. The Everglades were ablaze; an area 35 miles wide was threatening homes. "Lucky Jim" had survived again despite a car bomb, water bomb, car crash, street protest, volcanic eruption, coach collision, a love hotel, gangsters in Peru, arrests in Ecuador and Columbia, airlines going bust, dust storms and a mugging.

13

Interact with a visitor from Outer Space -

Religion, a positive or destructive force within society?

*"No one religion can claim to be better than another as
all are based on doing good for others". Dalai Lama.
"Just enough religion to hate one another but not enough
to love one another". Jonathan Swift.*

In the introduction to this book you were invited to interact with the people
and events encountered in my journeys through 100 countries. The concept
of interactive reading is that you are challenged to form an opinion. Religion
is one such topic that can raise a heated exchange irrespective of ones personal
beliefs or lack thereof. Consider the persecution of Buddhists in Tibet, the State
of Emergency in Nepal and the poverty of people in Ahmedabad, India. Evaluate
the part religion plays in these countries and also in America, South Africa,
Palestine/Israel, Mexico, England, China, Nigeria and Pakistan.

I came across the idea of creating a hypothetical space person as a defence,
after being conned, in a subtle way, to evaluate religion during a stay at a hunting
lodge in the Chitwan National Park in Nepal. A member of the local
intelligentsia came to the lodge with an invitation to attend a monthly meeting
of his group in the village hall. Apparently news of my history of travel had
filtered through the grapevine. Delighted to accept such an opportunity to meet
with local people I went like a lamb to the slaughter.

The group was about 40 strong drawn from all the local villages, they all spoke
English and represented a mix of religions. The majority were Hindus with one or
two Muslims, Sikhs, Parsis, Buddhists, Jews and Christians. Settling down to enjoy
listening to a lively debate my host whispered that it was customary for a visitor to
be invited to address the audience on some religious topic. I had five minutes to
think of something stimulating and knew that whatever approach I took was sure to
upset someone! The five minutes thinking time was nearly up when the idea of

looking at religion through the eyes of a visitor from outer space hit me. I would combine my experiences in Tibet, Nepal and India and relate them to the influence of religion. I knew that if I tried to present my personal view of the major religions I would be challenged by each of the religious representatives so my starting point was to present a view expressed by the Dalai Lama at a conference in London. He said that he would never try to change a person's religious belief. *"No one religion can claim to be better than another as all are based on doing good for others"*.

If the alien visitor landed in Lhasa, the Holy City of Tibet, they would find the local people oppressed by the Chinese. Over the years the Tibetans have been persecuted for being Buddhists. In addition to not having religious freedom they have no political/governmental power. The climate is harsh, Lhassa is 10,000ft above sea level, oxygen is rarefied, and soil quality is poor. The majority of the people live in poverty, so poor that when they die the poorest cannot afford to bury family members but adopt sky burials. The dead are positioned in a chair in their home for three days as the family pay their respects. The body is then taken a short way up the mountain and chopped into small pieces and left for the birds to eat. A practical reason for this is also that with so little fertile soil, priority is given to seed planting rather than graves. Only the rich can afford a coffin and the travel costs of transporting a body down the mountain to more fertile ground.

Thousands of Tibetans have been killed or imprisoned by the Chinese. Their spiritual leader the Dalai Lama is in exile. Many Temples were destroyed and religious symbols plundered. Despite this spiritual cleansing by the Chinese the Buddhists survived and it could be claimed that religion sustained them in the face of a harsh regime. Temples have been rebuilt and Buddhist Monks are now allowed to practice publicly.

The relaxation of the oppression of religion in Tibet has also had a moderating influence over the Chinese, both in Tibet and China. Prior to the Communist Revolution of 1949 China was known in religious terms as the "land of the three ways", i.e. Confucianism, Taoism, and Mahayana Buddhism. A consequence of the Revolution was that the Communist Authorities persecuted followers of the "Three ways". Gradually over the last 20 years all three faiths are re-emerging openly alongside Marxism which has displayed all the influence and appeal of a fourth religion.

Following the 1949 revolution the authorities had adopted three different responses in repressing the followers of the "Three ways". Confucianism was condemned, Taoism was controlled and Mahayana Buddhism tolerated.

Confucianism was primarily concerned with respect for superiors, with a just and kindly disposal to the elderly. There was the duty of a son to care for their parents and to venerate their ancestors. Taoism presents a mystical interpretation of the world and involves the worship of nature. Mahayana Buddhism brought *"the possibility of salvation to all by grace through faith and devotion"*. Having reviewed the "Three Ways" our visiting alien may be puzzled as to how a political ideology, Marxism, became accepted as a religion alongside the "Three Ways".

If Lhasa were the only contact the alien had with humans it would no doubt ponder on man's inhumanity to man and how slavery and religious persecution is acceptable.

If the alien were to have landed in Kathmandu in Nepal they would have found a different set of circumstances basically involving a Civil War between Royalists and Communists. Less than three months prior to my visit the country was rocked when four members of the Royal Family, the King the Queen and two sons, were killed in a family dispute. The killer was another son who was subsequently killed by the guards. The Royal dynasty had ruled the country for centuries. This event encouraged the Maoists to become active and try to take over the running of the country. The Maoists are strong in the countryside where farm workers, without an education, are easily exploited. Attacks are increasing on towns and the Government capital of Kathmandu. Only one week ago a major battle had taken place when more than 100 Maoist terrorists were killed due to the superior weaponry of the army.

The alien would be living in a Government declared "State of Emergency". A night curfew was in force, four bombs had exploded in the city in the past week. Everyone, including tourists and the alien have to carry identity cards at all times. Nepal is predominantly Hindu but Buddhist temples are prominent. Tibetan refugees are supported and a small number of Christians practice their religion. The elite are truly elite with 72% of the population living in poverty and without basic reading or writing skills. Corruption within the administration is high as illiterate people are exploited.

The alien's report would no doubt include reference to a society based on privileges of birth and education where the rich get richer and the poor get poorer. Only the faith of the masses sustains the harshness of poverty.

If the alien had landed in Ahmedabad in Western India the level of poverty in a major city would no doubt appal them. Like in other Indian cities people live on the street. If you attempt to walk on the pavement you would be walking through someone's home. Every spare area of dirt around the city is a home or a rubbish dump. Lean to shelters made of cloth or cardboard offer minimal protection from the elements. I saw a traffic island, triangular in shape, no more than 14ft at its largest was occupied by a family of all ages with their only possessions being a ragged settee, a lean-to cardboard shelter and a wood fire where dinner was cooking. Added to this the traffic island was at a major junction surrounded by massive traffic congestion. This family was living only inches from speeding vehicles belching out fumes, making excessive noise from faulty exhaust systems and honking their horns every few seconds. The combination of noise, pollution, exposure to the elements, lack of sanitation, money, education or work, paints an appalling picture for our alien to take away.

Landing in Ahmedabad rather than London, Birmingham or New York would make the aliens report totally different. Compare a typical street scene in Ahmedabad with say Birmingham. Driving down the street you will encounter cows and goats wandering aimlessly across the traffic looking for food on the open waste tips. The cow, as a sacred animal, is safe from harm or interference. People step into the road to avoid walking through the homes of street dwellers. The most common form of transport are motor scooters with motor cycles and 3 wheel tut tuts a distant second and third respectively; private cars are in the minority. Battered buses are packed to their limits, there is no glass in the windows and metal bars prevent people getting on and off illegally. However people still cling to the outside of a bus for a free ride. Carts are pulled by people, camels, bullocks or tractors. A caravan of camels passing through the City centre carrying the villager's produce to market is a common sight. Dust fumes and the incessant blasting of horns makes any journey through the city streets an ordeal.

Anarchy is never far from the surface. Accidents involving the mass of direction changing vehicles are common with instant justice being administered. I came across a bus which had knocked down a pedestrian, a large crowd gathered and witnesses, who blamed the bus driver, dragged him from his seat and started kicking and punching him. Others set fire to the bus that had quickly emptied to witness the confrontation. The police eventually rescued the driver. Our visiting alien will hopefully not take this as a normal example of the correct judicial process.

While India can claim to be a democracy it is still dominated by the Caste System that segregates and discriminates against large sections of their population. The Hindus and Sikhs share an uneasy relationship since independence from the British in 1947. Independent India's short history is dominated by race riots against the Muslims that led to Partition and the creation of Pakistan and Bangladesh. The ongoing dispute in Kashmir continues as they strive for independence.

Throughout India our alien will see thousands of Hindu temples and shrines that are decorated with garlands of flowers and gifts of food poor people can ill afford to buy. A more disturbing form of worship is of celebrities. The Indian cricket star, Sachin Tendulkar is named as a God and treated as such by million's of Indians. An example of this adulation can be witnessed during any match he plays. Whenever Tendulkar comes out to bat or on to bowl or just fields the ball, the crowd goes wild. If he moves toward the boundary edge a whole mass of supporters leave their seats and rush to the chain link fencing that surrounds the pitch. They cheer and chant his name and just a small twitch of his hand in acknowledgement is greeted with a roar of approval. Although there may be 50,000 people present they all take the gesture as personal contact with their God. The same sort of treatment is being directed to Bollywood movie stars. Where will it end? What must our alien think of people worship?

Against this background of poverty what does the alien report back? The newspapers are dominated by claims of corruption and incompetence. Money that had been set aside to improve sanitation in Ahmedabad has not been spent with the result that many more will die because of the annual mosquito epidemic and the resulting malaria.

Parliament was suspended because fighting broke out in the chamber as the opposition called for the resignation of a Minister because of alleged corruption in the purchase of coffins. Examples of corruption are regularly featured in the Indian press. If the people cannot trust their elected representatives is it any wonder that corruption is found in many Government services including the police? I have experienced corruption and therefore feel justified to raise this issue.

One of the key messages our alien can take away is that power can corrupt and that a handful of people in power can abuse the people they are supposed to represent. Billions have been spent by India and Pakistan in developing weapons of mass destruction, both have atomic weapons that would not only kill millions of their own people but could jeopardise the whole of mankind. How can India justify spending billions on a space programme just to put an Indian into orbit when their own people are starving, living on the streets, dying early and whose quality of life is only sustained by their religion?

Karl Marx described religion as the *"Opium of the masses"*. In the examples given he could have been right. He also said that if there weren't a God then people would invent one. Marx did not have to invent a God as he was brought up in a Jewish/Christian family. Marx believed it was possible to create an ideal society, a classless utopian paradise. The reality was different, using Marxism as a political banner 30 million Russians were killed on Stalin's instructions and 75 million Chinese died under Mao Tse Tung's leadership. Although Marxism has been universally discredited it is still followed in 2005 under Mugabe's brutal regime in Zimbabwe.

It is hoped our hypothetical alien is of a higher intellectual level than the leaders who are corrupt and control the lives of their subjects in a number of countries worldwide. Is it reasonable to conclude that a superior being would not judge mankind well on what they encounter in Tibet, Nepal and India?

The sixty minutes of my unscripted talk seemed to pass in a flash. No doubt they had been expecting me to say nice things about their individual religions that could be turned against their neighbours beliefs. In fact I had turned the tables and challenged them to look positively at other religions as the Dalai Llama had urged. I closed by repeating his words, *"No one religion can claim to be better than another, all are based on doing good for others"*.

In fairness to the citizens of India, Tibet and Nepal I have since superimposed into my lecture notes what our alien would have found had they visited other countries whose lifestyle and politics are influenced strongly by religion.

If our alien had landed in South Africa prior to the end of Apartheid in 1993, what would they have thought of people being treated so badly because of the colour of their skin? The lives of the native population of South Africa were corrupted in the mid 1600s when settlers from Holland and England set up trading posts. Their original intentions may have been honourable but just like the Aborigines in Australia and the Maoris of New Zealand, their numbers were decimated by European diseases, their land was taken, the mineral resources plundered and the fit and strong taken into slavery.

The settlers were accompanied by missionaries who would endeavour to convert the native population to Christianity and away from their so called Pagan gods and forms of worship. Although a significant number of black South African natives did become Christians it did not guarantee them freedom from slavery or freedom to live in areas dominated by white settlers, other than as servants. They were confined to ghettos on the outskirts of big cities in townships of cardboard and scrap metal. Parts of the major cities such as Cape Town were no-go areas for black people; there was even segregation in churches. It was not until 1993 that Apartheid, the official name for the Government policing of racial segregation, would be consigned to the scrap heap. Oppression based on the colour of a person's skin ended. It has taken more than 300 years to free the native Africans and it has been a campaign of non-violence led by religious leaders such as Bishop Desmond Tutu that had triumphed. A belated plus in the logbook of the alien for Christianity in a multi-racial society where the colour of a persons skin was no longer an issue.

If the alien visited America today they would be faced with many contrasting interpretations of religion. The historical victims have been the American Indians who were stripped of their lands, killed in large numbers and herded onto reservations as Europeans plundered their natural resources, including gold. The American Indians were considered as savages and in need of conversion to Christianity. Their treatment has been in the conscience of American politicians and religious leaders for a long time. The current situation in America shows a wide disparity in the living conditions of American Indians. In California a small number reside amongst some of the wealthiest people in the country. Their asset was land and the development of Las Vegas saw the elders of their Tribes become overnight millionaires. In contrast, in Nevada and Arizona the American Indians still live on the reservations. Unemployment is in the 50-60% range, alcoholism runs at 75%. Serious crime figures are on the increase and death rates among the police on reservations are four times higher than in the rest of the USA. Many Nevada Indians cannot speak English.

The introduction of Christianity to America has created numerous outcomes. The people in the area described as the "Bible Belt" have adopted a hard line approach to the interpretation of the Bible, (as have Nigeria). This is reflected in their reactions to the September 11th Twin Towers attack. Their fear of outsiders has hardened and Muslims have become targets of hate. The television analysis of America's reaction, in "Children of Abraham", featured a white American on Death Row. Immediately after the September 11th attack he went out onto the street and indiscriminately shot and killed two Muslims and seriously injured a third just because they had brown skin. The killer justified his actions, as a devote Christian, to the principle of "an eye for an eye".

In the same programme it was speculated that President Bush believed that Americans were the chosen people to bring Christian values to the world – that America was chosen to cleanse the world of terrorists – a divine purpose – God's gift to humanity – it was God's purpose that America was chosen.

In contrast to the hard line Bible Belt approach in the USA is the Interfaith Alliance. Their members believe America provides light in a world of darkness. Immigrants of all races and religions have flooded in and have been welcomed. By understanding and respecting other faiths and customs it brings harmony to the world.

Two contrasting opinions are offered, the first by the late Martin Luther King", *It is not a question of violence or non violence - it is non violence or non existence".* Secondly, Jonathan Swift – *"Just enough religion to hate one another but not enough to love one another".*

In America, as in other parts of the world, there are two mindsets:
1. Interfaith Alliances who are open to dialogue and discussion with other faiths.
2. Fundamentalists who see everything in black and white – they believe they have the truth. They are growing in number. Zealots believe their view of the world to be authentic.

There is a clear link between politics and religion in America based on the 2004 re-election of President George Bush. Early in the campaign Bush said *"This country must not fear the influence of faith in the future of this country". "We must welcome faith in order to make America a better place".*

Religion and politics are now firmly rooted in American life, consider the following facts;

90% of Americans profess faith in Christianity. 50% of the population attend church at least once a week. Christian novels outsell all other topic titles in America. TV preachers gain higher ratings than mid week soap operas on the networks. There is tax relief on donations to churches of up to 10%.

Preachers who led the Civil Rights Movement now preach for bans on sodomy, gay marriage, stem cell research and, in extreme cases, inter racial dating. Lt. Col Garry Brandl, Battalion Commander, proclaimed at the opening American attack on Fallujah in Iraq, *"The enemy has got a face. He's called Satan. He's in Fallujah and we are going to destroy him"*.

The fact that 90% of Americans profess faith in God is exploited by the business community. Television preachers earn massive salaries as viewers are encouraged to support religious causes. Commercialism is blatant as births, deaths and marriages are marketed. Some companies have been set up to exploit people's fear of death and grief for a deceased family member. Rich people who believe they can be reborn once a cure for the illness that may kill them is found are turning towards Cryonics. When they die their bodies are encased in capsules which are topped up with Nitrogen every five days to preserve them.

If a family has £1,500 to spare the ashes from a cremated body can be screened for minerals that are compressed into a small diamond which is fitted onto a ring to be worn by a family member. The scattering of ashes following cremation can sometimes be a problem during times of strong winds. Bio-disposal floating urns have been developed so that the ashes of a family member can be launched into the sea, a lake or river so that nature can take its course.

Video headstones are claimed to be the next big marketing ploy. Prior to death a video recording is made on whatever topic the person wants to be seen or heard. They may be making a death bed confession, be imparting a gem of wisdom on the meaning of life, giving advice to younger family members, describing highlights of their life, expressions of love or anger related to people or events etc. Anyone will be able to access the recording. The developers of the initiative envisage strangers visiting graveyards and playing a series of videos for a wide variety of reasons - interest, entertainment, morbid curiosity, enlightenment etc.

In Grand Rapids, Michigan, drive in funerals have been introduced. Mourners drive into a field near a woodland Church and tune into the service on their car radios. The respect for the marriage ceremony is also being diminished, particularly in Las Vegas, with commercial wedding Chapels in casinos and hotels.

American funeral innovations have spread to Sweden. They have developed a freeze-dry process called promession which involves firstly freezing the deceased before their coffin is lowered into a vat of liquid nitrogen making both very brittle. By vibrating the coffin everything disintegrates into a fine powder. A magnetic field applied to the powder removes metals such as mercury that is found in tooth fillings. The remains are placed in a biodegradable coffin made from maize or potato starch. The coffin is buried in a shallow grave that turns to compost in 6–12 months.

This process has attracted the green movements interest with local authorities running out of space in cemeteries. In Jonkopling they are planning to turn their crematorium into a "promatorium". They believe it will save millions as it eliminates the need for mercury filters to meet emissions targets. Although the process is currently illegal in the UK if support is gained the Department of Constitutional Affairs will review the idea. It could lead to "Forests of Remembrance" where nutrients from loved ones are used to enrich the earth.

The aliens report on America should make interesting reading. At one level is the battle for the hearts and minds of Americans as the Zealots and those supporting Interfaith Alliances lock horns. There is now a clear link between carrying a Christian banner and the election of the world's most powerful leader. Finally there is the blatant commercialism of rituals linked to death and marriage where the only motive is financial gain. Las Vegas is the centre of such commercialism. If you believe there is a God do you support the Fundamentalist or the Interfaith Alliance approach to religion?

If the alien had landed in Palestine in 2004 they would have found Muslim Fundamentalists, in the name of Islam, strapping bombs to their bodies and travelling into Israel to kill, indiscriminately, as many Israelis as possible. Women and children were not being spared in such attacks. If the alien were to engage Fundamentalist Muslims in conversation, such as members of Hamas, they would be faced with conflicting interpretations of the Koran within Islam.

A Fundamentalist Muslim will claim a male suicide bomber can expect a reward in Heaven of 72 virgins but they do not offer similar rewards to women who become suicide bombers. The relative part of the Sacred Scripture of Islam can however be translated so that "virgin" can be interpreted as "mates" or "angels" and there is no actual reference to suicide or suicide bombers. The Hadith, the tradition of words and deeds of Mohammed, considered to be the second most important foundation of Islam, forbids suicide. Fundamentalist Muslims will try to hide behind the act of Shahdid, (Martyrdom), by saying that carrying a bomb into enemy territory is not suicide but an act of Jihad (Holy War).

There have been numerous statements from senior Muslims decrying the suicide bombers but the practice continues with extremists committing suicide in the name of Islam in other parts of the world. While the split between Zealots and the Inter-faith Alliances is splitting the Christian church in America its impact is minimal when compared with the physical harm being caused by Muslim Fundamentalists in the Middle East.

The violence in Palestine is not of course confined to Muslim Fundamentalists. There have been Jewish atrocities during Army attacks that have resulted in the killing of innocent women and children.

The visiting alien, armed with the above assessment, must surely question issues such as the actions of suicide bombers acting in the name of religion. They must also question the claim that three-quarters of the world's refugees are Muslims fleeing other Muslims.

If our visiting Space alien were to visit Mexico they would encounter philanthropy. Although not physically destructive it is certainly wasteful in many situations. Philanthropy as a concept, when linked to religion, may puzzle a visiting alien. Large sums of money have been donated to glamorise/glorify buildings associated with religion that many would say is a waste. The cynics would say the donors are seeking a place in Heaven and a monument to themselves on Earth. Examples include the Temple De Santo Domingo in Pueblo, Mexico. It is considered one of the most exquisite Dominican constructions in the world. An American woman paid six million dollars to restore the Chapel that features gold covered statues. The Chapel only accommodates 200 people each Sunday - probably the same 200 people every week. In the area surrounding the Chapel there are thousands of people living in poverty. Could the money have been better spent on facilities that addressed the needs of the majority - health care, education, and welfare?

A second example is at the Catholic Church in Tepotzothan where mahogany statues are covered in gold leaf. The Church is situated in a similar area of poverty and only accessed by a small number of people. Assuming our visiting alien comes from a planet that believes in a Heaven and Hell they could report back that a place could be bought in Heaven, a privilege only available to the rich.

If the alien had arrived in England in June 2004 they would have found the Channel 4 TV documentary, presented by Theologian Dr Robert Beckford, "God is Black", both informative and disturbing. The programme makers were claiming that the Anglican Church was being split in two. On the one hand the liberal arm of the Anglican Church in England had lost a third of its congregation in recent years, that its congregation was ageing and lacking a major influx of young people, while the Evangelical Fundamentalist arm of the Church was attracting growing and younger congregations. The driving force for such changes is claimed to be Nigeria whose Anglican support has increased to 50 million making it the world's new religious power base. Churches that can accommodate 120,000 worshippers are being built. Up to a million worshippers are attending single outdoor services in Lagos. In England 10,000 people are attending Nigerian led services in Kingsway where tented areas are being installed to cope with the numbers attending with the service being relayed by CCTV.

The leader of the Nigerian Anglican Church is highly critical of the liberal interpretation of the Bible in England, particularly the recognition and acceptance of homosexuals within the church. The Archbishop of Nigeria claims that "*Nigeria is the heartbeat of Christianity*". The bible is being interpreted as missionaries presented it to Nigerians from England 150 years ago. Nigeria is now sending missionaries to England to reclaim the Victorian interpretation of the Bible and to reinforce the belief that "*homosexuality is an abomination*".

Christianity is being "marketed" in Nigeria and is led by the man they call their prophet, TB Joshua. People who are seriously ill are coming to him from all over the world in the belief that he will cure them. His team of disciples includes young white people from England. The raising of large sums of money in both Nigeria and England by missionaries is a central aim of their work.

The mass appeal of the Anglican approach to Christianity in Nigeria has prompted the growth in organisations such as Reform and Alpha in England. Claiming to be Evangelical Fundamentalists Alpha predicts a membership of six million worldwide within the next 10 years. Reform claims to be leading the "*battle for lives and souls of the Church of England*". They offer firm leadership based on the Bible including support for the opinion that "*homosexuality is an abomination*". The main victims of this homophobia are being driven to set up their own churches for gay and lesbian Christians.

The number of black churches in the UK has risen from 18 to 3,000 in nine years. Research has shown that people from the West Indies did not feel welcomed in white churches. In the style of Pentecostalism, they started in homes, met in Town Halls, Community Centres etc. Figures from 2004 show that in the Anglican Church there are only two black Bishops out of 120. There are 500 members of the Synod of which 12 are black representatives. It was not until 2005 that the Rt. Rev. Dr. John Sentanau, the Bishop of Birmingham, became the first black Archbishop when appointed at York. A victim of Idi Amin's regime in Uganda he came to the UK in 1974. In the Catholic Church there are 500 Priests, only 20 are black. The visiting alien, having viewed "God is Black", will no doubt have difficulty in coming to terms with the division in the Anglican Church and the persecution of a small percentage of the population based on their sexuality.

If our alien had landed in Pakistan they would have encountered the persecution of half of the Muslim population because of their gender. Women who commit adultery are banished from their homes whilst a man's indiscretion is ignored. A woman who kills her husband for adultery can be stoned to death whilst a man who kills his wife for the same reason is treated leniently under the excuse of purging "family honour".

Girls in rural areas of Pakistan are denied education as it is considered irrelevant to their expected roles in life. They have no freedom to choose a marriage partner, being subject to an arranged marriage at an early age. They are not allowed to go out socially with boys. Even while working in the fields they are chaperoned by adult female family members. Their clothing is also prescribed and consists of a full length, one piece, black garment that covers everything except their eyes. This ensures no flesh is exposed that might *"influence the interest of the opposite sex"*.

It would be interesting to read the alien's report on a visit to Pakistan. Although women are starting to escape the shackles of gender persecution, particularly in Pakistan's main cities, it could still take many years for the entire Muslim world to follow suit.

The issues reviewed during the alien's imaginary short tour emphasise the diversity of life styles on our planet and the power of religious leaders. These issues have included political ideology, being governed by Royal consent, celebrity hero worship, caste separation, the power/corruption equation, colour of a person's skin, treatment of resident natives, Christian and Muslim fundamentalism/inter-faith alliances, gender, homophobia, philanthropy and commercialism.

I was hoping our alien could have joined me on my tour of West Africa in late 2004 and particularly to visit Nigeria to see the other side of the Nigerian Christian crusade to England. They could also have witnessed the continuation of witchcraft and voodoo in Togo and Benin and child slavery in Nigeria. Unfortunately the visitor's visa had expired and their departure date was non-negotiable. You, however, will be able to read the results of my research in the final essay.

Based on the examples of the way an alien may view religion around the world I think it is fair to claim that they would view religion as both a positive and destructive force. If the most senior religious and political leaders cannot resolve the issues that create the destructive forces then an inevitable holy war will erupt. In the era of nuclear weapons this could result in Armageddon, if we are to survive the current religious conflict the interfaith alliances would seem to be our only solution.

What do you think?

14

Surviving in South East Asia

Racial conflicts in Malaysia, Sri Lanka and Borneo
Brutality of the Khmer Rouge in Cambodia
Vietnam War Crimes Museum
Attacked by an Orang-utan

Three visits to South East Asia are featured in this essay. The first in 1995 to Singapore, the second in 1999 to Thailand, Cambodia and Vietnam and the third in 2001 to Sri Lanka, Malaysia, Sabah, Borneo and Brunei. A number of dramatic incidents occurred during these visits. The Sri Lankan Air Force started bombing Tamil terrorists in the north of the island in retaliation for a series of suicide attacks in Columbo. In Borneo the notorious headhunters, the Dayaks, were engaged in ethnic cleansing of the Madurese. Racial tensions erupted in a riot whilst in Kuala Lumpur when a Malaysian funeral procession encountered a Hindu wedding parade, six were killed in the riot. In Bangkok there was a major explosion at an oil refinery that took five days to put out.

Singapore proved to be a good stopping off point to sample life in South East Asia during my first journey to Australia in 1995. My first impression was of the humidity, the worst I've encountered, it was necessary to take two or three showers a day.

Singapore remains engrained in the memory of the few British prisoners of war alive today. Historians still speculate whether the surrender in 1942 after just seven days of fighting cost more or less British lives. The Japanese brutalised allied prisoners for surrendering, a decision they considered dishonourable. Confirmation of the Japanese fanaticism and sense of dishonour in surrendering is reflected in the discovery of two Japanese soldiers on the Philippean island of Mindanao in 2005. They didn't know the war was over and had been hiding for the last 60 years. The soldiers aged 85 and 87, had been forbidden to surrender by their commander for fear of a court-martial.

Singapore was liberated in 1945 but their problems didn't end there. From 1948 they were engaged in a twelve-year guerrilla war for independence. Today there are no signs of armed conflict. A modern city has grown with tourists in mind. Singapore claims to be the cleanest country in the world thanks to strict laws against dropping litter. A fine and 12 hours of community service cleaning the streets is the punishment.

One of my top priorities was afternoon tea at the Raffles Hotel. The hotel survived the war and was used by the British and Japanese in turn. Its international reputation attracts many famous visitors. Some previous celebrity guests feature in many mounted photographs including Charlie Chaplin, Rudyard Kipling and Somerset Maughn. The hotel has taken a liberty with the wording of Kipling's quote. *"Feed at Raffles, sleep at Raffles"*. He actually wrote in his book, *"Sea to Sea, "The Raffles Hotel, where the food is as excellent as the rooms are bad. Feed at Raffles and sleep at Hotel L'Europe"*. I can't comment on the rooms as I stayed at the YMCA but I did enjoy the tea and cakes whilst watching the world go by.

My first stop on the 1999 tour was Bangkok in Thailand. The air pollution was so bad it took two days to acclimatise. In contrast to this was a great passion by the Thai people for fitness with a mass of continuous joggers around the lake in the city and hundreds playing football and volleyball nearby.

Thailand claims to be the "Land of Smiles", there are plenty when money changes hands. Whilst touring the King's palace visitors are encouraged to buy a small cage of birds on the pretext of giving the birds their freedom and bringing visitors good luck. The birds are in fact homing pigeons that come home to roost to be sold again the next day.

As the country is renowned for floating markets I took a day tour involving a motorised canoe on a local canal followed by a visit to a crocodile, snake and elephant farm. There was extra water traffic due to the King's birthday with many decorated water floats. The canoe wove in and out of rows of boats selling food, drinks, clothes, toys etc. The animal farms were entertaining but dangerous. A play enacted involved elephants and soldiers attacking and defending a fortress. It was very realistic with cannon shots and sword fights. In another event elephants played football - wearing coloured shirts of famous footballers. The crocodile show included trainers wrestling a crocodile and putting their head in its jaws and a snake charmer played with snakes crawling across his body.

The Rose Garden Resort featured a large auditorium that staged a series of performances including a Thai wedding, traditional dance and music and martial arts fights with swords and sticks. Elephants concluded the performance by carrying logs and stepping over spectators lying on the ground. Two months after my visit one of the elephants charged into the crowd killing two English tourists.

One attraction not sampled involved entering a large enclosure, the home of two enormous tigers. It's claimed that they are so tame that you could be safely photographed with them in the enclosure. They looked well fed but I decided not to take the chance of being added to their next menu. On the subject of food one aspect of traditional Thai cooking was the temperature the food arrived at your table. Although food is cooked at normal temperature it is allowed to cool before serving. Thai cooks believe that food is easier to digest when cool but at this temperature it would be returned to the kitchen in an English restaurant.

A full day mini bus tour took in the coastal resort of Pattaya, 100 miles south of Bangkok. It is one of the biggest and most popular tourist resorts. It was one of the few occasions I spent a few hours on the beach, as there was little else to explore. A 75 minute boat journey to an off shore island turned out to be a low point of the tour. Firstly we had to wade out to a small boat and were ferried to a larger boat. The further we travelled the rougher the sea became. The boat was bouncing about with many passengers being sick; we all dreaded the return journey. It proved worse for me as I slipped and gashed my wrist and ankle, my only injury of note in visiting 100 countries.

On returning to Bangkok I discovered there had been a major explosion at an oil refinery on the outskirts of the city. Five people were killed and many injured. It was the worst fire experienced in the city and raged for five days.

Religion plays a major role in the lives of the Thai males. Buddhism is followed by 95% of the population. The religion emphasises the potential of the individual to attain Nirvana without the aid of saints or gurus. Orange robed monks are common sights everywhere. Every Thai male is expected to become a monk for a short period between the time he leaves school and the time he starts a career or marries. Men under the age of twenty may enter the Sangha (Buddhist brotherhood), as novices. Their family earns great merit when he takes his robe and bowl. Traditionally the time spent in a Wat is three months starting in July, the Buddhist Lent. However, the current trend is to spend as little as a week or 15 days to accrue the merit as monks. There are about 32,000 monasteries and 200,000 monks in Thailand.

My visit coincided with the opening of the Sky Train Monorail System. There were teething problems with ticketing, instructions and access but I could see that it would be a great asset to the city and brilliant for sight seeing with its elevated view. The alternative method of travel is to ride in a three–wheeled motorcycle taxi. It is a real bone shaker, totally open and exposed to fumes from the other vehicles that surround you and though it is cheap and exciting, is not for the faint hearted.

An angry debate conducted in the press at that time concerned the film, "Anna and the King", a remake of the musical "The King and I ". That film was banned in Thailand as it was considered not a true representation of what happened. It is claimed that Anna made most of it up. The new film is also banned. The King it referred to was the ruler of Siam, which is now Thailand.

My childhood was coloured by the war in Burma, Malaysia and Thailand during World War II. These countries were often mentioned as my Uncle Sam Morris had been a Regimental Sergeant Major in the British Army fighting in the area. Fortunately he was never captured but had seen the conditions of allied prisoners held by the Japanese. Almost as a pilgrimage I took a full day visit to the bridge over the River Kwai, immortalised by the film of the same name. It was a bridge originally built by prisoners of war as part of the Japanese plan to build a railway that linked Bangkok and Rangoon in Burma. The bridge was subsequently bombed to destruction twenty months after it was finished, (not immediately after completion as shown in the film). To mark the site is the Jeath Museum that is a realistic construction of a prisoner of war hut. Monks now run the museum as a temple. The word "jeath" is made up of the first letter of the nations involved in building the bridge, Japan, England, America, Australia, Thailand and Holland. The word "jeath" was constructed as "death" was considered too emotive.

The railway was built through a jungle and across mountains, it was 260 miles long and 30,000 British prisoners were used to construct it, 8,500 of whom died. The Japanese also used 200,000 imprisoned labourers from India, China, Indonesia, Malaysia, Singapore, Burma and Thailand, of whom 80,000 died. A further 15,000 captured Dutch soldiers were also involved in the railway construction. Every year in the spring a weekend long sound and light show is held to commemorate the dead.

After touring the museum I walked across the single-track bridge over the River Kwai. There was an hour and a half rail journey north towards Three Pogoda Pass on the Burma border. My plan to stopover in Burma was scrapped due to the recent Burmese student hostage taking at the embassy in Bangkok. Diplomatic relations between Thailand and Burma had ceased following the attack and land journeys between each country were prohibited. The train terminated at Kanchanaburi following a winding journey through the jungle and along a mountainside track. The achievement of building the railway was incredible.

On returning from the Burmese border the final stop of the day tour was the main war cemetery where British and Dutch victims are buried. The epitaphs were very moving, the ages of the victims ranged from 19 to 51.

During the final two days in Bangkok I investigated the practice of purchasing a bride. Throughout the city elderly Western men are seen accompanied by beautiful young Thai women. In some instances they were married while others hired the women like Geisha girls in Japan. Agents approach single male tourists in bars and cafes with picture catalogues and details of age, language skills etc.

Another temptations for lone travellers are the massage parlours. I did enjoy a Thai massage; not the kind you may be thinking of, but a foot massage based on reflexology using oil, hands and a small stick that on occasions was rather painful. The massage parlour was on the main street on Siam Paza and was glass fronted onto the main pavement. For an hour and a quarter I enjoyed my first professional massage watching the people walking past who in turn were watching what was happening to me. I was surprised to discover that happy hour was adopted by shops in Bangkok where everything is reduced by 10% for an hour after an announcement over the loudspeakers. It didn't apply to massages.

I took a one-hour flight to Phnom Penh, Cambodia's capital on a plane with only a handful of passengers. I obtained a visa and hotel accommodation at the airport. The Harvic Hotel was a short drive from the airport. The traffic was dominated by Motos, 100cc motorbikes. They act as taxis with drivers and passengers not wearing helmets. The accident rate was high and you can often see four adults riding with a child sitting on the petrol tank. Apart from six principal main roads the side roads are rolled earth on top of rocks with frequent potholes. There aren't any streetlights on these side roads so walking at night is dangerous with the only light from open bars and shops. Large holes in the pavement expose deep drops into drainage sewage systems.

It is the only capital city I have visited where I was unable to locate at least one westernised shopping area of hotels and malls. A few tourist hotels were dotted around the city and tourists stick out like a sore thumb in their western clothes and only go out on tourist coaches under supervision. My usual old clothes made me less conspicuous but I was still approached by beggars. Children with missing limbs are victims of many of the mines planted by the Khmer Rouge during the war. Photos of Princess Diana's visit to Cambodia to lead the campaign against landmines were displayed across the city.

I spent the first day exploring near the hotel by foot. Places visited include the Wat Phonon; a hill temple built in 1373 that gave the city its name, the Royal Palace where the King resides, and the Silver Pagoda which has a floor made from silver and houses a 90kg solid gold Buddha and an emerald Buddha. As 90% of the population are Buddhists I wondered whether their beliefs had been questioned after the brutality of the Khmer Rouge.

I hired a car on the second day to visit the Toul Sleng Museum of Genocidal Crimes and the Killing Fields. The museum was formerly a high school that became the world's most infamous detention centre used by the Khmer Rouge under Pol Pot between 1975-79. During that time the Khmer Rouge undertook the worlds most extreme ethnic cleansing programme killing two million out of the countries seven million population. At least 17,000 men, women and children were tortured and killed in that detention centre alone. The cells remain intact along with some torture equipment. An enormous wall map of Cambodia made from human skulls was displayed. The majority of the educated classes were killed in a policy geared to give power to the peasants. The criteria for arrest and torture included knowing a second language or just wearing glasses. The ultimate aim was an uneducated working class who would do what they were instructed without question. The Khmer Rouge government ruled for four years. At the end of 1978 Vietnam invaded Cambodia and overthrew the Khmer Rouge.

My ten-mile journey to the Killing Fields took ninety minutes due to the poor road conditions; some holes were bigger than a car. Thousands were brought there to be murdered and buried in mass graves. Eighty-six graves containing 8,985 corpses have been uncovered. A large glass sided shrine in the centre of the graves contains hundreds of skulls. They are intended as a reminder that the genocide reign must never happen again. Some leaders of the Khmer Rouge are still to stand trial. One problem causing the delay is the lack of laws in Cambodia to address genocide. Local press reports show a group known as Khmer Seri are still active in the northern jungle and that an army post has been attacked and a soldier killed. Two of the main killers recently surrendered and live in a town in the north known as *"a retirement home for former Khmer Rouge killers"*. The Prime Minister Hun Sen, a former low ranking commander of the Khmer Rouge, initially fled to Vietnam in 1977 to avoid internal purges. He is under pressure from the UN to bring in an international panel of judges to ensure justice. It is feared that the two self confessed leaders will walk free.

Across the main streets of Phnom Penh hang large banners in English and the Cambodia language. The messages show the government's concern about the treatment of children and the rights of trade unionists and traders to belong to unions or business associations. Reports show that more than one quarter of children under 14 is employed in hazardous work and never go to school. Families encourage the use of child labour in order to survive and employers use children as cheap labour. A report on the problem featured an eleven-year-old boy who had been working in a brick factory. There was no training or protective equipment and when feeding in the clay, his hand got caught and his arm was ripped off. The family was matter of fact to the injury as they all worked in the brick factory and accepted injury as a strong possibility in their working day. It is against this background of family approval for child labour that the Government is trying to get children into school until they are at least fourteen years old. Other street banners draw attention to everyone's right for fair treatment and a call to ban all forms of discrimination. They also condemn the child sex trade and the sale of children into slavery.

Things that are taken for granted in most countries such as roads, is a major drawback for economic development in Cambodia. It does not matter if you are the Prime Minister or a lorry driver; the maximum speed you can travel is 10mph in most cases. Cyclists regularly overtake cars, even pedestrians sometimes. At the time of my visit only one road in the whole city was in good condition, the road from the airport to the city centre. There is a logic in this as visiting politicians, businessmen, national leaders etc can at least travel to and from the main government offices. If they go nowhere else they may think all the roads in the city are of a similar standard.

Phnom Penh is one of the most difficult countries ever encountered in terms of crossing the road. Although zebra crossings are marked, no one takes any notice. Virtually every road crossing has to be done on the jog. Motorcyclists are the main problem as they do not observe one side of the road but zigzag from side to side. The forecourts of petrol stations are treated as part of the road in order to cut corners. While a lot of cities in India and Africa have shantytowns and poor living conditions they have some areas where life is good. Deprived living could be seen across the whole city of Phnom Penh.

Television is a fascination, street bars overflow with men watching TV on the bar wall. Very few can afford such luxury at home. Even in my so-called luxury hotel there was no hot water although a flushing toilet was one benefit the majority are denied. The markets were crammed full with hardly any space to walk. *"Pa Pa buy this, Pa Pa buy that"*, rang out every few yards. Chickens were killed and dressed to order, "fresh" meat hung from rods exposed to all kinds of insects. Jewellery, watches and fruit and vegetable stalls all competed against each other for sales.

Cambodia has beaten the UK in the introduction of a novel form of entrepreneurial education. I came across a street containing former shops, each with its front shutters raised. They had been turned into classrooms, where 100 students sat outside at benches listening to the teacher holding a microphone and writing on a white board. They were working to instruction sheets chanting words by rote. These were in fact English classes at $2 an hour. The English language newspaper, "Cambodia Today" ran some of the classes and the students used copies of the newspaper as worksheets. There were at least thirty classes held simultaneously at one-hour intervals throughout the day. The government did not provide these business ventures and the teachers did not have to be qualified, many were probably moonlighting from their normal jobs. A great disappointment to me was the lack of newsagents and cake shops as the contents of both are considered luxuries. Children walk around selling newspapers mainly to tourists. According to reported figures only 48% of the population can read or write.

During the short flight back to Bangkok I reflected on my time in Cambodia. Was it really the most depressing country I have ever visited? Has the brutality of Pol Pot and the Khmer Rouge drained the people of their will to achieve? Is anarchy the result of the Pol Pot regime when city dwellers resort to hanging a known criminal from a lamppost in protest against a corrupt prison service? Are villagers adopting tactics of the Khmer Rouge when they take the life of a herbal doctor because they believe him to be a witch doctor? Can the Cambodian government, through legislation and investment in education, raise a once proud nation from its knees? My opinions may have been coloured by the fact that in 15 days time the rest of the world was to enter the 21st Century whereas Cambodia seemed trapped in the 19th Century in many respects. The current lack of negative news in 2005 hopefully means that they are making progress free from the Khmer Rouge.

On arrival back in Bangkok my priority was to secure a visa to go to Vietnam. I was fortunate that not many people wanted to visit Vietnam as just one person dealt with visas. The queue built up every time the clerk went walkabout, but eventually the visa was confirmed and a flight and hotel was booked for Ho Chi Minh City, (Saigon). Items not permitted into the country included newspapers, magazines or books that could affect the *"morale of the Vietnamese people"*.

I spent the first day on a walking tour made difficult by long street names and maps not to scale. Christmas songs could be heard and pictures of Father Christmas were displayed in shops. Four great philosophies and religions have shaped the spiritual life of the Vietnamese people, Confucianism, Taoism, Buddhism and Christianity. All four share the celebration of Christmas.

The next day I joined a guided tour of the city. The first visit was to the Reunification Hall, part of South Vietnams Residential Palace. Saigon surrendered to Russian made tanks on April 30th 1975 as they approached the Palace. One of those tanks is preserved on the lawn. The tour also took in the former US Embassy and the Notre Dame Cathedral where mass was taking place.

The War Crime Museum displayed horrific photographs of Americans torturing their opponents. American tourists were reminded of the folly of the US Administration under President Johnston. A group of GI's were shown holding the heads of guerrillas they had decapitated. A prisoner was shown dragged along the road strapped to an American jeep. Author Robert S McNamara wrote in his book *"In Retrospect"* - *The tragedy and lessons of Vietnam.* *"Yes we were wrong, terribly wrong. We owe it to future generations to explain why".*

Other rooms in the museum were devoted to photos of public protests from cities all over the world including London and New York. The USA mobilised 6.5

million young people who took part in fighting. Nearly eight million tons of bombs were dropped over Vietnam plus 17 million gallons of dioxins were sprayed over croplands. Nearly three million Vietnamese were killed and four million injured. Over 58,000 Americans died in the war. The 1973 Paris agreement ended America's role in Vietnam. Contrary to the agreement that ended the war the Northern Forces attacked across the 17th Parallel in January 1975. The take over by the Communists was soon followed by large-scale repression. Hundreds of thousands were imprisoned without trial in forced labour camps known as re-education camps. Over the next fifteen years thousands fled the country creating a flood of refugees, the boat people I had met in Hong Kong.

When America becomes involved in peace keeping crusades their record in Vietnam comes back to haunt them. Afghanistan and Iraq are two recent examples where their troops, supported by Britain are struggling to establish a stable and democratic society that benefits the majority of citizens. If America doesn't take the lead who will overthrow the Taliban or the Saddam Husseins of this world? Trade sanctions have been tried and failed. How long will it take and at what cost before Iraqi people can enjoy the freedom we have? The American government supported by allied forces has taken on this moral crusade and many believe they deserve the public's support.

A water puppet show was light relief after the museum. This is now unique to Vietnam. Performers controlling the puppets are unseen underwater. After lunch we visited Giac Lan Pogoda, China Town, Binh Toy Market, Ben Thank Market and Thien Han temple. The temple is dedicated to a Chinese goddess of the sea; Hong Kong tourists take this temple seriously. Its ironic that this was the case as Hong Kong authorities have been unwelcoming to Vietnamese refugees who fled to escape the Communist government. Our guide made four attempts to flee by boat, each time being captured and on the final attempt he was sentenced to two years imprisonment in a re-education camp. He had previously been a college lecturer but now earned a meagre wage as a tourist guide.

I found only one English speaking newspaper, the Viet Nam Niens. Such papers usually provide insights into a country and its lifestyle. This publication was hopeless, consisting purely of stories from abroad from Reuter's sources and announcements of visiting trade delegations.

The currency at that time was the Dong. There were no coins in use as one dollar was worth 14,000 Dong. By changing just $71 I became a Dong millionaire! As usual there was some kind of catastrophe or natural disaster during my visit. This time major flooding dominated the central Vietnam plains. The floods were not featured on the government TV channel but on CNN. A minor example of government censorship.

Departing Saigon there were reminders of the cities troubled past. Concrete hangers remain that were used for protecting planes from bombing attacks. Numerous anti aircraft guns remain facing upwards. My guide claimed that people in the South were grateful for the effort of the Americans in trying to prevent the Viet Cong Communist Forces taking over. Nearly all the fighting took place in the jungle bordering Laos and Cambodia. Only one bomb fell on Saigon during the whole war leaving the city virtually undamaged. It is ironic that the bomb landed on the American Embassy.

The triangular tour completed I returned to Bangkok for my flight home. On the flight to Paris an unusual thing happened. At 4am, with the plane in darkness except for floor lights and everyone sleeping, I was half awake when I felt a hand on my arm and an English voice say *"Excuse me - sorry"* I was in the aisle seat with two passengers to my left, one being a woman sitting next to the window. I was wearing an eye mask and so assumed it was the woman returning from the toilet. Standing up to remove my mask I felt a person's presence in the aisle, I took off my mask to find nobody there with everyone asleep around me. This was my first ghost/spirit experience. I cannot offer a logical explanation.

My third South East Asia visit was in March 2001. Problems started with a brief stopover in Colombo on the way to Malaysia and Borneo. This time dramatic events had taken place a week before my arrival causing disruption to my flights. The Sri Lankan Air Force had started bombing Tamil terrorists in the North and the British government had banned fund raising organisations linked to Tamil terrorists from operating in the UK.

After two days of sightseeing in Colombo I resumed my flight to Kuala Lumpur, the Malaysian capital. As the plane prepared to land the usual messages about luggage and mobile phones finished with *"Anyone caught carrying drugs in or out of Malaysia will be sentenced to hang. "Thank you for flying Sri Lankan Airlines". "Have a nice day"*!

Every city seems to claim to have something bigger than its neighbour, the recently opened Twin Towers in Kuala Lumpur claimed to be the world's tallest building. The two towers are side by side with a skywalk linking them between the 44th floors. Naturally everyone wants to boast of travelling up the twin towers and make the sky walk but the planners didn't anticipate this new tourist attraction and potential money-spinner as they only installed one lift to the skywalk that carries just 20 people at a time. At 9.30am and 2.30pm every day people queue for the 320 places in the lift for the next four-hour session. By a stroke of luck I was 30th in the queue at 1.30pm just as it was starting to form. Considering the mathematics of the exercise I queued for one hour then waited 15 minutes for my group to go up and down. Imagine the person 310th in the queue with 30 minutes outside in the blazing sun and a four-hour wait indoors! There is no charge for the journey although most of the queues consist of tourists expecting to pay a fee to ride up the worlds tallest building and 'walk the sky'.

If driving a taxi was used as a comparison between Malaysia and Borneo then Malaysia is top of the league as they observe speed limits, traffic lights and road markings. Borneo is relegated as their drivers drive on the horn, overtake on the inside and rarely consider pedestrians. Overtaking on the inside is very scary, on one occasion we were travelling at high speed inside a line of cars that were stationary as they had stopped for pedestrians – that in itself was a novelty. The car I was in braked at the last minute and skidded as four pedestrians came into view. They jumped for their lives.

The role of Britain in the development of Malaysia is significant. While Britain abused their power when exploiting the export of tin and rubber they did establish positives such as administration, legal and educational systems that have survived today. Allied troops also drove out the Japanese during World War II. A large memorial commemorates the sacrifice made by British soldiers.

After the war Malaysia gained independence from the UK in 1948 through political means. For the next twenty years they were engaged in civil war with the Chinese Communists. Having won that battle at great cost they have developed into one of the most successful economic countries in Asia. One prime example regards the growth of Kuala Lumpur. While other major cities get bigger and more congested Malaysia is building a new city thirty miles from the present capital linked by a super highway and a new rail system. Building a new international airport was the first step. Establishing a new administrative government centre with matching housing and recreation facilities is well advanced. The new city will be state of the art in terms of every public service.

Racial tensions still exist in Kuala Lumpur. During my stay two groups of Malaysians and Hindus attending a wedding parade and a funeral procession respectively, erupted into violence as they passed in the street. Six people were killed. Racial violence is still common place across Malaysia with additional problems between Indonesians and the Chinese.

I took a short flight to Kota Kinabalu in the Sabah area of Borneo to visit the Outward Bound Centre. A pleasant surprise was to see Colin and Sue Bailey's names in the visitor's book. They are exceptional supporters of Outward Bound and the Duke of Edinburgh's Award and live a few miles away from my home in Birmingham!

In the foothills on Mount Kinabala I felt privileged to see the worlds largest flower, the one metre wide rafflesia. I was recommended to stay at the nearby Sepilok Jungle Resort that houses the orang-utan sanctuary, one of only four in the world. The resort was the most beautiful and tranquil place I've ever stayed. I visited the orang-utans feeding area situated on a raised platform in the forest. The warden warned everyone not to touch the animals wandering freely. I got within a few feet of one of the animals holding my camera to my eye and waving the other hand to get his attention. Suddenly my hand was grabbed by the orang-utan and I was pulled to the ground, I was shocked by the strength of his grip. The warden came to my rescue giving me a good telling off. The orang-utan had lived up to the translation of its name the *"wild man of Borneo"*.

At the time I was grabbed by the orang-utan I was not aware that the same fate had befallen the American film star Julia Roberts when she visited Camp Leakey in 1997, the other orang-utan camp in Borneo. Just like me she had crouched down in front of an adult orang-utan holding out her hand to attract its attention. Her hand was grabbed and Julia Roberts was pulled to the ground, it took four wardens to drag away Kusasi, the "Orang-utan King". Unlike me she was not told off by the wardens as her support for the Programme and her celebrity status was highly valued. The words of Julia Roberts closely echoed my own - "it happened so fast, he was unbelievably strong". The future of the orang-utans in Borneo is at great risk as their natural jungle habitat is being destroyed by logging companies. The Rain Forests are being cut down to meet the world demand for Palm Oil, a key product in the production of lipstick and soap. There is a touch of irony about a beautiful woman such as Julia Roberts, who uses those products, campaigning on behalf of the orang-utans and their forests.

This was my first physical contact with apes although early in my travels I visited the Rock of Gibraltar and saw the resident apes. There is a legend that should the apes die out on the Rock that British rule would swiftly follow suit. The release of secret government documents in 2004 from the National Archives show that apes played a part in World War II when Allies were powering into German occupied territory. The Prime Minister, Winston Churchill, was very superstitious and worried about the ape populations decline. Writing to the British Colonies Governor in 1944 he demanded that, *"The establishment of the apes should be maintained"*. Files revealed his concern for their health, feeding habits and sex lives. Since 1944 there has been six monthly updates on the Barbary ape population which have become a matter of humour. Today there are at least 160 apes on the Rock, an impressive recovery since Churchill's memo.

Whilst relaxing at the Sepilok Jungle Resort the fighting continued in south Borneo which is administered by Indonesia. The indigenous Detaches, armed with spears and swords continued to wage their campaign of ethnic cleansing of the Madurese migrants. More than 500 had been killed and more than 50,000 had fled the country over the past two weeks. The Indonesian police killed protesting mobs of Detaches outside the parliament buildings. The Madurese were industrious and had taken over more land and secured the best jobs. The Detaches were jealous and started killing them by beheading. Government forces were trying to return order by attacking the Detaches. The New Sabah Times read, "*Detaches in vengeance burn police posts*".

Tourists were not allowed to travel south by road because of fighting. As I still wanted to see more of the country I caught an express boat down the coast to Bander the capital of Brunei. Brunei is the smallest country in the world but also one of the richest due to oil. Its ruler, the Sultan of Brunei, has an estimated £19 billion fortune. I had previously met him in England when I was Midland Regional Officer of the Award Scheme during his visit to RAF Cranwell in Lincolnshire. He was shopping for jet fighter planes. A qualified pilot, the Sultan co-piloted one of the jets. I was puzzled why he wanted more jets as Brunei's population is only 250,000 and they are not in a position to threaten other countries. As part of his visit he met with young people from the Duke of Edinburgh's Award and watched a range of activities demonstrated in a hanger. I was explaining the activities when I noticed that one of his shoelaces was undone so I discreetly mentioned this to a member of his staff. The group suddenly stopped and the most senior officer approached bent at 90 degrees and bent down further to tie the Sultan's lace. Apparently no citizen of Brunei must approach the Sultan with their head held level or higher than his. The massed ranks of the media captured this moment and it was in all the national papers the next day.

There was little of interest to see in Bander other than the Omar Ali Saifuddin Mosque, resplendent with its golden dome and positioned on an artificial lagoon. Brunei is a strict Muslim country with a dress code for women and no alcohol for men or women. Returning to the jungle resort that evening I had enjoyed a trouble free mini adventure with no signs of the Detaches and Madurese fighting. Once again I had survived and I returned home via Kuala Lumpur intact.

15

Three American Adventures

Triangles based on music, gambling, entertainment and obesity
Tributes to the Civil Rights Movement
Sporting welcome in Barbados
Life in Cuba under Castro

Three main tours of America have been undertaken. The first in March 1998 involved New York, Buffalo and Detroit. On its completion it was extended to take in cricket in Barbados and a study of politics and prostitution in Cuba. In November 1999 the theme was music, taking in New Orleans, Nashville and Memphis. In March 2000, the theme included gambling, crime and entertainment taking in Las Vegas, the Grand Canyon and San Francisco. There have been other stopovers in America including two in Los Angeles and two in Miami, both featured in other essays.

There were a number of dangerous situations encountered including the mugger with a revolving eye, the out of control hotel lift, a drug crazed street attacker and earth tremors in San Francisco. The one big disappointment was being the thickness of a wall away from an interview with Castro in Cuba.

A triangular format of focussing on three adjacent cities works well in such a large country as America. One of my most successful trips focussed on music. The first stop was New Orleans for the pleasure of traditional jazz, second was Nashville for country and western music and thirdly Memphis for blues and rock'n'roll. This triangle began in November 1999 with a flight into New Orleans.

New Orleans traditional jazz is so infectious; to visit the home of black music brought to America by the slaves from Africa was very uplifting and inspiring. The first priority was to go on a river boat shuffle on the Mississippi River with a traditional jazz band playing on deck as we dined. The second highpoint was to walk down Bourbon Street, the main area for jazz clubs, where street players entertain the queues of people waiting for entry to the clubs. Most outdoor cafes on the waterfront have a resident jazz band playing, creating a vibrant atmosphere. The top place to visit was Preservation Hall, considered one of the world centres of traditional jazz. On stage there is always a core band and a steady stream of musicians join in and jam all evening. Classics such as 'Tiger Rag', 'St Louis Blues', 'I Aint Got Nobody', 'Georgia On My Mind ' and of course 'When The Saints Go Marching In' get the feet tapping. It was a wonderful evening's entertainment.

A second popular night time activity are midnight walking tours around the French Quarter including Bourbon Street and Canal Street. The walks are based on stories of haunted buildings, vampires, voodoo and psychic magic. At the start of the ghost tour we were all issued with a bead necklace that had been blessed to protect us from evil spirits. Even though the ghost stories may have been embellished the historical facts about the French Quarter were interesting.

The preoccupation with the dead is partly attributed to the geography of the city. New Orleans is built on a swamp and the city is at least 2ft below sea level. They have an average of 5ft of rain a year and huge barriers have been built to reduce the occasions when the city floods. One result of the high water level is that graves cannot be dug without them filling up with water. The solution was to build rows of white mausoleums covered in carved angels and other symbols.

The cemeteries are the *"Cities of the Dead'* according to Mark Twain. Some of these mausoleums are more than 100 years old and are bought and sold on the open market like houses. The burial process works on the principal of 'one year and one day'. The body goes into the top of the structure, a sealed chamber whose design generates temperatures of 200 degrees Celsius in the summer, so speeding up the decomposition process. After a year and a day all that remains are the bones and they are pushed through the end wall and they drop onto metal crossbars in a chamber below. The small particles drop through the crossbars immediately while the rest drop over a period of time as they turn to dust. The bottom chamber, still above ground, retains the dust of bodies from the last hundred years. On the outside of the mausoleums are listed the names of all who were buried there. Some are wholly owned by clubs and societies. Families too poor to access such a tomb have to rely on cremation.

A taxi driver added to my knowledge of the burial rituals by explaining that the Catholic Church in New Orleans was traditionally opposed to cremation. This is being relaxed because coffins that have been buried in the ground have 'floated' to the surface because of the water base. Normally embalming fluid is applied to the body for the seven-day period of mourning but if too much is applied it slows down the decomposition of the bodies. The taxi driver said that his father was treated with too much liquid and he set like concrete and so would never turn to dust. He had to be cremated instead.

An afternoon was spent on a Cacun Boat sailing through the Louisiana Swamplands. Wildlife witnessed included alligators, snakes, egrets, white tailed deer, mink, and nutria. The boat got within touching distance of swimming alligators and a baby alligator was caught by the boatman and passed around for photographs.

New Orleans is known as the "Fat Capital" of America where 38% of the population is 20% overweight. Residents don't seem to mind their size and brag about the size of their meals and bodies. My visit coincided with Thanksgiving Day, America's big day rivalling Christmas in terms of importance for families. The day is dominated by turkey, including the traditional release of a sacrificial turkey by the President at the White House.

The Louisiana Superdome is worth a visit; it is the biggest covered stadium in America at that time. It seats 78,000 and the seats are moveable to alter the shape and size depending on the event held there. The Rolling Stones had attracted the biggest ever audience.

On reviewing this essay in September 2005 I was devastated to see the wreckage caused by Hurricane Katrina. Blithely I had mentioned that the city was built on a swamp and was below sea level, that graves couldn't be dug and how interesting it was to walk down Canal Street and praised the design of the Superdome. Pictures have shown that New Orleans is wrecked. The Superdome became the temporary home for thousands of people as their homes have been destroyed. There is anarchy on the streets as gangs of looters, gunmen and rapists have taken over the city. Food and water are in short supply as people fight over the little there is. Canal Street has become a canal, as have many of the streets in the city.

There can be no excuses for what has happened. Hurricanes are not uncommon in the area. A city built below sea level on a swamp will always face flooding. The sea barriers were not high or strong enough to cope with the volume of water generated by Hurricane Katrina. It will take years to rebuild the city and the lives of the people.

A short flight took me to Nashville, America's Country music home. On arrival I encountered a massive street protest outside Capital Hall against the new State Income Tax. On hearing my accent I was presented with a microphone linked to a live broadcast and asked to compare the proposed State Income Tax with the UK's Poll Tax. Taking the middle road I suggested that State Tax could support the disadvantaged. There were obviously not many disadvantaged people in the audience as I was booed loudly!

I visited many of the main country music venues including the Grand Old Oprey, the Ryman Theatre, the New Theatre and the Country and Western Hall of Fame. The Opreyland Hotel was also a major attraction. It is the biggest covered area hotel in the world with 2,000 rooms. You can take a canal boat trip around the rooms and the large convention centre.

My top musical experience was attending a show based on the life and music of Patsy Cline, her most famous hit being "Crazy". The visit concluded with a day in the Nashville County Criminal Court as an observer and then to my first ice hockey match. The court deals with people who attack civilians in the street while the ice rink provided a legal opportunity to attack opponents for entertainment.

It is ironic that Las Vegas places America near the top of the world's gambling league table while gambling is prohibited in some American states including Tennessee. Even the lottery is banned. On Saturday night's fleets of coaches leave Nashville and travel over the Mississippi border to visit casinos.

The next flight was to Memphis, the home of Elvis Presley and rock and roll. It is also the capital of Rhythm and Blues made famous by Jerry Lee Lewis, WC Handy, BB King, Carl Perkins, Howlin' Wolf and Otis Redding. No visit to Memphis is complete without a visit to Graceland, home of the late Elvis Presley, who clocked up 130 Gold Records and starred in 31 films. Elvis's grave is within the grounds at Graceland. It would have been a major problem had he been buried in a public cemetery as people still send flowers and visit his grave more than 20 years after his death.

Beale Street in the heart of Memphis is incredible; the sound of rhythm and blues and rock n' roll comes from every shop, restaurant and bar. The street is sealed off from traffic as people flood in to the live shows and to dance to street bands. Musical instruments signed by many of the great stars and old posters featuring great musicians hang on every restaurant wall. I chose a different restaurant every evening to enjoy a different band.

The most fascinating shop on Beale Street is Schwabs Dry Goods Store, 120 years old and still going strong. The inside of the shop is like stepping back in time and reminded me of similar shops in Walsall, 60 years ago. All the stock was just jumbled up, with minimal lighting, rock bottom prices and a lot of the goods on sale way beyond modern usage.

There were two other memorable contacts not linked to music. I visited the National Civil Rights Museum, formerly the Lorraine Motel where Dr Martin Luther King was assassinated by James Earl Ray in 1968, shortly after Dr King's famous "I have a dream" address to the world. Outside the museum I met a woman who had been evicted from the motel when it became a museum 11 years and 322 days previously. She lives on the pavement sleeping on her only possession, a sofa. She told me that she was protesting as she thought Dr King would rather the money have been spent on the poor rather than a museum. The museum traces the struggle of black people to gain equality and features a segregated bus, café, and washrooms etc. I wonder if six years later she is still maintaining her protest?

The significance of the bus in the museum was highlighted by the death of Rosa Parks. Dr Martin Luther King Jnr. rightly remains known as the person who led the fight to end segregation between black and white Americans but it was Rosa Parks who launched the first mass civil rights action. It started in Montgomery on December 1st 1955 when she refused to give up her seat on the bus to a white passenger. Refusing to be treated as a second class citizen as a black American she was arrested, convicted and fined $10. Black residents boycotted the bus system in protest and were led by Rev Martin Luther King, who at that time was only known within his community. The boycott lasted 381 days and ended when a US Supreme Court decision ended the law that separated whites and blacks when using public transport throughout the southern states of America.

Rosa Parks was persecuted for having led the fight, lost her job and received death threats. She eventually moved to Detroit with her family where she received the respect she deserved, a school and road were named after her. President Bush's words should be added to the display board on the bus in the Memphis museum. "Rosa Parks was one of the most inspiring women of the 20th century. She will always have a special place in American history".

The second contact was extremely unnerving, it was a Sunday afternoon and I was walking down a deserted side street when a man approached. He wanted money and his hard luck story involved revolving one of his eyes. He had been stabbed in the eye during a card game and was playing on sympathy to get money. Fearful that I might become the next stab victim I pretended to see someone in the distance and shouted to the imaginary person to wait for me. Fortunately it fooled the would-be robber and I was safely away.

The American triangle undertaken in March 2000 was to Las Vegas, the Grand Canyon and San Francisco. The flight into Vegas airport was spectacular, the surrounding desert and rock formations giving the impression of landing on the moon. On arrival at the airport you are immediately confronted with targets for your money. Slot machines are everywhere, in the luggage retrieval area and even before you reach customs officers. The same approach is adopted in hotel lobbies before reception, in theatres before reaching your seats. Flashing signs advertise big wins on the slot machines, sometimes as much as one million dollars. The approach was so brash and exploitative that I set myself a target to resist every slot machine that I encountered during my visit. It was a target I was to achieve.

Apart from the constant pressure to gamble the first thing that caught my attention was the lack of tourists from abroad. Almost all the visitors were American with just a few Japanese. The second thing was the lack of children; it was a city designed for adults. The third observation related to obesity. While the people of New Orleans are proud of their title the "Fat Capital" of America, a large number of Las Vegas tourists from all over America were also obese which makes America the "Fat Country" of the world. This is not meant as a criticism, it's a fact recognised by US politicians and doctors and is a matter of national concern.

Theatre restaurants were very impressive with top quality entertainment. I chose a different show each night and attended the opening night at Caesar's Palace of "Smokey Joe's Café", starring Gladys Knight. In the audience were Stefi Graf and Andre Agassi. The show at the Flamingo featured the New York Radio City Rockettes. At the Stratosphere was "Viva Las Vegas", a tribute to Elvis and Michael Jackson. In the light of Michael Jackson's trial in 2005 will such tributes be more or less popular?

Casinos and hotels also provide entertainment themes to attract customers. Treasure Island Casino featured a battle between two ships complete with cannons and special effects. Large crowds gather to see the show repeated during the afternoons and evenings, one of the ships sink at the climax.

Casino visitors can attend classes to learn the basics of the various games. I was particularly interested in the craps table. In 1966, whilst en route to Italy with a group from the Twenty Two Club, we stopped off at the main casino in Monte Carlo. Despite not understanding the rules I bought £5 of chips and placed a number of small bets. Players around the table took turns to roll the dice continuing until the banker won. I was eventually presented with the dice that I rolled. After five straight rolls of the dice without the banker winning I noticed the pile of chips on many of the numbers growing higher. The crowd around our table grew bigger and more bets were placed. I continued to throw winning dice, apparently I was "on a roll!" players were leaving the table with large piles of chips to cash in. Eventually I threw numbers that meant the bank finally won. I estimated that some of the players won thousands of francs. Although I had failed to break the bank of Monte Carlo I had at least boosted my modest £5 to £20.

A great day out from Las Vegas was a coach trip to the Grand Canyon. It involved a three-hour drive through the desert to a small Indian reserve on the top of the West Ridge of the Canyon. We were served a meal of chicken, rice and beans cooked by our Native American hosts. They no longer live at the reserve and earn a living entertaining tourists before they return each evening to their modern homes in the city. All that remains of the traditional Indian culture were the arts and crafts made for the benefit of the tourists and for profit. The Grand Canyon was awesome. Standing on the top of the steep red stone cliffs provided a picture of the immense power of the forces of nature. Helicopters swooped along the bottom dwarfed against the massive sides of the Canyon. The Canyon is 277 miles long, 18 miles across at the widest point and has a maximum depth of 6000ft. The Colorado River runs along the valley.

One of the most memorable characters on this trip was our coach driver whose hypertension was not very reassuring. Throughout the six-hour journey he hardly stopped talking over the intercom. Learning about the passing landmarks was interesting but we also had a crash course how to play the slot machines and how to win at Blackjack. His gambling advice was obviously not very good as he told how his wife had tried to kill him for losing their $45,000 life savings. She had thrown him out so he was now living in a motor home. The more irate he became about his wife the more involuntary his arm movements became, very disconcerting whilst travelling at 60mph through the desert.

The third leg of the tour was to San Francisco. I stayed at the Nuro Hotel in Geary, a seedy area with people living in doorways. Beggars were very aggressive; some even came into restaurants pestering the customers. Alcohol and drug abuse is a big problem with street dwellers. I was walking down a street in the early evening following two men who were just a few paces ahead. Suddenly a wild-eyed, long haired, bearded man leapt out of a doorway and ran shouting at them. He knocked them both to the ground and ran off still shouting. I was lucky not to have been attacked.

The Nuro Hotel was being renovated, but at $40 a night it was good value. The lift was very old and scary with a large metal door that had to be slid manually. I was travelling down with a woman passenger when six big young men got on at the floor below with enormous rucksacks. As the lift started to go down we suddenly accelerated which the woman commented on. Jokingly, inspired by fear, I shouted that we'd all better jump in the air before we reached the bottom. Without thinking we all jumped in the air before the lift came to a sudden halt. It finished 3ft below the ground floor level and we all clambered out on our hands and knees. Perhaps without the jump we might have plummeted through to the basement floor and all killed or injured.

A highlight was a boat trip to Alcatraz. A tour of the cells was enhanced by personal tape recordings featuring former famous inmates such as Al Capone and Machine Gun Kelly. Our guide, a former warder was very dismissive of films made about Alcatraz. The central character in the "Birdman of Alcatraz" never kept birds in prison, although he did breed them at home before arrest and he did learn to read and write in prison. In reality he was a *"suicidal homicidal maniac"* who spent most of his time in isolation, as he was a danger to prisoners and staff. There was only one successful escape from Alcatraz, although three escaped there's no evidence that they survived the swim to shore. Nothing has been heard of them and they are presumed drowned.

Earthquakes are a constant and major concern in the city; it was virtually destroyed in the 1906 earthquake. The rubble from damaged buildings was laid on the beach area with houses, shops etc built on the landfill. All new buildings have the ability to withstand high-level earthquake activity. The Golden Gate Bridge can move 27ft sideways in severe weather conditions, (a 100mph gale). There is a weekly earthquake report; there were 22 earthquakes during my weeklong stay, all around 2.4 on the Richter scale.

A coach tour to the Napa Valley took in three major wine making areas. It was a contrast to be calm and relaxed after the fear of walking around some parts of the city. The small town where we stopped for lunch was an oasis of tranquillity. I was surprised to discover that all grapes produce a clear white liquid irrespective of the colour of their skin. A speedy process of crushing the grapes produces White wine with their skins skimmed off. Red wine is left in the vat with its skins; the red colour comes from its skins fermenting. Red wine takes at least 18 months to process compared to the 6 months needed for white. Champagne is made from white wine with gas added to give sparkle. The Napa Valley proved to be an ideal place to conclude my tour.

In March 1998 New York was my first stopping point. The following weeks would take in Buffalo and Niagara Falls, Detroit, Brighton, Miami, Barbados and Cuba. My base in New York was the YMCA Vanderbilt which was not only cheap but ideally placed for Times Square and Broadway, (a 20 minute walk), the United Nations Building, (a five minute walk) and a ten minute walk to Grand Central Station. The YMCA is infamous for accommodating the killer of John Lennon who spent the night preparing for the assassination the next day.

One of my priorities was to visit a Jazz Club in Harlem but I was advised that no taxi would enter Harlem after dark for fear of being attacked. The YMCA was able to offer a place on a tour that would start in the afternoon and end with a meal at a Jazz Club in Harlem in the evening. The afternoon tour took in the Bronx and there were stops off at Central Park, St John the Divine Cathedral and the Apollo Theatre, where all the top stars have appeared including Buddy Holly. The final stop was the Church where Nelson Mandela, Mother Teresa and Princess Diana met for the only time together.

Thanks to the protective name of the YMCA, we made it successfully to the Jazz Club deep into Harlem. One of the great entertainers of all time, Ray Charles, had appeared at the club at a time when he was trying to establish himself. There was a basic four-piece band that was joined by others as the evening progressed to engage in a big jam session. Beef, beans and rice was served as we soaked up the electric atmosphere. It proved to be a tremendous evening in an area that many Americans would never dream of going to because of the reputation for crime.

Day two involved a tour of Broadway and Times Square. Radio City was impressive; the theatre seats 6,000 and is home to The Rockettes, the famous dance troop. Preparations were under way for the visit of President Clinton the next day to celebrate the 75th anniversary of Time Magazine. Many of the people featured on previous front covers were invited including Mohammed Ali and Sophia Loren. The technology of the moving stage on hydraulic rollers was years ahead of its time and it had been was copied by the US Navy in the design of the decks on aircraft carriers. The Rockettes were rehearsing for the next night and one of them posed for pictures and answered questions.

The most efficient way to see New York is via a tourist bus; a pass will cover two days of journeying. Key Places visited include The Empire State Building, Greenwich Village, Soho, Chinatown and Canal Street. As a fan of the TV show, "Hill Street Blues", I was able to see some of its featured sites. The World Trade Centre still bore some scars of the 1996 terrorist attack; work was still ongoing to strengthen the building. Little did I know that the next devastating terrorist attack would take place on September 11th 2001.

I took a ferry to the Statue of Liberty and Ellis Island. There were very few tourists at this time of year so queues were short. I climbed the 254 steps up 22 floors to the top of the Statue of Liberty. The climb was worth the effort to see a panoramic view of New York from the statue crown. The only surprise was discovering the statue wasn't a casting or a sculpture but a model made from copper plate. Metal straps and rivets held it all together.

The museum on Ellis Island contains the records of all the immigrants that landed there seeking a new and better life. Immigrants were inspired to travel to America by the following words written in the book, "The Declaration of Independence", that is held in the left hand of the Statue of Liberty. *"Give me your tired, your poor, your huddled masses yearning to breathe free…"* 17 million immigrants answered that call during the period 1892-1954. It is estimated that 40% of the current American population of 100 million can trace their ethnic roots from the records held in the pedestal of the Statue of Liberty or on Ellis Island.

Other highlights of my stay included a tour of the United Nations Building and sitting in the General Assembly where so many mammoth issues have been debated and voted upon for many years. A show on Broadway was a priority and I was able to get a ticket for an afternoon matinee of the hit musical "Chicago" at the Shubert Theatre. The theatre, built in 1913, has hosted some of the great entertainers of all time including Barbara Streisand, Al Jolson, Paul Robeson, Rex Harrison and Fred Astaire. As a sports buff a visit to Madison Square Garden was a must.

Travellers will no doubt recall occasions when you meet someone interesting while abroad and end up exchanging addresses with the invitation to 'call anytime'. Only once have I taken up such an offer. While in Istanbul I met two sisters Paula and Mary Rose from New York. They were such an interesting couple that I telephoned them when I arrived and we met for a meal at the YMCA and had a wonderful three hours of non stop talking about our respective travels abroad.

My final excursion took me to Buffalo near the Canadian border to experience one of the great natural wonders of the world, Niagara Falls. The sense of power from the cascading water and the noise as it crashed below was tremendous. I took the opportunity to enter the passageways behind the falls as well as to sail up to the falls in a tourist boat. The plastic mack that was issued to protect my clothes from the spray became a valuable addition to my luggage for future travels.

On returning to New York I then travelled to Detroit to meet up with my daughter Leigh who was working as a nanny in Brighton for a year. Her host family, Ken and Cheryl Lingenfelter, kindly invited me to stay. The weather in New York had been quite mild but in the Mid West there was severe weather with extensive flooding in some states and 6ft of snow in others. Despite the change in weather I still visited a number of places of interest, fitting them around Leigh's timetable of looking after four children (including five-year-old triplets!) A massive undertaking which she completed with great skill. The Henry Ford Museum displayed the limousine in which John F Kennedy was travelling when he was assassinated. A trip to the theatre reminded me of home. The play, "Murder by the Book" was set in London.

At the time of my visit the big issue was President Clinton, Monica and the cigar. All the public opinion polls showed that 70% of the population supported Clinton and didn't care about his relationship with women. Yet in every conversation I had with Americans in various cities, they were all highly critical of Clinton and thought he should resign. Was it a coincidence that I only spoke to critics or were the polls wrong? Were the same people changing their opinion when challenged to justify their support for Clinton?

Key political issues of the time were the treatment of Native American Indians, the constitutional rights of citizens to carry arms, the issue of fascism, particularly among young people still influenced by Hitler and finally the move to ban tobacco. Events focussing peoples minds included the Columbia School massacre when 13 were shot dead. More recently the atrocity on the Indian reservation when 17 year old Jeff Weise, who was obsessed with Hitler, armed himself with two handguns and a shot gun and indiscriminately shot 10 teachers and pupils as he walked through Red Cake School before killing himself. With respect to the tobacco, Congress are still trying to pass a bill to declare tobacco as an illegal drug for those under 18 years of age. The implications to cigarette makers are enormous, as they have already faced a number of multi-million dollar lawsuits due to cancer.

After the three-day stay my plan was to fly to Barbados. Leigh drove me to Detroit airport in driving snow. Due to the snow the 30-seat plane was stuck on the runway for three hours waiting for a de-icing truck to spray the plane. It arrived in Cleveland three hours late and my flight to Miami had gone so I was diverted back to Newark (New York) for an alternative Miami flight. On arrival in Miami I found the flight to Barbados had gone so I had to book into the Airport Hotel for an overnight stay.

Whilst sitting in Newark airport they announced that anyone giving up their seat for a later flight would receive $500. For fear of missing the Barbados flight I did not take up the offer. As I still missed my Barbados connection I had also missed out on $500. A totally frustrating and expensive day.

I finally arrived in Barbados at 6.30pm. The heat was tremendous even though it was dark 15 minutes later. The "Barmy Army" had just arrived on a London flight; they all seemed very reasonable, unlike their reputation. I chatted with the Chairman and his wife. The "Army" had originated in Australia four years ago whilst I was in Sydney.

A Duke of Edinburgh's Award colleague met me at the airport with an invitation to the British Embassy for a drinks reception with the English and West Indian Test players. After the reception I had a short drive around the south coast to the Croton Inn about 100 yards from an expansive beach. The hotel was basic, situated on a major road with lots of traffic noise, but adequate for my needs. I was told that there was currently a drought but that night there was a tremendous storm, so I had experienced snow, heat and tropical rain all within 36 hours!

On the first day of the Test Match I had to pay over the odds for a ticket from a tout. The second day I located the ticket office inside the stadium. In the office I spotted Geoff Boycott, the former England batting star and started a conversation with him while he walked into the Weekes, Worral and Walcot Stand. I followed him and sat in a spare seat to watch the last two sessions without charge. The match finished in a draw when rain on the fifth day prevented any play with England in a strong position. Despite vast amounts of alcohol being consumed the behaviour of all the supporters was excellent and the atmosphere brilliant. There was not a trace of racism, lots of friendly banter as the matches' fortunes ebbed and flowed. It was typical of the warm welcome and friendship extended by the majority of Barbados residents I encountered.

The one area of Barbados life I found dangerous was travelling by local mini-bus. They were licensed to hold 11 but the least I experienced was 19. The drivers travelled at ridiculous speeds, racing in and out of the town centre and along the coast road. A bus packed with such a number could cause massive injuries in an accident. The single decker official buses were also packed solid. They just keep piling them on until everyone is packed like sardines. When passengers wanted to get off the bus about a dozen had to vacate to allow them to alight at their stop.

Back at the Croton Inn, fish was the main attraction; freshly caught Marlin or Flying fish served up with rice and vegetables with entertainment provided by the resident jazz band. Another treat was to walk along the golden sand after breakfast under a blazing sun, a far cry from the snow in the American Mid West.

The final destination of my tour was Cuba. At the Barbados airport the England cricket team and media commentators were mixed in with the tourists. It must have been frustrating for highly paid sports stars to queue like us mere mortals. Due to international and political restrictions I had to fly via Miami and Cancun in Mexico to Havana. Tourism in 1998 was a major source of income for Cuba. Since the collapse of the Soviet Union Cuba had lost the massive financial support that had allowed it to develop under Castro. The ten-year blockade of Cuba by the USA in an attempt to overthrow Castro had almost crippled the economy. In view of the need to encourage tourists the treatment I received at the airport was draconian. A burly female security guard with a moustache took a dislike to me and gave me the full treatment, my worst airport welcome.

Cuba is so desperate for foreign currency that it is the only country I have visited where it is not necessary to change money into the local currency, (Pesos). All transactions are carried out in dollars, as Pesos are worthless elsewhere in the world and can not be changed back to sterling or dollars.

A mini bus took me from the airport to the Hotel Vedado which, like many buildings in Cuba, looked rough on the outside but was fine inside. A Cuban band was playing in the bar creating a welcoming atmosphere, my room was clean and tidy and provided my best nights sleep in a week after my noisy ground floor roadside room in Barbados. The roads from the airport into Havana were wide, tree lined and in good condition. The traffic was light despite a city population of 2.5 million. It turns out that the city has fewer cars per head of population than any other major city of the world and reflects the poor standard of living. The majority of cars were old and battered.

I booked a tour of Havana and found that I was the only passenger. The guide took quite a lot of assurance before believing that I was a genuine tourist and not a member of the Secret Police. One of my many questions related to home ownership. The guide explained that if a young man or woman wanted their own home they would have to leave their job for two or three years and join a housing construction team working for no pay. Once the apartment was built they would return to their normal job. 10 per cent of their salary would then be paid to the government for the next ten years. Although they would eventually pay for the home they would not be allowed to sell it, as it still belonged to the government. They could swap homes without money changing hands but if they moved abroad or died the home remained the property of the government. This was a tough example of life under Castro's Marxist regime.

Castro is rarely seen in public, his home is a closely guarded secret and his attendance at an event is never publicised in advance except for two national events each year. There have been numerous attempts on his life and he is getting quite old. It is believed that Cuba, one of the few remaining Marxist States in the world is nearing its end. On the death of Castro there will no doubt be a power struggle that will hopefully restore democracy, boost the economy and the standard of living for the people. While visiting the Criminal Court I was just the thickness of a wall away from talking with Castro, his secretary tried but failed to set up a meeting as I waited outside his office on the top floor of the court building. Eventually the door flung open and Castro and his bodyguards marched past without a look in my direction.

The city is made up of a combination of old colonial buildings in decay and new hotels being built. Some of the lavish buildings of the pre-revolution era were handed over to Castro's associates, a number have become embassies. Some streets look like areas of Beirut in decay; others look clean, modern and spacious.

One of the most depressing results of the poverty is how desperate people will use their bodies as a saleable commodity. Children and adults approach persistently as you walk down the street. The first time I was approached by a lad of about eight I was left in a state of shock when he asked, *"Do you want a blow job mister?"*

Religion plays a smaller part in the lives of Cubans than in other Caribbean countries. It is estimated that only 5% of the population follow the Christian faith whereas in Barbados, the churches are packed, they have gospel programmes on the radio with passionate sermons quoting the bible. This is typical of poor countries where religion gives hope and support but this was not apparent in Cuba. It would be interesting to know if this is a result of Marxism. Hopefully the Pope's recent visit has given a boost to the Catholic Church in Cuba.

It is ironic that one of the most respected people in Cuba was the American author Ernest Hemingway. His home was turned into a museum on his death and the bar where he drank is a major tourist attraction. Despite the ten-year blockade by the USA, Hemingway is considered a hero; I was unable to find out why.

A full day mini coach tour of the flat lands and the mountainous areas around Havana was undertaken. On leaving Havana we passed through one of the prosperous suburbs where the houses are very grand and well kept. There was a policeman in a booth at every street corner and often an armed soldier in front of individual houses.

Out in the country the main crops are tobacco, sugarcane, and seeds for making rum. They are few mechanical aides such as tractors; the ground is ploughed by oxen and harvested by hand. The first stop was a factory making cigars. The process involved firstly stripping the main leaf vein from the leaf. The best quality cigars are rolled by hand although mechanical methods are used for cheaper brands. Rows of people sat on benches rolling the leaves into cigars, trimming them to length and attaching a name band. It turns out that dusky maidens rolling leaves with their thighs is a myth. They do however stack the flattened leaves on their thighs.

Next was the rum factory. The process starts with small fruit like a blackcurrant that ferments for six months in barrels before alcohol and spices are added. Further fermentation can take seven years for the strongest and smoothest rum. We then stopped for a lunch of pork, rice and beans and were entertained by Cuban musicians and dancers. This was followed by a drive to a mountain cave network that was the home of Cuban Indians hundreds of years ago. The caves led to an underground river where boats completed the journey.

On returning to Havana I tried an alternative hotel for my evening meal. Half way through the meal a guy at the next table with two young women started a conversation, could one of the women sit with me because he was leaving and if she were to sit alone the police would remove her. We tried to converse, she in Spanish, unsuccessfully. Apparently she wanted to spend the night with me-which I declined. I carried on with my meal and she sat silently. A few minutes later two more of her "friends" joined the table. The Manager came over and appeared to threaten to throw them out. They came to some sort of compromise and the three sat chatting to each other, checking out new entrants in the restaurant and ignoring me. You can probably guess what their employment was.

I spent the last day on a walking tour of Havana, first stop the Capitolio that was the Parliament building before the Revolution. It is the replica of the White House in Washington. The main chamber remains as it was before the dictator

Batista, an army sergeant, took-over in 1929. Elections were reintroduced in 1993 and the Parliament building is once again in use with somewhat limited powers. Next stop was the Museo de la Revolucion - commemorating the Castro led Revolution of 1959 when he and Che Guevara overthrew the Batista dictatorship. The original Landrover Castro drove into Havana is displayed with a tank, a boat, improvised farm tractors adapted as fighting vehicles and two aeroplanes. A video showed the recent return of Che Guevara's remains and of other freedom fighters from Bolivia. Che volunteered to join the Bolivia Independence struggle after freeing Cuba; he was killed in action. The video pictures of the military funeral were incredible and the precision marching based on the John Cleese walk impressive.

Reflecting on my stay I had found the Cubans reluctant to discuss their life under Castro for fear of the Secret Police. Many opponents have been jailed without trial for opposing Castro. The lack of religion, with only 5% of the population churchgoers, appears to have undermined the moral standards of behaviour. Prostitutes frequently approached me; research shows that young women turn to this lifestyle to ensure a basic standard of living. The next Revolution will hopefully be based on democratic grounds that will release a spiritual uplifting to the population and strengthen the Church's influence. Castro may have raised the standards of education and health but at what cost to the suppression of the human spirit that requires a massive budget to maintain control through the Army and Police? Just as Marxism collapsed in Russia so must it collapse in Cuba. Surely Cuba can no longer stand-alone and must introduce free elections to give its people hope. Could you survive the Cuban lifestyle? Would you become a revolutionary and fight for freedom if you lived in Cuba?

On arriving home I once again thanked my lucky stars for surviving a number of dangerous situations but even more that my home was in England not Cuba.

16

Around the World in 40 days

Tamil Terrorist attack in Colombo
The Vicar eaten by cannibals in Fiji
Ringing the Peace Bell in Hiroshima
Adrift in the China Sea

In March 2002 I undertook my own "Around the World" tour inspired by the writings of Jules Vernes and his Phileas Fogg character that took 80 days. Using a circular air ticket costing £820 I journeyed to Vancouver, Los Angeles, Fiji, Auckland, Christchurch, Melbourne and Hong Kong. Taking advantage of linking domestic flights and sailing's I added Japan, Macau, Sri Lanka and United Arab Emirates to the journey.

During the 40-day tour I encountered the following events and situations:

The vicar who was eaten by cannibals in Fiji leaving only his shoe. The oppression of Maoris and Aborigines by invading European settlers. Comparing Kamikaze pilots with Middle East modern day suicide bombers. Ringing the Peace Bell in Hiroshima to remember sacrifices made by Allied Forces. A cyclone in Fiji and a typhoon in Japan. A helicopter landing on Mount Cook. Drifting in a damaged turbojet in the China Sea off the coast of Macau. Hiding under my bed whilst under attack from Tamil Terrorists. A desert safari and dune buggy racing in Dubai and the day that never happened, March 10th 2002.

Time in respect to GMT/day/night/local time, produced some unusual situations during the circular tour. Departing from Heathrow at 5pm in darkness the plane passed through a period of daylight before arriving in Vancouver at 6pm as night fell again. The actual flying time was nine hours but in that time two periods of blackness and one of day light were experienced. Even more unusual was the flight from Los Angeles to Fiji that left at 10.30pm on the 9th March and arrived in Fiji at 5.15am on the 11th March. The flight was ten hours but by going through the International Date Line the 10th March never happened. I hope I didn't miss anything important!

During this trip I would experience all four seasons, the first being winter. The weather in Vancouver was bitterly cold. The city is unique within Canada as it is at sea level and experiences only two small snowfalls a year of around two-three inches that usually melts in a few days unlike the rest of the country. Travelling just 20 minutes out of Vancouver to Grouse Mountain there was 6ft of deep snow with hundreds of snowboarders and skiers in action. To reach the snow line there was an eight-minute sky lift cable car ride. One of the treats at the top was a motorised sleigh ride.

A guided city tour displayed a clean, well-planned and courteous place. I was surprised to discover a cricket ground at the edge of the harbour at Stanley Park. The small contoured ground was typical of an English village ground. The world's greatest batsman, Sir Donald Bradman, once played there describing it as one of the most picturesque grounds he'd ever played on. I imagine a few balls were hit into the harbour in that match!

The three-day stop over concluded with a visit to the Provincial Court to witness Canadian justice in action. The start of a trial involved a motorist charged with murder. The bizarre background to the trial can be found in the Crime and Punishment essay.

The next stop was a two-day visit to Los Angeles. March was a quiet time so I was able to explore Universal Studios and Disneyland without much queuing. I enjoyed King Kong, the 8.3 Earthquake, Star Wars, Splash Mountain, Thunder Mountain Railroad and the Flintstones Show. The whole day was the most exhilarating entertainment of its kind I have ever experienced.

My flight to Fiji was delayed due to a cyclone passing over the island. When it was considered safe to fly I arrived in Nadi at 5am in driving rain and the temperature in the 80s, what a contrast to the Vancouver snow. The damage from the cyclone was evident with uprooted trees lying in the roads leading from the airport. A stretch of palm trees on the beach had been completely uprooted. The cyclone had passed by the end of the day so I was able to enjoy three days of pure relaxation. I experienced the Fijian Meke Show (traditional dances and singing by villagers), the Fijian fire walking ceremony and a beach BBQ featuring a Polynesian Dance Show. There were five different restaurants to cater for all tastes, five night clubs, beach massage, horse riding, scuba diving, miniature golf, archery, canoe racing, spear throwing, touch rugby and children's clubs. I found it difficult to distinguish between men and women employees, at the hotel, particularly from the rear as they wore similar hairstyles and skirts.

During a museum visit I was intrigued by a single shoe belonging to the Rev Thomas Baker that was displayed in a glass case. The Reverend Baker had been eaten by cannibal's 136 years ago. In October 2003 Fiji publicly apologised for killing and eating the British Missionary. Rev Baker had offended the local Chief by touching his head so his punishment was being roasted and served with chutney, herbs, fruit and vegetables. His bones were broken to provide marrow and his clothes and shoes were also cooked with the exception of his one shoe. Perhaps it was too tough, hence the expression, *"as tough as old boots!"*

My next flight was to New Zealand in the luxury of first class, one of the rare occasions I have been upgraded. The extra space, special food and wine, personal television and gifts made it a very pleasurable experience. On arrival in Auckland I had a quick dash to the domestic airport for a connecting flight to Christchurch. Arriving at 8pm I was shocked to find that there wasn't a spare bed in the whole city. After visiting 100 countries it remains the only time I couldn't find accommodation from an airport information desk. Facing the prospect of a five-day stay on a bench at the airport during the England v New Zealand Test match was a shattering thought. An airport officer came to my rescue after phoning friends for ideas. A bed was found at Meychelle Manor, 25 miles outside Christchurch and a £25 taxi ride away. It proved to be a wonderful location, part of a deer and ostrich farm. There were only four guestrooms with breakfast served with the owner's family. The speciality was venison sausages with bacon, eggs and tomatoes. I hired a car to avoid taxi fares to and from the Test Match and used the car for touring after the game. If you're visiting New Zealand for a sporting event be sure to book ahead to guarantee a hotel bed.

England won one of the greatest Test Matches ever; records were broken every day. Hussain was the first day star with a 100. Hoggard the second day star with seven wickets. Thorpe with a double hundred and Flintoff with 147 the third day stars. Caddick was the England fourth-day top performer with six wickets but, even though England won, the star of the day was Nathan Astle with the fastest double century in history of cricket.

An anti-clockwise tour of the South Island took in Arthur's Pass, Greymouth, Hokitika and to the Fraz Josef Glazier for an overnight stop. I took my first ever helicopter flight and flew around Mount Cook and landed in the snow on the mountaintop. At take off in the valley it was in the 80s, at the top, it was freezing The scenery was spectacular as we swooped down through the valleys where "Lord of the Rings" was filmed.

The journey by road then continued via Lake Paringa, Haaste Pass to Wonaka, Linda's Pass, Omarama, Twizel, Lake Tekapo, Farlie, Pleasant Point and the sea side resort of Timaru.

The New Zealand government has made major progress to address the plight of the Maoris. Like the North American Indians and the Australian Aborigines the Maoris were thrown off their land and their numbers disseminated by

European diseases. Once the sole occupants they now only represent 10% of the 10.3 million population, a figure dwarfed by 44.5 million sheep. The government recently made a public apology for their treatment, paid millions in compensation and gave an area of the South Island to the Maoris. Perhaps the fact that New Zealand was the first country in the world to give women the vote was a contributing factor in the Government's compassionate response to the treatment of its native population.

My Australian base was Melbourne the Garden City, a multi-ethnic city with a population of three million. The city prospered during the Gold Rush in the 1890s when people from all over the world flocked there attracted by "gold fever". The city was able to build many fine buildings and parks from the sale of gold.

A tour of Melbourne Cricket Stadium was impressive with a Museum devoted to cricket and the 1956 Olympics. The stadium's record attendance was 127,000 when Billy Graham lectured there. The record for cricket and rugby is 98,000 all seated.

A real bonus was to see "Mamma Mia" at the Princess Theatre just 100 yards from my hotel. The packed audience was soon on their feet swaying and dancing to the hits of Abba. At the interval street entertainers kept the atmosphere alive outside the theatre. At the end of the performance a row of horse drawn carriages pulled up to return people to their hotels.

The second day in Melbourne was spent on a coach tour that included a river cruise on the Yarra, a city tour and a visit to the Blue Dandenog Range to see wildlife that included the Kookaburra, Crimson Rosella and Kangaroos. The only disappointment was not being able to fit in a visit to Ayers Rock.

I had previously visited Australia in 1995 spending three weeks in Sydney with two very good friends, Vic and Maisie James who had emigrated from England more than twenty years ago. During that visit I spent a lot of time investigating the early arrival of convicts from England at the Penal Colony and now a tourist attraction known as The Rocks. The Penal Colony consisted of 568 male convicts, 191 female convicts, 200 Marines, their wives and children. Not only did the boats bring convicts but they also introduced smallpox, which killed half of the Aboriginal population that lived in the Sydney area. The transport of convicts ended in 1840, a total of 83,000 having been sent. Charles Darwin described the venture as *"a success unparalleled in history"* in his book "The Origin of the Species". The Aborigines would no doubt disagree. Tools discovered show that the Aborigines have lived in Australia for 45,000 years, in the 21st Century they struggle to survive. Old Sydney Town was a must visit, it was the only opportunity to discuss with the Aborigines their former life style and the depths to which many had descended despite increased Government funding to maintain their culture.

The traditional tourist attractions were explored including the site of the 1842 Gold Rush at Bathurst. Walking tours included Bondi Beach and an embarrassing walk from Spit to Manly Harbour that passed through a nudist beach. Once started the walk had to be completed because of he steep cliffs at the edge of the beach and so, staring straight ahead, I walked as briskly as possible trying to avoid eye contact with the nudists.

One of the surprises was to hear that bush fires in the Blue Mountains which feature prominently every year in the British TV news, were in fact good for the environment and were nature's way of regeneration. It is only when the fires spread toward housing areas that concern rises.

Other memorable events experienced in Sydney included a visit to the Opera House to see a performance of Puccini's "Turandot", watching the Gay Mardi Gras, walking across the harbour bridge along the gantries, seeing sharks and crocodiles in the Sydney Aquarium and a different kind of 'shark' in the Sydney Supreme Court.

Returning to the 2002 world tour my departure from Melbourne would take me to Japan. Tokyo is the most expensive city that I have ever visited with even the most average accommodation three times as costly as in England. Fortunately it was the low season and I was able to cut a good deal at a decent hotel, Alcyone, in one of the main shopping areas of Ginza. The famous Kabuki-Za Theatre was just around the corner from my hotel. A guided tour of the theatre would cost 10,000 Yen (£50) but by doing the tour myself, having a McDonalds's meal costing £3 and a seat at the back of the theatre for £4 I managed so save £43. Although the Theatre performance was in Japanese the costumes and dancing made it a worthwhile experience. During the performance two things puzzled me. The first was the almost strangulated voices of the female characters. I later found out that in 1667 women were banned from appearing on stage so men played all the female parts. This gave rise to the tradition of transvestism in Japanese Theatre. The second puzzle was the large exodus of the audience between acts. Apparently they choose which parts are boring and go off to a bar or café, returning when a more lively act is to take place.

Coming out of the theatre I was faced with heavy rain as a typhoon was blowing in off the East Coast. Winds of 100mph were recorded and there had been reports of seismic activity in the area of Shimizu, 100 miles south of Tokyo. The locals live under a continuing threat of earthquakes and in my hotel room, along with fire instructions, was information on what to do in the case of an earthquake. My room, on the ninth floor, had a steel ring cemented into the wall by the window to be used with ropes if necessary. I will have to practise my abseiling the next time I visit an Outward Bound Centre. Tokyo was almost totally destroyed by an earthquake in the Kanto area in 1923 and so the residents concern is well founded. In August 2005 an earthquake struck north-eastern Japan triggering small tsunamis and shaking skyscrapers in Tokyo, 190 miles to the south. The earthquake had a magnitude of 7.2.

The hotel was amazingly quiet; I seemed to be the only guest in the ten-storey building. Every day they changed the carpet in the lift to read the correct day. They provided a new toothbrush and toothpaste each day and I finished with a good stock to take home. I asked for a copy of the English language "Japanese Times" and the next time I passed reception I was given a copy, plus a "Daily Yomiuri", with much bowing on their presentation.

Armed with a rail pass that I purchased in England, (this is much cheaper than buying it in Japan), I started the first of a number of train journeys by travelling to Veno, North East of Tokyo. This is one of the main cultural centres of Japan. Veno Zoo houses the two giant pandas received as a gift from China that I had seen in a zoo in Peking in 1993. A new experience for me was a talking bus stop. It consisted of a computer on a pole that you type in your question such as "What time is the next bus due?" The answer then appears on the screen and it also speaks in English or Japanese.

The "Japanese Times" was a source of pleasure each morning, Japan has the worlds second largest newspaper readership behind Norway with 580 copies per 1000 people to Norway's 598. The UK's figure is 314, Germany 306 and the USA 209. A study showed that 82% of Japanese men and 58% of women read newspapers on a daily basis, spending an average of 39 minutes per day. People in their 60s spend 54 minutes a day whereas those in their 20s spend only 25 minutes. At home I spend more than an hour a day reading the morning and evening newspapers.

Two cultural differences between the UK and Japan regard blowing your nose and eating. It is considered very bad manners to blow your nose in public and Japanese people with a cold wear a white face mask to avoid spreading germs. When eating it is normal to do so with your mouth open so that you make as much noise as possible as a sign of appreciation. As I prefer to eat with my mouth closed they must have thought that I disliked the taste of the food. Sometimes they were right.

On arrival back at my hotel from Veno I found that the police were closing off the streets. Within 10 minutes a massive 3-hour carnival procession started with marching bands and decorated floats. There was a great atmosphere to end the day on.

The underground Metro system was very impressive. As well as being punctual and clean the behaviour of the passengers was notable. On the London Underground passengers stare straight ahead to avoid conversation and eye contract. On Tokyo trains they close their eyes during the journey only opening them to get off at their destination. Rows of apparently sleeping passengers provided an amusing sight. In London if you dozed off your bags would be under threat but in Tokyo there is no problem due to the low amount of such crime.

A fascinating place was the infamous Yasukuni Shrine dedicated to the spirits of all-Japanese soldiers and civilians who had given their lives in defence of the Japanese Empire. Many of the 2.5 million souls honoured by the shrine died in Imperialistic Wars. It seems astonishing that such a small nation should in turn attack Korea, China, Russia, the USA and British Protectorates. Like Germany they were seeking global domination, and but for the atom bomb they might have succeeded.

Nearby was the Military Museum that displayed a one-man submarine intended for a Kamikaze attack and a plane of the type used for suicide attacks on US and British ships. The planes were also used in the attack on the US fleet at Pearl Harbour. There are pictures of the pilots and sailors, with items of their personal belongings, in praise of their suicide missions. Generals were also featured who had committed suicide by falling on their swords. It is claimed that a mixture of the Shinto religion and government propaganda inspired such action. A similar combination of theology and politics is driving the suicide bombers in the Middle East today in the name of Islam.

The rail pass was used to travel North on the Tahoku Shrinkansen, a super express bullet train, to visit Sendai on the main island of Honshu and to Kyoto and Hiroshima in the south. Bullet trains are very comfortable as they travel at 200mph. The sound was minimal and the journey was so smooth that there was no surface movement on the liquids resting on the table. The carriage layout was similar to a plane; the seats recline and can be reversed depending on the direction you are travelling. The coaches had air conditioning; two coaches had cafes and refreshment trolleys travelled up and down continuously. Mobile phones were banned in the main carriages. This was a relief as everybody had one, including the children. If you wished to make a call you had to go to a small compartment at the end of the carriage where coin operated telephones were also available. On entering the carriage the conductor announces himself, bows, checks the tickets and bows again before leaving. After 400 miles the train arrived in Kyoto on time, an inspiration for British Rail.

One of the highlights of Kyoto was a "Walk in Kyoto, Talk in English" a five hour walking tour led by Johnnie Hillwalker, the winner of numerous international awards. The group of 14 was from America, Australia, England and Korea. The first stop was Higashi-Honganji, the biggest Buddhist temple in the world. Japanese Buddhism seemed tailor-made for the work mad society. They believe that everyone will enter paradise, whether good or bad, so you don't need to attend service or pray. Priests can be male or female, single or married and live in the temple grounds. Marriage in Japan is in decline. The fashionable thing to do is to marry in a Catholic Church, have children blessed at a Shinto temple and to have your funeral at a Buddhist temple. Elementary schools are shutting down as the birth rate has dropped to 1.4 children per family.

We visited Gojyorkuen a local Geisha area. The lifestyle of the Geisha girls is in decline. Girls enter an apprenticeship between the ages of 17-25 and when they graduate to full Geishas they can be hired through a booking office, often in pairs to entertain parties of men after dinner at a restaurant or teahouse. Most Geishas never marry and traditionally do not accept sexual assignations. The decline in the Geisha lifestyle is reflected in the closure of many Geisha bars and only one Geisha Theatre remains in Kyoto. Geisha means a person practised in the arts, principally dance and music.

The lone Korean woman in our party had to endure a visit to Mimizuka, a large mound covered in grass with a stone carving at the top. The mound contained thousands of ears brought back by the Japanese from the 16th century Korean War.

Johnnie Hillwalker pointed out that Kyoto had been the centre of Japanese civilisation for over 1000 years. It was spared Allied bombing during World War II and remains a living museum of Japans artistic heritage. It was on the list of four cities targeted for the first Atom Bomb. It was third on the list but survived after Japan surrendered following the dropping of the second bomb. Recently released American documents show that Hiroshima and Nagasaki, (where the atom bombs were dropped) and Kyoto were deliberately spared traditional bombing raids so that once the Atom bombs had been dropped they could measure their impact as weapons on undamaged buildings. It was intended as a scientific and military experience. The decision to drop the Atom bombs was taken when it was known that Japan had no intention of surrendering. The Japanese instruction went out *"100 million deaths with honour"*.

I took the bullet train to Hiroshima. No one can deny the tragedy of Hiroshima but the Japanese single minded fanaticism would have led to the *"100 million deaths"* on the Japanese and Allied sides in maintaining a war they started while looking for domination of Asia. Countless more Allied service men and women could have died the longer the war progressed.

It was refreshing to see parties of school children touring the Hiroshima Peace Park and Museum. Hopefully the futility of war is a message that grows with them. I joined them in ringing the Peace Bell. Hiroshima had been totally rebuilt, the only remains were a charred and twisted skeleton of the Industrial Promotion Hall renamed "A Bomb Dome and a Peace Memorial Park". A Peace Flame burns in front of the Memorial Cenotaph, never to be extinguished until all nuclear weapons are abolished. Do you think that will ever happen? Was the dropping of the Atom bombs on Japan justified?

It was a strange experience walking around Hiroshima wondering what people were thinking about the white English-speaking tourists. Those over the age of 60 would have some memories of the dropping of the Atom Bomb. The Memorial Museum was totally open about the events that built up to the dropping of the bomb, unlike the shrine in Tokyo. The Government introduced a policy of spiritual mobilisation during the war to deny freedom of thought. It was intended to heighten the Japanese spirit and perhaps helps explain the suicide missions and why Generals would fall on their sword rather than admit defeat. One of the slogans for the general public was "Doing without until victory".

A further excursion was taken from Kyoto on a bullet train to Kobe via Osaka. Kobe is the main sea port in Osaka that hit the headlines on 17th January 1995 when an earthquake measuring 7.2 on the Richter Scale hit somewhere under Awaji Island, offshore of Kobe. Of a population of 1.5 million, 5,000 died and 300,000 were made homeless. The media savaged the Government for the rescue services inadequate response. There was great alarm all over Japan because buildings, expressways and tracks of the Shinkansen railway had not stood up to the shock waves of the earthquake. In Tokyo, 20 years of complacency vanished overnight and strengthening programmes commenced immediately. There remains very little evidence of the effects of the earthquake in Kobe.

On the return journey to Tokyo the bullet train passed Mount Fiji, the highest mountain in Japan. I did not realise that there was a family connection, the first woman to climb the mountain was Lady Parkes, the wife of the British Ambassador. Great, Great, Granny Parkes sounds quite a woman! The mountain top clearly stood out above the clouds covered in snow. It is in fact a volcano and although it has not erupted since the 18th Century, the neighbouring mountain of Asama frequently rumbles and belches smoke.

The flight out of Tokyo took me to Hong Kong. When I was last there in 1987, the place was on tenterhooks as the Chinese were about to take over Hong Kong from the British. Many members of the Hong Kong business community had sought refuge in other countries fearing that the Chinese would strip them of their wealth and nationalise their companies. Many of their fears proved to be unfounded.

The changes since 1987 were mainly material. A new airport has been built and more skyscrapers were under construction. Goods are no longer made in Hong Kong and it had now become the world's biggest supermarket. Goods from around the world come in and out of the enormous dock side terminals to be dispatched globally. The "boat people" refugee camps have gone and all the Vietnam refugees returned home. Refugees from Mainland China are still prohibited from crossing the border into Hong Kong. Accommodation remains limited in terms of space. Cooking is so difficult that most people eat out for every meal. Restaurants are packed from early morning to late evening. Horse racing is the only form of gambling with betting controlled by the Government with any profits used to create welfare programmes. Hotel rooms are extremely expensive.

Many countries seem to be experiencing an explosion in youth crime. However, the greatest concern in Hong Kong was the high suicide rate amongst young people. A newspaper report stated, *"The problem we face is no longer about delinquency but about teenager's values. They simply do not treasure life and do not respect others"*. The report covered a suicide pact of three girl's aged 14 and 15. In 2001 there were 984 suicides in Hong Kong, including more than 30 teenagers aged between 10 and 19. Some academics compare suicide to an infectious disease as it infects people from all backgrounds. It infects not only so-called problem youths from deprived backgrounds but those raised in good homes by caring parents. Events regarded as trivial to adults are enough to push youngsters over the edge - a broken relationship, poor exam results or even a scolding from parents can be a reason for suicide. Dr. Dennis Wong Sing-Wing said, *"Young people in Hong Kong are too vulnerable. They do not have the skills to control their emotions, and no abilities in problem solving"*. Wallace Shui Ka-Chum agrees that the notion of high-risk youths is a thing of the past. *"In this case, we can see no risk factors with the three teenagers, there were no signs to indicate suicide. We teachers and academics all feel helpless about this situation. Many teenagers have been contacted who have negative values, and some even think death is romantic. Many young people do not love life. They think study is torture, work is hard and staying alive torture"*. The blame has been attributed to the lack of time allocated in schools to promote Civil Education; the limited time parents spend with their children and their lack of ability to communicate with them.

On the last day I visited the island of Macau, which has always been part of China and was allowed to develop into one of the world's biggest gambling centres. It is situated an hour from the China coast towards Vietnam. Only rich people and criminals used to be attracted along with the accompanying corruption. It had become an important source of international currency hence the Chinese government turning a blind eye. Being off the mainland it didn't compromise the Communist ideals in exploiting capitalism. Its popularity has declined since China took over Hong Kong with the Chinese Government no longer having to pretend such capitalist activities were not taking place. Floating casinos were the first sight as the turbojet landed. The streets were deserted compared to Hong Kong and it looked like a ghost town.

Two years later the "ghost town" image would be dramatically changed following the opening of a mega casino on the island by the Las Vegas based Venetian group. It has proved so popular that the $250 million cost of building the casino has been recouped in just 12 months. No doubt bidders for one of the proposed Mega casinos in the UK are rubbing their hands in anticipation of big profits from their investment.

In retrospect a boat trip on my final day was not a good idea with an evening flight booked. There was a sense of relief when the turbojet set off from Macau on time but the feeling was short lived. Ten minutes into the journey there was a loud explosion and the ferry stopped. The captain announced the jet engine had sucked up floating debris and although there was no fear of the ferry sinking we were drifting across shipping lanes whilst waiting for a rescue boat. Tugs eventually towed the ferry back to Macau and a second ferry was taken to Hong Kong. Fortunately I had built in a safety time margin so that the two hours delay didn't affect my evening flight.

To break the long flight home I arranged stops in Sri Lanka and the United Arab Emirates. Arriving at Colombo airport was like entering a war zone with armed soldiers and roadblocks surrounding the airport. Vehicle checks were made at road blocks on all approaches to major towns, places of administration and worship.

Travel plans in Sri Lanka were based on time rather than distance. Due to the roadblocks, narrow and pitted roads, no motor ways or dual carriageways, journeys were tortuous. The high temperatures and hazardous driving conditions made travelling very tiring. Highlights of the tour north of Columbo were visits to the Elephant Orphanage, the Hill Station at Newara Eliya at 7,000ft, the Mosque of the Sacred Tooth, (which had recently been car bombed), a tea plantation and processing factory.

It would be unfair for me to criticise the Sri Lankan administration on such a short visit but it was apparent that they had problems. The following comments are taken from a report by five High Court lawyers. "*A number of leading Politicians, senior Police Officers, senior Army officers and High Court Judges are corrupt. The Government has no real wish to end the Tamil Tigers conflict, thousands of Army jobs would be at risk, massive arms budgets would be reduced giving less opportunity for bribery in negotiating contracts. The corruption at highest level cascades down to minor officials, even Probation Officers accept bribes to write favourable reports".*

The last night produced a dramatic end to the visit. At 8.30pm gunfire rang out around my hotel in Columbo. My flight was due out at 4am so I had tried to get a few hours sleep. My hotel, built in 1875, was situated near the docks. On hearing the sounds of gun battle I hid under the bed as spasmodic firing continued for thirty minutes. When the firing ceased I went to reception but was given no explanation for the exchange of fire. Days later, when back in England, I found that Tamil Tigers were involved in an attack on the docks.

Listening to the sound of high velocity bullets brought back memories of the German bombing raids on Birmingham in the 1940s. Cowering in the air raid shelters there was the fear of whether the next bomb might drop on you. Not knowing what was going on raised thoughts not only of my safety but on practicalities such as whether the roads would be open to the airport, if it would be safe to travel, if the airport would be closed etc. Even after the shooting stopped there was still the fear that it might start up again. At 1am it was time to go to the airport. The hotel staff still offered no explanation. There were numerous roadblocks where checks were made. Everything must have worked out successfully as my flight departed on time.

The world press reported what happened that night, months before the local press due to censorship in Sri Lanka. Two suicide bomb attacks had been reported during my stay that had taken place six months previously. The police, through torture, it is claimed, obtained "confessions". The freedom of press in the UK is just one of the many advantages of living in a free society.

Dubai was my final stop before returning to England. Within minutes of arriving at the Airport Hotel I had booked a Desert Safari and Dune Drive. Dune Bashing involves four-wheel-drive Land Rovers racing over sand dunes across the desert at high speed. Six passengers and the driver are wedged together as the vehicles drop over the top of massive dunes. Deep in the desert we arrived at a bamboo fort where a barbecue was being prepared. Camel riding was the first attraction followed by the handling of falcons used for hunting. By now the black sky was dotted with bright stars. We were ready for a feast of lamb, chicken, beans, fish and flat bread with vegetables and soft drinks. The evening concluded with Arabic music with a belly dancer inviting spectators to join in.

On the second morning a guided city tour included beaches, markets and the camel racetrack. The tallest landmark is the Burji Al Arab Hotel built on the seabed 100 yards from the beach with three underground car parking levels. It's a seven star hotel, and costs $3000 per day and is fully booked for the next two years.

Although Dubai has had a port for many centuries the new City of Dubai is only twenty years old. Due to the discovery of oil massive wealth came to the area and modern buildings geared to tourism and trade developed. The country is so wealthy no one pays tax, there is no import and export duties and welfare services are free for residents. Parts of the city resemble Las Vegas in terms of building design and materials used. Two major tourist attractions are the Gold and Spice markets. The oldest part of the City is Fort Al Falidi built 150 years ago and now a modern museum. At ground level it retains its true style and original building materials. Below ground, the old city life is recreated with craftsmen demonstrating traditional craftwork. Space age technology was also incorporated with life size holograms projected that portray life styles from hundreds of years ago.

During my world travels I have collected audio tapes featuring the music of the people who have inhabited their countries for thousands of years. Although I am not a musician I can recognise the same sounds that are common to people living thousands of miles apart. How could the sounds be so common to each other when the means of travel by native North American Indians and the Aborigines of Austrialia, the Maoris of New Zealand and the people of Kenya were denied to them all the time? Did the inhabitants of Africa migrate by foot to Australia, New Zealand and North America?

The answer would appear to be "Yes" if the National Geographic review of the evidence undertaken by James Shreeve in the March 2006 edition under the title "The Greatest Journey Ever Told – The trail of our DNA," is accepted. The writer reports that most paleoanthropologists and geneticists agree the modern humans arose 200,000 years ago in Africa and that some of those humans started migrating over land and ice across the Middle East, Australia, Asia and Europe and eventually the Americas. This could account for the commonality of the music of Africa and the Aborigines, Maoris and North American Indians.

No further mishaps were to occur with a smooth flight home that concluded my Phileas Fogg adventure. I wonder how Jules Verne would relate to my 21st Century "round the world trip?" I had visited ten countries in 40 days thanks to jet travel.

17

Sport - The Opium of the Masses?

A constructive or destructive force within society?
Can sport be defined as a religion?
The political exploitation of sport?
World Cup Black Magic

The title of this essay is the re-hash of the original opinion expressed by Karl Marx that religion was the opium of the masses. If sport acts as a drug as suggested then I am a sports addict. The sports that I am addicted to are football, from playing to refereeing for over fifty years, cricket, from player to umpire, for the same period and golf for a mere twenty-five years of playing, now a member of a group of four retired gentlemen known as the "Last of the Summer Winos".

In the introduction of this book I described my approach as "interactive". I want to involve you in issues encountered during my world travels. The twin titles of this essay present an ideal opportunity for you to be a member of a jury. I will act as Prosecutor, Defence Advocate and presiding Judge, in that order. As the Prosecutor I will rely on historical events supplemented by my own experiences. As the Defence Advocate I will rely almost entirely on my personal involvement as a player or spectator. As the presiding Judge I will summarise the big issues prior to leaving you to come to the decision - guilty or not guilty?

The introduction on behalf of the prosecution. Statistically sport has overtaken religion if the measure of such issues can be decided by TV viewing figures. Occasions such as the Football World Cup Final and the Olympic Games produce a mass world wide audience only rivalled by natural disasters such as the recent Indian Ocean Tsunami.

The effect of sport on the day to day life of people throughout the world has been reviewed by academics seeking explanations for the mass hysteria that can be generated. Hundreds of books have been written comparing sport and religion. Television programmes probe issues such as the Channel 4 documentary, "Hallowed be thy name" where the question "Is football the new religion?" was probed by Mark Dowd. Prior to the World Cup in Japan The Sun newspaper recruited a London Minister to lead mass prayers on behalf of its readership for the speedy recovery of a broken bone in David Beckham's foot. Have you ever prayed on behalf of your favourite sports team in the hope of securing victory?

Sports stars achieve God-like status, examples being the former Liverpool player Robbie Fowler, his fans wore replica shirts with the word God on the back. There is even a church in Brazil dedicated to the "hand of God", the self confessed offender Diego Maradona. Those supporting the view that football is the new religion make comparisons of the change in the role of Church buildings within the community. Traditionally the Church would have been both the sanctuary and the hub of contact for those seeking help. The life of the community would have revolved around the church building. Many now believe football stadiums have taken on that role. People's ashes are scattered over the pitch and wedding ceremonies held within the ground. Stadiums now become assessable seven days a week, not just on match days. Could you see yourself taking part in events as described or being so committed to a Club that you would change your name to include the club's or a player's name?

Can sport be defined as a religion? Is it fair to compare tribal violence and hatred generated between religious Fundamentalists with the behaviour of football hooligans? Is it alarming when school children, taking part in a survey on who are their role models, that the majority name sports stars and hardly anyone names a religious figure such as Jesus Christ?

The principal evidence for describing sport as a destructive force can be found in the political history of football. It has been used as a Fascist tool by three Military Dictators in the 20th century.

The most infamous is Hitler who used the 1936 Olympics in Berlin to promote his master race ideology. Although Germany won the majority of the medals he was infuriated by the success of the black American Jesse Owens who won four Gold medals and stormed out of the stadium.

Hitler used sport to pacify Europe prior to 1939. He tried to present himself as a sports loving non-aggressive leader. Hitler only ever attended one football match, Germany v Norway at the 1936 Olympics. Germany was expected to win but lost, Hitler was predictably furious. After annexing Austria in 1938 Germany included five star Austrian players in their team for the 1938 World Cup in the hope of better success. The one Austrian player who might have brought that success was Sindalar, the Beckham of his day, but he refused to play for Hitler. He died in mysterious circumstances in 1939, through poisoning.

In 1938 England played Germany in Berlin, winning 6–3. The British Foreign Office ordered the English players to make the Nazi salute during the opening ceremony. This was a major publicity coup for Hitler.

Mussolini used the 1934 World Cup in Italy to promote his regime. To ensure that Italy won the World Cup Mussolini chose the referees for the games involving Italy. He had dinner with the Swedish referee he had chosen the night before the semi-final. It was accepted that the referee had been bribed to favour Italy. During the semi-final the referee headed the ball towards an Italian player to set up a goal scoring opportunity. The same referee was appointed by Mussolini to referee the final. No referee has since been allowed to referee a semi-final and a final. The referee was invited into the Royal Box before the kick-off, again something that has never been repeated. Italy won the Final 2–1 against the Czechs.

Franco came to prominence in 1938 when he led the Spanish Civil War. In 1939 Hitler provided bombers to support Franco's attacks. As a reward to Hitler, Spain remained neutral during World War II. Franco adopted Real Madrid as his team and this support rallied his opponents against Fascism in the Catalan Region to support Barcelona. This rivalry continues to exist and explains why passions roused today are greater than in any local derbies in the UK. Thousands of people were killed in the Spanish Civil War.

In 2005 there are worrying signs that Italian football is attracting more Fascists to an already established hard core of supporters who revere the memory of Mussolini. Right-wing revivalism has become fashionable again. Black shirted volunteers guard Mussolini's grave that attracts 200,000 visitors a year. The most popular Italian calendar in 2004 was one featuring Mussolini that sold 350,000 copies. One of the countries most feared groups are the "Ultras", a notorious gang of neo-Fascist hooligans who follow Lazio FC.

Violence flared in the 2005 European Champions League when Liverpool supporters were attacked by Juventus fans in retaliation for the Heysel disaster in 1985. The same month there was a riot in the San Siro Stadium between Italian supporters of AC Milan and Inter Milan. The AC Milan goalkeeper was felled by a flare.

In respect to the authorities allowing spectators to bring flares into stadiums, it is farcical. I remember attending the Mallorca v Real Madrid game with my son James on holiday nearly 20 years ago. Stewards watched as supporters of both teams attached flares to the perimeter fencing that were discharged as players came onto the pitch. The potential to injure players was extremely high.

In Spain football supporters are regularly abusing black players. Despite public address appeals calling for racist chants to be stopped, the response has been an increase in such abuse. One of the worst examples was at the 2004 Real Madrid derby match between Real and Athletico.

A more subtle approach was taken by Russia during the Cold War as they used sport as part of a public relations campaign aimed at its own people, as well as the Western Alliance, to show that Russia and Communism was superior in all aspects of life.

Foreign office documents released by the National Archives in the U.K. under the 50-year rule show that football, in the form of Arsenal was a political subject back in 1954. At that time the nuclear arms race was at fever pitch as Soviet tanks, under the direction of Krushchev, were crushing the worker's rebellion in East Berlin.

The Russian opponents were Moscow Dynamo who duly won 5-0. Leaving nothing to chance the Russians had arranged numerous strength sapping excursions prior to the game, returning the team to their hotel in the early hours of the morning after supplying them with copious amounts of alcohol. A similar fate befell French and Danish teams who also complained that they had been entertained so royally that they were in no state to play football and suffered heavy defeats.

When evaluating destructive forces in sport the position of the media is pivotal in terms of how information is conveyed to the public. The British media has a reputation for building up sportsmen and women and when they reach the top of their game they look to knock them off the pedestal that they, the media, have created.

Sport has had limited success in being the subject matter of film and TV drama. Amongst the exceptions have been "Chariots of Fire", the "Rocky" boxing series, "Tin Cup" featuring golf, a couple of American baseball films and football's "Bend It Like Beckham". One memorable TV drama from my perspective featured a referee on a public park pitch being subjected to all the abuses experienced by many referees on every weekend of the season. Finally coming to the end of his tether he scores the winning goal in the last minute by heading the ball into the net from a corner. Signalling the goal he walks off the pitch leaving 22 stunned players. As a football referee I have felt tempted on the odd occasion, when trying to control poor sportsmanship to do exactly the same. Fortunately, such games are rare and my faith in sport quickly returns.

Another destructive element of sport is how it has been a target for terrorists and corruption. Diego Maradona, the self-confessed 'hand of God' cheat in the World Cup match against England, was expelled from the 1994 World Cup for drug taking. Colombian player Andres Escobar was assassinated for scoring an own goal in a major tournament. The culprits were drug barons engaged in heavy gambling. Athletics and cycling were also rocked by drug scandals in the lead up to the 2004 Athens Olympics.

The "Black September" terrorists massacred Israeli athletes at the Munich Olympics. An anarchist exploded a bomb at the Atlanta Games. Hooligans were the root of the Heysel Stadium disaster during the Liverpool v Juventus Cup Final. British hooligans went on the rampage in Belgium in 2000.

An interesting piece of sporting journalism was encountered in Zimbabwe in 2005 that highlighted the Juju craze that is spreading across Africa within sport and the business community. The Football World Cup is due to be played in Africa in 2010. It is claimed that African countries that qualify for the finals could have an advantage over teams from around the world. It was the Zimbabwe Herald that drew attention to the Juju craze. It reports that some business people with an insatiable desire to get super rich are crossing the Limpopo River into South Africa seeking "special supernatural powers" to enhance their businesses.

It is also claimed that some successful football coaches are consulting n' angas prior to big matches. Some teams have been reported to abandon matches claiming that a particular stadium is jinxed. It is an African traditional belief that there is only a certain amount of luck in society with each individual receiving a portion. To obtain extra luck some footballers are turning to black magic. There have been claims that witchdoctors have made fortunes selling their "special powers" to clubs and players alike. It is not uncommon to see a n'anga going around the stadium before a match or to see players grouped in a corner performing certain rituals purportedly to enhance their performance.

The Zimbabwe National African Traditional Healers Association President, Professor Gordon Chavhunduka, confirmed that Juju was a common practice, prevalent in most African countries. Zimbabwe was no exception. "The idea of using Juju and goblins for the sake of business is common in African culture".

Non African coaches may laugh at the use of Juju and the potions but what about the view that being given something to take care of one' s worries is therapeutic in its own right even if the potions are of no use, i.e. the placebo effect.

In making the case that sport is a destructive force it is necessary to point out that animals are also victims in some countries. In the following examples even the description of the activity as a "sport" is debatable. The following examples have been personally researched or encountered.

Bull fighting is undertaken in a number of countries with Spain being the most prominent. The word "sport" is questionable from a number of perspectives - not just from the cruelty angle. The majority of sports allow participation by millions of people playing at their own level of ability. In Spanish bull fighting only a handful of people get to participate. One visit by a tourist is usually sufficient for them to make up their mind about its credibility as a sport. Bull fighting is also a major attraction in Peru and in Venezuela it is the fourth most attended activity. A more humane version of bull fighting is to be found in Portugal where a team of matadors wrestles the bull into submission without the use of any weapons. The bull is not killed in the ring. Two "sports" not attended in Malaysia were cock fighting and fish bombing. Cock fighting is still a regular sport despite it being illegal. A press report featured a police raid and subsequent fining of 32 men of RM300 (£70) or one month in prison. A large sum in terms of local wage rates. A major campaign is underway to ban fish bombing. By dropping explosives into the water small fish not needed are also killed. Large areas of coral reef are being destroyed that has taken thousands of years to form.

During my two visits to Pakistan, a "sporting" option not taken up was a chance to witness a bear baiting event. The Pakistan Government banned bear baiting in 1988 but an investigation in 2004 by The World Society for the Protection of Animals showed that bear baiting is in fact growing. There were 10 known events in 2002 and more than 20 in 2003. The WSPA has set up a sanctuary for rescued bears.

Bear baiting involves a tethered Asiatic black bear and takes place in an arena watched by thousands of men. The bear is defenceless, its teeth and claws have been removed and two ferocious dogs, bred for the purpose, are trained to attack the bear. Their fangs sink into the bear's muzzle and they tear through the ears as they try to gouge out the bear's eyes. Each fight lasts three rounds of three minutes before the bear is carried away with flesh hanging from what remains of its nose. The release of photographs from a recent event has led to further pressure on the Pakistan government from across the world to ban this "sport".

The final example of cruelty focuses not only on animals but on their jockeys. Whilst in Dubai I visited a Camel Racing Track to see the camels racing and training. The shocking thing was the jockeys were five and six year old boys. Naturally they have only a short career. These children are bought through the slave trade in Asia. Once they become too heavy for racing they are cast out and become beggars and child prostitutes. International pressure put on the Government to stop this form of slave trade has proved successful. By the end of 2005 children will be replaced by mechanical jockeys controlled by a remote control fixed to the saddle. That concludes the case for the prosecution.

The case for the defence will focus on activities and events visited over the past 45 years. The three main sports are cricket, football and golf. One off events based on opportunism are polo, sumo wrestling, tango dancing, kite flying, donkey riding, dune buggy racing, rugby sevens, outdoor chess, motor racing, speedway, baseball and ice hockey.

On arrival in a country I immediately scan the local papers for scheduled events. Some of my travels were deliberately timed to coincide with sporting events such as cricket matches. Test matches have been attended in India, Pakistan, Sri Lanka, South Africa, West Indies, New Zealand, and Australia.

There is sometimes an element of luck involved in arriving in a country at the time of a special sporting event. A prime example was an early morning arrival in Hong Kong that coincided with the final of the Hong Kong Sevens, an internationally famous rugby tournament. England, Scotland and Wales had all progressed to the third day that saw the quarterfinals, semi-finals, and Final of the three competitions. England were the eventual winners beating Fiji 33-20 in the Final.

The six hours of play were a sell out so it was necessary, and well worth paying over the odds, to buy a ticket from a tout. Once in the stadium the thing that struck me was the behaviour of the multi-racial spectators who were consuming massive amounts of alcohol throughout the day without a trace of the type of violent behaviour associated with international football matches. Does this reinforce the theory that football is used as an excuse for gangs of hooligans to rampage around the world quenching their thirst for racial violence?

Other opportunist events encountered included the Hungarian Grand Prix in Budapest and the pre-qualifying event for the Motor Race around the streets of Toronto, Canada.

It came as a surprise to find that in Japan baseball is the main spectator sport so I took the opportunity to watch the Final of the Japan Series between Yokohama Bay Stars and Seibu Lions. There was a capacity crowd of 30,000 for the second of the seven match Series. The Bay Stars had won the first 9-4 and won this second match 4-0. The crowd reaction was incredible with almost non-stop rhythmic chanting and drum banging for nearly three hours. By the end of the match I had sufficiently grasped the rules to appreciate the tactics.

A second Japanese sporting highlight was to attend a Sumo Wrestling event. Sumo wrestlers are treated like Gods. One question left unanswered was "Do fat people become Sumo wrestlers or do thin people make themselves fat to become Sumo Wrestlers?" The Japanese are generally short in height and slight in build. There are very few who could be described as overweight. The contradiction of these facts are Sumo wrestlers, some of whom are over 20 stone in weight.

Sumo Wrestling is Japan's national sport and can lay claims to being the world's oldest sport. Its roots lie in the realms of mythology. Before becoming a sport in the 6th Century, Sumo was practised as a form of deviation and a way of invoking the goodwill of the spirits. The pre-fight rituals demonstrate the Shinto origins of Sumo and serve to raise the psychological tension between the fighters to fever pitch although there was no signs of unruly behaviour from the spectators.

A third Japanese highlight was to witness Samurai Mounted Archery. This is a Shinto ceremony dating back 1,400 years. Dressed in period costume the Archers first paraded through the streets of Kyoto. Unlike other Carnival processions world-wide the parade passed in silence. The parade was followed by the archers riding across open ground at full speed firing arrows at the targets. The Samurai tradition is to never surrender but to commit suicide by falling on their sword, this doesn't apply to the Samurai archers if they fail to hit the target.

Chess is a major sport in Venezuela. Large crowd's gather around street cafes dominated by tables set up for chess. In Christchurch, New Zealand, a giant chessboard is painted on the ground in the main square where chess pieces, half the size of an adult, are moved around the board. Tourists queue to test their skill against local opponents.

Kite flying is a popular sport in Pakistan and Afghanistan. The fourth most popular in Pakistan and third in Afghanistan. It is more popular than football in both countries and is undertaken by adults as well as children.

Polo was observed "live" for the first time in Argentina. It is extremely elitist and an expensive sport dominated by members of the higher financial echelons of society. This is in total contrast to street Tango dancing which is considered by the "lower classes" as their sport, second only to football.

One additional surprise whilst in Argentina was the opportunity to watch a cricket match in Buenos Aires between Belgrano North XI and Belgrano South XI. Does the name Belgrano ring a bell? If you need a clue think of the Falklands War.

One of only three riding experiences was riding a donkey up a mountain in Greece. The second mounted experience was as a teenager riding the milkman's horse whilst it was pulling a milk float. The third was riding a horse through Petra in Jordan. The Greek Mountain track was extremely narrow and dangerous. Being in need of two artificial hips at the time of the ride it was extremely painful so I soon dismounted and walked alongside the donkey. I had previously assumed that it is through chivalry that the man led the donkey with his wife riding-it now seems to be more like self preservation as it is was less dangerous.

During a visit to Nashville I made my first ever visit to an ice hockey match, Nashville Predators v Montreal Canadians, a 6-1 victory for the home team. The venue was the Gayland Entertainment Centre which seats 20,000 fans. The hockey was fast, exciting and sometimes brutal with fistfights. The crowd was equally macho and stereotypical of American Deep South males. Although their aggression was directed at the players there was no way they could reach them because of high surrounding fencing. It was just a form of posturing.

As it was my first ever ice hockey match the lady in the ticket office found me a seat directly at the side of the players cage. That meant I had a close up view of the player's actions as they were sent off or substituted, and was just inches away as they smashed each other into the safety fence.

Although I haven't attended any Olympic Games I have visited stadiums in Los Angeles and Montreal where past Games were held. The Olympics represents one of the finest examples of sport being a constructive force in society. Participants from nearly every country take part irrespective of political or religious ideologies. The Olympics are the sporting equivalent of the United Nations.

It was claimed that the 2004 games in Athens meant that the Olympics had come home. The modern day events however bore no resemblance to the Greek games of 776 BC when the main events were chariot races that often lead to deaths and giants wrestling in the nude. They did not run marathons at that time.

The modern games were started in 1896 by the French Baron de Courbertin, and it is claimed he was not inspired by Homer but by the book "Tom Brown's Schooldays". The ceremony of the Olympic torch was not passed down by the Greeks but was invented by Hitler for the 1936 games in Berlin.

Courbertin was not the first to revive the Olympics; the English Olympics, spelt Olympicks, started in 1612 on a hill outside Chipping Norton in the Cotswolds. The creator was Robert Dover. Although he claimed the games were based on the Greek model there were many differences. The English Olympiks were held every year rather than every four years, competitors were clothed and events such as shin kicking and head standing were very popular. Also included were hunting, dancing, cards and chess. The English Olympiks are once again going strong and shin kicking has been revived!

Can golf be held up as the flag bearer for sportsmanship and camaraderie and therefore a positive force within society? There have been numerous opportunities for me to play golf while abroad and I have never been confronted by bad behaviour. To play the St Andrews Course in Scotland is an ambition for many but perhaps more so if the course of that name and design is in Trinidad. The course had two considerable differences to that in Scotland, wonderful colourful Rhododendrons and as the sun sets, the emergence of fireflies that glow like miniature torches.

Playing golf in Iceland is a real challenge because soil is at a minimum. The fairways are volcanic rock with a light covering of moss. I was provided with a small mat on which the ball is placed to prevent causing damage to the clubs. Mats were also issued in The Gambia as golf is played on sand. The Greens, (Browns), are rolled mud and earth with gentle contours smoothed in by hand to provide a putting challenge.

In Singapore golf mad businessmen can play throughout 24 hours as the Course near the airport is floodlit. Twenty-four hour golf is also popular in Japan where they have produced multi-storey-driving ranges due to the lack of space. In an area surrounded by high netting, at one end is a concrete structure that consists of rows of platforms on top of each other. Up to 400 golfers can be seen hitting balls from platforms up to ten storeys high. Some multi-storey buildings also have rooftop driving ranges for use of their employees. One problem with multi-storey and roof top driving ranges is the noise of the clubs on the balls. I found ear plugs helpful!

The Travel Company "Solo's" provides excellent golfing holidays. So far I have spent a week playing in Tunisia and a week in Corfu. One of the events involved 36 competitors, with women outnumbering the men 3-1. Each day was a different format with players rotating partners. The number of putts taken by teams of two decided one of the Competitions. One of the more outlandish women said to her male partner, "Sink that putt and I will sleep with you tonight!" The ball was at least 20-yards from the hole. He sank it and she did! Once the story got around some of the men were volunteering to play with her the next day whilst others confessed they would have deliberately missed the hole!

A few statistics for golf buffs. What is the longest hole in golf? The record is held by American Floyd Rood who played golf from to coast to coast across America in 114,737 shots on the 3,397-mile hole. It took him one year and 114 days. South Korea are building the world's biggest golf complex consisting of 540 holes which means golfers can play a different Course every day for a month. They hope to capitalise on the tourist influx to the Beijing Olympics. The current largest golf complex is the 180-hole site in Mission Hills, China. It covers an area equivalent to 2,444 football pitches.

Golf remains one of the highlights of my week - rain or shine, only snow curtails my year round pleasure. The key factor in my weekly games is the camaraderie rather than the scores. My group "The Last of the Summer Wino's", celebrate birthdays, anniversaries, the birth of grandchildren, (including my granddaughter Lily) and are all toasted with a bottle of wine after the 9th hole. My colleagues are Tony Leadham, Ian Taylor and Stan Sheffield. They each bring a touch of colour to the proceedings. Ian holds the record for the longest distance travelled by a golf club. Tony has fallen off a bridge and also into a ditch. Stan retreats to Spain every so often seeking inspiration. Dennis Curley is our first reserve in case any of the Wino's go to the great golf course in the sky. Dennis entertains with the occasional delivery of a ball onto an adjacent road.

We are a permanent fixture at Boldmere Golf Course at 9.32am every Thursday, following another group of stalwarts named the "Hamstead Hackers". The Boldmere Course is the most profitable Municipal Course in Birmingham. The café is famous for its bread pudding.

There is a fascinating link between a previous team I used to play with and the "Wino's". Aidan Ronan, an exceptional Award Officer and long standing friend, and the late Arthur Watson were in the team. Arthur was a valued friend and neighbour who died before his time. I actually drove him to hospital for a scheduled operation but complications set in and he died in hospital. Arthur was a keen ornithologist. About four years ago I started to notice a particularly large crow that always seemed to be around the 10th fairway. By way of a joke I would speak to the crow, addressing it as Arthur. I think the others thought I was daft talking to a bird but gradually they began to notice the same bird in the same place every week. I usually have a banana at that part of the course and "Arthur" will now fly up to me to retrieve the skin. Believers in reincarnation would claim Arthur had come back as a bird.

Cricket has provided me with many wonderful opportunities and memorable and exciting moments. The impact of cricket on society should not be underestimated. In 2004, after ten years of hostility between India and Pakistan over a border dispute, India sent a team to Pakistan. The tour was greeted in both countries as a great success. The only major international incident in more than 100 years was the "Bodyline" MCC tour to Australia. The leg theory tactic employed by Douglas Jardine nearly led to Australia leaving the Commonwealth. As Corporal Jones from "Dad's Army" might *have observed, "They didn't like it up 'em!"*

My first introduction to organised cricket was with the Beacon Cricket Club who used to play in Red House Park in Birmingham just after World War 2. As a 10-year-old I used to join in the practice sessions by retrieving the ball from beyond the boundary. There were a number of characters in the team including Harold Dyson. Harold was an ex RAF rear gunner from Bomber Command. He had two artificial metal legs and because he could not run very fast he would be positioned close in front of the batsman in the hope of either taking a catch or in putting the batsmen off. If the ball was hit at his legs there would be a loud metallic sound. Much to the amazement of the batsmen Harold would nonchalantly pick the ball up and throw it back to the bowler. Once while on holiday, Harold sent a telegram home that read;

"Send new leg, one broken".

Another character was Terry Wood who developed a number system when batting to try to make up for his poor eyesight. If it were a fast bowler he would count to four and then swing the bat. If it were a slow bowler he would count to six. This method proved effective on some occasions with scores in the 20s and 30s. One of the other players suffered from Lumbago. He was involved in a last wicket stand and the scores were level when he went for a quick run. Halfway down the wicket, his back locked and he fell down in the middle of the pitch doubled up. His team-mates could not straighten him up so they put him in the back of a car and took him to hospital. Ron Rabone had a reputation for dealing with injuries hence his nickname, "Doc". On one occasion he had to treat himself when, in attempting to catch a high ball, he split his eyebrow. He reacted by using a safety pin to pin the wound together before driving himself to hospital. The days of do it yourself surgery have long gone as we enter a period of litigation driven by the American "ambulance chasing" culture.

The early experiences and encouragement received at Beacon C.C. held me in good stead for a lifetime's involvement in cricket across the world. There have been moments of high drama, nail biting finishes, elation and disappointment, but there was always members of the opposition to share your joy or sadness in a sporting manner.

One colourful character encountered at the Test Match in Faislabad, Pakistan, was known as "Uncle Cricket". I had seen him on television back in England many times. He wears a full-length bright green one piece gown, a green skull cap, has a long white beard and carries a huge Pakistan flag. I chatted with him and found out that he was formerly a social worker but was now employed by the Pakistan Cricket Board as a Public Relations Officer. He is allowed to move freely around the ground and encourages the crowd to clap and chant pro-Pakistan slogans. The television cameras continually focus on "Uncle Cricket" as there is always plenty of action surrounding him. The Cricket Board paid his expenses to visit England for the World Cup.

One of the great days of Test Cricket was experienced in Sri Lanka at the ground in Columbo. The third day of the third and final Test against Sri Lanka was sensational. The start was delayed because water had been put on the pitch overnight illegally leading to claims of cheating. The Sri Lankan press reported the start was delayed due to dew on the pitch! When play commenced 22 wickets fell for 229 runs with England winning by 4 wickets in the last over of the day. England won the series 2-1 after being one down in the first Test. The crowd, with English supporters in the majority, celebrated in style.

Another great Test Match was watched in Christchurch, New Zealand. Despite the fastest double hundred in the history of Test Cricket by New

Zealander Nathan Astle, England won by 98 runs. There were two unusual features about the match. Firstly, the game was played at a Rugby Stadium (Jade). Secondly, a prepared cricket strip was lowered into position by a crane in the middle of the ground after an equal amount of turf had been removed. After the game the cricket strip was removed and the rugby turf replaced. This was the first ever use of a specially prepared wicket as far as England were concerned. The second major issue was that the maximum number of spectators on any day was only 5,000 with 4,000 of those from England. The implications for Test Cricket in New Zealand are bleak.

Cricket at the Sydney ground has been dominated over the years by the barracking of the predominantly male Australian occupants who sit on the grassy bank known as "The Hill". During the 1995 cricket tour England failed to qualify for the Final of the One-Day International Series. Australia "A" were to play Australia "B" in the Final. This is the only occasion I am aware of when the "Barmy Army" ducked a challenge and did not attend. I did sit on the Hill, keeping my mouth shut, to see for myself what antics they got up to. Without the English to bait the Australian males amused themselves by chanting the names of the players imploring them to "Give us a wave". Depending on the response the players were either cheered or booed. All very juvenile. The only other targets were the young Australian women as they paraded past. The day spent on the Hill emphasised the chauvinistic nature of Australian men.

The first floodlit cricket match encountered was in Cape Town in 1993. It was South Africa's Inter State One Day Final. There were two notable features. The first was the high proportion of women and girls in the crowd. The second occurred towards the end of the night when alcohol was having an effect. In addition to the "Mexican Wave" the spectators threw all their litter into the air. Whilst paper wrappers were not a problem empty beer cans landing on your head were. It was all very good natured with everyone having a good time, (except for those getting cut heads).

The Prosecutor has claimed that football is a vehicle for Fascism and hooligans. It is true that three 20th Century dictators have exploited football and its supporters for their own ends. It is also true that there have been deaths caused by hooliganism. I would argue that such behaviour is restricted to no more than 2% of so called football supporters and that football should not be described as a destructive force in society.

Football is recognised as having the biggest world wide following of any sport. Attending football matches abroad can be dangerous when travelling alone but so far I have escaped unscathed. I always follow these basic rules; dress down and don't wear clothing carrying any logo. On arrival at a ground without a ticket take advice from the police to establish which area is for home supporters and which is the safest area. In the ground don't start a conversation or make eye contact with your neighbours until you have decided they are reasonable people. However tempting never applaud good play by the opposition and only jump to your feet when those around do! As the game progresses and you are accepted as "one of them" it is enjoyable to swap football stories from around the world.

Amongst the most dangerous grounds encountered was the Stadium in Buenos Aires, Argentina where I saw River plate lose 4-1 to Boca Boys. The stadium held 80,000 and had a 5ft high wall, 10ft high fencing and a trench around the pitch. Spectators stood behind the goals as there were no seats in that area. Firecrackers exploded, enormous banners were passed overhead and kites were flown. In the last 10 minutes there were 5 cautions and a sending off as the game exploded into violence. This time it was the players who were the problem not the supporters.

Health and Safety issues are at a minimum in some countries. The Phnom Penh stadium in Cambodia is an accident waiting to happen. There are steep steps to the top of the "Olympic" stadium. All seats are concrete slabs without covering. Glass panelling is shattered with the risk of getting cuts everywhere. The slightest rush of spectators must surely end in disaster.

There was no sign of physical danger or violence at the Tokyo National Stadium where I saw a J League match between Verdy Kawasaki 0 - Yokoama Flugels 3. The stadium seats 80,000 although J League fixtures only attract between 5,000 and 17,000 spectators. The majority of players were Japanese with just one Brazilian and African in each team. The stadium is uncovered so it was fortunate that the light rain that morning had stopped by the 7pm kick-off. The standard of play was at English Division 1 level. Both sets of supporters were beating drums at opposite ends of the stadium trying to out play each other. Unlike South America there was no sign of violence, no armed soldiers, water cannons or safety fences. League games are not allowed to end in a draw. The team that wins in 90 minutes gets three points. The team that wins in extra time, (golden goal), gets two points. The team that wins the penalty shoot out gets one point. Before the game a giant screen flashed instructions about not using fireworks and what to do in the event of an earthquake!

In conclusion, wearing my Defence Advocate hat, I urge you, as a member of the Jury, to consider the following examples of the positive influences on the people living in the UK at the conclusion of the following sporting events. It was claimed that large areas of business were brought to a standstill at the climax of a recent Test Match in South Africa. David Lloyd and David Gower gleefully reported during a Sky Sports transmission that office desks were being vacated as millions were watching the climax. Readers who can remember England winning the football World Cup in 1966 in the dramatic Final at Wembley against Germany will recall the sense of euphoria that swept the country. Other recent TV moments that united the country were the Olympic exploits of Kelly Holmes and the round the world record breaking sailing of Ellen Macarthur.

At another level I have observed, over the past 45 years of involvement in youth work, many success stories where young people became leaders in their chosen career paths. They cite the basic personal development skills they acquired through youth sport as a major factor in their subsequent achievements as adults. Nobel Prize winner, philosopher and author, Albert Camms said, *"What I most surely know in the long run about morality and the obligations of men, I owe to sport"*.

It is extremely gratifying to witness the ways in which many people are giving their leisure time to voluntary work, much of it sport related. Do you have a positive experience linked to youth sport that has helped you in later life? I remain an optimist in believing that sport is a constructive force within the life of a Nation.

Summing up as the presiding Judge I would not only draw your attention to the evidence presented but pose the following questions for you to address. Can sport be likened to a drug because it can spark off both peaceful celebrations or violent anti-social behaviour? Because sport has been hijacked in the past as a Fascist tool by military dictators and used by terrorists as a public platform does it mean sport must be labelled as a destructive force? Has sport become the new religion around which the community now moves towards in greater numbers? When is a sport not a sport? Is sport a constructive force in raising the spirits of a Nation? Does sport have a positive influence on the personal development of young people that is repaid by voluntary work as adults?

As a member of the jury cast your vote.

18

Residing in the home of Osama Bin Laden

Afghanistan, Turkey, Iran and Pakistan –
Four of the most volatile countries on Earth
Has the liberation of Afghanistan been justified?
What next – a bullet or a smile?

Three of these four countries don't appear as recommended tourist destinations in most guides while the fourth: Turkey is approached with caution. The fascination to me of all four countries was the threat that they pose to world security. They are all continually prominent in the media. Their internal conflicts that could bring down governments remain unsolved. Conflicts such as the attempt to overthrow the Al Qaeda warlords, who still control large parts of Afghanistan and continue to feed the world's heroin supply. The Kurdish fight for independence in Turkey and the unification of Cyprus. The border conflict in Pakistan led by the Kashmiri freedom fighters and the attempts to suppress drug smuggling of the Mujahideen rebels on the Afghan border and Pakistan's treatment of women and the enslavement of children.

Armed with the Western media's version of these events, I wanted to see for myself what life was like for an average citizen of these countries. I wanted to mix with the people who were most affected by the current fighting and political manipulation, and gain the viewpoint of the man and woman on the street as closely as they would allow. There were dangerous moments, car bombs, street shootings and motoring incidents and risks were taken in photographing prohibited sights. These events were balanced by residing in Osama Bin Ladens' former base, attending a trial in a Tehran Court, being the first Western Magistrate to attend a trial in Kabul and visiting three of the Seven Wonders of the Ancient World. The lasting memory will however be of the welcome and the kindness shown by the very people that I wanted to meet.

The first stop on the November/December 2000 tour was Istanbul in Turkey. Tensions between Turkey and Greece remained high at that time over the Ocalan

Affair. Early in 1999 Turkish Special Forces had snatched Abdullah Ocalan, the Kurdish guerrilla chief from the Greek embassy in Nairobi, Kenya. Ocalan was the leader of the Kurdish Workers Party fighting for self-rule in the Kurdish Southeast. In that same area the Kurds were being butchered in poison gas attacks by Saddam Hussein. In addition to the Kurdish problem Turkey and Greece were still in dispute over the Turkish invasion of Cyprus in 1974 and the annexing of the North of the island. Greek Cypriots were forcibly expelled from their homes in the north of the island and their homes given to Turkish families from the mainland. Add to that the dispute with Greece over the Aegean Islands and you have a picture of tension, anger and mistrust that was only being held in check by the United Nations and the European Union.

Although tourists were being discouraged to visit Turkey at that time, I only experienced one direct terrorist attack while in Istanbul or when touring down the countries West Coast. Warnings to tourists were well founded as Al Quaeda linked terrorists bombed the British Consulate in Istanbul killing 33 in November 2003. Six tourists were killed in a mini bus attack in July 2005 at the west coast resort of Kusadasi and 20 were injured in nearby Cesme the same month.

Turkey is known as the bridge between Europe and the Middle East with Istanbul and the Bosphorous River being an unofficial borderline. One of the enjoyable experiences was to cruise down the Bosphorous stopping at Besiklas on the European shore and Kanlica on the Asian shore. Istanbul has many impressive buildings going back centuries including the Blue Mosque and the Topkapi Palace, the home of the sultans who had ruled Turkey when they were a major military and political force. In the palace is the gold casket containing the Prophet Mohammed's cloak. The palace is divided into three courts with a harem that consists of 300 extravagantly decorated bedrooms.

The Grand Bazaar will captivate anyone interested in shopping; it is not the place to pop into just to browse, as you are likely to get hopelessly lost among the 65 streets and 4,500 shops. If you are looking for a carpet you will be swamped for choice and had I bought a fraction of those that were presented to me I would have needed a jumbo jet of my own to get them back home. A smaller item that I did indulge in was apple tea; the Turkish version was so refreshing that I took some packs home. Despite extensive searches of health food stores back in England I have never found a brand of apple tea that matched the Turkish version. Buying anything in Turkey at this time was tricky because of the large denomination notes that were in use, as a result of high inflation. The highest value note in circulation was the 20 million lira note that amounted to just £8 in Stirling. If you were not careful you could finish up with a large wad of Turkish notes of very little value. It is only now that the currency has been revalued with 2.4 Turkish lira to the pound.

On the final day of my visit complacency about my safety was jolted when a Kurdish Separatist detonated a car bomb just two streets away from the Grand Bazaar. I started to have second thoughts about attending a football match that same evening between two of the cities rival teams, Galatasary and Fenerbache. I reasoned that such a high profile game at the Ali Semi Yen Stadium would attract a massive police presence and that apart from getting drawn into disputes between the supporters I would be reasonably safe. The stadium was on the outskirts of the city so I took a taxi to the ticket office. The stadium was the one where Leeds Utd had played earlier in the year, and where two of their supporters were killed in knife attacks in Taksim Square prior to the game. Taking advice from a senior police officer I positioned myself within the area of the home supporters. The players emerged onto the pitch from an underground tunnel so that they could be protected from any missiles thrown by the crowd. Police with riot shields and batons surrounded the pitch in the wide area between the pitch and the crowd. Fire engines complete with water cannons were positioned behind the goal facing the crowd. The game passed without any major incidents although there was lots of verbal abuse between the rival fans that I couldn't understand. I assumed it was abuse from the hate and anger on their faces. I left a few minutes before the end of the match to get a taxi and to avoid any possible gang fights.

The tour of West Turkey started with an overnight sleeper coach to Izmir via Canakkale, (the stopping point for those wishing to visit the site of Troy or travel across to the war graves of Gallipoli). I had been warned not to accept drinks on the coach from fellow passengers as the contents could be drugged. The intention being that while asleep the "friend" would make off with my luggage at one of the regular stopping points.

Using Izmir as my base I visited Selcuk to see the Roman ruins of Ephesus including the Temple of Artemis, one of the Seven Wonders of the World and the Basilica of St John. Five miles from Ephesus is the chapel where it is believed that the Virgin Mary spent her last days. This building was not identified as such until the 1890s when an invalid German woman saw a vision of the building. The woman had never visited Turkey or even left Germany. In 1967 the claim was authenticated when the Pope visited the site.

The next step on my tour was Bodrum where the massive Crusader Castle dominates the harbour. The castle links with the island of Rhodes, which was also the base for the builders of the castle, the Knights Hospitaller of St John. Bodrum is the site of another of the seven wonders of the Ancient World – the Mausoleum, the tomb of King Mausolus. The tomb was completed in 354 BC but wrecked in an earthquake in the 13th Century. A permanent reminder of the King is that his name has entered modern usage as a description of a tomb, Mausoleum.

236

The final stop was to be Marmaris, a destination popular with package holiday tourists from England. My main interest was to catch the ferry to the island of Rhodes, two and a half hours away. Although Rhodes is a Greek Island with the conflict with Turkey ongoing I was surprised not to need a visa. Pulling into the harbour the first striking sight was the Crusader fort battlements. It had been in 1523 that the Crusaders were driven out of Rhodes and Marmaris by Suleyman the Magnificent. The knights then relocated to Malta.

It is claimed that the site of the Colossus of Rhodes, another of the Seven Wonders of the Ancient World, is located somewhere on the island. Records show that the 100ft plus tall statue was built between 292-280 BC, and that it collapsed during an earthquake 56 years later. Some claim that the Colossus dedicated to the Sun God Helios is a myth. The appearance and dimensions seen in ancient documents seems to contradict each other. There may never be a definitive answer.

Having completed my journey down the West Coast of Turkey I caught a flight from the nearby Dalaman airport back to Istanbul. From there it was a flight to Tehran in Iran. On arriving in Tehran I seemed to be the only tourist in the city. Whilst looking for a guided tour I tried an agency dealing in airline tickets. There were no guided tours but the agency were able to find a retired English speaking Indian oil field manager with a supporting car and driver. Because of his Indian background he was prepared to talk politics and even got me into the Tehran Court of Justice. The former manager had settled in Iran thirty-five years ago. Fortunately he was content to stay in Iran with his family because he would not have been allowed to leave because of his extensive knowledge of the oil industry. He was however pleased to discuss issues he had lived through including the American hostage siege at their former embassy, the Iran/Iraq War, the Middle East crisis involving Israel, the lack of a democratically elected Government and the Courts sentencing powers, based on the Koran. He believed that the students who had stormed the US Embassy were "used" by the government in a pointless exercise that had subsequently cut off sources of international investment in the country. The war with Iraq had been another pointless exercise costing thousands of lives and wasted money that could have been spent on developing the country. Signs of unrest against the stranglehold of the government controlled Secret Police are emerging with growing student protests.

Iran at the time of my visit was a dictatorship controlled by Islamic religious leaders. The former King, the Shah of Persia, was overthrown in a Revolution led by the clerics around thirty years ago. Although the majority of Iranians would not publicly admit their dissatisfaction with the level of control over their lives, such as the restraints, low standard of living, secret police, the death penalty for political activity etc, my guide had no such problems. He believed that the rigid censorship and media control was slowly breaking down. Young people found ways to access satellite television and the Internet. Students were growing in confidence and were leading street protests that subsequently led to the first free elections. However the election of President Mahmound Ahmadinejad in 2005 was not a "free election" as many potential nominees were barred from taking part. The prospects of a more restrained view towards peaceful co-existence under the new President are not good. He praises suicide bombers and has declared that Islam will take over the world. It is claimed that Iranian death squads are operating in Iraq to undermine the Allies efforts to bring democracy and self government to the country. In defence of its Islamic policies the Government claim that the world crisis of the spread of AIDS, the world's fourth biggest killer, could be stopped if every country adopted Islam because it forbids casual relationships and sexual activity outside marriage.

It was under former president Ayatollah Khomeini that Iran started the modern cult of suicide bombing. During the eight year war with Iraq he recruited 12 year olds to clear minefields knowing they would die. Murals to 13 year old Hossein Famedeh can be seen across Tehran. He is recognised as the first "suicide warrior" of Iran. Hossein strapped explosives to his body and threw himself under an Iraqi tank. It is claimed that Iran has a military garrison set aside to exclusively recruit and train volunteers for "Martyrdom".

Relationships between Iran and the United Nations are deteriorating due to Iran's insistence of continuing with a nuclear programme that they claim is peaceful and only intended to produce electricity. The fear is that the generators will produce weapons grade uranium.

During the tour of Tehran I visited the mountain range in the north of the city. The Caspian Sea lies behind the snow topped mountain range. Narrow, shallow, fast flowing canals flank most main roads running north to south through the city. The water is melted snow and helps to wash away litter left on the streets. We made a number of stops including the Shah's former Palace, which is now a museum. The Jewel room contained incredible wealth belonging to previous Kings over the past 200 years. The Jewel guide was very discrete when asked if the government could ever sell off this decadent treasure to bail out the economy, *"the Government has the power to do anything"* was his response.

On passing the former American Embassy I asked my driver to slow down so I could take photos of the bullet pitted walls painted with anti American slogans, this was an illegal activity and could have got me locked up. Considering the camera was tucked in my armpit the photographs turned out particularly well. The Americans were held hostage for 444 days and it almost led to an American invasion of Iran.

My visit to Cambodia was still fresh in my mind and I couldn't help but compare it to Iran. Despite Iran being more advanced there are some interesting parallels. Both have no American or British influences in term of shops, fast food restaurants, international newspapers, magazines or films. Officially TV programmes from abroad such as CNN and BBC are banned. Both countries have raging inflation, three years ago the pound was worth 2,800 Rials, now it's valued at 11,000 a decline of almost 400%. Airport security is mammoth with military roadblocks and fighter planes sharing runways with commercial flights. Armed soldiers are in view around all government buildings.

Iran was more advanced in the quality of roads, pavements and street lighting etc. Driving however was chaotic and crossing the road life threatening. One problem is the wide carriageways separated by barriers to create one way streets. I was in a taxi that reversed for nearly a mile at 40mph down a four-way carriageway with traffic swerving out of the way and blasting their horns. The driver concluded by turning up a one way street the wrong way again causing more cars to swerve just to take a short cut to the airport saving a few minutes.

On a lighter note, the Iranian driver of my hire car had developed a tactic to avoid getting more than one parking ticket a day. Early that morning he had parked in a restricted area and received a parking ticket. Traffic is so dense that drivers find it difficult to park legitimately. The fine is equal to £2, a lot of money in a low wage economy. There is no way of avoiding fines as parking tickets are logged on a central computer. If someone wanted to renew an annual tax licence on their car any unpaid fines would show on the computer and the fine increased 3 times. Non-payment results in no car tax and subsequently no car. The little dodge employed by my driver would be to park in a restricted spot every time we visited a new place of interest. He would put the parking ticket under the windscreen wipers as though it had just been issued. It worked every time and he got away with one parking fine all day.

The final stop on my tour was to the National Football Stadium. Football in one of the most popular sports in Iran. They have qualified for the World Cup Finals on two previous occasions. Although no matches were played during my stay I was able to tour the Azadia Stadium, to watch players training. The stadium is basic in term of safety especially when there are 100,000 spectators in the ground. At the end of a qualifying match against Japan in 2005 five fans were crushed to death and forty others seriously injured as they rushed to exit the ground.

Iran's population is 98% Muslim and with the month of Ramadan starting the day I arrived it placed restrictions on me when walking around the city alone. Muslims fast between sunrise and sunset so it wasn't possible to eat or drink in public during that time for fear of causing offence. As the sun set large queues formed outside bakeries and food stores.

I found accommodation at the Pars Hotel through the airport information desk. The hotel was plain with white walls and brown threadbare carpets in the bedroom and white tiles throughout the bathroom. There weren't any locks on the bedroom door so I wedged a chair against the door for peace of mind. The spartan conditions reminded me of East Germany in the 1960s. At least it was cheap at £60 for four days plus breakfast. It was my first exposure to carrot jam!

There were four TV channels, none in English. Programmes featured large groups of people doing communal exercises to music in matching tracksuits, again very East German. On the final night on a channel usually blank I discovered an English language film starring John Travolta. It was a bland film unlikely to cause offence however every few minutes a message appeared in English stating that no one should be watching this film or have a video version. If anyone had a copy they were to telephone a number in confidence. American and British films were considered a corrupting influence for showing too much flesh or for low moral activities that offend the Koran's teachings.

If Iran wished to boost tourism and hence the economy they would be at a major disadvantage as hardly anyone speaks English. Not only is English not taught but also the lack of English language films, TV, newspapers, music etc means people can't practice and teach themselves. The only advantage for me was that no one approached me to buy anything. It was fascinating watching my Indian guide bartering with Persian carpet dealers. This was the biggest covered Bazaar in the world. While the Tehran market was packed with Iranians the Istanbul market was packed with tourists spending currency to boost the Turkish economy.

The feeling is that Iran is heading towards another Revolution based on democracy. There were growing reports of student protests and jails full of political activists. In time the masses may erupt when the declining economy and harsh regime becomes unacceptable. That time didn't come in 2005 as the newly elected President Mahmound Ahmadinejad is considered a hard liner against western influences. In many ways women remain second class citizens. Women's veils are of three designs. One shows the full face, one just the eyes and the other completely covers the face. The majority wore a one piece black robe showing the face and the gown reaching to the floor so not to arouse men by exposing hair or other parts of their body. Could the next Revolution be led by women to throw off their shackles?

The anti US/UK feelings are due to the support given to Israel against the Palestinians even though the Allies brought Saddam Hussein to defeat over Kuwait and so weakened Iraq's ability to attack Iran. The English language Iran News and Iran Times were full of anti-Israel stories of the crisis in the Middle East. The press was also amused by the Presidential election fiasco in the USA. They claimed that if Gore were elected he would bomb Pakistan to destroy their atomic weapons capacity. If Bush was elected he will be bound to support Israel as wealthy Jewish businessmen back him. The government controlled press was calling for all Arab countries to ban all US products and not undertake any trade. Recently many newspapers were closed down as they voiced criticism of the Iranian government and their editors were imprisoned. The Iran News survived by featuring censored international news.

It took three days to solve the Coca-Cola mystery. Cans were on sale everywhere despite the ban on US products. It transpired that the Coca-Cola design had been copied and a similar drink placed in the cans. The same copycatting had been done with Mars bars and Twix. No doubt the companies are powerless against this breach of copyright.

During my time in Iran there were a number of occasions when I felt my safety compromised. There was a constant atmosphere of fear and mistrust as the main population remains under the constant observation of the secret police and live under strict conditions that restrict their liberty and freedom of speech. By taking a risk photographing the US Embassy I felt I had, in a small way, put up two fingers to the government's oppression of their people.

My next step was Faisalabad in Pakistan, north of Karachi and near the disputed border area of Kashmir and India. Kashmir is fighting for an independent state, free from India and Pakistan. The Mujahideen rebels and the armed forces kill each other on a daily basis. This had been going on in the Northern Territories for many years with thousands killed.

There was another flashpoint, out of bound for tourists, the border between Afghanistan and Pakistan. Fighting was regularly taking place as drug runners tried to get through with heroin to feed the world market. The second problem involved sectarian fighting between groups within Pakistan. At any time here, in Faisalabad or any major city a bomb could go off in a car, bus or in a packed market place.

I had chosen to be in Pakistan at this time to indulge my passion for cricket. The second Test match was about to take place. Faisalabad is Pakistan's third biggest city and the country's main industrial and textile centre. Prior to partition from India it was a small market town. Guidebooks now describe it as the "Manchester of Pakistan" (without the nightlife). I'm sure the people of Manchester would not be pleased with this comparison!

I stayed at the Prime Hotel, rated 3 star in Pakistan but not in England, but at £12 a night you shouldn't complain. You even get your own pet lizard in the bathroom! At least there was BBC World on TV for news and ESPN for international sport. It was the kind of hotel you didn't know what to expect next. An English guest woke up one morning and without putting on the light swung his feet out of bed into water a foot deep. His room had been flooded from a shower overflow with his clothes floating around the room! What a shock start to the day. His only item of dry clothing was the trunks he slept in.

Traffic and pollution are tremendous as vehicles compete with herds of goats, donkey drawn carts and motorised rickshaws. These two stroke engine boxes on wheels are cheap but a dangerous way of getting around the city. Massive street markets add to the congestion. Three incidents occurred on the way to the Iqbal Stadium. Firstly I saw a donkey lying stretched out on the ground having collapsed pulling a cart piled high with wood. It took eight bystanders to lift the cart off the donkey enabling the animal to stagger to its feet. The second involved a motorised rickshaw; it is always a rough ride due to potholes in the road so when we crashed into another rickshaw it was no big deal. The two drivers got out and had a big row as they surveyed the damage before we continued our journey. Thirdly, as I approached the main perimeter fence of the stadium on foot a large crowd was milling about. Suddenly the police charged the crowd and lashed out with long batons. Two tear gas shells were fired into the crowd to make them disperse. A police officer, spotting me getting swamped by the retreating crowd quickly pulled me out of danger and guided me toward the stadium.

The Iqbal Stadium is new with a modern design holding 20,000 people. There was a huge police/army presence. Having got through the first perimeter I was confronted by a large crowd trying to get through a second set of gates. No one had tickets and were all trying to talk their way past the guards who every few minutes would clear everyone away beating them with their big sticks. I had no ticket, my only advantage was being white. Once through this second perimeter I approached the entrance to the stadium. I asked a senior police officer where I could buy a ticket. He laughed, shook my hand wearing sparkling white gloves and said, "This is Pakistan, you don't need a ticket". He shepherded me through he VIP entrance into the main pavilion. While sitting in the elevated seating area I noticed that the 20 strong Barmy Army had been given an area to themselves on the boundary edge complete with soft chairs, bottles of Pepsi and packets of crisps, all free of charge. After the lunch interval I went down onto the grass to join them.

On the second day of the match I did exactly the same and again got in free. Amazingly this was all down to being white; I was treated with exaggerated respect, possibly on the belief that in some way I was linked to the sponsors. The Barmy Army were on their best behaviour as they had heard of the reputation of the police in dealing with trouble makers and knew that they could finish up with a beating or be put in jail if they misbehaved. There were no more than 150 English supporters in the crowd of 20,000 and most of them were locked away in the pavilion on an expensive cricket tour. It is a big advantage that no alcohol is allowed in public because it meant that the crowd remained good spirited throughout without any aggression associated with some sporting events. Beyond the boundary rope there was a 10ft high steel fence all round the ground. This is to ensure that the crowd can't invade the pitch during inter state matches. The ground is divided into sections separated by high steel fences. There are separate areas exclusively for women, as they are not allowed to sit with the men in public even if they are married to them.

At the cricket stadium a steady stream of people would come up, introduce themselves and discuss anything and everything in a cheerful and positive manner. They are rightly proud of their progress as an emerging nation. It is only since 1947 after partition from India that they have been an Independent State. There was still a strong affection for the previous British rule in India.

At the conclusion of the Test Match that ended in a draw it was time for a flight to Karachi. After the cheap flea pit hotels of Iran and Faisalabad it was time for a touch of luxury. By a stroke of luck a brand new luxury hotel, the Carlton, had recently opened on the beach area. They were trying out the facilities and wanting to build up a reputation so they were offering six star accommodations for 2,500 rupees rather than 56,000 rupees. This worked out at just £30 a night bed and breakfast. There was a golf course, health club, marina and six different dining areas. It was a real treat to play golf at the Defence Authority Golf and Country Club on the edge of the Arabian Sea. It was the first time I had ever hired a caddy. For the princely sum of 80 rupees (£1) only one ball ended up in the Arabian Sea thanks to his advice.

There were two English language newspapers, Dawn and News, both critical of many facets of the administration of the country. They have exposed corrupt political leaders and police officers. They were also campaigning on behalf of women. A press headline read, *"Haunting biases continue to hound us"*. It focused on the prejudices and injustice suffered by women particularly in rural communities. A few of the key points contained in the report written by Sikandar Bohi, are as follows.

"The birth of a girl can bring on an air of sadness within a family and in some tribes there is a tradition of hitting the father's head seven times with a pair of shoes. For a son parents may receive handsome gifts from relatives and friends. Inequality between genders

exists at every step. It is preferred that boys eat first and they get the choicest selections. In some tribes women are not allowed to eat meat because it would make them strong sexually. Women are not allowed to go out of the house without permission from a male unless it is for economic gain such as working in the fields. Tribal women are denied education - Girls once educated will go astray and write love letters and flee away with someone. Another problem is that very young girls are married to much older men, it is not uncommon to be betrothed from the age of three. Girls are "sold" into marriage. If a girl is beautiful and physically strong her price would range from 200,000-300,00 Rupees, (£2,700-£4,300). A girl less endowed can be purchased from 75,000-150,000 rupees, (£1,000-£2,000). Women have to work harder than men in village society but are paid less than men for equivalent work. Tribal societies are quick to judge women in regard to their "purity". In case a bride falls short for any reason she is either killed or divorced by the bridegroom the morning after the wedding".

Sikander Bohi concludes her report. *"We have entered into a new millennium, but unfortunately we have moved into it laden with traditions, attitudes and discriminations of eras long past. We have not unburdened ourselves against prejudices and injustices nor brought wisdom into our future. It is high time we took measures to eradicate antiquated medieval laws. It is time for the State, its functionaries and civil society to initiate practical steps to forge ahead instead of bowing under pressure from quarters not given to change for selfish reasons and gains".*

The tradition of arranged marriage is not a Muslim custom but due to the influence of Hindus who shared India for centuries before the establishment of the State of Pakistan. Arranged marriages are declining within the educated classes. There is virtually no recorded crime by women or girls. Prostitution is forbidden under Islam hence the lack of such Court cases. Pakistani society is strongly patriarchal and only partly because its Islamic. Women are held to be lowly and precious, meant to be mothers and housekeepers, yet to be protected with ones life. The ideal marriage, (usually arranged in the early teens), was traditionally between first cousins on the father's side.

The American influence is slowly spreading across Pakistan. Coca-Cola and Pepsi are commonplace and KFC, McDonalds and Pizza Hut are opening up across Karachi. Dunkin Doughnuts had just opened and was deserted apart from myself in the middle of the day; it would have been more sensible to wait for Ramadan to end before opening. The day after my visit a press report described how two businessmen were shot dead at the nearby Metropolitan Hotel, just 100 yards from where I had been sitting. It was a reminder to be continually on alert when moving around the city.

The move to establish democracy was once again gaining momentum with reports of fragmented political parties forming alliances. They had put pressure on the military to relinquish power and allow free elections. Lawyers have joined in the campaign by striking. The problem appears to be a lack of public figures capable of running the country free of previous records of corruption. The last military coup of 1999 was the fourth in a country only established in 1947.

Pakistan is desperate to encourage tourism. Reports affecting tourists include a survey by the International Labour Organisation showed that 3.3 million children between five and fourteen years old work outside the home. Child labour is not just confined to family farming but to carpet making, leather tanning and sports equipment. Large numbers are "bonded labourers", working in servitude to pay off their parents debts. Examples of corruption in education have been highlighted in reports finding that government funding wasn't reaching its targets. Comparing government figures independent researchers found 16,000 ghost schools, headteachers and school staff. The report claimed that children were taught poisonous nonsense, rural school buildings are used for storing onions and potatoes and a whole new university has been abandoned as it fell down (before it was even used).

Statistics from 1998 show that only 428,000 tourists visited Pakistan whilst 2,398,000 visited India and 1,007,000 to Iran. Only three countries fared worse than Pakistan, Bangladesh, war torn Sri Lanka and the remote Maldives. Only 13% of visitors came to holiday in Pakistan while 57% visited relatives. Tourism earns only $76 million and Pakistan visitor's abroad spent $218 million, a deficit of $142 million. To show how significant these figures are in terms of the economy France received 61.5 million tourists and the USA 44.8 million. Even China attracted more than 22 million and smaller countries such as Malaysia, Thailand and Indonesia attracted between four-six million each. The tourism problems have been identified as image, lack of natural and historical features, fears of sectarian violence, corruption within the government, army and the police. It is very sad, as the "ordinary" people I encountered were all helpful, cheerful and kind. A surprising statistic is that Americans travel overseas less than any comparable country. The numbers who even hold passports is an extremely small percentage of the population.

The third Test Match against England was held at the National Stadium in Karachi. It looks impressive from a distance but close up it is dirty and run down. It seats 50,000 and is floodlit. The ground had large areas of empty seats with around 3,000 people present including 150 English supporters. With so few present it lacked atmosphere and the presence of armed police with machine guns was unnecessary.

On the fourth day a decent crowd finally attended creating an exciting atmosphere. The ground was a third full with around 14,000 present. They clapped and cheered in rhythm to try and encourage their bowlers as they struggled to dismiss England. A new computerised score box was used for the first time that could show replays on a large screen. Half way through the day it broke down when rats chewed through the power cables. There is no news of the fate of the rats.

While many people find the tradition of children in Pakistan being bethrothed into marriage at a very young age difficult to understand an even more difficult practice to comprehend is vani. This marriage tradition has been highlighted by three sisters, Abda, Amna and Sajda Khan, who have threatened to commit suicide if forced to marry when coming of age. Vani is the pratice of being promised in marriage whilst children to the enemies of their family. The tribal custom of vani is a method in which blood feuds are settled with forced marriages. The brides will spend their lives paying for the crime of one of their male relatives and live like slaves.

The story involving the Khan sisters began 14 years ago when the girls' uncle killed a neighbour. The Tribal Council who dealt with the crime offered to pardon the offender in exchange for the vani of his three nieces. The victim's family refuse to release the vani sentence stating. "They have betrayed us by asking to be released from the vani, they have insulted our honour. If the vani is not fulfilled the two families will start fighting again and more than 200 people could die".

The Pakistan Government banned vani early in 2005 but it is claimed the ban is not being enforced by the police. The Khan sisters are leading a campaign to overcome their plight. Abda Khan said "if the government does not help us we will commit suicide. We will burn ourselves alive to protest vani. I know this is prohibited by Islam but so is vani and God will forgive us". The sisters have the law, religion and family on their side. What they have against them is the weight of tradition, tribe and partriarchy. Much will depend on whose justice will prevail.

On departing Karachi I reflected on a conversation I had with a team of construction workers at my hotel. They were extremely careful when travelling to Karachi for fear of kidnapping. Their fears were confirmed in a conversation with a Canadian businessman I met in Dubai on the way to Karachi. He was met by an armed bodyguard at the airport and his company had a million dollar ransom insurance cover for him. I had survived my month in Turkey, Iran and Pakistan. Was I "Lucky Jim" or "Unimportant Jim?"

In September 2004 I decided to venture into Afghanistan which borders Iran, Iraq and Pakistan making it one of the most volatile areas in the world. I had been biding my time in terms of believing when it would be safe. Friends, family and colleagues thought I was mad.

The journey to Kabul involved a flight from Birmingham to Islamabad, Pakistan, on to Peshawar and then to Kabul. My arrival coincided with the release of 375 Pakistan prisoners from Kabul while over the border in Iraq 47 were killed in gun battles in Baghdad. Three were killed in the west Afghan city of Herat as two UN buildings were attacked by 1,000 protesters following the dismissal of the Governor Ismael Khan, an anti Soviet fighter and warlord. It was quite a welcome.

Deteriorating security had contributed to a low voter registration for the parliamentary elections so they were delayed until next January. The country has never had an election, for centuries it was ruled by a Royal dynasty. The dynasty ended with the invasion by Russians that led in turn to the Taliban freedom fighters who drove the Russians out before taking over. The Taliban introduced a brutal regime based on Islamic Fundamentalism with self-appointed warlords ruling the country. The Taliban were overthrown by a coalition involving US and UK forces in 2001 although their war lords still control large areas of countryside used for harbouring Osama Bin Laden's Al Queda network of operations and training camps.

Despite the delay for parliamentary elections the presidential election was due to take place on October 9th 2004. In an attempt to ensure the elections smooth running the US has increased its troops to 20,000 with NATO also providing 2,000 troops. So far 10 million people had registered to vote out of a population of 25-28 million. The actual number is unknown, as there hasn't been a registration of voters before. There were worries that some people had registered twice. Literacy levels are low across many rural areas. Many had not experienced an election before and do not understand the concept of voting. There are worries that voters are vulnerable to manipulation from warlords. Warlords remain the biggest worry, as they are heavily involved in the resurgent opium trade using profits to buy weapons for their private armies. Their annual income from drug trafficking is estimated at $2.3 billion, almost eight times the governments tax revenues.

There were 18 Presidential candidates including the interim President Hamid Karai who was installed by the US to stabilise the country prior to an election. Other candidates include a poet returning from exile in France, a female doctor, a religious conservative and a warlord infamous for driving nails into his opponent's heads during the 1990s civil war.

Refugees returning from Iran are a massive problem, every evening mini buses pour into Kabul in their hundreds. Refugees report of leaving Iran reluctantly and of being "sharply encouraged" by the Tehran authorities. They receive 18 dollars each as a hand out on arrival. They are warned about landmines of which the countryside is infested. More than 1 million Afghan refugees have returned from Iran since April 2002. In recent weeks there had been an average of 4,000 a day. Jawad, a refugee aged 23 who spent 22 years in Tehran said, *"Any kilometre you are coming into you think you are going 10 years backwards. I could not have ever imagined what it was going to be like"*. His sister Fatima, 32, added, *"There is dust and no sanitation, kids get sick. I did not imagine how much had been destroyed"*.

The Afghan *"Back to School Campaign"* has begun again with half a million children returning in September to the Northern and Eastern Provinces. There are two academic years, one running from March to December in areas with cold winters and the second from September in areas where the summer is too hot to hold classes. Special programmes have been introduced to promote the importance of education especially for girls. At the Helmand Province the attendance by primary school girls is only 10%. Afghanistan has seen a steady increase in the number of children attending school since the fall of the Taliban in 2001. Today more than four million children are enrolled in classes, a third of them girls. Surveys in 2003 showed that net girl's enrolment rates had reached 35% and there are indications that Afghanistan could reach the Millennium Development goal of parity by 2005. Despite these successes more than a million girls of primary school age are still not attending school. Reasons include the distance to school from home, inadequate facilities at those schools that do exist and the perception that education has no value for many rural families.

The battle to overcome the Taliban is not yet won. The Operational Commander of the US led Forces said that Al Qaeda chiefs are still commanding operations in parts of Afghanistan. Major General Eric Olson, implicated Osama Bin Laden's terrorist's group in a deadly car bomb attack in Kabul the previous week that killed six people. The General said that the battle against the remnants of the ousted Taliban regime was far from over. It is hoped a successful October Presidential Election will discourage other militants from disrupting the delayed Parliamentary Elections next January.

There is no professional sport in Afghanistan. The National Stadium in Kabul is only used for political rallies, not sport. There are no national sports coaches, no training facilities and no international rating. A small group took part in the Olympics in Greece but no medals were gained. Those who competed were relatives of officials. Football, cricket, volleyball and table tennis have begun in some schools. Following a series of trials a squad of 14 adult cricketers have been selected and will play their first match as an Afghanistan team during a tour of Bangladesh.

The first sign of being in an occupied country was seeing patrolling US gun carriers outside the airport. Talks have been held with Pakistan urging them to increase co-operation against Islamic militants along their border and to stop them attacking Afghan. US gun carriers are also found outside a new mosque being built in the city centre.

A report by a UN expert on Human Rights records that many Afghan warlords are violating human rights. Actions include executions, torture, arbitrary arrest, inhuman detention, seizure of private property and the trafficking of women and children. Fractional fighting in western Afghanistan has left thousands of returning refugees stranded at the Iran border for days.

A taxi drive to the Supreme Court in Kabul ended in drama. Driving is chaotic with drivers relying on their horns to signal their intentions as they weave in and out of the traffic. My driver took a wrong turn and suddenly we were heading the wrong way against four lanes of on coming traffic all flashing their lights, sounding their horns and weaving from side to side to avoid collisions. The police eventually stopped the taxi and arrested the driver leaving me stranded to find another taxi.

There are victims of the war begging on the streets all over the city. At one major road junction controlled by an ageing police officer the same two beggars sat in the middle of the road every day with lines of traffic passing on each side of them. They appeared to be war veterans having missing limbs. It looked more dangerous sitting in the road than fighting a war as only inches separated them from the lorries and cars racing past. There appeared to be no restrictions on how high a vehicle was piled with products. A taxi had a bed strapped sideways on the roof with the ends protruding on each side.

I booked into the only recommended secure hotel outside the centre of Kabul, the Hotel Continental. A large sign outside the hotel showed an automatic weapon with a red cross through it and stated "No Weapons". The hotel was built in 1969 by the UK Company Taylor Woodrow. Prior to the liberating invasion by US/UK troops three years before, the top two floors of the hotel had been occupied by Osama Bin Laden and his senior staff. It was his home and centre of operations with a large communications dish on the roof. The dish is now used by the BBC and other international television stations such as CNN.

The room opposite mine on the second floor had been turned into a studio for the transmission of all BBC TV news stories with an engineer on duty 24 hours a day, seven days a week on a six week rolling shift. The Arabic TV station, Al Jazeera, that has shown British hostages and has transmitted statements from Osama Bin Laden was known to the engineer. The TV station is highly regarded in the world of telecommunications and many of its staff are former BBC employees. Al Jazeera has a TV studio in London overlooking the House of Commons. An interview was transmitted from there involving the cleric who is banned from public speaking in England while he fights extradition to the US for a trial.

Banking was a problem in Kabul, there were no ATM's and for the first time on my travels VISA and Credit cards were not accepted. I had to visit five different banks before I could find one to change £ into $, the only currency accepted by the hotel.

A pleasant surprise was to discover the Duke of Edinburgh's Award Scheme was being piloted in Afghanistan. A half-day was spent with the Award Officer during which I was able to give advice on promoting the Award. In return I learnt a lot about life in Kabul and of the aspirations of young, thrusting business people. I was also able to visit a women's centre where craft skills were being taught that would allow them to secure employment. There was a unit where the children of the women trainees were being looked after and also classrooms for students to develop their language, reading and writing skills. None of their activities would have been allowed under the Taliban warlords.

Britain's colonial past in Afghanistan was to be seen in the British cemetery. In 1839 Britain had sent soldiers to Kabul to try to maintain order. By 1841 they were in retreat in the face of a public uprising. The troops marched towards India but it is claimed that only one of 16,000 troops survived the journey.

At the weekends hundreds of kites can be seen flying over Kabul, it is a pastime shared by adults and children alike. In some areas of the city war damaged buildings can still be seen, pock marked by missile hits and very reminiscent of Beirut.

During my stay in Kabul I had great difficulty in sleeping but it was not because of noise or a lack of comfort. At the airport on departure I struck up a conversation with a UN Aid Worker who had been manning a refugee station on the border with Iran and was flying to Peshawar in Pakistan for a welcome break. She attributed my sleeping difficulties to my raised level of adrenaline. While I had been walking around Kabul I had subconsciously been at a high level of fear as if I was expecting to be attacked at any moment.

The flight home gave plenty of time for reflection particularly as I was upgraded to the first class section. This also happened on the outward flight from Birmingham where I was escorted to the front of the queue. It turned out that I was the only white person on the plane and perhaps racial prejudice was working in my favour. Had I been sensible in going to Afghanistan at this time? Would I be able to see if the Coalition Forces had been justified in liberating Afghanistan in 2001? I finished up with 12 questions based on human rights issues. If you agree with the thinking behind the majority of these questions I suggest you will be reassured that the liberation of Afghanistan was justified.

Is there a right to a basic education that allows all citizens to enjoy the benefits of reading and writing? The majority of the population can do neither; it is a right that we take for granted.

Is there a right for women to be treated equally? The right to education, to vote in elections, to wears clothes of their own choice, to be able to show their faces, to earn a wage through employment outside the home, to access public transport and entertainment without restrictions, to participate in sport. It is only since 2001 that girls have been able, by right, to go to school. At least 1 million girls of primary school age are still not in education.

Is there a right for all citizens to have access to clean drinking water and for sanitation that is effectively channelled to process plants rather than into open sewers?

Is there a right for women to be free to marry the person of their choice and not be subjected to arranged/forced marriages?

Is there a right for a free health service for all and sufficient medical staff to cover the basic illnesses?

Is there a right to free democratic elections where citizens have a choice of candidates and are able to express their views on the broad-based issues that effect their lives? The election in 2004 was the country's first.

Is there a right to travel on adequate road surfaces with street lighting? Very few roads have smooth tarmac surfaces and virtually all side roads in Kabul are dirt tracks, which are like obstacle courses.

Is there a right to participate in sport or other forms of recreation? There is no professional sport in the country. No football, cricket, hockey, swimming, athletics, etc for adults to support or follow. There are no leisure centres, swimming pools, tennis courts, training facilities, qualified coaches or access to equipment. It is only since 2001 that sport has been introduced to schools.

Is there a right to access radio, television or the Internet for information and knowledge of what is happening in the outside world?

Is there a right to a free press and to have freedom of speech?

Is there a right to roam the countryside free from the fear of stepping on indiscriminately laid landmines?

Is there a right to live in peace, free from the influence of the Taliban warlords who still control areas of the countryside through torture, executions and the trafficking in drugs, women and children.

If you agree these are 12 basic rights we take for granted then the liberation of Afghanistan was justified. Having seen for myself, without media influence, I am convinced that through the UN, developed countries have a responsibility to uphold the human rights of citizens on this planet.

Although at this time, September 2005, I have been unable to get a visa or consider it safe to visit Iraq I believe the liberation of Iraq was justified for many of the same 12 reasons above. The response to the first free elections in Iraq in 2005 is a positive sign. Let the people decide, not the terrorists.

19

Journey's End in West Africa

100 Countries visited – Ghana reunion
Reality of modern day slavery, voodoo and corruption
Royal funds for trees and monkeys myth destroyed
Nigerian missionaries lead Anglican revival in the UK
A Near Death Experience with King Mboutcheko in Cameroon

Having visited 95 countries over the last 45 years I wanted to reach a target of 100 in the grand fashion. Although I have favoured triangular programmes in recent years, a five country overland tour along the coast of West Africa seemed a possible challenge. There were a number of options linking countries, some more dangerous than others. The final choice was Ghana, Togo, Benin, Nigeria and Cameroon. They all operated an African version of the Duke of Edinburgh's Award and by offering my experiences, time and knowledge of the Award Scheme to the National Co-ordinators of these countries I would in return receive advice and support that would make the visit more enjoyable. I was visiting as an Award volunteer and paying all my own expenses.

In the first instance my Award colleagues were able to provide me with letters of introduction to secure visas from their UK Embassies. I discovered it was possible to hold two passports simultaneously so I used one to circulate around the Embassies in London and at the same time used the other to visit countries such as Afghanistan and Pakistan. The visas were quite expensive, costing nearly £200.

My hosts were very helpful in locating modest but comfortable low cost accommodation and providing access to hire cars, some of which I would pay for. The real bonus was to access young people and their teachers/Award leaders by giving promotional talks in 10 schools and colleges. Meetings were held with Government Ministers so that I could extol the virtues of the Award Scheme in an attempt to secure additional funding for the host countries. A number of small dinner parties were a bonus. Thanks to the links with the Award Officers I was to meet some exceptional people doing outstanding work through the Scheme. I learned far more than any conventional tour could have provided and made some very good friends.

In the final days of November 2004 before departing on what might be my last adventure, I was given a number of reminders of the volatile state of life across Africa. Ghana was my first destination, its neighbour, Cote d'Ivoire, formally known as the Ivory Coast, was in a state of war with the French administrators as the French were trying to put down a revolt by Government forces who had used their Air Force to kill nine French Aid workers. The French retaliated by destroying the governments Air Force. The events seemed destined to deepen the crisis that had already pitted Muslims against Christians, Northerners against Southerners and Ivorians with deep roots in the country against those whose parents and grandparents had immigrated seeking work. Looting was taking place led by the Young Patriots. The 400 British citizens living in the country had been evacuated to Ghana and 8,000 French citizens had fled the country.

The crisis involving Rwanda and the Congo continued claiming 4.5 million lives to date. UN Peace keepers were patrolling the border in an attempt to stop the fighting. The Rwandan President claimed that the only way to bring peace to the area was to fight a war! He claimed it would prevent further genocide of the ethnic Tutsis if their opponents were wiped out.

Two days before my arrival a major incident occurred in Tome, the capital of Togo, another of the places I was to visit. A public demonstration at the Presidential palace was against 11 years of Government rule during which the promised democratic free elections had not taken place. During the demonstration 216 sustained injuries and 13 were killed.

A state of emergency had been declared in the North Dafur State of the Sudan because of the military escalation by the rebel fighters. The conflict had been raging for 21 months with more than 70,000 either killed or dead from hunger or disease. The conflict revolved about the marginalisation of Black Africans by the Arab led Government. Khartoum's response to the latest rebel attacks had been to release the Janjaweed, the Arab militia who had been blamed by Western officials and Aid workers for the killings, rapes and widespread violation of human rights.

In South Africa, Archbishop Desmond Tutu, speaking at the Nelson Mandela annual lecture, warned that South Africa is sitting on a powder keg because millions are living in *"dehumanising poverty"*. He claims that attempts to boost Black economy ownership were only benefiting an elite minority. He also claimed the Black Economy Empowerment Programme was, *"further enriching already wealthy blacks. Gruelling, demeaning, dehumanising poverty experienced by millions of South Africans was the biggest threat to the country's security"*. Acknowledging what had been achieved since the end of apartheid he concluded that, *"Unthinking, uncritical, kow towing party line towing is fatal to a vibrant democracy"*.

Mugabe was sabre rattling in Zimbabwe accusing Prime Minister Tony Blair of meddling. *"The enemy will not stop its imperialist manoeuvres - we must be vigilant to resist him"*.

Tension still exists in some parts of Nigeria. Sharia Muslim riots have taken place twice between Igbo Christians and Hausa Muslims. 300 were killed in one night of hand to hand fighting - including 24 Britons.

HIV/AIDS remains a major deterrent to some considering a trip to Africa. Although medication exists to treat Aids, the cost is beyond most Africans. The 2004 campaign is focused on girls/women who are the biggest group of victims. World Aids Day concentrated on how Aids spreads, stigmatisation reduction, methods to reduce discrimination and prevention strategies. The fact is that since many people are not prepared to be faithful to their spouses but continue to engage in unprotected sex, the spread of Aids will not stop.

Against the above summary of the life threatening events across Africa my five-country adventure started with my arrival in Accra, Ghana, via Amsterdam. A few days before my departure I was discussing the trip with Prince Philip at the Award General council in Liverpool. Concluding the conversation he said, *"Good Luck, I wish you a successful trip"*. And turning away added cryptically *"You'll need It"*.

How true!

Ghana is considered one of the friendliest and easiest countries to get around in West Africa. The area was previously known as the Gold Coast as it was gold and ivory that attracted invaders from the UK and Europe. In the 16th Century slaves replaced gold as the principal trade, supplying European plantations in the Americas. The battle for independence was led by Kwame Nkrumah from 1949 onwards. Independence was gained in March 1957. Major changes came in 1979 with the emergence of Flt Lt Jerry Rawlins who led a military coup with the aid of junior ranks - a most unusual occurrence. Military coups are normally conducted by senior officers.

My first contact with Ghana was in 1971 when I was a part time Award worker for Staffordshire. An exchange programme involving D of E participants was established and I supported a candidate from Pelsall in the West Midlands. The exchange has continued for over 30 years with groups visiting each country in turn. My contact in Ghana, Ernest Safo, was an Award participant who visited England in 1974. We would have met at events across Staffordshire including the one at the home of Lord Lichfield at Shugborough Hall. It was an amazing reunion after all this time.

The first promotional element of the trip included visits to a girls school in Aburi and to the Nungua Community School in Accra, in both cases I was asked to speak at an assembly about the countries visited and the participation of young people in D of E activities. The story of Mother Teresa being the most interesting to the school children. Other engagements included meeting government ministers to encourage greater funding for the Award Scheme to allow specialist work with young offenders and those with special needs to be undertaken. Training workshops for leaders were run, the site of an Open Award Centre/Outward Bound Centre was visited and a dinner party held under a full moon with Jenkins Awumee, Africa's representative on the D of E International Council.

Visits to places of particular interest to me included the Accra Supreme Court. Outside is a memorial to three judges who were murdered by anti government rebels. Some of the killers were never caught and are believed to have been serving senior politicians. The court in which I sat as an observer was dealing with a fraud case. The woman judge was sitting alone although there was provision for up to 9 judges to sit on trials involving serious issues. The trial by jury option has been retained but lay magistrates sitting in Magistrates Courts have long gone. All the magistrates are now qualified lawyers.

Travelling around Ghana I came across a number of banners that would fall foul of the Advertising Standards Agency in the UK. They read "*The Association of Registered Entrepreneurs*", "*The Institute of Charismatic Church Leaders*", and "*The International School of Language*" (hung outside a small village shack) .All three signs raise questions about their credibility and take up. Most bush taxis carried Christian messages. With the election just days away, an imaginative slogan read "*Vote for Jesus*".

The treatment of children is still a major issue. A training workshop was held in Accra on the subject of child labour. It was targeted at fisherman, farmers, the Police Service, Parliamentarians and civil society organisations. It was claimed that 2.47 million children in Ghana aged between 5 and 17 were engaged in work activities. Most are engaged in prostitution, drug peddling, domestic work, farming, fishing, street hawking, stone breaking, forestry and animal rearing. The workshop attracted just 18 delegates. With so little interest in the plight of children is it any wonder that they remain in a form of slavery.

Election campaigning was well under way in Ghana. The elections due to take place the day after my departure. A big scandal emerged involving the former President of Ghana, Flt Lt Jerry Rawlins, who was accused of attacking the District Chief Executive for Bongo. Following the front-page news a hasty cover up followed to ensure the former President was not charged by the police.

The next leg of my journey was to Togo. On departing my hotel it was quite a shock to receive an account totalling 2.4 million Cede. Fortunately in dollars it was a more manageable sum of $272.

The departure from Ghana to Togo was to be by car. The journey took three hours, had I been travelling by bus it would have taken twice as long. Ernest escorted me to the border for the hand over to my hosts in Togo. Traffic congestion in Accra is horrendous with numerous jams. Once onto the open country roads the driver came into his own racing through villages with the wrecks of mini busses, lorries, and cars dotted along the roadside. It was one of the most frightening journeys I have ever experienced. The rule of the road appeared to disregard pedestrians. In the villages there were no traffic lights, zebra crossings or give way signs. As we raced through the villages at 70 mph the wandering sheep, goats, dogs, children and adults all dived for cover. One woman was part way across a road when she suddenly realised she wouldn't make it. With a pirouette that a top ballerina would have been proud of she dived for the side of the road. Our eyes locked for a split second as she reversed into the dust.

At the Togo border Michel Adopre of the Award Scheme greeted me. A promotional event was immediately attended at the British School of Lome where the achievements of the English head teacher over the past 20 years have been incredible, so much so that Mr Ian Sayer has been decorated as tribal Chief Senou 2nd. A forum involving a senior government minister was attended to explore the possibility of creating a link between the President of Togo and the D of E. This was followed by a dinner party with the purpose of recruiting sponsors for such a new operating authority. Unfortunately something I ate at the party did not agree with me and I spent an uncomfortable night diving in and out of bed to be violently sick. One of my hosts was a doctor so the next morning he supplied something to settle my stomach. For much of the rest of the time in West Africa I was living on French bread rolls and bottled water as the problem flared up every so often. In the space of three weeks I lost a stone in weight.

One of the personal issues I wanted to explore was voodoo. The Lac Togo area of Tome is the centre of the voodoo cult. By arrangement with my hotel I joined a visiting French businessman in sharing a taxi to an Ewe funeral. The funeral rites focus on the conception of life and death. When a person dies their djolo, (reincarnated soul) comes back in the next child born into the same lineage while their luvo (death soul), may linger with those still living, seeking attention and creating havoc. To stop the luvo from lingering the funerals involve three nights of drumming and dancing followed by a series of rituals to help free the soul of the deceased and influence reincarnation.

Before going to the funeral we were both warned by a hotel representative not to take any type of food, drink or tobacco offered. I had a good excuse anyway considering my health problems. My French colleague did not heed the warning and accepted and smoked a roll of leaves. Within 10 minutes he had joined the 'mourners' and was involved in frenzied dancing before eventually collapsing with exhaustion. With the aid of some of the dancers we carried him to a taxi so that he could be returned to the hotel. There was no sign of him at breakfast the next morning.

The car journey to the Togo/Benin border took two hours and fortunately the driver this time was more restrained. At the border I was met by the Award Scheme President, Hippolyte da Silva, who took me to Contonou and my next hotel. The hotel had seen better days, the room was dull, the sink overflowed, the window would not close completely, and there was a lot of noise from the car park and poolside musicians. It was going to be a difficult stay.

Benin is the birthplace of voodoo and was once the seat of one of West Africa's most powerful kingdoms. Its power declined in 1894 when it became a French Colony. Independence was granted in 1960. A military coup was followed by 20 years of military controlled Marxism. The first free elections were held in 1990.

A number of Award activities were undertaken, the most memorable being to visit the Tovi-Nonvi Community School situated in a swampy and forsaken area. On arrival at the school there was a guard of honour with pupils clapping and singing "Welcome Brother Jim". At the school assembly where I was to give a talk, it was announced that "Brother Jim" was the first prominent person from within Benin or overseas to ever visit the school – three cheers were then given for "Brother Jim". To mark my visit a wooden statue of Prince Philip is to be carved and will be positioned at the entrance to the school. A bust in my image is to be carved and will placed at the entrance to the Technical and Arts Centre currently under construction. On departing from the school another guard of honour was in place with the pupils clapping and singing "Farewell Brother Jim". It was one of the most moving experiences of my life.

Another important engagement was a meeting with the Minister of Sport, Leisure and Youth to encourage more Government funding for the Award. There was also a leader training session to address new volunteers. On hearing that I needed to change some money, my guide took me to a house with armed guards at the entrance. It was not what I had expected; it was certainly not a legal operation. Unwittingly I had become involved in money laundering and my guide was a government official!

An independent visit was made to the port of Ouidah, the main centre in Benin for the study of voodoo. There are two types of voodoo-happy or BO (evil), both have historical links with slavery. Voodoo was exported to Haiti by the slaves who were shipped from Ouidah. It is renowned for feverish drumming and highly charged dancing by costumed fetish priests. Human skulls are used as musical instruments. There are two museums displaying voodoo and slave artefacts. The Temple Des Pythons was full of sleepy snakes, certainly not a place for the faint hearted.

Slavery continues in many parts of Africa. It is claimed that 200,000 children were sold into slavery in Benin alone during 2003. Wealthy black families buy the children as servants from local village families. Selling their children provides a source of income that overrides any love that they have for their off spring.

During my travels across Ghana, Togo and Benin I had noticed tables positioned at the side of the road side on which was placed large and small bottles of a dark peach coloured liquid. Eventually I asked one of the drivers what fruit the liquid was made from. Stifling a laugh he told me that the bottles contained un-refined fuel stolen from the Shell pipelines in Nigeria. It was a lot cheaper than that sold at garages but produced much more pollution and caused damage to the engines. Another interesting motoring feature were the two wheeled scooter taxis. The drivers wore yellow shirts with a registration number on the back. The 50/100cc scooters carry one or two passengers and they wait in taxi ranks just like conventional taxis. They are highly dangerous as they weave in and out of traffic and I was fortunate that I never needed to hire one.

The next stage of the journey was to travel from Benin to Nigeria via car. Time keeping was a major problem due to traffic congestion and the general relaxed attitude towards being on time. After an early breakfast we were on the move by 8am arriving at he Nigerian border an hour later. My Nigerian hosts were not as prompt and a three and half hour wait at the border in blazing sunshine was an anxious time. Was I to be stranded at he border? Should I head back to Benin? Should I catch a bus to Lagos? It was a great relief when my guides eventually arrived. The four-hour journey to Lagos was made more difficult by the frequent roadblocks. There were checks by immigration, customs, narcotics, etc looking out for drugs, petrol or refugees. Not all the roadblocks were legal; out on the open road away from the police roadblocks, men armed with automatic weapons would set up a barrier and collect a toll. If the police appeared in the distance, they would grab their make shift barrier and dash off into the jungle.

On arrival at Lagos I was put on a flight to Abuja, the capital of Nigeria. The 50-minute flight was a delight after all the previous road journeys and their dangers. There was a large welcoming group at the airport led by the National

Director of the Award, Miss Jophia Gupar. A group of children in traditional costumes were playing musical instruments and singing a welcome song. I was given a large basket of fruit that is a traditional welcome gift. A large crowd gathered to see who the 'celebrity' was that was getting star treatment.

Abuja was a very modern city in African terms with wide roads and modern buildings. My accommodation was at the Christian Mission at the Ecwa Wuse Church. An early night was called for, as my programme for the World Aids Day celebrations was to start at 6am the next morning. There was a notice in my room listing the house rules: No Alcohol, No Smoking and No Free Women! Is there such a thing as a free woman?

A 5.30am call ensured I was on the road to the World Aids Day celebrations at the Eagle Square Stadium that would start at 6.30am. All the National Youth Organisations were on parade along with organisations supporting women's groups. In the order of 3,000 people were present including Government Ministers and the Vice President who was listed as the principal speaker. Just as the speeches were about to start the announcer expressed surprise and delight when a cavalcade of cars roared into the centre of the stadium. It was the President making a surprise visit. He jumped out of his car and circled by bodyguards started running round the stadium on a lap of honour. Over coming their surprise the spectators poured out of their seats to race after the President. What a sight, a lap of honour joined by at least 2,000 of the audience. On completion of the run the President, in his mid fifties got back into his car and roared off to another engagement. Not the sort of thing that Blair or Bush would undertake!

The Youth Forum was held in the afternoon at Cinema Hall with at least 1,000 young people and leaders present. The theme was "*Women and the fight against Aids*". There were a number of presentations including a drama depicting someone who had discovered they had caught Aids, a male voice choir singing self penned anti-Aids advice, displays of traditional dance etc. As the guest of honour I was asked to draw parallels between the lives of young people in Nigeria with those encountered in other parts of the world and incorporating the world threat of Aids. After more than two weeks on tour I was now well versed in the style of speaking inspired by religious zeal. The opening statement is always delivered powerfully and purposefully. The intention being to grab the audience by the scruff of the neck and rouse their passion for whatever cause was being presented. My opening punchline was to be, "*I wish you could see what I see - I wish you could know what I know*". What could I see? 1,000 young people supported by teachers and youth workers who through the Award Scheme, were leading the fight against Aids. I praised the partnership between young people and their mentors. The country could be proud of them. What did I know that would help them come to terms with their place in the world and the fight against Aids? In general terms I could compare the work other young people were doing in 98 other countries. I could also highlight the influences of those who guide their early development and those who would shape their lives as adults.

Their earliest mentors were of course their parents, grandparents and members of their extended families. The next to influence their lives would be teachers and youth workers. Show them respect and appreciation for what they do on your behalf. As they become adults they will come under all sorts of conflicting sources of information. These sources will vary depending on the country of residence. Examples would be the conflicts that exist between the traditional church and the religious fundamentalists. The differences between a Government policy and an ideology, a free or controlled press, the link between drugs and crime, military intervention in countries such as Afghanistan and Iraq, the difference between terrorists who kill innocent people in suicide attacks and a campaign of non-violence that led to the scrapping of apartheid in South Africa. Purely in terms of the fight against Aids would be the consideration of the growing movement in America to say "no" to all sexual relationships outside marriage.

The closing speaker of the conference reinforced the "Say No" policy by giving an impressive presentation that summarised the current situation in the whole of Africa and personalised the reality of the consequences to individuals such as himself. He started by presenting the statistics. HIV has taken the greatest toll on its youth, more than 70% of those infected in Africa are youths with girls and women the biggest group of victims. He was 21 years old and had HIV/AIDS. He explained how he had reacted to the news and how he had adjusted his lifestyle. He was not afraid of dying, he was continuing with his life without the use of medicines. He was aware of his low white blood count and that the condition could lead to his death because of the inability to fight other illnesses. He was devoting the remainder of his life to educate others not to become Aids victims. It had been a privilege to share the platform with such an inspiring speaker. At the end of the rally the biggest I had addressed since starting a new career as a public speaker, it was time to give three magazine interviews, two radio interviews and a TV show appearance.

There were a number of other engagements linked to the Award Scheme including a meeting with a close confidant of the President of Nigeria. Mr N. O. F. Chukwu, the Chairman of the Award Scheme in Nigeria occupied a complete floor in one of the top hotels in the city. His importance was reflected in the permanent eight-man police bodyguard. Advice was given on how to raise the profile of the Award and how to secure funding from multi national companies.

The success of the Award Scheme in Nigeria in leading the fight against HIV/AIDS showed the importance of making the Award relevant to the needs of its people.

A private audience was gained with the leader of the Evangelical Church in Abuja, Rev Same Tugba Afthryba. I wanted the Nigerian perspective on the moral crusade and claim that TB Joshua was a true prophet The Rev criticised TB Joshua who claimed the power to cure people, believing he used the occult or was in league with evil forces and that the Pentecostal Church was exploiting the so-called powers of Joshua. He would never go to Joshua for treatment.

The Reverend was asked if he believed that Nigeria was leading a worldwide moral crusade to return the Anglican Church to the strict interpretation of the Bible. The Rev responded by quoting a report from Transparency International that showed that Nigeria was the third most corrupt country in the world. "*It seems that once people put on a uniform they become separated from the Bible - they do not respond to the commandment "Thou shall not steal"*. Because a significant number are involved in corruption it contradicts the view that Nigeria is a God fearing country.

The Reverend was scathing about the hypocrisy of Islam. He claimed that Islamic leaders make an example of poor people by stoning them to death for adultery when well off Muslims have four wives who often had relationships with other men. Some contracted AIDS from these other men but were never charged under Sharia Law.

I came across numerous examples of corrupt practices amongst officials. On the Benin/Nigeria border I was asked to pay £10 if I wanted to pass into Nigeria. There were no senior officers in view to complain to and I had to pay. At the airport in Lagos I had cleared the formalities and was heading for the transfer bus to the plane. The plane was due to take off in less than five minutes. An official ordered me to stop, stating that the plane had a shortage of fuel and unless I paid 40 Euros I would be held back for a flight five hours later. Under such circumstances, with people waiting for me at the other end and no policemen in sight I had to pay up. I was so angry I decided that I would refuse future requests for money by threatening them as a magistrate or just to laugh off the approach so that when asked by a corrupt official "*What have you got for me*" I would reply "*You've got me, I'm here to help as a volunteer*". That shuts them up sheepishly.

One of the achievements in terms of religious unity has been the joint funding and building of a large church in the city centre of Abuja. It is an Ecumenical Centre shared by Anglicans, Catholics, Methodists, etc. The construction is almost complete although it is behind schedule as there have been a number of heated debates on the design, which religions would access the building and what religious practices would be observed.

Crime is a major issue, particularly the involvement of the police, armed forces and Government officials. A number of examples are featured in the essay devoted to Crime and Punishment. Traditional gang led crime is also a big issue, particularly in the area of the docks where cargoes are raided as cargo ships arrive. A major success was achieved during my visit with 200 cultists having been arrested with many being charged with murders linked to raids on ships. An amnesty has been declared with the arrest of the gang leaders and as a result there has been a mass handover and destruction of weapons.

Another area of Government concern is the continued increase in child trafficking. Officials are investigating all non-Government Organisations involved with street children. It is believed that under the pretence of rescuing homeless street children and providing them with food, clothing and a bed, they are really shipping them abroad as domestic and sex slaves. This modern day slavery is organised by black Nigerians and involves members of their own race.

During my travels down the West Coast of Africa I have made a number of references to dangerous driving and poorly maintained cars. The majority of cars are imported as second hand with no service records. Two examples of the consequences of driving like people possessed in unsafe vehicles occurred on the same day. There were 80 people hanging on to a trailer as they hitched a lift home. The lorry pulling the trailer crashed and 16 of the 80 were killed. A multiple crash caused by a burst tyre saw another 13 people killed in a separate incident.

On arrival back in Lagos I looked around for the official who had forced me to pay an illegal fuel tax to get on my flight to Abuja. I was hoping to get him arrested now that I had time to spare, but he was not on duty. After a night in a Lagos hotel the magic day dawned when I was due to set foot in my 100th country – 4th December 2004. My flight to Douala in Cameroon arrived 3 hours late, a fact that was to impact later on my programme. Cameroon comes from the Portuguese "River of Prawns", the place that the Portuguese had sailed into, in 1472. Cameroon achieved independence from the French in 1960. Whilst in immigration my host King Mboutcheko, from the Kingdom of Bafoussam, and National Director of the Award Scheme, was waiting with his colleague Chief Puis Ambe from the South West Province. The King and the Chief are very active, the King has five wives and 18 children, and the Chief has four wives and 15 children. We immediately set off to attend a major Award Rally organised for my interest. There were displays of dancing, singing and poetry plus speeches of greeting. Amongst the gifts received was a framed certificate containing the Diamond Award, it is the highest Award of its kind in Cameroon. It was to mark my 45 years as a volunteer Youth Worker and Award Officer, plus the achievement of having visited 100 countries. The framed certificate takes pride of place alongside my MBE on my wall at home.

After the great Award rally the proceedings took a nosedive. The car of King Mboutcheko was really battered and would not have survived a an MOT in the UK. The intention was at 7pm, just as it was getting dark, to drive the 200 miles North to Yaounde, the capital of Cameroon. It took nearly an hour to escape the stop/start traffic jams around Douala before hitting the open road. There were no streetlights and the car had a defective near side headlight. It was difficult to see where the side of the road ended and the jungle began. There were a number of stops to reposition the dangling bulb to give some sort of illumination. On one occasion the car would not start and we had to get out and push. There was also the problem of villagers walking along the edge of the road and numerous occasions when they had to dive for cover as the car came too close to the edge. Sometimes the sound of bushes against the side of the car signalled that the car had strayed too far to the right. I tried to take my mind off the possibility of crashing by reflecting on the life style of the villages we passed. At about 20 mile intervals there would be a collection of wooden shops and a single open fronted bar. The shops would be illuminated by a single bulb with the bar shedding the most light against the dark background making it the focus of attention. I assumed that those gathered at the bar were enjoying the highlight of the day – social companionship. The atmosphere in the semi darkness was magical, the same sort of feeling you get sitting around a campfire with friends, miles from anywhere. The nightmare journey did not end until 1am. The reason the drive had to be completed was that I was to speak with the Minister of Youth and Sport at a breakfast meeting at 8am. I managed to squeeze in six hours sleep.

The meeting with the Minister went well, particularly when I was able to correct a major misunderstanding about the role of Prince Philip and Prince Edward. In recent years there had been a visit to Cameroon by Prince Philip to hand over a large cheque on behalf of the World Wild Life Fund, to preserve a rain forest. Prince Edward had also visited and handed over a cheque to protect a troop of monkeys who were being hunted to extinction. I was asked why the Government in Cameroon should support the Award Scheme when it is awash with money and being supported by one of the richest families in the world. If they, the Princes', could afford to support monkeys and trees they should also support young people. In countering this misrepresentation I explained that Prince Philip, for example, has links with 98 different charities including Outward Bound, the World Wildlife Fund and Lords Taverners etc. When he brings money to protect a rain forest it is not his money but money donated or raised by supporters of the WWF. The same applied to Prince Edward. The Award in Cameroon needs the support of the Government as it operates on a shoestring.

The second major event in Yaounda was to attend a large rally organised by the Gold Award holders Association. Activities included a display of Karate, a play featuring the fight against Aids, and traditional singing. Another talk on my world tour was my contribution to the event. References to Mother Teresa and Nelson Mandela gained the most interest.

The two-day visit to Yaounda concluded with a visit to a small Game Reserve, the only one visited during the whole of the five-country tour. The star attraction was the "King of the Jungle", a fully-grown two year old lion and his mate. The 200-mile journey back to Douala was much more enjoyable as we were travelling in the clear light of day. Every small deserted village I had described on the outward journey was now a large open-air market, a mass of colour and excitement.

Transparency International's reports of 1998 and 1999 claimed that Cameroon has the most corrupt administration in the world. I personally did not have any bad experiences. The people I met were charming, helpful and full of smiles. The young people participating in the Award programme were as good as ambassadors as could be found anywhere in the world. In saying that, looking at a single days newspapers shows that there are still major problems:
"THE SEASON OF BLACKMAIL AND VOODOOISM"
"Since the October 11th Presidential Elections, CPDM militants are working around the clock to blackmail their comrades and gain favour from President Biya. The election was heavily rigged by an ambitious elite with the complicity of administrative authorities".
"CATHOLIC CHURCH; SAME HOUSE DIFFERENT ROOMS"
Cardinal Tumi "The election was a masquerade". Arch Bishop Bakol "Election the will of the people". "One of them is lying ",
"CAMEROON LOSES 32 BILLION. FCFA IN PETROLEUM FRAUD"
The estimated amount lost through fraud.
"CAMEROON LEADERS ARE SLAVES TO POWER, SAYS PRIEST"
"Father Lado Ludovic speaking at Holy Mass. He regretted that through Christian rule, Cameroon, the society had become rife with moral bankruptcy. The majority of Cameroonians are wallowing in abject poverty while the leaders are busy siphoning the country's resources and embezzling public funds with impunity. We are sitting on a time bomb. Poverty is a source of violence. In heaven there is no beer, no sex, he warned. The time to be spiritually awake is now".

Throughout the tour of these five West African countries the issue of Government corruption was raised time and time again. In June 2005 the Finance Ministers of the leading G8 Financial Nations agreed to wipe out the debts of African countries and to invest around £30 billion in aid to fight starvation and disease. The dilemma is how to ensure that any new money does not get misappropriated by corrupt leaders in purchasing extravagant properties, private jets, fleets of expensive cars, etc. The need for aid to Africa is overwhelming. The latest survey shows that 25 million people are currently affected by HIV/AIDS across the whole of Africa. This total is growing by four million new infections a year with 2.2 million related deaths each year. The average life expectancy age in Africa has dropped from 62 to 47. Some 11 million children have lost at least one parent. The total of 2.2 million that will die in Africa in 2005 is nine times greater than the number who died in the Asian Tsunami in 2004. Unless the problems of Africa are addressed this figure of 2.2 million will grow not just this year but next year and the year after.

One of the frustrations of the continuing spread of HIV/AIDS across Africa is the lack of adequate funding to find a cure for the disease. Anti-retroviral drugs that stabilise the condition have been developed for use in America but the cost of these drugs is beyond the means of 97% of Africans. In the absence of scientific support witchcraft prevails. Ineffectual folk remedies are peddled by witch doctors. One such treatment encourages those infected to have sex with babies as a way of banishing HIV/AIDS!

The death toll and levels of poverty across Africa are not all related to HIV/AIDS. The following situations/circumstances beg the question about the lack of substantial financial support to offer solutions. Where is the funding for the science that could lead to the control of the plagues of locusts that regularly destroy the crops of Africans creating starvation greater than that caused by the Tsunami? The plague of locusts that destroyed crops across Africa in 2004 was the biggest for 45 years.

Where is the UN action to stop child labour and child sex/domestic slavery in Africa? How effective is the UN in resolving Africa's long running insurgencies and civil wars? It has taken 20 years and the loss of 1.5 million lives to come up with a solution to the conflict in the Sudan. Civil Wars still rage in Algeria, Ethiopia and Rwanda/Congo where 4.5 million lives have been lost with the virtual elimination of the ethnic Tutsis. Zimbabwe is allowed to use the restriction of food supplies causing starvation to hundreds of thousands in their country for political reasons. The Government has confiscated successfully managed farms and given them to Government supporters who lack the skills to maintain the previous levels of food production.

Two African countries suffer the world's worst human rights abuses, Equatorial Guinea and Angola. According to the OECD 28 out of 50 of the world's poorest countries are in Africa. One of the reasons these African countries are poor is down to International Trading Agreements that work against farmers. The price received by the farmers barely covers production costs with the coffee pickers getting a pittance. By imposing International controls of the coffee chain from picker to drinker the villagers could enjoy a higher standard of living and be able to access education, health care, and a better quality of food for their family.

Although I am not a fan of Bob Geldof he has brought Africa back to the top of the agenda of the most successful financially developed countries. There have been doubts cast about the previous campaign he organised as to whether all the money raised reached its target. Ethiopia received millions from the first Live Aid Concert yet remains in debt with claims that the money did not reach the most deprived citizens. The same problem will be faced again, how to manage and control aid, free from corrupt national African administration? I believe that the approach adopted in the regeneration of Afghanistan is more reliable. One of the major problems in Afghanistan is the lack of a unified network of roads to allow for the movement of people and goods. A major road is currently being constructed between the capital Kabul and the city of Kandahar. No money changes hands between China, the funder and Afghanistan. The Chinese bring in all the equipment and construction materials together with skilled labour. They create work for the unskilled local people, which bring in valuable revenue. There is no opportunity for corruption; external funding totalling billions of dollars is secure.

The last adventure on this West African journey was during the drive from Yaounde to Douala, where I would fly to England the next day. On many trips I have taken there comes a defining moment. On this occasion it was while travelling in an old car at 60mph on the open road around 50 miles from Douala. The driver was King Mboutcheko and one of his five wives was sitting in the back with me. There was a loud bang as a front tyre exploded and the car went out of control. In the space of a few seconds as the King fought to stop the car from dropping down a steep embankment I experienced a series of flashbacks. The Immigration Officer at the Benin/Nigeria borders whom after disputing my age said; "You must have been blessed". The talks I had recently been drawn to give about Mother Teresa that I always ended with the words she had said to me, "God bless you". Back on the road with all these events flashing before my eyes, and the tyre blown out, the King finally managed to hit a short stretch of crash barriers side on and this straightened up the car, preventing it from crashing down the embankment. We all got out and sat quietly at the side of the road reflecting on what had happened and how we had all escaped death or serious injury.

That night resting in my room I reflected on another escape. While I believe there is a God, I can support a number of interpretations of religion and the way that God watches over us. Although my praise of the work of Mother Teresa has been concentrated over the past few days, it presents food for thought that I may be a 'blessed person'. When I had set off for Africa I had no prior intention to describe my contact with Mother Teresa, but when asked to address a school assembly at a moments notice it had been an instinctive response that the audience might find such a story of the selfless work of Mother Teresa inspirational. Because the talk had gone so well I repeated it on at least 10 other occasions. An alternative view of my escape would be that this was just all co-incidences and that I am just "Lucky Jim" as labelled by the press. I prefer the former view rather than the latter.

The 24-hour return flight from Cameroon involved four flights via Lagos, Accra, Amsterdam and onto Birmingham. Arriving back in Birmingham was a massive relief. It had been my toughest trip ever and one that I would never repeat, but would however look back with affection for the kindness and generous welcome received in all five countries.

Although I have now reached my target of 100 countries I have no intention to hang up my travel bag and notebook. I am sure that there are other adventures awaiting me. Since my visit to Cameroon in December 2004 I have been reviewing my travels of the past 45 years.

There have been a number of re-writes and fine tuning of the book over the past 12 months to ensure accuracy. Alongside the time spent writing I have visited a further nine countries. The triangular tour of Estonia, Latvia and Lithuania has been incorporated. Likewise I have included the overland tour of South and East Africa which involved visits to South Africa, Tanzania, Mozambique, Zimbabwe, Zambia, Botswana and Zanzibar Island. Hopefully the results of these visits have fitted seamlessly into the essays on Crime (5), Apartheid (10), Propaganda (11) and Sport (17).

My favourite country in the world? The answer is England closely followed by Wales. In my view nothing rivals England in terms of its democracy, freedom of speech, social order, sense of community, access to International sport, theatre, dance and cinema. Four seasons of contrasting weather patterns and the beauty of the countryside and waterways also add to its appeal. In Wales a favourite walk is along the beach at Aberdovey in the early spring or late Autumn when the only sounds are of the waves and the sea gulls. A place to unwind, for reflection, meditation and to plan my next overseas adventure.

The overriding achievements of the 45-year long tour? The first are the achievements of the young people who I accompanied. Even on the shorter trips I could see them growing in stature as they coped with a new culture and environment. I believe they became more compassionate as they worked alongside people less fortunate than themselves.

In material terms receiving the MBE from the Queen on November 13th 1997 stands out. When the letter from 10 Downing St arrived inviting me to accept the award I was ecstatic. As the offer was confidential I couldn't tell anyone except my family. I remember driving that day down the M1 singing at the top of my voice. I don't know what the other drivers must have thought! It wasn't the medal itself but what it represented in terms of my childhood, living conditions, place in society and what my parents would have thought. The Royal family and the Parkes family were a million miles apart. On Christmas Day we would stand when the National Anthem played on the radio before the Royal Christmas message.

The Investiture at Buckingham Palace was a wonderful occasion. On the morning of the Investiture a telemessage from Buckingham Palace read, *"Many congratulations on your well deserved Honour"*. Philip. Although I was receiving the lowest award and the press were focussed on Nursery Nurse Lisa Potts receiving the George Medal and the subsequently disgraced Paul Burrell being recognised for his services to Diana, Princess of Wales, it didn't matter. Nothing could diminish my sense of achievement.

The future? At the age of 69 my days of taking groups abroad have gone. This does not mean I cannot travel by proxy. During my interactive speaking engagements I hope to inspire others to engage in international adventures so they can gain a "Whole world perspective on life". I am visiting Saudi Arabia, Sudan, Eritrea, Yemen and Oman this autumn, I will still umpire, referee and play golf regularly and chase after my granddaughter Lily. There is much to commend in becoming an Urban Explorer. It keeps those little grey cells stimulated.